GW00649427

Heresy and Inquisition in the Middle Ages
Volume 2

Heresy, Crusade and Inquisition
in Medieval Quercy

YORK MEDIEVAL PRESS

Heresy and Inquisition in the Middle Ages
ISSN 2046–8938

Series editors
John H. Arnold, Department of History, Classics and Archaeology, Birkbeck College, London
Peter Biller, Department of History, University of York

Heresy had social, cultural and political implications in the middle ages, and countering heresy was often a central component in the development of orthodoxy. This series publishes work on heresy, and the repression of heresy, from late antiquity to the Reformation, including monographs, collections of essays, and editions of texts.

Heresy, Crusade and Inquisition in Medieval Quercy

Claire Taylor

THE UNIVERSITY *of York*

YORK MEDIEVAL PRESS

First published 2011

A York Medieval Press publication
in association with The Boydell Press
an imprint of Boydell & Brewer Ltd
PO Box 9, Woodbridge, Suffolk IP12 3DF, UK
and of Boydell & Brewer Inc.
668 Mt Hope Avenue, Rochester, NY 14620, USA
website: www.boydellandbrewer.com
and with the
Centre for Medieval Studies, University of York
www.york.ac.uk/medieval-studies

ISBN 978 1 903153 38 3

A CIP catalogue record for this book is available
from the British Library

The publisher has no responsibility for the continued existence or accuracy
of URLs for external or third-party internet websites referred to in this book,
and does not guarantee that any content on such websites is,
or will remain, accurate or appropriate.

Papers used by Boydell & Brewer Ltd are natural, recyclable products
made from wood grown in sustainable forests

Printed in Great Britain by
CPI Group (UK) Ltd, Croydon, CR0 4YY

Contents

Illustrations

This book is dedicated to the memories of Jean Duvernoy and of Janet Hamilton, for their contributions to our understanding of European dualism in the Middle Ages.

Acknowledgements

My thanks go to York Medieval Press for the opportunity of appearing in this series, and in particular to Peter Biller and John Arnold, series editors, for their guidance, patience and excellent suggestions; and to Caroline Palmer of Boydell & Brewer. Philipp K. kindly proofread penultimate drafts. Remaining errors are my own.

I owe a great debt to fellow heresiologists who have helped the ideas in this book take shape, particularly John Arnold and Peter Biller again, and also Bernard Hamilton, Rob Lutton, Bob Moore, Andrew Roach and Lucy Sackville. I am indebted also to my colleagues in the School of History, University of Nottingham: in particular Karen Adler, Ross Balzaretti, Julia Barrow, Gwilym Dodd, Richard Goddard, Rob Lutton, Spencer Mawby and the Belief and Ideology Research Network (BIRN). As always, we learn from our students, and I would like to single out Faye Taylor in particular, soon to complete an impressive PhD thesis, and also my Special Subject students.

Thank you also to my family, Victor, Christine, Joe and Andrea Taylor; to Simon Constantine, Konni Behr, Anna and Clara; and to the Simonian family. The biggest thank you is to Michael Craven, still fighting.

Prefatory Note on Words

For the most part I have translated words in other languages, but there are some instances in which I do not translate Latin terminology. I have used the Latin *perfecti* for Cathar initiates (literally 'the perfect', the singular for men being *perfectus*, the feminine forms being *perfecta* and *perfectae*, singular and plural respectively), and *credentes* for their followers (literally 'the believers', singular: *credens*). Their use is in part a historiographical convention, as I discuss in Chapter 1. As such, there seems little point in using another such convention, more arbitrary, which is to translate the word into English 'the perfect'. Translating *haereticus* (plural *haeretici*; feminine singular and plural: *haeretica* and *heareticae*) always and only as 'heretic' is problematic too, and this will also be discussed in Chapter 1. Some words, such as *castrum* (Latin), cannot be translated in a single word anyway, but are explained when referred to initially.

In terms of personal names, I use the modern French where we have it. Some Anglophone scholars make the leap from Latin, in which the vast majority of names were recorded, into modern English, for example from 'Raimundus' to 'Raymond'. I prefer to use the French, hence 'Raimond'. This approach has the effect of linking us to both the French scholarship and also to the region, as does using modern French adjectives such as 'Cahorsin' (of Cahors) and 'Quercinois' (of Quercy), and French ways of referring to regions such as the 'Cahorsain'.

Finally, a note on place-names. A great many of these occur in this work. In my index the extant place-names are given with the modern commune within which they lay, where they are not communes themselves. As well as a map of medieval Quercy, a map of the Bouriane is also included, because of the detailed attention paid to that area.

Abbreviations

Arch, mun. de Cahors	Archives municipals de Cahors
BSEL	*Bulletin de la société des études du Lot*
CF	*Cahiers de Fanjeaux*
Chanson	Guillaume de Tudela et al., *La Chanson de la croisade Albigeoise*, ed. and trans. E. Martin-Chabot, 3 vols. (Paris, 1960–72)
CO	*Cartulaire de l'abbaye cistercienne d'Obazine (xiie–xiiie siècles)*, ed. B. Barrière (Clermont-Ferrand, 1989)
D	Paris, Bibliothèque nationale de France, Mss. Fonds Doat.
DCBC	J. Duvernoy (ed.), *Cahiers de Bernard de Caux, 1243–1247*: http://jean.duvernoy.free.fr/text/pdf/bdecaux.pdf
DPC	Duvernoy, J. (ed. and trans.), *L'inquisition en Quercy: le registre dea pénitences de Pierre Cellan, 1241–1242* (Castelnaud la Chapelle, 2001)
GC	J. H. Albanès (ed.) *Gallia Christiana novissima. Histoire des archévêchés, évéchês et abbayes de France*, 7 vols. (Montebéliard and Valence, 1895–1920)
HGL	C. de Vic and J. Vaissète (eds.), *Histoire générale de Languedoc*, revised by A. Molinier, 16 vols. (Toulouse, 1872–1904)
HHMA	Wakefield, W. L. and A. P. Evans (ed. and trans.), *Heresies of the High Middle Ages* (New York, 1969 + rprt. 1991)
IRC	Albe, E. (ed.), *Inventaire raisonné et analytique des archives municipales de Cahors*, 3 parts: 1 (Cahors, 1915); 2. *BSEL* 41 (1920), pp. 1–48 and *BSEL* 43 (1922), pp. 1–28; 3. *BSEL* 47 (1926), pp. 1–150. Volume 1
PL	J. P. Migne et al. (ed.) *Patrologiae cursus completus, series Latina*, 217 vols. (Paris, 1852–1904, with 4 vols. index and 5 vols. supplementum 1958–74)
P&P	*Past and Present*
PVC *Histoire*	Pierre des Vaux-de-Cernay, *Histoire Albigeoise*, ed. and trans. P. Guébin and H. Maisonneuve (Paris, 1951)
PVC *History*	Pierre des Vaux-de-Cernay, *The History of the Albigensian Crusade*, ed. and trans. W. A. and M. D. Sibly (Woodbridge, 1998)
PVC *Hystoria*	Pierre des Vaux-de-Cernay, *Hystoria Albigensis*, ed. P. Guébin and E. Lyon, 3 vols. (Paris, 1926–30)

RHF   *Recueil des historiens des Gaules et de la France*, ed. M. Bouquet
et al. (revised L. Delisle), 24 vols. (Paris, 1738–1904)

Song   *The Song of the Cathar Wars*, trans. J. Shirley (Aldershot, 1996)

Map 1. Medieval Quercy

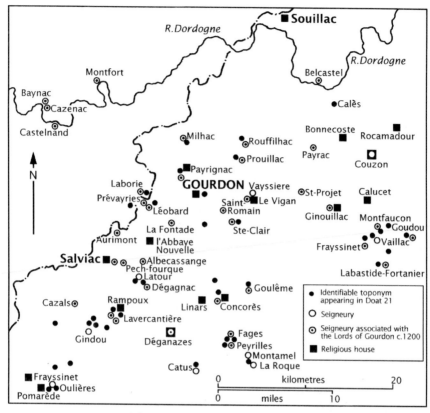

Map 2. Gourdon and its sphere

XV

The House of Gourdon

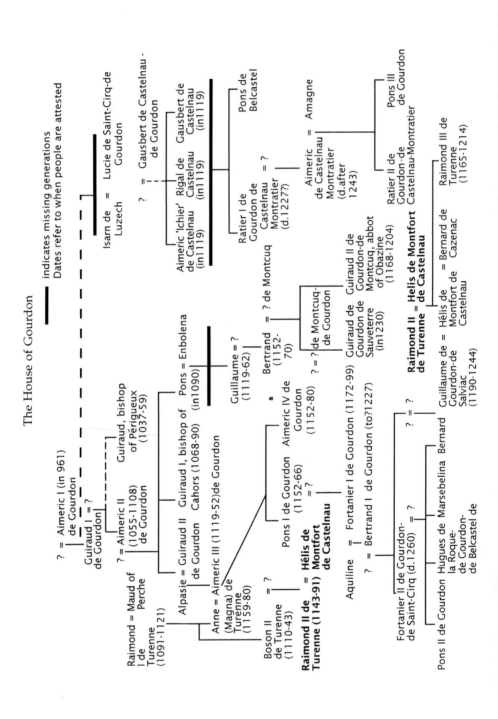

indicates missing generations
Dates refer to when people are attested

Introduction

Around Easter time in 1242, the deponent Pierre de Penne appeared in front of the Dominican inquisitor Pierre Seilan at his court in Montcuq, in the medieval county of Quercy. What he said, we cannot know exactly. What was recorded, we likewise cannot be sure. But almost certainly his vernacular deposition was translated into Latin and distilled into what we do have, the following summary of his crimes:

> Pierre de Penne saw heretics many times in many places, and ate and drank with them often, and sent them bread, fruits, and other things. He believed them to be good people and that they in their sect would be saved. He ate bread blessed by them. He said also that the mercenary Loubaix was as likely to go to heaven as Martin of Tours, and he had said this to the priests who bought wax in honour of St. Martin. He believed that no one could swear an oath or kill without sin. *Item*, he didn't believe in any of the sacraments of the Church and believed that the heretical church was the only church, that no one in the Roman Church will be saved, but that everyone was saved in the heretical church. *Item*, he said that God does not destroy what he has made, nor would it disappear. He said also that he adored heretics, and that previously he had denied being put under oath or question. *Item*, he said that he himself had preached heresies to other people many times.[1]

This is what was set down in the inquisitor's register of sentences as justification for one of the heaviest penalties he passed: an exile of seven years, to be spent at Constantinople in support of the conquests of the fourth crusade. As we shall see, almost every word of the summary is significant in terms of what the sentence tells us about its declared subject matter: Pierre's actions in relation to both heretics and priests; which heretics specifically (two sects operated in Quercy: Cathars and Waldensians); his beliefs about saints and

---

[1] D21, fol. 217r–v. On D21, see below. Loubaix was presumably either a well-known mercenary of the region or a well-known fictional character. The vernacular 'routier' is given for 'mercenary'. The routier was a common feature of Occitan life and the region's small armies would be made up of many of them. Furthermore, because of the mass seizure of southern castles during the Albigensian crusade there were many *faidits*, dispossessed knights, who were sometimes forced to hire out their services. Thus *routier* does not carry the amoral connotations that 'mercenary' does. 'Adoring' heretics was a ritual and commonplace form of veneration of Cathars, and a feature of depositions, and was used by inquisitors as a measure of the extent to which a witness adhered to this sect specifically. On both *routiers* and ritual, more will be said below.

sinners; about the authority of the Roman church; that God did not make things that then died or were destroyed; about ritual; and about how people negotiated the inquisitorial process. We shall also see that every aspect of the text both relates to and sheds light on other events in Quercy that took place before Easter 1242, and to wider discourses informing the record of such trials. Even though Pierre was an otherwise relatively obscure figure, of whom we know only a little more through the content of other people's depositions, he and people like him are vitally important to the historian of heresy and the exploration of the contexts in which heresy both emerged and was imagined. Through him we glimpse structures and value systems operating in the society in which he lived – the ones that Pierre Seilan was interested in, at least – at a particular point in its history. Also, we see some of what he thought about them and how he responded to them.

I came to read the depositions of people in Quercy while writing about the Cathar heresy in the Agenais.[2] Both counties are the most northerly in Languedoc, bordering Aquitaine, specifically Périgord and the Limousin, and they are bisected by the river Lot and tied into the Garonne-Tarn-Aveyron communication network. Hence, aspects of their political, cultural and economic life were intertwined. There is a wealth of primary source material for Cathars in Quercy, for whom far more has survived than for the Agenais. It reveals that their 'heretical' lives were also interrelated. I observed that the heretics of Quercy appear to have operated under the authority of the Cathar bishop of the Agenais, Vigouroux de la Bacone, who was noted many times in Quercy.[3] The sources also suggested a specific chronology for the spread of the heresy within Quercy and stress the presence of another group of heretics, the Waldensians, apparently not active in the Agenais but every bit as significant as Cathars in some towns in Quercy. Waldensians are sometimes overlooked by historians of heretics. Not only were they nowhere near as ubiquitous as Cathars in Languedoc, they were far less glamorous and strange.

In his edition of Bibliothèque nationale de France ms Lat. Fonds Doat 21, the manuscript in which Pierre Seilan's sentences for Quercy survive and within which Pierre de Penne's sentence is to be found, Jean Duvernoy observes that a much more extensive study of the evidence revealed by this manuscript could be undertaken than has previously been attempted by historians of heresy in Quercy, although some onomastic work has been done

---

2 C. Taylor, *Heresy in Medieval France: Dualism in Aquitaine and the Agenais, c.1000–c.1250* (Woodbridge, 2005); C. Taylor, 'Authority and the Cathar heresy in the northern Languedoc', in *The Origins of Heresy and Persecution in the Middle Ages: Essays on the Work of R. I. Moore*, ed. M. Frassetto (Leiden, 2005), pp. 139–54.

3 For his career, including in Quercy, see originally Y. Dossat, 'Un évêque Cathare originaire de l'Agenais: Vigouroux de la Bacone', in his *Église et hérésie en France au xiiie siècle* (London, 1982), pp. 623–39. See also Taylor, *Heresy*, pp. 177, 178–9, 181, 225–31 and below, in particular chapter 7.

by them.[4] He suggests that this is a task for someone already a historian of Quercy. Jörg Feuchter began this in the case of Montauban specifically shortly afterwards.[5] I also hope to be able to fulfil some of the potential suggested by such a project.

The earliest scholarship on the Cathar heresy identifies a 'dualist' belief system in southern France in the late twelfth century; that is to say, the concept of two supernatural entities, two 'principles' in conflict with each other. One of the themes of the book is whether or not there was such a thing as empirically observable 'dualism' in Quercy. Was it in fact the fancy of medieval clergy, an oppositional value in relation to which they defined 'orthodoxy'? Or is it in fact the creation of historians?

Such possibilities dominate modern scholarship on heresy and will be addressed in Chapter 1 in detail and throughout. We introduce the historiography with the earliest scholarship, which suggested Balkan and dualist origins for western heresy. The second half of the twentieth century began with an attack on this model by Raffaelo Morghen, who asserted that heresy was an expression of extreme piety and the desire for reform within the western church.[6] Antoine Dondaine reasserted the dualist case essentially in its traditional form, but more methodogically – although his methods are seen as flawed today – and with the use of new sources.[7] The dialogue between these two models then occupied a period in which historians created and shored up meta-narratives to account for the increase of sources referring to heresy in the eleventh century: dualist, apocalyptic, socio-economic,

---

4   DPC, 25. He is referring to the work of Edmund Albe, especially *L'hérésie albigeoise et l'inquisition en Quercy* (Paris, 1910). He also refers to Yves Dossat's edition of the deposition of Guillaume Donadieu d'Elves, in *CF* 3 (Toulouse, 1968), pp. 290–98, within H. Blaquière and Y. Dossat, 'Les cathares au jour le jour. Confessions inédites de cathares quercinois', *CF* 3 (Toulouse, 1968), pp. 259–98; and to G. Passerat, 'Cathares en Bas-Quercy: entre l'église de l'Agenais et celle de l'Albigeois' (Carcassonne, 1995), 149–65.

5   See, for example, 'Le pouvoir de l'inquisition à travers ses peines. Le cas de Montauban (1241)', in *Inquisition et pouvoir*, ed. G. Audisio (Aix-en-Provence, 2003), pp. 237–55, and as cited below. In this, Feuchter noted the dramatic implications that Pierre Seilan's sentences would have had for a town like Montauban. He observes that most notable families contained people who were condemned, and that the inquisitor thus transformed the whole governing caste at Montauban into a group of penitents. But he also suggests that the town was able to negotiate with the inquisitor and that the sentences in Doat 21 may have been commuted into building work on churches, and as such that the penitential pilgrimages never took place. Feuchter's monograph on Montauban, *Ketzer, Konsuln und Büßer: Die städtischen Eliten von Montauban vor dem Inquisitor Petrus Cellani (1236/1241)* (Tübingen, 2007), was published during the late stages of my research for this book; while I have engaged with his francophone articles, I have not attempted to integrate his most recent findings into my own text.

6   R. Morghen, *Medioevo cristiano* (Bari, 1951).

7   A. Dondaine, 'L'origine de l'hérésie médiévale: à propos d'un livre récent', *Rivista di storia della chiesa in Italia* 6 (1952), 47–78.

concerning clerical reform, even neo-Platonic. I discussed these models in some depth in my first monograph.[8]

However, in the 1970s there also began a critical tendency towards deconstructing heretical texts and considering the *process* by which they were authored as being as significant as the *assertions* – for they could logically only be assertions – that they made about 'heresy'. This was not merely the result of generalised post-modern anxieties within the discipline but was an important and justified approach, because in 1972 Robert Lerner demonstrated that the fourteenth-century 'Heresy of the Free Spirit' was entirely constructed within inquisitorial discourse, specifically that of the 1311 Council of Vienne.[9] The implications of this for heresiology more widely were enormous, and so at the same time as scholars of Cathar history and belief such as Bernard Hamilton,[10] Malcolm Lambert,[11] Christine Thouzellier[12] and Jean Duvernoy[13] were doing the vital work of identifying further sources to help us understand its nature, origins and transmission, a new, alternate meta-narrative was emerging: that there were no 'real' medieval heretics after all. Such was the starting points of those leading post-modern revisionism concerning earlier movements, people such as Guy Lobrichon[14] and those in Monique Zerner's seminars.[15]

Nonetheless, the evidence on twelfth- and thirteenth-century heretical movements was considered relatively uncontroversial until around 2000 in the Anglophone world. It was generally accepted that they fell into the category of social and clerical reform – in the cases of the Paterines and heresiarchs such as Henry of Lausanne, Pierre of Bruis and Arnold of Brescia – and of Balkan-inspired dualism, or 'Catharism', in France, Italy, the Rhineland and maybe even England. As such, the most fundamental conclusions about eastern and western dualism drawn by Hamilton, Duvernoy et al. for

---

[8] See Taylor, *Heresy*, pp. 55–101.

[9] R. E. Lerner, *The Heresy of the Free Spirit in the Later Middle Ages* (Los Angeles and London, 1972).

[10] See the collection *Monastic Reform, Catharism and the Crusades (900–1300)* (London, 1979).

[11] See *Medieval Heresy: Popular Movements from Bogomil to Hus* (London, 1977), now in its third edition, retitled as *Medieval Heresy: Popular Movements from the Gregorian Reform to the Reformation* (Oxford, 2002).

[12] See *Catharisme et Valdéisme en Languedoc à la fin du XIIe et au début de XIIIe siècle* (Paris, 1966) and *Un traité cathare inédit du début du XIIIe siècle* (Louvain, 1961).

[13] See *Le catharisme I: La religion des Cathares* (Toulouse, 1976), *Le catharisme II: L'histoire des Cathares* (Toulouse, 1979) and also 'Le problème des origines du catharisme', in his *Cathares, Vaudois et Béguins: dissidents du pays d'Oc* (Toulouse, 1994), pp. 39–52.

[14] Most notably in 'The chiaroscuro of heresy: early eleventh-century Aquitaine as seen from Auxerre', trans. P. Buc, in *The Peace of God: Social Violence and Religious Response in France around the Year 1000* , ed. T. Head and R. Landes (Ithaca and London, 1992), pp. 80–103.

[15] See the collected essays in *Inventer l'hérésie? Discours polémique et pouvoirs avant l'Inquisition*, ed. M. Zerner (Nice, 1998), pp. 7–13.

the twelfth century were modified but not significantly challenged by the Anglophone scholars following them, people such as Malcom Barber[16] and even R. I. Moore, who was and is still by far the most convincing of the sceptics concerning the earlier movements.[17]

In the Francophone world, however, doubts about the twelfth century were indeed creeping in. Anne Brenon[18] called into question the significance of core dualist beliefs in the success of the movement. Monique Zerner and others challenged afresh the documentation concerning a key event in Cathar history, the Council of Saint-Félix de Caraman.[19] Jean-Louis Biget agreed that there were dualists but considered them home-grown, with social circumstances accounting for the central logic of their cosmology.[20] Like Biget, Uwe Brunn questioned the historical validity of the term 'Cathar'.[21] This scepticism concerning the roots of Catharism entered Anglophone scholarship with the work of Mark Pegg and his assault on the persistence of scholars in relating reports of 'heresy' to each other and considering that they might be connected,[22] and his suggestion that inquisitors in the Lauragais were themselves responsible for constructing whatever heresy they discovered there.[23]

In both languages, therefore, there are those who would have western dualism seen as something derived from inquisitorial sources in just the way as the 'Heresy of the Free Spirit' was. For my part, I think this has gone too far. As well as drawing on the greatest heresiologists such as Hamilton, Duvernoy and Moore, I find some of the most recent historiography concerned with inquisition sources also affirming their use as a source for information about heretical phenomena, including the work of John Arnold,[24] Peter

---

[16] M. Barber, *The Cathars: Dualist Heretics in the Languedoc in the High Middle Ages* (Harlow, 2000).

[17] See *The Origins of European Dissent* (London, 1977) and subsequent work, but *cf.* his 'Nicétas, Emissaire de Dragovitch, a-t-il traversé les Alpes?', *Annales du Midi* 85 (1973), 85–90, before he was convinced by Bernard Hamilton's work on the Cathar council of Saint-Félix de Caraman.

[18] See especially *Le vrai visage du Catharisme* (Portet-sur-Garonne, 1988), pp. 109, 122–8.

[19] *L'histoire du Catharisme en discussion: le 'concile' de Saint-Félix (1167)* (Nice, 2001).

[20] See the articles collected in *Hérésie et inquisition dans le midi de la France* (Paris, 2007).

[21] *Des contestaires au 'Cathares': Discours de réforme et propaganda antihérétique dans le pays du Rhin et de la Meuse avant l'inquisition* (Paris, 2006).

[22] See 'Historiographical essay: On Cathars, Albigenses, and good men of Languedoc', *Journal of Medieval History* 27 (2001), 181–95.

[23] See *The Corruption of Angels: The Great Inquisition of 1245–1246* (Princeton and Oxford, 2001).

[24] See *Inquisition and Power. Catharism and the Confessing Subject in the Medieval Languedoc* (Philadelphia, 2001); 'The historian as inquisitor: the ethics of interrogating subaltern voices', *Rethinking History* 2 (1998), 379–86; 'Inquisition, texts and discourse', in *Texts and the Repression of Medieval Heresy*, ed. C. Bruschi and Peter Biller (York, 2003), pp. 63–80.

Biller,[25] Caterina Bruschi,[26] Louisa Burnham,[27] Christine Caldwell Ames,[28] and Julien Roche.[29] This informs my discussion of historiography and methodology in Chapter 1. I conclude that the sources do indeed relate to a reality. However, I explore this with reference to Quercy specifically, using a methodology that cannot necessarily be reproduced elsewhere, for reasons to be discussed, and I make no claims to be writing a new positivist history of European Catharism.

Although the more sceptical school on Occitan heresy has not turned its attention to Waldensianism, logically it must do so. There cannot be a Waldensian-filled, Cathar-free Languedoc. Probably they have escaped attention because the earliest largest set of data for them is also Pierre Seilan's Book of Sentences. In other words, we know most about them in Quercy, but, like the Cathars there, they have not been the subject of a systematic study in a regional context. I have little fear for them! Even were it not impossible to account for their presence in the sources for Quercy except by accepting that they were indeed active in Quercy, Peter Biller has demolished the deconstructionist case in relation to medieval Waldensianism more generally.[30]

In terms of my methodology, I hope to demonstrate that it was in part through systematically contrasting the two movements – specifically their teachings and practices – that inquisitors identified one from the other, and that we can do likewise. This would have been a very flawed methodology indeed on the part of the medieval clergy if they themselves had *created* 'the Cathar'. Of course medieval clergy were not so stupid or so cynical, and there is a reality behind their recording of Catharism, Waldensianism and Roman Christianity. The relationship between the three doctrines and what they tell us about popular belief is therefore another theme of this book.[31]

As a starting point in demonstrating what 'Catharism' and 'Waldensianism' were, we begin with what historians have traditionally come to understand them to be. I make use here of a historiographical portrayal of coherent, self-aware movements, in southern Europe and in Languedoc specifically,

---

25 P. Biller, 'Through a glass darkly: Seeing medieval heresy', in *The Medieval World*, ed. P. Linehan and J.L. Nelson (London and New York, 2001), pp. 308–26; P. Biller, 'Goodbye to Waldensianism?', *Past and Present* 192 (2006), 3–33.

26 C. Bruschi, '"*Magna diligentia est habenda per inquisitorem*": precautions before reading Doat 21–26', in *Texts and the Repression of Medieval Heresy*, ed. Bruschi and Biller, pp. 81–111.

27 L. A. Burnham, *So Great a Light, So Great a Smoke: the Beguin Heretics of Languedoc* (Ithaca and London, 2008).

28 C. C. Ames, *Righteous Persecution: Inquisition, Dominicans, and Christianity in the Middle Ages* (Philadelphia, 2009).

29 J. Roche, *Une église cathare. L'évêché du Carcassès: Carcassonne, Béziers, Narbonne, 1167–début du XIVe siècle* (Cahors, 2005).

30 Biller, 'Goodbye to Waldensianism?'.

31 As it has been for Feuchter in his work on Montauban, in particular his 'Le pouvoir de l'inquisition', explicitly at pp. 238–9.

painted most compellingly in the case of Catharism by Duvernoy himself[32] and by Bernard Hamilton,[33] and in the case of Waldensians in Languedoc by Duvernoy,[34] Anne Brenon,[35] Peter Biller[36] and Yves Dossat,[37] and also of works on their interaction, notably that of Christine Thouzellier,[38] and in the case of Quercy, Duvernoy again.[39]

Cathars and Waldensians

According to the historiographical model inherited and improved on by Hamilton, Duvernoy and many since, Catharism was brought to western Europe by missionaries from Asia Minor and Byzantium, or by westerners encountering the heresy in the east in the decades leading up to the 1140s.[40]

---

[32] Jean Duvernoy has written more extensively on the topic than anyone else. See most significantly the works cited in note 13 above.

[33] I remain convinced by his case for the direct and deliberate influence of eastern dualists on Catharism, both in its development in the twelfth century and its interference again in the early 1220s. See 'The Cathar council of Saint Félix reconsidered', in his *Monastic Reform, Catharism and the Crusades (900–1300)* (London, 1979), pp. 23–53; 'Wisdom from the east: the reception by the Cathars of Eastern dualist texts', in *Heresy and Literacy, 1000–1530*, ed. P. Biller and A. Hudson (Cambridge, 1994), pp. 38–60. This work is significant for Quercy in that is the only historical model through which evidence for Vigouroux de la Bacone's career makes sense (see chapters 5 and 6 below).

[34] J. Duvernoy, 'Aux origins du valdéisme: une profession de foi de Valdès', in his introduction to Durand de Huesca, *Liber antiheresis, Archivum Fratrum Praedicatorum* 16 (Rome, 1946), pp. 232–5; 'À l'époque, l'Église ne poursuivait pas les Vaudois: éssai de chronologie de valdéisme languedocien', in his *Dissidents du Pays d'oc: Cathares, Vaudois et Béguins* (Toulouse, 1994), pp. 153–61.

[35] '"Vaudoisie" en Languedoc, xiie–xive siècle', in *Le Pays cathare*, ed. J. Berlioz (Paris, 2000), pp. 125–46 (pp. 138–9, 145–6).

[36] P. Biller, *The Waldenses, 1170–1530: Between a Religious Order and a Church* (Aldershot, 2001).

[37] Yves Dossat was the first to work on Waldensians in Quercy specifically. See 'De Vaudès à Saint François à Montauban', *CF* 8 (Toulouse, 1973), pp. 403–13 and 'Les Vaudois méridionaux d'après les documents de l'Inquisition', *CF* 2 (Toulouse 1967), pp. 207–42.

[38] *Catharisme et Valdéisme en Languedoc.*

[39] 'Albigeois et Vaudois en Quercy d'après le registre des pénitences de Pierre Seilan' (originally 1964) in his *Dissidents du pays d'Oc: Cathares, Vaudois et Béguins*, pp. 85–97.

[40] For the earlier scholarship see especially Stephen Runciman's *The Medieval Manichee* (Cambridge, 1947). Runciman goes too far in viewing Catharism as belonging to an unbroken chain in the dualist tradition beginning in the ancient world (although Paulicians certainly influenced Bogomilism), Elie Griffo's work is rather esoteric, for example *Les débuts de l'aventure cathare en Languedoc (1140–1190)* (Paris, 1969) and *Le Languedoc cathare (1190 à 1210)* (Paris, 1971). Among other widely referenced scholarly accounts to build on the work of Hamilton and Duvernoy are those of Barber, *The Cathars*; Lambert, *Medieval Heresy*, and *The Cathars* (Oxford and Malden, 1988); Moore, *Origins*; M. Roquebert, *L'épopée cathare*, 4 vols. (Toulouse, 1970–89); W. Wakefield, *Heresy, Crusade and Inquisition in Southern France, 1100–1250* (London, 1974). Not all of the best-

Their doctrine, Bogomilism, was 'dualist'. Specifically, they believed in the existence of a good god who created human souls and an evil god who created the physical universe and imprisoned these souls within carnal bodies. Over him, the good god had no influence. It followed from this heretical cosmology that Christ was not made human and only appeared to suffer and die. Cathars were the western adherents of this belief system, and believed that at death the soul was reincarnated in another body, human or animal.

The only way to escape this endless cycle of reincarnation was to die as a *perfectus*. Initiation into this elite was through a period of study followed by the laying on of hands by an established *perfectus* in a ceremony called the *consolamentum* (the 'consoling' or 'consolation').[41] This ritual transformed the initiate into a *perfectus* or *perfecta* themselves. Thereafter they had to live a life of extreme abstinence, owning nothing personally, renouncing sexual pleasure, killing no living thing, refusing to swear oaths and following strict dietary restrictions (no meat, eggs or dairy products, although they did admit fish),[42] including frequent and arduous fasting. Any lapse undid the *consolamentum* and the process of initiation had to be begun over again. Likewise, anyone who had been consoled by lapsed *perfecti* had to be reconsoled. *Credentes* hoped to be 'consoled' shortly before death and thus to die in the perfected state themselves, but without the necessity of leading an ascetic life. This is referred to in depositions as 'dying in the hands' of these heretics.

In 1177 Count Raimond V of Toulouse (1148–94) appealed to the Cistercian order and to the kings of France and England to help him against the heresy of 'the two principles' which had emerged in his lands. The Aquitainian viscount Raimond II of Turenne, whose family will be referred to frequently in the following chapters, was involved in the resultant royal mission to Toulouse in the following year. His role would seem to have been to provide the implicit threat of legitimate violence that lay behind it.

The sources refer to two distinct heresies at Toulouse in the late 1170s, and neither is Waldensian. Persecuted as 'Arian' was Pierre Maurand. His sect appears to have vanished after this episode. But 'among other things' the mission discovered was a sect which taught 'that there were two gods, one good, the other evil; the good had created only invisible things, those which could not be altered or corrupted; the evil had formed the heavens, the earth, men, and other visible things'. They were also donatists, rejected sex

---

known scholarship adheres to this model, by any means. See, for example, Brenon's *Vrai visage du catharisme*, and works cited in chapter 1 below.

41 Plural: *consolamenta*. While male and female *perfecti* were theroretically equal, human souls not being gendered, in normal practice only men performed the ceremony.

42 The reason often cited for eating fish is that medieval people did not know that fish reproduced sexually, although I am not sure of the basis for this assertion. Certainly Cathars did not consider fish to be 'meat' and did not avoid it (see chapters 5 and 6 below).

even within marriage and opposed infant baptism, although, when pressed, they denied all of this.[43] Their leaders were Raimond de Baimac and Bernard Raimond, the latter probably the Cathar 'bishop' of Toulouse.[44] Arian tenets are not observed in this second sect. A case can be made that clergy vaguely labelled various heresies as 'Arian',[45] but from his description Roger of Howden clearly saw the difference.

Raimond de Baimac and Bernard Raimond got off relatively lightly in 1178. But they were challenged when captured again at the siege of Lavaur (Tarn) in 1181, an affair sometimes termed a 'crusade'.[46] This time they converted formally and become canons in Toulouse, one in Saint-Etienne and the other in Saint-Sernin.[47] Had they been taken on a second occasion after 1184, however, they could have been executed. Pope Lucius III's decree *Ad abolendam*, anathematising both Cathars and Waldensians, decreed that relapsed and recalcitrant heretics should be burned at the stake.[48]

All this was probably long before heresy entered Quercy, which we can only safely date to *c.*1200. In the many missives and missions, accusations and condemnations hurtling between Rome, the clerics in Languedoc, kings and local rulers in the late twelfth century, there is no mention of Quercy. The first we hear is evidence in inquisitorial depositions that there were enough Cathars in lower Quercy by *c.*1204 for a large and important gathering to be held there, one which the inquisitors certainly saw as significant because they drew evidence concerning it from a number of witnesses.[49]

The Waldensian heresy began in the Lyonnais when a merchant of Lyons, Valdes, gave up his worldly affairs and took it upon himself as a layman to preach the gospel in the vernacular and live strictly by its precepts.[50] The

---

43 *Chronica magistri Rogeri de Houedene*, ed. W. Stubbs, 2 vols. (London, 1868–71), II, 150–5; W. L. Wakefield and A. P. Evans (ed. and trans.), *Heresies of the High Middle Ages* (New York, 1969; rprt. 1991), pp. 194–200 (p. 198). See also Gervase of Canterbury, *Opera historica*, ed. W. Stubbs (London, 1879), pp. 270–1; *PL* 204, cols. 235–42; *PL* 199, 1120–4. Arians believed Christ to be lesser than the Father, not equal within the Trinity as Catholics believed. Donatists believed that priests must be sinless or their supernatural powers were undone, rather as dualists believed of their own elect with regard to the effectiveness of *consolamenta*.

44 See below, pp. 199–200, for discussion of the use by Cathars and their enemies of titles such as 'bishop' and 'deacon'.

45 Y. Congar, 'Arriana haeresis comme désignation du néo-manichéisme au xiie siècle', *Revue des sciences philosophiques et théologiques* 43 (1959), 449–61.

46 For example, *HHMA*, p. 197 note 28.

47 *The Chronicle of William of Puylaurens: The Albigensian Crusade and its Aftermath*, trans. W. A. and M. D. Sibly (Woodbridge, 2003), chapter 2, p. 12.

48 X 5.7.9, *Corpus Iuris Canonici*, ed. A.L. Richter and E.A. Friedberg, 2 vols. (Lepizig, 1879; rprt., Graz, 1955), II, cols. 780–2 (council of Verona).

49 See chapters 4 and 7 below. Malcolm Lambert has identified another reference to heresy in Quercy that could have been dualist. It is an abjuration of faith in a mid twelfth-century manuscript of Moissac: *Medieval Heresy*, p. 65.

50 On Waldensianism in Europe generally the period in question, see Biller, *Waldenses*;

heresy spread rapidly, throughout southern Europe in particular. From the statement of orthodoxy elicited from Valdes in the 1180s, he accepted the doctrine of the trinity, the old and new testaments, the incarnation and the authority of the Catholic Church; the sacraments, including their validity whatever the moral status of the priest performing them; that the devil was made by an act of God's will and not through nature; that the dead would be resurrected in their own bodies and that masses and good works benefited them; and that eating meat was not a sin. In other words, there were clear differences between the beliefs and practices of the two sects, Waldensianism and Catharism. The Waldensian profession of faith distances the suspected heretic from the key traits of dualism, and was updated in 1208 and 1210 to the same effect.[51]

Waldensian brothers and sisters insisted on personal poverty. Like the *perfecti*, they were modest in clothing and humble in appearance, but were distinguished from the former because of the unusual way they customised their footwear, cutting leather away so as to resemble sandals,[52] in the period before wearing distinctive clothing became dangerous for both sects. Women had a far higher profile than Catholic nuns, certainly preaching and travelling with men, and of course being accused of immorality as a result.[53] But what *was* heretical was that they vociferously preached the gospels without papal or episcopal licence, something specifically addressed as heretical in *Ad abolendam*.[54] As such, the Waldensians were only officially 'heretical' from 1184.[55] Aside from this, Waldensianism was a 'simple, gospel-based movement … a would-be reform movement drawn into heresy by the inadequacies of ecclesiastical authority'.[56] However, Waldensians came to reject all violence, even judicial,[57] and by the early thirteenth century they too denied the authority of unworthy clergy, stopping just short of Donatism.[58] By the 1190s

---

E. Cameron, *Waldenses: Rejections of Holy Church in Medieval Europe* (Oxford, 2001), esp. pp. 11–35, 49–79; G. Audisio, *'Les Vaudois'. Naissance, vie et mort d'une dissidence (xiie–xvi siècles)* (Turin, 1989), translated by C. Davidson as *The Waldensian Dissent: Persecution and Survival c.1170–c.1570* (Cambridge, 1999), esp. pp. 6–39; Lambert, *Medieval Heresy*, pp. 70–85.

51   *HHMA*, pp. 220–8; A. Dondaine, 'Aux origines de valdéisme. Une profession de foi de Valdès', *Archivum Fratrum Praedicatorum* 16 (Rome, 1946), pp. 191–253; Cameron, *Waldenses*, pp. 17–21; Lambert, *Medieval Heresy*, pp. 72–3; Audisio, *Waldensian Dissent*, p. 16.

52   Cameron, *Waldenses*, p. 32.

53   Biller, 'The Preaching of the Waldensian Sisters', in his *Waldenses*, pp. 125–58.

54   Audisio, *Waldensian Dissent*, pp. 11–13; Cameron, *Waldenses*, p. 21.

55   Cameron, *Waldenses*, pp. 21; J. Duvernoy, '"À l'époque, l'église ne poursuivait pas les Vaudois", pp. 153–61, *passim*.

56   Lambert, *Medieval Heresy*, p. 70.

57   They may even have influenced Cathars in this: P. Biller, 'Medieval Waldensian abhorrence of killing pre-c.1400', in his *Waldenses*, pp. 81–93.

58   Cameron doubts that they were quite as extreme by c.1200 as Alain of Lille implies in

Waldensians were established in many small towns of Languedoc, openly flouting the proscription of preaching, as exposed in an investigation of the sect by the archbishop of Narbonne. They preached against both Catharism and Catholicism and by 1215 were so far removed from the authority of the bishops, in spite of their orthodox interpretation of the Bible, that anathema was pronounced against them at the Fourth Lateran Council.[59]

Waldensians were well established in Quercy in *c.*1200, as we discover from what Peter Biller notes was the first significant set of trial records for Waldensians, the inquest by Pierre Seilan in 1241–2.[60] It was once considered that Durand of Huesca, one of their leading theoreticians, who converted back to Catholicism in 1207, was from the neighbouring Rouergue. This has been corrected.[61] Nonetheless, after his reconciliation he recruited men from Saint-Antonin, Najac and Saint-Paul to a new, orthodox body, the Poor Catholics. Cameron notes that these are all Occitan place-names.[62] They are more than that. Saint-Antonin and Najac lie on the south-eastern edges of Quercy, and although there are many 'Saint-Pauls' in Languedoc, there is also one in Quercy near Castelnau-Montratier and one at a castle of that name at Moissac, on the Tarn. The lords of the latter, who greatly influenced secular society at Moissac,[63] were to play an important role in future events.

Certainly, by the 1230s Quercy was one of the Waldensians' most important spheres of operation, and in that context we hear of them carrying out ritual and other activity just as other Christians did but which marked them out from Cathars, such as celebrating the Last Supper by eating meat as the disciples did and preaching on Good Friday and Easter Sunday, as significant feasts.

The Story in the Sources

Against this background of historiographical generalities about the two heresies we can make sense of some of Pierre de Penne's observations. From what we hear about what God created and destroyed, on ritual, and on the sacraments, we can say that the heresy being described was Catharism. That is certain if we accept that the inquisitorial methodology was to distinguish

his 'Work in Four Parts against Heretics,Waldenses, Jews and Saracens', composed in the 1180s or 1190s at Montpellier: *Waldenses*, pp. 25–8, 33, 71. Lambert considers them more clearly Donatist after 1205: *Medieval Heresy*, p. 85.

59 Cameron, *Waldenses*, pp. 24–5, 27 note 26, 34–5; Lambert, *Medieval Heresy*, pp. 77–9, 80, 83; Lambert, *Medieval Heresy*, pp. 80, 83; Audisio, *Waldensian Dissent*, p. 16.

60 Biller, 'Goodbye to Waldensianism?', 4.

61 See Lambert, *Medieval Heresy*, p. 83 note 40; *cf.* Cameron, *Waldenses*, p. 53, and Audisio, *Waldensian Dissent*, p. 36.

62 *Waldenses*, p. 52.

63 DPC, p. 231 note 331.

one sect from the other and both from Catholicism; that is to say, the methodology that produced the kinds of source for Languedoc more generally that have informed historians' understanding of what Catharism and Waldensianism were. But both the inquisitor and the historian might draw too fine a line between devotional forms. Some of what Pierre said could also refer to Waldensians, or simply be an expression of anti-clericalism, or both. The sources have to be approached with a methodology in mind that can address these possibilities, and also that can admit the possibility that 'heresies' were not encountered, engaged with or practised to the exclusion of each other; nor, in fact, to the exclusion of 'orthodoxy'.

For example, in 1243 Bernarde Targuier of Castelsarrasin was recorded as telling the inquisitor Bernard de Caux that men and women of every social standing would come from the town of Villemur, in the northern Toulousain (Haute-Garonne), to mass at Corbarieu, just south of Montauban in Quercy. But, on coming out of the church, they would go straight away to listen to the preaching of Bernard de Lamothe, *hereticus*.[64] In its way, this account touches on several key themes addressed in modern heresiology and, as with Pierre de Penne's record, there is far more to say *about* Bernarde's anecdote than there is *in* it.

Firstly, there is its context, the inquisition: the court in which Bernarde stood and the dynamic between her and the inquisitor. Then there is the weighty technology of the written record and the obstacles and opportunities it both afforded the inquisitor and affords the historian. There is Bernarde, who she was (a townswoman, a commoner), whom she was described as being related to (she was the widow of the heretic Pons Gran and mother of his two children, and the daughter of one man called Guillaume Targuier and the sister of another),[65] what she knew (plenty) and what else this frightened woman would reveal about her friends and neighbours, some of them implicated in the scene she had just set. Her motives, and what she told and what she concealed, may or may not be apparent to the historian even though, along with fear, family and so on, they will have informed her evidence. But the implications and repercussions of the evidence form part of a wider narrative of heresy at Montauban, Corbarieu and Villemur. As such, through the individual deponent we can learn something about Quercy, just as we can contextualise her evidence within what we know about Quercy from other sources.

Then there is the story itself and what it reveals about medieval religiosity. It illustrates well that people did not necessarily choose between confessions, let alone identify clearly what was heretical or orthodox about them. We also possibly have an insight into what made the heresy popular with the laity:

---

64 D22, fol. 2v.
65 See D22, fols. 1r–3r, 15v, 22v, 41v–42r.

the Latin mass was an obligation and listening to a Cathar preach in the vernacular was another experience entirely and was undertaken voluntarily. That is what appears to be the case. But then there is the issue of religious authority. They went to *listen* to Bernard, not to talk to him as an equal. How do we know that they did this voluntarily and felt no overriding obligation, as they did in church? Bernard de Lamothe, a lord of the Montauban region himself, was Cathar deacon of Villemur. Furthermore, he was of a family of notorious heretics – his niece Arnaude de Lamothe is one of the best known and the most cited example of the activity of women within the heresy (see Chapter 4). Then there is Corbarieu itself. What Bernarde knew, and what Bernard de Caux also did by this point in the inquisition's work, was that Corbarieu was one of the most important sites in heretical Quercy. It was not only a location where Cathars preached, but was where many of the living and the dying went to be consoled themselves. It was perhaps too important *not* to visit and its heretics too powerful socially to be ignored.

The individuals, the families, their confessional leanings; the priests and monks and their failings; the heretics and their teachings and rituals; the towns and those dominating them; the nobles and the commoners: Bernarde's spoken testimony could be comprehended by the historian as it was by the inquisitor, as a window in the courtroom onto a wider narrative that is as much social and political as it is 'heretical'.

Before further discussion in Chapter 1 of how we should use sources for medieval Quercy and its heretics, we should ask what kinds of sources they are and what their value is in relation to one another. For the most part they fall into three types: narratives, charters and depositions of people like Bernarde Targuier, as well as summaries of such depositions like that of Pierre de Penne. These types of sources view events from very different perspectives. The history of the period as gleaned from narratives is like a core sample taken from the earth, consisting of coloured bands representing distinct periods. Looking along their length, 'reading left to right' (to the westerner), these are very much 'one-thing-after-another' sources, most of them closely focused on the specific events of c.1209–c.1229; the events are date-specific bands visible in the core sample.

If narratives are core samples, charters are cross sections taken across its bands. They represent specific points in time when something started, changed or ended. They tell us who changed it or initiated it and who witnessed and acknowledged it. They are very different from narratives even where they relate to the same events; whereas narratives can tell us what happened next in the story the charter does not know what will happen next, only what its enactors wanted the future to look like: that is to say, who should hold what property, who was going to 'side with' whom, and against whom or what in the future.

But in the case of depositions and their summaries we need a different simile. The reality of everything up to the point of deposition – the contextual memory of the deponent – is like the bottom of a 'figure of eight'-shaped hour-glass. It is filled with knowledge about a lifetime of events and the causes and effects of events. In the middle, at the narrow point, the witness stands alone in front of the inquisitor. It is where the consequences of those earlier events come together, although the deponent is pre-occupied with only a sub-set of those earlier events: the things that had got them into trouble. Although the deponent is being induced to discuss the past, they are nonetheless very focused indeed on the present and, of course, the future. The top half of the glass represents this future and is empty as yet, and may never be filled with anything but fear on the part of the deponent and those they loved, or with the pain of exile or incarceration, or even agonising death at the stake. In this sense, the future informed what the deponent said arguably more than the past and present did. It is the historian's privilege to know, in some cases, what came next, and to place an interpretation on it. Chapter 1 deals in more detail with the nature of the sources and what kinds of methodologies and theoretical models we should use in exploiting them. It also discusses the sources for the history of Quercy itself and what historians have done with them. It concludes with an outline of the history of Quercy in its formative period, noting key political and clerical structures governing its development before the twelfth century.

The model through which we have come to understand *why* heresy flour-ished in Languedoc, as opposed to how it got there, has several key elements.[66] One is the role of minor noble families dominating *castra*, which are the forti-fied small towns so characteristic of much of Languedoc, who were engaged in an anti-clerical and highly secular culture.[67] There was also a handful of more precocious urban centres, such as Toulouse and Agen, thriving on trade and usury. These were moving away from comital and clerical control towards communal self-government through the ambitions of consular bodies.[68] Heresy, it is argued, was transmitted essentially through the elite

---

[66] For elements of the generalised understanding of the medieval Languedoc in the context of Catharism, in addition to the more specific literature below, see H. C. Lea, *The Inquisition in the Middle Ages* (London, 1963), I, 66–8; Griffe, *Les débuts de l'aventure cathare*, pp. 172–208, and *Le Languedoc cathare*, pp. 23–6; Roquebert, *L'épopée cathare*, I, pp. 95–126; J. Sumption, *The Albigensian Crusade* (London, 1978), pp. 15–31; Barber, *The Cathars*, pp. 34–70; Lambert, *Medieval Heresy*, pp. 90–4, and *The Cathars*, pp. 63–80; Moore, *Origins*, pp. 232–7; L. Paterson, *The World of the Troubadours* (Cambridge, 1993), pp. 66–89; J. Given, *Inquisition and Medieval Society: Power, Discipline and Resistance in Languedoc* (Ithaca, 1997), pp. 5–9, 118–19; Duvernoy, *Le catharisme II*, pp. 195–7.

[67] Singular: *castrum*. For social structures see the work of Elizabeth Magnou-Nortier, for example: 'Fidélité et féodalité méridionales d'après les serments de fidélité (xe–début xii siècle)", *Annales du Midi* 80 (1968), pp. 457–84 and 'La noblesse Toulousain: essai sur son histoire médiévale', in *La noblesse au moyen age, 11e–15e siècles*, ed. P. Contamine (Paris, 1976), pp. 154–74.

[68] On commercial towns and heresy see most notably J. H. Mundy, *Liberty and Political*

family networks in such towns.[69] Leading families even established houses for the sectarians of their family and social circle. This was comparatively cheap in comparison with orthodox religious patronage, the heretics living austerely and meekly, partially earning their own living[70] and being awarded the epithet 'good men and women' – which they shared with the Occitan elite more generally – or 'good Christians'. By contrast, it has been suggested, the region's clerics were indolent and, alternatively, pampered or pauperised, rarely attending their flock but nonetheless demanding both tithes and reverence from people often unable economically to commit to them and typically unwilling to do so on ideological grounds. As such, *perfecti* were at the heart of social solidarities created in the confessional sphere and 'une pratique religieuse, une volonté de conformité de vie des Apôtres'.[71]

So, the austere sectarians were apparently integrated within networks of support so extensive that Cathars were apparently to be found in every type of settlement and community by *c.*1200, and key to this were the roles of minor nobles and of orthodox religiosity. However, heresy, like all social phenomena when explored through historical methodologies, should be understood within specific contexts, not generalities. Chapter 2 therefore makes observations about the history and nature of society in Quercy in the twelfth century. On the face of it, the county accords with an accepted, generalised picture of shared 'Occitan' identity attributed by historians to the commercial centres and *castra* making up the Cathar heartlands of the Toulousain and Lauragais. But a detailed exploration of Quercy's development stresses its distinctiveness as a region and also its internal variations. It establishes specific social and political relationships in place by *c.*1200. Significantly, it establishes that twelfth-century Quercy had a vibrant orthodox religious culture, in stark contrast with what we think characterises societies vulnerable to 'heresy'.

Quercy's own 'heretical history' is first discernible in *c.*1200, a generation or more after the first Cathars entered Languedoc. The sect then expanded northwards into the central and upper parts of the county during the

Power in Toulouse 1050–1250 (New York, 1954). For Agen, see Taylor, *Heresy*, esp. pp. 161–70, 177–86.

[69] On families in this role see especially Anne Brenon, *Les femmes cathare* (Paris, 1992) and 'Catharism in the family in Languedoc in the thirteenth and fourteenth centuries: an investigation based on inquisition sources', in *Urban and Rural Communities in Medieval France*, ed. K. Reyerson and J. Drendel (Leiden, 1998), pp. 291–304. See also Given, *Inquisition*, pp. 149–52.

[70] On the significance of Cathar economic activity see Andrew Roach's 'The Cathar economy', *Reading Medieval Studies* 12 (1986), pp. 51–71. See also L. Kaelber, 'Weavers into heretics? The social organisation of early thirteenth century Catharism in comparative perspective', *Social Science History* 21 (1997), pp. 111–37. The idea that Cathars earned their own living will be challenged in the case of Quercy.

[71] A. Brenon, 'Le catharisme méridional: questions et problèmes', in *Le Pays cathare*, ed. Berlioz, pp. 81–100 (p. 90).

northern-French-dominated Albigensian Crusade (1209–29), during which many knights of central and upper Quercy became active southern partisans. The crusade ended in 1229 with the Peace of Paris and Count Raimond VII of Toulouse performed homage for Quercy to the French king, saving the rights of the crusader-bishop of Cahors, Guillaume IV de Cardaillac (1208–34). Chapter 3 discusses the impact of these wars on Quercy and the circumstances under which its nobles came to tolerate even very high-ranking religious dissidents, and in some cases actively to encourage them. Thus Catharism did not establish itself in Quercy simply because of the nature of its message and the admiration inspired by its first missionaries and converts. As elsewhere in Languedoc, it occurred because some social groups were willing, because of their own particular circumstances, to reject Catholic authority, both secular and clerical. Minor nobles fell victim to the social and political transformation wrought by the crusade in the Agenais and Quercy, not least the imposition of rigid vertical ties of dependence largely alien to the region. These changes and the resistance to them were, in turn, to impact on and subvert patterns of toleration of the heresy. Thus for many noble and knightly families 'heresy', or the toleration of heretics, was a socio-political choice. We shall see that it was an ill-advised one in most cases: a stubborn cutting off of the nose to spite the face. This toleration of heresy, which we learn about through narratives and depositions, became a low-level but significant feature of quercinois society in an era in which the charters, in contrast, make it *appear* as though the dominant discourse was that of noble–clerical alliances and the rise of urban aspirations more typical of medieval France.

Chapter 3 concludes with a discussion of the inquisition as an outcome of a socially disastrous war. Its records for Quercy in particular provide the focus for Chapter 4, where we shall draw out in some detail the evidence given by specific people in specific places about themselves and specific other people. We will encounter more people like Pierre de Penne and Bernarde Targuier and learn something of their activity in the crusade years and early inquisition. The material in this chapter is structured around the depositions and the summaries of depositions as they were organised for the record by the inquisitor. The focus is, therefore, very much on the 'facts of the matter' as they appeared to Pierre Seilan and Bernard de Caux: who did what and believed what, who knew about it. The historian, like the inquisitor, also learns what formally constituted the sets of relationships deponents were part of, be they familial, political or urban.

Chapter 5, in contrast, looks at the evidence in thematic terms. It focuses on what we could call the 'social life' of heresy and explores devotional cultures in Quercy. We will see that we cannot talk of 'heretical families'. In fact, the evidence more typically contains many examples of divergent beliefs and allegiances within single families. But while the inquisition wrongly considered individuals within such groupings as automatically tainted and suspect, we should not go too far the other way in assuming a naive or ambivalent eclecticism on the part of members of these families. What emerges is that it was individuals, rather than families, who were devoted adherents of one or the other sect. Socio-economic aspects of the 'heretical life' are also examined.

Another great contribution to our understanding of heresy is that of Bob Moore and his view that the persecution of such movements needs to be understood in the context of the rise of medieval bureaucracies. Persecution was a feature of the bureaucracies from the early eleventh century, reaching its apogee in the thirteenth, corresponding to the re-emergence of statecraft after perceived chaos at the end of the Carolingian era. Both the identification of 'otherness' and its destruction by authority is not, he reasons, a natural extension of an innate intolerance of diversity within a given society, as Durkheim had it. It is instead, as Weber understood it, initiated and imposed from above by these bureaucracies.[72] More recently he admits less of a contrast between the two models, because persecution, while imposed and not 'natural', became institutionalised and as such played a role in defining who was *within* and *beyond* society: that is to say, *protected by* or *threatening to* Christian political order. In Moore's words, 'persecution began as a weapon in the competition for political influence, and was turned by the victors into an instrument for consolidating their power over society at large'.[73] In Chapter 6 we shall see this process come to fruition under a variety of competing authorities: local, urban, papal, Dominican, episcopal, comital and royal.

We will focus also in Chapter 6 on how individuals and groups of people responded to these forces. They attempted to negotiate their relationship with the inquisitor, for example, in ways similar to those highlighted generally by James Given and also by Jörg Feuchter,[74] but also through strategies specific to their own social position and networks of affinity and the weapons these afforded them. This final chapter also discusses what the evidence from Quercy tells us about the distinctiveness of Catharism organisationally; in short, was there a distinctive structure hierarchy that we could call a Cathar 'church'? We explore further the relationship between the heretics and their supporters. Finally, we establish how heresy and its legacy of oppression had affected Quercy as a society by *c.*1245, when major inquisitions in the region had done their work.

---

[72] The case is pursued throughout his *The Formation of a Persecuting Society: Power and Deviance in Western Europe, 950–1250* (Oxford, 2008).

[73] *Formation*, p. 146.

[74] Feuchter follows Given in seeing the inquisitorial process as a 'negotiation' of power': 'Le pouvoir de l'Inquisition', p. 236.

1

Investigating Medieval Quercy:
Questions about Sources

In this chapter we address the evidence and methodologies available for studying those medieval phenomena classified, in different contexts, by historians and by medieval clergy as 'heresy', and also for studying the medieval county of Quercy. We also note what has been established previously about Catharism and Waldensianism in Quercy.

Recording Society and Heresy in Medieval Quercy

Medieval Quercy corresponded closely to the modern departments of Tarn-et-Garonne and Lot: that is to say, the region between the Dordogne and the Garonne-Tarn-Aveyron basin. Before the fourteenth-century creation of the diocese of Montauban, it corresponded essentially to the diocese of Cahors and to the most northerly part of the diocese of Toulouse. The boundary was in fact the gates of the quercinois town of Montauban.

In terms of conceptualising its social, political and confessional orientation in the high Middle Ages it makes sense to regard Quercy as having six different geographical spheres, contrasting with each other in some important ways. They are lower Quercy, the Vaux, the Bouriane and what we could call the Cahorsain-Lot, Limousin-Quercy and Eastern-Quercy (see Map 1, p. xii). The first three terms are names used by the people of the region historically. Identifying twelfth-century networks of lordship and religious affinity shows these distinctions to be appropriate for our purpose too. The latter three are terms I suggest as useful, again on the basis of identifying political and other features typifying these geographical spheres. These regions responded differently to the presence of, firstly, heresy and, secondly, the Albigensian crusade.

We have three main kinds of sources available: charters, narratives and inquisitorial depositions. Charters provide almost all of the available evidence before the thirteenth century. They tell us who held what property, in what sense, until when and who held it next. They also tell us things such as who was allied to whom, and why, and what they pledged to do together. Others tell us what lords of towns had to offer or concede in order to secure the cooperation of townspeople. Charters also give us hundreds of names of quercinois people and their relative positions within an event. These charters fall into two main categories: those relating to donations made in favour of abbeys, and those relating to secular activity by individuals, families and towns. Of the extant documents, most of those surviving the revolutionary period[1] were distributed within the new network of French communal and departmental archives, in this case those of the Lot (at Cahors), the northern two-thirds of which was the medieval Quercy. In the archives of Tarn-et-Garonne (at Montauban) far less survives for this period.

Many such charters are reproduced in antiquarian collections, the most important of which for Quercy is the *Histoire générale du Languedoc*.[2] In spite of its southern orientation, *HGL* is not sympathetic to protectors of heresy or opponents of the crusade. Its authors describe the involvement of Bishop Guillaume IV in the war as giving Quercy 'une légitime indépendance' from the heretical 'fauteur' Raimond VI.[3]

In spite of Duvernoy's request for a thoroughly integrated history of quercinois heresy and society, historians are in fact already exceptionally lucky to have had as one of the Lot's most important archivists and local historians one of the few scholars also to have written on heresy in the region. He was the canon Edmond Albe (d. 1926).[4] Several more of Quercy's archivists have done important work on the high medieval evidence. L. Combarieu, departmental archivist in the 1870s and compiler of several inventories of Quercy's communal archives, edited an important charter relating to the town of Cajarc as well as the consular record of Cahors known as *Te igitur* and an invaluable historical dictionary of place-names of the Lot.[5] Before this, Emile Dufour had

---

[1] An important archive which did not survive was the communal archive of Castelnau-Montratier, destroyed in 1793: see L. Limayrac, *Étude sur le môyen age. Histoire d'un commune et d'une baronnie du Quercy: Castelnau-Montratier* (Cahors, 1885), p. iii.

[2] *HGL*, VI, 1, 3–5, first compiled in *c*.1730. The theme of heresy is central to its medieval material, evident even in its structure: volume six opens '1. Origine & de l'hérésie dans le province', followed by an account of the 1165 Council of Lombers. *HGL* also observes the first recorded 'heresy' in Quercy, that of Ulfald, who lived in the tenth century and asserted that the soul dies with the body. His heresy was apparently refuted by Bishop Durand of Cahors (d. 953): *HGL*, III, 157.

[3] *HGL*, VIII, 287.

[4] Editor of *IRC*. Part one was published at Cahors in a volume in 1915: *IRC* i. But *IRC* ii, iii, and iv were published in *BSEL*, respectively in 41 (1920), 1–48; 43 (1922), 1–28; 47 (1926), 1–150. See also E. Albe, *Les institutions religieuses de Gourdon* (Gourdon, 1926).

[5] Editor of *Inventaire sommaire des archives départementales antérieures á 1790: Lot*, 3 vols. (Cahors, 1883–1900), 'Inventaire mss. des archives communales de Cahors' (Cahors, 1864) (unpublished guide, AD Lot) and other unpublished guides to the departmental archives at Cahors (see bibliography); *Charte des coutumes de Cajarc* (Cahors, 1879); L. Combarieu and P. Lacombe (eds.), *Te Igitur* (Cahors, 1888; *Dictionnaire des communes du Lot* (Nîmes, 2000: rprt. of Cahors 1881). I am indebted to my research student Faye Taylor for the long-term loan of the latter valuable resource for the purposes of writing this book.

edited some previously little used charters.[6] Slightly later, a full inventory of the archive at Montauban was produced by M. Maisonobe.[7]

Like other French departments, Quercy had several histories composed and re-edited using such documentation in the second half of the nineteenth century, when there was quite a flurry of them.[8]

There are four key narratives of the Albigensian crusade and inquisitorial period, three of them composed by southern French authors and one by a northerner. The latter is the Latin chronicle of a young Cistercian, Pierre, of the abbey les-Vaux-de-Cernay, who followed his uncle and abbot, Gui, on the Albigensian crusade.[9] Pierre was with the army for most of its major engagements and negotiations. His is a relatively easy source to use. He had an enthusiastic eye for detail, and his fanatical pro-crusader stance never wavers. As such, we can read him for factual detail about events and campaigns and discount most of his observations on southern French society and its confessional preferences.

---

[6] *Documents inédits pour servir à l'histoire de l'ancienne province de Quercy* (Cahors, 1868).

[7] *Inventaire sommaire des archives départementales antérieures á 1790: Tarn-et-Garonne* (Montauban, 1894).

[8] The 'great men' school of historiography was well-served by C. Lacarrière, *Histoire des évêques de Quercy, des saints, des monastères, des principaux événements du Quercy* (Nîmes, 2004; rprt. of Martel, 1876). L. Ayma's translation and re-working of G. de Lacroix's history of the bishops, published around the same time, is more worthy of note: *Histoire des évêques de Cahors*, 2 vols. in 4 (Cahors, 1878/9: translation of *Series et acta episcoporum Cadurcensium*, G. Lacroix (Cahors, 1621). Likewise useful is the more general work by G. Lacoste: *Histoire générale de la province de Quercy*, 4 vols. (Cahors, 2004: rprt. of Cahors, 1883). See also that of his contemporary and friend J.-L. Lacabane: *Observations sur la géographie et l'histoire du Quercy et du Limousin à propos de la publication du Cartulaire de Beaulieu* (Paris, 1862). Very important, although not without its flaws, is E. Dufour's history of Cahors itself: *La commune de Cahors au moyen âge* (Marseille, 1976: rprt. of Cahors, 1846). Best used cautiously is Limayrac's monograph on Castelnau-Montratier. See, for example, his characterising of the Middle Ages as 'a time of progress, patriotism and freedom': *Étude sur le môyen age*, p. xxxv, and the lords and people of medieval Castelnau as 'defenders of the Church': *Étude sur le môyen age*, p. 7. Roger Bulit's early twentieth century examination of the lords of Gourdon is essential: *En pays de Bouriane: Gourdon en Quercy, des origines au xixe siècle* (Gourdon, 1997: rprt. of Toulouse, 1923). However, it too is not entirely flawless and does not always supercede an earlier work on these lords by Combarieu and F. Cangardel: 'Gourdon et ses seigneurs du xe au xive siècle', *BSEL* 6 (1880), and published as a volume at Cahors in 1881. More recently, the traditional narratives have been evaluated and added to by J. Lartigaut, whom I have used extensively. Most significant is his *Histoire de Quercy* (Toulouse, 1993). See also *Les campagnes de Quercy* (Toulouse, 1976) and *Puy-l'Evêque au Moyen Age. Le castrum et la châtellenie (xiiie–xve)* (Beynac, 1991). A. Ligou produced a significant history of Montauban: *Histoire de Montauban* (Toulouse, 1992). Also useful is M. de la Torre's guide to the various communes of the department of the Lot: *Lot: le guide complet des ses 340 communes* (Paris, 1990), unpaginated.

[9] PVC *History* (English translation). For the Latin edn: PVC *Hystoria*. The French translation has some important footnotes: PVC *Histoire*.

A second narrative, from the perspective of a southern French troubadour, could hardly provide more of a contrast. Known as the 'Song of the Albigensian Crusade', this performance poem, though also partisan, is less easy than Pierre's chronicle to pigeonhole and interpret. It is pro-crusade and anti-Cathar in its early sections, which are composed by Guillaume de Tudela, but anti-French and more tolerant of the heretics and their supporters in the passages composed after 1218 by an anonymous continuator.[10] From 1198 to 1211 Guillaume was based at Montauban, which makes him an especially useful source for Quercy.[11] An anonymous later thirteenth century narrative chronicle in Occitan follows the Song very closely, but occasionally contains information from other sources.[12]

A third narrative is that of Guillaume de Puylaurens. It focuses on the efforts of the church to combat heresy, from the first preaching campaigns of 1206–7 and the efforts of bishops to the crusade itself and finally the inquisition from its establishment in the 1230s into the 1270s. In spite of covering some seventy years' worth of events, it is far briefer than the two major narratives. It touches on important events in Quercy and, in spite of the late date of composition, is an invaluable source even for the events which took place when the author was an infant. Many others he witnessed at first hand. But Guillaume was not a southern partisan. Indeed, he blames his countrymen for bringing the wrath of the papacy upon itself, whatever the faults and excesses of the crusaders.[13]

Finally, Guillaume Pelhisson's chronicle deals with the inquisition in the period 1229–44, and is an essential work for understanding its early operational context in Quercy. It is also an insider's view. Pelhisson, who died in 1268, was an inquisitor himself, probably from 1234, and Jean Duvernoy notes him as a key source for the inquests in that year by Pierre Seilan and Guillaume Arnaud at Moissac (1234), Cahors (1235) and Montauban (1236). There are known to be a few inaccuracies in his work in terms of chronology, and some of these impact on our knowledge of Quercy, although Jean Duvernoy and Yves Dossat have made sense of most of them. This evidence is important

---

10 For the Provençale, with facing French translation: *La Chanson de la croisade albigeoise,* ed. and trans. E. Martin-Chabot, 3 vols. (Paris, 1960–72), hereafter abbreviated as *Chanson*. See also *The Song of the Cathar Wars*, trans. J. Shirley (Aldershot, 1996), hereafter abbreviated as *Song*.

11 J. Balteau et al. (eds.), *Dictionnaire de biographie française* (Paris, 1929–), XVII, pp. 191–2; Taylor, *Heresy*, p. 190.

12 *Histoire de la guerre des albigeois*, Anon., in *RHF*, XIX, pp. 114–92 and *HGL*, VIII, pp. v–vi, 5–205.

13 *The Chronicle of William of Puylaurens*, trans. Sibly and Sibly; *Chronica magistri Guillelmi de Podio Laurentii*, ed. J. Duvernoy (Paris, 1976). See also Y. Dossat, 'A propos du chroniqueur Guillaume de Puylaurens', in his *Église et hérésie*, pp. 47–52, and 'Le chroniqueur Guillaume de Puylaurens était-il chaplain de Raymond VII ou notaire de l'inquisition toulousaine?', in his *Église et hérésie*, pp. 343–53.

because we do not have inquisitors' registers for this period, although we know they were made, because Guillaume Pelhisson makes a point of telling us that the many confessions made in various locations were recorded in books.[14] So we know that registers were in use this early but were perhaps something of a novelty, worth commenting on.

Those registers of the 1230s would have contained trial records from Quercy, including depositions, but only one set of documentation from this decade survives. It is the earliest extant trial documentation of the medieval inquisition, the depositions and letter of penitence of a key supporter of heretics in Quercy, Pons Grimoard, seneschal to Count Raimond VII of Toulouse. Guillaume Arnaud's meticulousness allowed his confession and recantation to be consulted a decade later by the inquisitor Bernard de Caux. The incriminating documents from the 1230s were then copied into de Caux's register, and the original lost. De Caux's register was lost also, as was that of Pierre Seilan, inquisitor in Quercy in 1241–2. Indeed, the records of almost every other inquisitorial trial had been lost or destroyed by the time of the Revolution. What was still extant in the Dominican convent in Toulouse by October 1669 was transcribed for the French crown into Bibliothèque nationale de France mss Lat. Fonds Doat before the friars' archive was destroyed.[15] In terms of material relevant to Quercy, Doat 21 contains Pierre Seilan's register, Doat 22 Bernard de Caux's and Doat 23 that of an otherwise unknown Brother Ferrer, or Ferrier.

Doat 21, folios 185v–312v, consists of 724 sentences passed by a peripatetic court that sat between May 1241 and March 1242 at Montauban, Moissac, Gourdon, Montcuq, Sauveterre, Beaucaire, Montpezat, Almont and Castelnau-Montratier. The majority of the deponents had came forward voluntarily during the period of grace, when confessing and recanting meant they would not be 'handed over to the secular arm' for corporal or capital punishment. The register is the earliest extant record of this process and consists of summaries of deponents' heretical admissions and crimes, and their punishments, most typically pilgrimages, to places as close as le Puy and as far as Jerusalem, and often also the support of paupers. It is far less detailed than most inquisitional records. A representative brief entry reads, in its entirety, thus: 'The sisters Arnalda et Geralda saw heretics and heard their words. They will go to Le Puy and Saint-James.'[16]

---

[14] Guillaume Pelhisson, *Chronique (1229–1244) suivie du récit des troubles d'Albi (1234)*, ed. and trans. J. Duvernoy (Paris, 1994), pp. 22, 56–9, 70–1. There is an earlier, English translation in Wakefield, *Heresy, Crusade and Inquisition*, Appendix 3, 'The Chronicle of William Pelhisson', pp. 207–36.

[15] The Doat manuscripts consist in total of 258 volumes of documents relating to southern France. Volumes 21–37 relate to the inquisition.

[16] D21, fol. 299r.

The exact nature and purpose of this register is not certain. It seems likely that it is a summary of a longer document containing full depositions. Jörg Feuchter suggests that it could have been an *aide-memoire* for the inquisitors, or may have served in drawing up letters of safe conduct for penitent pilgrims.[17] It seems likely to me that it is an early version of the *culpa*, a summary of the significant elements of a deponent's crimes read out just before sentencing,[18] to which the sentences were then added. There is reason to believe that the sentences were set down some time after the cases were heard, a point to be addressed in Chapter 7 below.

In the year after Pierre Seilan completed his mission Bernard de Caux began his posting in Quercy.[19] Evidence relating to witnesses, including fourteen from Quercy, was taken at Agen and Cahors from 30 November 1243 to 17 March 1245 and is preserved in Doat 22.[20] Included among this evidence is Pons Grimoard's letter of absolution. Dated 29 March 1236, it is the earliest inquisitorial record of any type. It vaguely outlines the nature of his association with heretics and is in essence a letter of safe conduct from Guillaume Arnaud and Bishop Pons Antéjac of Cahors (c.1236–7) so that he might safely complete part of his penance – pilgrimages to Santiago-de-Compostella, Nôtre-Dame de Rocamadour, Saint-Gilles and Nôtre-Dame du Puy – within two years. It survives by being copied by Bernard de Caux into the record of the 1244 investigation into Pons's more recent activities and thence into Doat 22.[21]

Doat 23 contains evidence for Quercy, some about one of the best-known Cathar women, Arnaude de Lamothe of Montauban, and information about the heretical life of Moissac, where the seigneurial family were important *credentes* and where Raimond VII's *bailli* (bailiff), Othon de Berètges, had undermined the inquisitors at his master's behest, as he revealed to Bernard de Caux.[22]

17 J. Feuchter, 'Pierre Sellan, un viellard expérimenté, in *Les inquisiteurs. Portraits de défenseurs de la foi en Languedoc (xiiie–xive siècles)*, ed. L. Albaret (Toulouse, 2001), pp. 41–55 (p. 51). It seems certain that this was not the *only* record of this lengthy inquest, because the practice of making copies of registers was quite common in the 1240s following an insurrection in 1235 at Narbonne, which saw townspeople systematically destroying registers: H. C. Lea, *The Inquisition of the Middle Ages* (London, 1963), p. 133.

18 Bernard Gui, *Manuel de l'inquisiteur*, ed. and trans G. Mollat, 2 vols. (Paris, 1926–7) and see Burnham, *So Great a Light*, pp. 54–5.

19 See Y. Dossat, 'Une figure d'inquisiteur: Bernard de Caux', in *CF* 6 (Toulouse, 1971), pp. 253–72, also published in his *Église et hérésie en France au xiiie siècle* (London, 1982), pp. 47–52; Y. Dossat, 'L'inquisiteur Bernard de Caux et l'Agenais', in his *Église et hérésie en France*, pp. 75–79.

20 In 1988 Jean Duvernoy transcribed and translated this into French and it is published an on-line as DCBC. Although it contains a few proofreading errors it is invaluable in being searchable.

21 D22, fols. 38r–40v, *HGL*, VIII, 1015–16; Guillaume Pelhisson, *Chronique*, pp. 92–3.

22 On Othon de Berètges see below and also Caterina Bruschi, *The Wandering Heretics of Languedoc* (Cambridge, 2009), pp. 172–3, 176.

These sources give us evidence about what sort of assumptions and questions were on the inquisitor's mind when he sat in the courtroom with the frightened witness in front of him, and what witnesses may have thought or believed about the world, metaphysical and otherwise. They also give us insight into what witnesses knew about events in the preceding decades, going back as far as *c.*1200. As such, they are as important for the study of individual lives, of families and towns, and even for political affairs, as they are for the nature of heresy.

The Doat Manuscripts: Interpretative Issues and Opportunities

The relationship between phenomena called 'heresy' by medieval clergy and the texts clerics produced concerning them is the subject of a key historiographical debate at present. The nature of the depositional evidence for heretical adherence both raises problems and offers opportunities.[23] I intend to take a 'glass half-full' approach to the evidence and exploit it cautiously but optimistically. To begin with, there are some essentially technical points to consider.

What we have and what we do not have
Peter Biller has noted that unlike what has become known as the 'Heresy' of the Free Spirit, was in fact entirely constructed by the council of Vienne, the Cathar heresy preceded clerical commentary on it. Yet 'it is this initial relief, the fact that the sources do relate to a reality, which constitutes the danger: by relaxing vigilance about how these sources have shaped that reality'.[24] So, we need to be clear about what sentences and depositions are and what they are not.

The sentences passed by Pierre Seilan and recorded in Doat 21 are a record of who was found guilty, and of what, and what penalties they faced. What they are not is a record of who appeared in front of the inquisitor. There is, accordingly, no record of who was found 'innocent'. If we could not tell this from the content of the sentences themselves, we could deduce it from the fact that the majority of the sentences delivered were passed on people whose family name we find only once or twice in the register. It would seem that most family members had given what J. Roche calls 'negative depositions':[25] that is to say, records of witnesses volunteering to speak up in the period of

---

23 As well as the works to be cited below, a good introduction to the discussion is Biller's 'Through a glass darkly'. See also L. Boyle, 'Montaillou revisited: *Mentalité* and Methodology', in *Pathways to Medieval Peasants*, ed. A. J. Raftis (Toronto, 1981), pp. 119–40; Given, *Inquisition*; Arnold, *Inquisition and Power*, esp. pp. 1–15.
24 'Through a glass darkly', p. 312, and see 'Goodbye to Waldensianism?', pp. 7–8.
25 *Une église cathare: l'évêché du Carcassès*, p. 10.

grace of whom it was accepted that they had never had any dealings with heretics of any sort, and whose words were therefore not recorded. Everyone recorded had committed a 'crime', and so some people in any given vicinity – we can not know how many – remain unknowable. They may have been marginal to the history of heresy, but not necessarily to the wider history of Quercy. But we only 'know' about quercinois society what was recorded concerning it.

This relates to depositions also. They are not transcripts: far from it. We do not have a record of the inquisitor's questions, although we can often deduce what they were. The deponent's reply to the questions, in the vernacular, was set down in Latin and in the third person. Probably the deponent could neither read nor understand the significance of the Latin text attributed to them, and yet, should they be tried a second time and found guilty, this record was what showed the inquisitor that they had relapsed and were thus be liable to be handed over to the secular arm. Hence, as James Given notes, inquisitorial documents were 'instruments ... not only of knowledge but of coercion'.[26] We have noted this in Pons Grimoard's case. Pétronille de Pierre Sanche claimed that she had been a *perfecta* but had been reconciled with the church through Bishop Fulk of Toulouse. She presumably claimed to have undergone a penance and not to have sinned again, because the scribe noted that this claim was to be followed up.[27]

A third factor also impacts on evidence for the 'social life' of heresy. The fact that the inquest of 1241–2 condemned hundreds of people to undertake pilgrimages, often of several years' duration, affected what Doat 22 and 23 can be a record of. Key figures in social networks were quite probably absent from the picture by the time of the 1243–5 inquests.

We also lack an obvious name for the phenomena for which we have evidence.[28] Those receiving the minor sentences in Doat 21 are designated *credentes* in the Latin sources and a distinction is made between these and *heretici* by the inquisitors. But issues arise from translating other terminology used by the inquisitor to identify religious dissidents. In Doat 21 both 'heretics' (*heretici*) and 'Waldensians' (*Valdenses*) are recorded. The latter were chaste and took vows of personal poverty and obedience, and, although they were forbidden to preach by the church, this was one of their main activities. After this, their similarity to the activities ascribed to the 'heretics' ends. They were treated differently by the inquisitors, too. Witnesses were asked whether they had encountered 'heretics' and/or 'Waldensians'. For example, one record reads 'Guillaume de Broile saw Waldensians and listened to their preaching. *Item*, he saw heretics in another place and assisted in discussion

---

26 Given, *Inquisition*, p. 39.
27 D21, fol. 244v.
28 On labels applicable to heresy in the northern Languedoc see especially Arnold's *Inquisition and Power*, pp. 138–49; Taylor, *Heresy*, pp. 171–2.

about (the New) Testament in the presence of Waldensians. He saw heretics and listened to their preaching and discussed creation with them ...'.[29] In other words, these are not interchangeable terms. Waldensians are not simply a sub-category of the inquisitorial 'heretic'. Furthermore, 'heretic' must refer to what historians have chosen to call Cathars, or *perfecti*. The question 'Did you adore heretics?' i.e. offer the ritual veneration, is evidently being asked where the record reads 'he saw heretics and he adored them', as, for example, in the testimony of Bernard Guiraud of Moissac.[30] The question was not asked concerning Waldensians and in any case would have been meaningless, because Waldensians did not practise the same ritual adoration as Cathars. Furthermore, the term *'credens'* is hardly ever used about Waldensian 'believers' or adherents. In evaluating the extent of attachment to this sect, the question 'Did you believe them to be good men?' is the only one asked.

This conceptual framework, in which dualist heretics were distinguished from Waldensians by clerics, was in place by the 1180s or 90s, for example in the *De fide catholica* of Alain of Lille, written somewhere between 1179 and 1202.[31] It was continued in a clerical treatise of *c*.1208, explicitly citing the diocese of Cahors as a place that is inhabited by heretics who asserted that there was 'a good God and a strange/malign god' and 'other heretics ... Waldenses'.[32] This account may have informed Pierre des-Vaux-de-Cernay's account of the differences between the heretics who, on the one hand, 'postulated two creators' and are called 'the Perfect' or 'Good men' and, on the other, the 'sect of heretics who received the name "Valdenses" from Valdius, a citizen of Lyon', but there are also important differences between the two accounts.[33] An anonymous manual for inquisitors of *c*.1265, which is based on practices of the 1230s and 1240s, was structured to deal separately with Cathars and Waldensians.[34] Euan Cameron observes that the 'continual dialogue between literary tradition and direct testimony' in the manuals resulted from inquisitors' application of established examples to trials that

[29] D21, fol. 263r. See DPC, p. 183 note 278 for Duvernoy's rendering of 'cuiusdam testamenti' as New Testament.

[30] D21, fol. 291r–v.

[31] *PL* 210, 301a–340a. Hilbert Chiu is an emerging expert on Alain of Lille and his as yet unpublished MA thesis is already proving influential: 'The Intellectual Origins of Medieval Dualism' (University of Sidney, 2009). I am most grateful to him for allowing me to read it.

[32] The statement, possibly by Ermengaud of Béziers is contained in A. Dondaine, 'Durand of Huesca et la polémique anti-cathare', *Archivum Fratrum Praedicatorum* 29 (Rome, 1959), pp. 268–71; *HHMA*, p. 230 (for the dating), pp. 231–5 (p. 231).

[33] *HHMA*, pp. 230, 235; PVC *History*, p. 14, and see pp. 27, 231.

[34] A. Dondaine, 'Le Manuel de l'inquisiteur (1230–1330)', *Archivum Fratrum Praedicatorum* 17 (1947), pp. 106, 144–5; Biller, 'Preaching', pp. 125–58 (p. 129).

they were themselves involved in.[35] In other words, distinguishing between the two groups of heretics was found to be necessary. Guillaume Pelhisson also refers to 'Cathars' as *heretici perfecti* and Waldensians as *Valdenses*, again distinguishing clearly and using terminology denoting a distinct status for the Cathar elect.[36]

Like medieval clergy, historians writing about heresy in Quercy need a terminology to use about western dualists to distinguish them from Waldensians, because the term 'heretic' is used too widely of dissident religious movements to be useful.[37] But we cannot simply call them 'good men and women', as deponents sometimes did in Languedoc more widely.[38] We have no evidence that they were designated as such in Quercy. The terms *bons omes* and *prodomes* mask and also normalise dissident belief rather than denote it, being used of people of high social status too generally for it to be wise for the historian of Quercy to use them. We do not find the term 'good Christians' in Quercy either, and it too is, in any case, too vague. Neither can we do as Jean-Louis Biget does. He considers the 'heretics' in the depositions to be dualists, but, because they did not use the term 'Cathar' of themselves, he prefers to use 'heretic' or 'dissident'.[39] His approach is viable for the geographical areas he addresses because Waldensians were marginal there. In Quercy, however, they were present in large numbers, so we have to distinguish 'dualists' from Waldensian heretics. I shall therefore use the term 'Cathar', noted by Eckbert of Schönau of dualists in Germany in the 1160s,[40] as most historians of Languedoc do. Eckbert tells us that they used this term of themselves and it seems highly likely that the southern French and Italian dualists were part of the same sect. But I accept that it is not an unproblematic designation.[41]

Finally, although the detailed depositions in Doat 22 routinely attribute dates to significant events – because the inquisitor, like the historian, was interested in when things took place, and when things changed and why – we lack this in the sentences of Doat 21. From the dates in Doat 22 we know that *credentes* were recalling events from as far back as 1204. But things changed in heretical society. Heretics began to be burned to death in 1209, were sheltered

---

35 *Waldenses*, p. 4.
36 Guillaume Pelhisson, *Chronique*, pp. 42–3, 56–7.
37 Arnold, *Inquisition and Power*, pp. 138–9.
38 Ibid., pp. 139–44.
39 He also rejects the term 'Albigensian' as a politically descriptive term employed by clergy and crusaders: 'Les 'Albigeois'. Entrée dans l'histoire', in his *Hérésie et inquisition dans le midi de la France* (Paris, 2007), pp. 142–69 (originally 1998).
40 *Sermones tredecim contra Catharos*, PL 195, 11a–98c, *passim*.
41 Uwe Brunn's rejection of the term 'Cathar' is central to his work on the Rhineland, where the term originated: *Des Contestaires au 'Cathares'*. See also Taylor, *Heresy*, pp. 171–2, for discussion of terminology for Catharism. Although it seems safe to understand *hereticus* as 'Cathar', the rendering of *hereticus* as 'parfait' by Duvernoy in his edition of D21 seems to go too far.

from the crusaders by defiant lords in the south, were hunted down routinely by royal and local forces from 1229, and they and even their most moderate supporters were dragged before inquisitorial courts from the mid-1230s. We can locate events within historical contexts such as these. For example, from Pierre Austorgue we learn that Waldensians preached publicly on the roads.[42] This surely relates to a relatively early period in the sect's activity in Quercy, because in the crusade period and in particular after 1229 this was extremely dangerous. We have very few references in any of the Quercy depositions to the distinctive garb of the *perfecti*, black robes, but Guillaume Faure de Pech-ermer of Castelsarrasin was to note specifically of Raimond Grimoard that he had seen him in the dress of a *perfectus,* and Guillemette de Sapiac would reveal that she had been dressed thus as a little girl. Raimond was a genera-tion older than Guillaume, and Guillemette was an adult when questioned, so we can safely suggest that both references date to the period before 1229, at the latest, when such distinctive dress had to be abandoned. Among the many questions that deponents were routinely asked about *perfecti*, matters of distinctive dress were rarely raised. This inclines me to the view that most references to heretical practice were relatively recent. Indeed, the inquisitors were most interested in events that had taken place since the inquests of the 1230s, as we shall see. The abandonment of heretical garb also helps us to make sense of several accounts in which deponents would claim not to have known that the people they were ferrying in their boat, for example, were *perfecti*, and that they realised only when it was too late. Such misunderstand-ings can have taken place only if *perfecti* were attempting to pass themselves off as ordinary people. Indeed, the inquisitor asked a whole battery of indic-ative questions to determine whether 'heretical' or 'innocent' activity had taken place, but in these highly formulaic schemata identification of heretics by their appearance does not register.

Assumptions about inquisitors and inquisition
Of course, the discussion above raises epistemological as well as technical issues. For example, might it be the case that inquisitors did not ask questions about clothes because the good men and women had *never* worn distinctive clothes? Conversely, how do we know that the formulaic questions asked to identify 'heresy' actually related to any real-world phenomena against which a deponent's evidence may have been measured? In other words, how do we know that we do not have another 'Heresy of the Free Spirit', constructed deliberately or accidentally by the inquisitor? Certainly, there were some very odd things believed in Languedoc, as we shall see. Being aware of this, M. Pegg refuses to use the term 'Cathar' because it assumes and thereby imposes uniformity on what might be a variety of religious phenomena,

---

[42] D21, fols. 237v–8r.

rather as J. J. Clarke observed of the colonial construction of Hinduism.[43] In using the word 'Cathar' we may be allowing the inquisitor to fool us into thinking that these phenomena that did exist were related and that they were dualist.

At some point in the process of seeking to 'know about heresy' as it is reflected in the depositions we have to make a judgement about the extent to which we trust that the inquisitors asked appropriate questions and recorded accurately what was answered. At some point we draw a line that admits certain evidence as 'reliable' and excludes other evidence. If we aim simply to take a 'common sense' approach we draw this line arbitrarily. 'Common sense' usually means interpreting something according to the historical consensus. At some points this need to be revisited, and this is indeed happening in the field of heresiology.

We also need to be aware of what we are doing if we try instead to draw the line ethically. We react strongly against the evidence because of how it was generated, rightly considering this illegitimate. For example, suspects who had apparently not confessed everything during the period of grace, and against whom someone else made an allegation, were summoned by the inquisitors for further questioning, but were told neither what the allegations were nor who had made them, and as such could do little to defend themselves. Such evidence would not be admissible in (most) modern courts of law. So should the historian rely on it either? We should detest inquisition for the harm it did to individuals, to communities, to peace, to cultural diversity and development and, in its later manifestations, to inter-faith interaction and to the arrival of 'renaissance'. But this is an ideological position – liberal and tolerant – that western modern scholars share. We cannot dismiss the value of inquisitorial records just because inquisitors did *not* share it.

Louisa Burnham has written most recently on how historians using the records of depositions made in Languedoc should approach them and, even though her work is on fourteenth-century Beguins, her observations are very relevant and instructive.[44] I agree with her, for example, that one thing we must never do is translate the Latin third person into the first person, in whatever language, as John Arnold has also argued.[45] It pre-supposes a close relationship between the historian and the deponent that overcomes the intervention of the inquisitor, which is indeed both ethically and methodologically flawed. Arnold was one of the first to deal with these issues of theory and methodology seriously, responding convincingly to more gener-

---

[43] Pegg, 'Historiographical essay', pp. 181–95; Pegg, *Corruption of Angels*, e.g. at pp. 17–19; J. J. Clarke, *Oriental Enlightenment: The Encounter between Asian and Western Thought* (London and New York, 1997), esp. p. 69. I am grateful to Spencer Mawby for this observation and reference.

[44] Burnham, *So Great a Light*, pp. 55–9.

[45] Arnold, *Inquisition and Power*, p. 5.

alised post-modernist concerns about the authenticity of the text and arguing that inquisitorial records pose additional problems.[46] Witnesses, he argues, were 'self-making' – that is, creating a version of themselves that they wanted to present to the inquisitor – and so we should attempt to observe this rather than reading and judging through either the inquisitor's or our own values. I aim to take this approach responsibly with regard to Quercy's deponents. But Burnham also cites the early modernist John Martin, who answers his own questions: 'How can historians use an archive of repression to reconstruct the history of dissent? Is not such an archive by its very nature so distortive that we cannot trust it at all?' with 'all texts … are at least in parts products of social and cultural life'.[47] If we also consider inquisitorial sources as being produced within the same events that they claim to document, we can make cautious use of them. But we cannot prove, philosophically, that they were not generated externally, thus creating the phenomena they claim to describe. I have no new model that solves all these problems.

However, I do think that we do our best work if we start by being convincing on what the texts were actually *for* from the point of view of those who actually set them down: the inquisitor, that is (not the deponent, most of whom, we can safely say, did not have a single word that they *spoke* recorded exactly as they spoke it). Then the texts are not part of an abstract genre and subject to the generalised rules of post-modern uncertainty, but rather to concerns relating to their specific historical context. Here, I would argue, we need to be flexible about what we think the texts were for, but this means not being overridingly hostile to them. We should consider that they were not in the first instance about coercion and terror. They were used in that way, but in the first instance they were about identifying and recording heresy. Otherwise they would not have served their secondary purpose – persecution and punishment – so well.

An example of our tendency to allow our feelings about the inquisitor to affect our historical judgement was Jean Duvernoy's location of the birth of the inquisition in the 1233–4 condemnation at Toulouse of Jean 'le Tisserand' by Pierre Seilan and Guillaume Arnaud. But he also noted that in 1233 these same inquisitors had defended the suspect Bernard Peytavi against allegations of heresy.[48] He thus implicitly perceives the origins of the process as being in condemnation, when it was arguably in investigation. In fact, for all our qualms about it, depositional evidence cannot lead us to the conclusion that anything apparently said by the defendant was not said, or that it was not true, or that inquisitors' conclusions about deponents' beliefs were inaccurate. While this may have been the case, as it may be for any legal evidence

---

[46] Arnold, 'The historian as inquisitor', pp. 379–86.
[47] J. Martin, *Venice's Hidden Enemies: Italian Heretics in a Renaissance City* (Berkeley, 1993), p. 10: Burnham, *So Great a Light*, p. 57.
[48] Guillaume Pelhisson, *Chronique*, p. 15.

given under duress, is the evidence in the depositions any more compromised than other sources for 'heresy', including those produced for polemical purposes rather than as records, such as Alain of Lille's treatise?[49] Both types of source were shaped by the same clerical meta-narrative, but served entirely different purposes. Indeed, the contents of chronicles and polemics are more comparable with each other than either genre is with depositions. It served the inquisitor's purpose best to collect evidence thoroughly and accurately, if not necessarily 'fairly'. An inquisitor held the soul of another person in his hands, and he was answerable to God for it. This did not make the inquisitor a nice person, but it probably made him careful.

There is another erroneous assumption about inquisition, an unhistoricised one which, ironically given the philosophical post-structuralism it is informed by, contributes influentially to the generalised grand concept of 'The Inquisition' spanning several centuries and many societies. Commenting on historiography that sees heresy as constructed in elite texts, as opposed to being reflected in them, Caterina Bruschi objects to the resultant tendency to see deponents as 'passive, naïve and helpless individuals'.[50] The deponent, in this schema, is 'pliable, ignorant and easy prey to the situation, skilfully dominated by the inquisitors',[51] explicitly an individual, blindly feeling the way through processes they cannot understand, let alone control. But the fact that medieval phenomena were, of course, constructed through elite discourse to *some* extent should not lead us too easily to the somewhat elitist conclusion that dualistic models for making sense of the universe were beyond the ken of ordinary medieval people, the very assumption that is essential to a portrayal of Catharism as a clerical construct rather than a historically locatable phenomenon.

Neither, I shall suggest, should the weight of the historiographical repugnance concerning the inquisition lead us automatically to sympathise with the underdog, the 'heretic': the gentle, pacifist, vegetarian, hunted, primitive Christian; the other-worldly victims of a clergy whose indolence and hypocrisy they exposed by their very existence. They were not necessarily the antithesis of what the clerics said they were. Truely 'heretical' or not, it is not a given that they were deserving of our sympathy.

The structure of depositions

Depositions were structured by a framework of questions about heretical ritual, lifestyle and belief systems. In Doat 21 the formula consists of a deponent's name, a list of their crimes, and what their penance was to be. There are relatively few records that do not confirm to this name–crime–sentence

---

49 See also Roche, *Une église cathare*, p. 118 and M. Roquebert, 'Le déconstructionisme et les études cathares', in *Les cathares devant l'histoire*, ed. M. Aurell (Cahors, 2005), pp. 105–33.
50 *Wandering Heretics*, pp. 6–8 (p. 6).
51 Ibid., p. 7.

formula. The content of the crimes as well as the structure of questions was often also highly formulaic. The knight Guiraud Gaillard apparently told Bernard de Caux that he had heard heretics say 'of visible things, that God had not made them, that the host was not the body of Christ, and that marriage availed nothing'.[52] These are possibly Guiraud's faithfully recorded words, transposed into the third person. But what he said corresponds almost exactly to numerous other depositions. Pierre de Noye, for example, is recorded as having said that heretics taught him 'of visible things, God had not made them, of the sacred host, that it was not the body of Christ ... and of marriage and baptism, that they did not save'.[53] We have seen that Pierre de Penne said likewise. It is certain that the deponent was asked 'What did the heretics say about visible things? And about the host?' and so on.

Records and summaries of depositions are also formulaic in that specific words – often verbs – are used over and over. We need to look behind these terms. John Arnold has stressed the significance of translating *audivit* as actively 'listening' rather than simply 'hearing'. I strongly agree, in the context he outlines, although 'hearing' too and not reporting it was a crime. Similarly, we can translate *vidit* as 'saw'. Though in purely grammatical terms *vidit* is an 'active' rather than a 'passive' verb, in a different register it may denote something more passive than active: heretics passing in front of someone's eyes, rather than being actively looked for. This is made clear by the context. Inquisitors considered even seeing a heretic and not reporting it to be a crime.

But because even the slightest contact with Cathars or Waldensians that went unreported was a crime in the eyes of the Dominicans this meant that almost everyone had committed it. Guillemette Lautier, for example, whose only crime had been that she 'saw heretics', was ordered to undertake pilgrimages to Le Puy and Saint-Gilles.[54] Because almost everyone must have been guilty of this crime at least, what we find is deponents themselves deliberately stressing the 'ordinariness' of being around heretics, as a contrast to 'believing in' them or aiding them. They were trying to negotiate down the cost of contact with heretics, but this process meant accepting that believing in or aiding heretics was a crime. For example, to protect his wife Bernarde, Guillaume Faure de Pechermer apparently told Bernard de Caux that in spite of his *own* belief in heresy, she had spoken to heretics but he did not think she had become a believer in them. Of his sister Guillelma, he tells us also that she never believed in the heretics, implicitly admitting that she must indeed have come across them.[55] 'Seeing' and 'talking to' heretics, on the one hand, and 'believing in' and 'helping' them, on the other, meant something different before and during the inquisition. We shall encounter other deponent strate-

---

52 D22, fol. 17v.
53 D22, fol. 29r.
54 D21, fol. 264v.
55 D22, fol. 9v.

gies, and, as we have seen in the case of Guillemette Lautier, deponents were not usually able to normalise even the smallest crime; all were significant to the inquisitor.

There are other 'special' words that inquisitors used to categorise types of events and behaviour. Peter Biller identified the several terms recorded by inquisitors for the various ways in which heresy, and as set of beliefs, was transmitted orally; *dico* (simply saying or talking), *monitio* or *admonitio* (suggesting moral content), *expositio* (suggesting commentary of scripture), *doceo* (teach), and *predicatio* (preaching in a private house or in public).[56] Such words helped inquisitors work out and communicate to each other textually how deeply deponents had been involved or exposed.

But we cannot assert that the *substance* of what deponents said was purely the result of the questions asked and answers recorded. Witnesses were coerced into giving evidence in the first place, and their testimony was manipulated in the court room and in the record to fit a certain *ideal type*. But it was not in the inquisitor's interest for them to be coerced into lying. Words used to trap and categorise a deponent served the record more immediately than they served the inquisitor using them. They told an inquisitor further down the line what 'kind' of adherent someone convicted had been, what their heretical 'score' was. But in the courtroom the inquisitor also had an impression of the specific qualities of the individual, as well as a mental list of questions to which the answer was 'yes' or 'no'.

Fortunately, on the odd occasion, some of this seeps through the 'box ticking' and we do not have to rely on formulaic testimony to form an impression of what deponents did, believed or witnessed. Paradoxically, the formulaic and contrived record can actually help us better understand the unique and individual. Where non-formulaic, 'uncontrolled' evidence is also present, we must consider this, by its very existence, significant too. Caterina Bruschi advocates dealing separately with what are quite probably contrived elements of depositions by using a kind of algebraic approach. Essentially, she compares depositions containing formulaic material and cancels out the near-identical material on either side of the imaginary 'equals sign', while paying very close attention to the surplus left over. This surplus is very probably significant even if we are not convinced by the rest.[57] A good example is where Pierre de Noye's account diverges from that of Guiraud Gaillard and others like it. He stated, between his observations about the host and the sacraments, that heretics had said that if hosts were of the body of Christ He must have been as big as *Monsgrandis* – presumably a large mountain

56 Biller, 'Preaching', pp. 140–1.
57 Bruschi, '"*Magna diligentia est habenda per inquisitorem*"', pp. 81–111. On acknowledging and using the 'windows' and 'grilles' through which we see the evidence, imposed on it by modern historians, medieval clergy including inquisitors, and the deponents themselves, see also Biller, 'Preaching', pp. 125–58.

known to all. And, in addition, he stated that they had said that the body would not be resurrected, and that no one was saved unless they died in the heretics' hands. Indeed, he had left the faith when he heard the heretics say that someone could believe whatever they wanted, but that they would still be damned unless they died in their hands.

In Pierre's case, we should observe that deponents usually had attributed to them a more positive formulaic, that they believed that one *could* be saved if they *did* die in Cathar hands. Pierre's divergence from what the inquisitor was used to hearing and recording perhaps gives us, as it perhaps gave them, an insight into, for example, why someone might leave the faith: Pierre apparently objected to the Cathars' monopoly over ways to be saved.

We should add to this that in the Quercy depositions there is not only formula with *some* 'surplus', like Pierre's, but whole depositions on cosmological matters that are surplus, alongside a minimum of formulaic content. Take Raimond de Rodolos's apparent assertion that Aimeric de Na Regina had said that God was not born of the Blessed Virgin; she just *seemed* to be pregnant and the child just *appeared* to be born. And that God is not present at the mass, only the cardinals and priests were, and this out of their love of the great offerings. Furthermore, according to Raimond, Aimeric had told Arnaud de Bressols this – about the Virgin and the mass – in a vineyard, and also at Guillaume Centolh's stall on the Castelsarrasin road. But Raimond did not believe it all to be true himself.[58] Here we get an insight into the way in which anti-clerical ideas might be expressed: a version of something believed about the Virgin birth, and a little snippet of evidence for social and economic history too.

It seems highly likely that such aberrations from the formulae were not recorded accidentally. They survive because they signified something of importance to the inquisitor. In Doat 21 in particular they made it past several editing processes, each time-consuming for the court. The inclusion of such accounts in the Doat documents can shed light on the extent to which we think ordinary *credentes* concerned themselves with theological speculation, and they possibly had a similar function for the inquisitor. They clearly mattered over and above simply condemning someone for vague crimes, formulaically expressed. Furthermore, they did not always implicate other people, so this was not the main reason for the inquisitors' recording them. They were recording beliefs and notions as they encountered them in part to build up their own picture of what was believed in Quercy. As such, while not neutral, these accounts are invaluable to us.

These are issues to which we will return. Before exploring more of the history and wider historiography of Catharism, we should briefly survey what historians have done already with the evidence for Quercy specifically.

---

[58] D22, fol. 31v.

Historians of Heresy

In terms of the secondary literature on heresy and inquisition more generally, Quercy has featured marginally, but see the works of Malcom Barber,[59] Yves Dossat,[60] Elie Griffe,[61] Bernard Hamilton[62] and Michel Roquebert.[63] The closest attention has been paid to the wider region by Edmond Albe, Max Aussel, Peter Biller, Jean Duvernoy, Jörg Feuchter, Georges Passerat, Andrew Roach and myself. Albe's work is a thorough and well-contextualised narrative rooted firmly in the full range of sources.[64] Jean Duvernoy has written twice specifically about heresy in Quercy, noting the significance of Doat 22 for Waldensians as well as Cathars, and has undertaken quantitative analysis, including using statistics deriving from Doat 21 indicating also who was attracted to each sect by gender.[65] Passerat made observations about the heretical structures to which Quercy belonged.[66] Roach uses examples from Quercy in his socio-economic work.[67] Biller has done some of the most important work in terms of using the Doat evidence for Quercy to explore heretical culture and also in terms of putting Waldensians in the picture.[68] Aussel used Doat 21 to explore social and economic aspects of heresy in the town of Gourdon, also employing a quantitative approach,[69] and Feuchter has done so for Montauban.[70] For my part, I have primarily considered the early thirteenth century heretics of Quercy in the context of their relationship to those of the Agenais, their neighbours to the west.[71] The work of these historians will be incorporated into the following chapters, but I intend to take new approaches.

---

[59] *The Cathars*, pp. 144–64.

[60] 'De Vaudès à Saint-François à Montauban, pp. 403–8.

[61] *Le Languedoc cathare (1190 à 1210)*, esp. 89, and *Le Languedoc cathare au temps de la croisade (1209–29)* (Paris, 1973), esp. p. 117.

[62] *The Medieval Inquisition* (London, 1981), esp. pp. 61–5.

[63] *L'épopée Cathare; Les Cathares de la chute de Montségur aux derniers bûchers, 1244–1329* (Paris, 1998).

[64] *L'hérésie ...en Quercy*.

[65] As well as DPC, see 'Albigeois et Vaudois en Quercy', pp. 85–97; *L'inquisition en Quercy: le registre des pénitences de Pierre Cellan, 1241–1242* (Castelnaud La Chapelle, 2001), pp. 9–28; *Le Catharisme I*, esp. pp. 267–73, 353–5.

[66] Passerat, 'Cathares en Bas-Quercy', pp. 149–65.

[67] For example, 'The Cathar economy', pp. 51–71.

[68] '*Curate infirmos*: the medieval Waldensian practice of medicine', in his *The Waldenses*, pp. 49–67 (e.g. p. 54); 'The Cathars of the Languedoc and written materials', in *Heresy and Literacy, 1000–1530*, ed. P. Biller and A. Hudson (Cambridge, 1994), pp. 61–82; '*Thesaurus Absconditus*: the hidden treasure of the Waldensians', in his *The Waldenses*, pp. 97–110 (p. 101).

[69] M. Aussel, 'Noël 1241: Gourdon au temps de l'inquisition', *BSEL* 117 (1996), pp. 91–117.

[70] Feuchter, 'Le pouvoir de l'inquisition', esp. pp. 240–1.

[71] Taylor, *Heresy*, part ii, and 'Authority and the Cathar heresy'.

Catharism as dualism

To generalise rather, there are essentially two ways of looking at the appeal of Catharism to medieval people. The traditional one is that it answered the philosophical question 'Where does evil come from?' Dualism offered a more immediate and easily comprehended solution than that of the Church fathers: the presence of evil is not God's doing. It is not what He wants for us. He made our souls in light and purity, but we have been trapped in the darkness and corruption of the material world, the creation of another god, His antithesis. Here, there is little but suffering, pain and then death. But even at death we cannot escape. Our souls transmigrate into another body, human or even animal. This is our fate without knowledge of the true state of affairs, as well as action taken in life to secure release from it at death. For medieval dualists, the engagement in certain rituals and strict abstinence thereafter from physical pleasure, from violence and from consuming the products of coition ensured this release.

Unless an Occitan parish priest was able to interpret Augustine for you – assuming he knew and understood the Patristic writings in the first place, which he probably did not – this is a comforting story. It is also a self-serving one. It absolves the believer, including the powerful, not only from responsibility for what is bad in the world, but demonstrates equally that it is futile to attempt to relieve the burden of others. Yet at its heart it is also empowering. We can alter our own fate: all this will pass if at the point of death a certain form of words is pronounced over us by one worthy to pronounce them. For the *credens* who was hereticated at the point of death, salvation was a matter of the performance of the correct ritual at the correct time, not a lifetime of correct practice, as it was for the *perfecti*, or of correct belief and striving towards being worthy of Heaven, as it was for the adherent to Roman Christianity.

This tendency towards recognising 'two principles' in the cosmos as understood by the traditional historiography emerged within a variety of medieval European and Asian societies. Most historians of Catharism locate its origins in Balkan and Byzantine Bogomilism and the transmission of its teachings westward by missionaries and emissaries, at the latest in the 1160s. The most famous was 'Papa Nicetas', who claimed to be the head of the Bogomils of Drugunthia when he arrived in western Europe.[72] This is the case in particular since the authenticity of the documentary evidence for his visit and participation in the Cathar conference at Saint-Félix-de-Caraman was established by Bernard Hamilton, who argued that the council marked a break with the 'moderate', or mitigated, dualism which had first been established in southern France, and the adoption of the 'absolute' dualism of

---

[72] In relation to the northern Languedoc see Taylor, *Heresy*, pp. 172–5, 177–86.

the Manichees, reborn in the medieval world with the Paulicians.[73] The case
for the authenticity of the document is very convincing, given the textual
and contextual evidence that Hamilton identifies (some of which touches on
Quercy, as we shall see), even if the significance Hamilton attributes to it is
not always accepted. Anne Brenon, for example, considers that it was not
so much a new doctrine that Papa Nicetas was concerned with, but rather
the organisational relationship of the western to the eastern sects, because
the *consolamenta* performed by western bishops needed to descend from one
whose own 'saved' status was beyond doubt (i.e. Papa Nicetas himself) and
not from one whose status had been corrupted, which is what Nicetas said
had happened.[74] So, there are essentially two traditional ways of interpreting
the Cathar council at Saint-Félix; as a change in doctrine, thereby necessi-
tating the reconsolation of the Cathar hierarchy into the new order so that
they could then reconsole their flock, or as the reflection of a power struggle
in the Bogomil churches, with Papa Nicetas taking the opportunity to gain
control of the western churches for his *ordo*. The conceptual integrity of the
documentation has been upheld more recently even by the group of historians most likely to be able to revive doubt on its origins, although their
opinions vary as to its implications.[75]

Whatever the case, knowledge and truth alone, even accompanied by the
appearance of leaders of exotic eastern sects, do not give rise to mass religious movements. Societal circumstances are crucial in their formation. There
has been an essential move in recent years to regard the Cathar heresy as an
expression of social discontent as well as alternative doctrine, and most historians now admit a combination of social and religious factors. This is significant, not least because it may have been dissidence rather than dualism that
appealed to *credentes* and protectors of Cathars. This, as we shall see, was the
case in much of Quercy. We find relatively little evidence of *explicit* dualism,
'absolute' or 'mitigated', in inquisitorial depositions, for all the attention paid
to it by Catholic polemicists. We cannot even say that Raimond de Rodolos,
for example, or the other deponents discussed above, understood the *significance* of what Aimeric de Na Regina told him, or that Aimeric did either, for
that matter. Interest in what heresy meant to ordinary people also informs
much sociological scholarship.

---

[73] Hamilton, 'The Cathar council', pp. 23–53. Moderates believed that the former had
somehow given rise to the latter. Both forms were present also in the Balkans, Byzantium
and in Italy.

[74] See *Le vrai visage du Catharisme*, pp. 109, 122–8; Duvernoy, *Le catharisme I*, pp. 105–7. See
also Taylor, *Heresy*, esp. pp. 173–4.

[75] See Monique Zerner et al., *L'histoire du Catharisme en discussion: le 'concile' de Saint-Félix
(1167)* (Nice, 2001). This seminar had already argued, convincingly in some cases, for the
'invention' of heresy by clergy in the eleventh and earlier-twelfth century: see M. Zerner
et al. (eds.), *Inventer l'hérésie? discours polémique et pouvoirs avant l'inquisition* (Nice, 1998).

Heresiology as sociology

Mainstream sociological explanations for the rise and role of Catharism rest on a few key, widely held truisms concerning features of Occitan society. It is interesting to explore these first through the eyes of Jean-Louis Biget. His position on the above issues is unique. He asserts that a thoroughly self-conscious dualist church, indeed 'Church', with its own clerical structures, arose from purely western origins, unrelated to Bogomilsm. He thus rejects the idea of heresy as something abstract and even partly disembodied from context, and considers tensions in twelfth-century Languedcoc *alone* enough to give rise not only to social and religious 'dissidence', as he sometimes calls heresy, but to a dualist belief system specifically.[76]

Firstly, he holds that there was widespread anti-clericalism. Priests, he considers, were ill-educated, worldly, indolent and typically despised, and the clergy had dashed expectations raised by the reforms of *c*.1050–*c*.1100. Furthermore, they were the enemies of two key social groups who were to take the heresy to their hearts; the knightly lords of *castra*, impoverished in part by the demands of the clergy for tithes, and the merchants of new towns, condemned by the same clergy for usury. The radical evangelism of the dissidents spoke to the spiritual needs of these groups in a way that Catholicism could not. However, he warns, we should not transform the good men into the champions of social reform as a result. Such a portrayal owes more to the sentimental construction of regional identity in the modern-day Languedoc and to Protestant historiography than it does to the sources.[77]

The picture he paints correlates closely with other historians' understanding of why Languedoc readily took up dissident religious ideas. It is generally accepted that it also had very decentralised political authority; a confusion of ties and contracts made the establishment of stable hierarchies difficult and, at the same time, produced a highly militarised culture. Violence was endemic at a local level as a result and, as always, it was a voiceless peasantry that suffered, even though personal freedom was threatened less in southern France than in some other twelfth-century societies. The survival of Roman legal practice, including partible inheritance among even female heirs, meant that large numbers of families struggled economically on increasingly diminished revenues. On the other hand, it meant that Languedoc was characterised by women able to dispose of their lands and incomes as they wished,

---

[76] For example, in his 'Les bons hommes sont-ils les fils de Bogomils? Examen critique d'une idée reçue', *Slavica occitania* 16 (2003), pp. 133–88, revised as 'Un phénomène occidental' in his *Hérésie*, pp. 63–105. See also 'Introduction: Le "catharisme", une histoire en devenir', in his *Hérésie*, pp. 7–35 (p. 7).

[77] See, in particular, 'L'anticléricalisme des hérétiques d'après les sources polémiques', *CF* 38 (Toulouse, 2003), pp. 405–45, revised as 'À la source, un anticléricalisme et un évangélisme', in his *Hérésie*, pp. 38–62. On Waldensians in this context see Biller, 'Goodbye to Waldensianism?', pp. 5–6 and 17, note 3.

and so they were able to forge independent economic relations with heresy and heretics, all the more so because there were very few female abbeys in Languedoc. Towns, on the other hand, thrived precociously and were relatively cosmopolitan, secular and open-minded. Cathars therefore answered spiritual and social needs better than a largely despised Catholic clergy could. The heresy was patronised and protected by networks of influential nobles and merchants, and propagated and nurtured within heretical families, especially by mothers and grandmothers.[78]

The above explanation is 'structuralist-functionalist' in traditional anthropological terms, the social function of the heretical doctrine in relation to the social fabric being central. Wherever dualism came from, the simple life of the adherents of this sect, its political neutrality, the devotional opportunities it offered women because of the notion of equality between un-gendered souls, and its 'status-blindness', deriving from the same philosophy, fulfilled an otherwise unrequited yearning to make sense of the world on the part of large sections of the Occitan laity. As suggested, this theoretical model perhaps implies that dissidence of some sort would have arisen anyway in later twelfth century Languedoc.

But while these generalised social features may well have made it more likely that dissident beliefs could have taken root and successfully flourished, historical phenomena are shaped by specifics as well as by generalities. Each region, town, family and individual was different, and this means that generalisations about them can only get us so far. The above model is in fact being contested, and three elements of it particularly so in the anglophone literature. The truism that is the 'Cathar family' is disputed by John Arnold, while Malcolm Barber problematises the generalised concept of a clergy inactive in the face of heresy, and also the natural relationship between heresy and towns, as do M. Lambert and B. M. Kienzle.[79] In Quercy none of these three

---

[78] See Moore, *Origins*, pp. 232–7; Barber, *The Cathars*, esp. pp. 68–9; Lambert, *The Cathars*, pp. 41, 64–9, and *Medieval Heresy*, 3rd edn, pp. 90–2; Roquebert, *L'épopée cathare*, I, pp. 95–126; A. Vauchez, 'Les origines de l'hérésie cathare en Languedoc, d'après un sermon de l'archevêque de Pise Federico Visconti (1277)', in *Società, istituzioni, spiritualità: studi in onore di Cinzio Violante* 3 vols (Spoleto, 1994), pp. 1023–36; Sumption, *Albigensian Crusade*, pp. 15–31; Given, *Inquisition and Medieval Society*, II, pp. 5–9; Taylor, *Heresy*, p. 150. Although it is commonly asserted that this contrast between the Cathars and the distant, worldly and disinterested clergy probably accounts for peasant adherence to the heresy, we must heed R. I. Moore's caveat that there is in fact 'nothing which permits a sustained assessment of the impact of the heresies on the greatest part of the population' (*Origins*, p. 237). This, and the dearth of secular documentation for this social group in Quercy, means that they are addressed here very little.

[79] Arnold, *Inquisition and Power*, esp. pp. 118–19; Barber, *The Cathars*, pp. 60–8; Lambert, *Medieval Heresy*, p. 90; B. M. Kienzle, *Cistercians, Heresy and Crusade in Occitania, 1145–1229* (York, 2001), pp. 38–9, 47–8 (*cf.* Taylor, *Heresy*, p. 181 on the differing *kinds* of towns that proved receptive to heresy, and p. 150 and note 24 on models of Occitan society more generally).

generalisations apply either, and neither do some other truisms in the gener-alised model: the lack of female abbeys, for example.

Furthermore, as we have seen, for the twelfth-century Languedoc in general it seems likely that what the clergy identified as 'heresy' was so much a part of the social life of its heartlands that it was not acknowledged as 'heresy' by the laity. Distinctions in theological form might have shaped real confessional phenomena in Languedoc, and were certainly noted by inquisitors, but were perhaps less important day-to-day than the routine comfort that 'belief' in itself provided.[80] This sort of understanding of 'heresy' asserts that a multi-plicity of religious formulations existed side-by-side, and that awareness of the contradictions between them did not necessarily matter until the arrival of the crusaders and inquisitors. The implication of this is that deponents and witnesses were operating within a different conceptual framework to the inquisitor. To the person on trial, even if they had not considered the heretics to be 'good men and women' themselves, it had been perfectly normal to see heretics about the place. Pérégrine, wife of Guillaume Gasc, for example, had associated with Waldensians at Moissac, but this was before the church was persecuting Waldensians, she said. She had believed that they were good people and that their faith was good, until she discovered that the Church did not consider them so.

Heresy and orthodoxy
This 'ordinariness' of heresy relates to more general observations by scholars of religion that 'heresy' is merely the flipside of 'orthodoxy': orthodoxy cannot exist without it, so they are inseparably linked conceptually. Whatever shape heresy takes, there is nothing objectively 'wrong' about it *in itself*, only in comparison with 'correct' belief. 'Falsehood' can only be attributed to it by someone with the ability to enforce the definition and distinction between falsehood and truth. The struggle between orthodoxy and heresy is therefore not about the definition of 'truth' over 'falsehood', but concerns ownership of the *right to define* what is true.

Thus Bernard Gui's observation that 'heresy cannot be destroyed unless heretics are destroyed'[81] is thought-provoking from several perspectives. One rejoinder to it might be that 'heresy' is produced by defining orthodoxy: Gui and others 'created' heresy in order to destroy it. This could be argued from a Durkheimian perspective. The vilification and ostracising of 'heretics', or other groups that are rejected socially and set apart, is part of the natural human process of creating and reinforcing collective solidarity and cohesion among the rest of the community, the vast majority. In this schema, the high-

---

[80] See, in particular, Brenon, *Le vrai visage*, *passim*, and 'Le faux problème du dualisme absolu', *Heresis* 21 (1993), pp. 61–74, and, more generally, 'Les hérésies de l'an Mil: Nouvelles perspectives sur les origines du Catharisme', *Heresis* 24 (1995), pp. 21–36.

[81] In Lea, *Inquisition of the Middle Ages*, p. 292.

medieval clergy expressed and acted upon the desire of the community to expel those with incorrect beliefs, thereby reinforcing solidarities among the 'orthodox' community. As Biget asserts, heresy was an 'instrument de l'unité de l'Église',[82] meaning the wider Christian communion.

But R. I. Moore transformed our understanding of persecution as a normal social process. Taking a Weberian stance, he demonstrated that it was the preoccupation of a new secular administrative elite. Persecution did not 'arise', but was the result of a top-down process. The deviant distinctiveness of heretics, like that of Jews, homosexuals and lepers, was 'not the cause but the result of persecution'.[83] While often apparently locating their starting point in Moore's model, usually by citing *Formation of a Persecuting Society*, some historians who like the idea that elites constructed 'heresy', not the 'heretics' themselves, in fact misunderstand Moore by stressing the activity of *clergy* driving the process. Guy Lobrichon argues of the eleventh century that the Cluniacs invented heresy;[84] Monique Zerner and others consider that it was the Cistercians, in the main, in the twelfth century;[85] Hilbert Chiu argues that it was the Paris scholars in the latter half of that century and that Alain of Lille specifically did not encounter Cathars, and was not even attempting to address a medieval historical phenomenon but an ancient one.[86] In the crusade years, Jacques de Vitry's anti-Cathar sermons addressed dualist beliefs including on the two principles, as well as the usual accusations of immorality, and these would surely strongly influence inquistors' understanding of Catharism.[87]

But Moore's model holds that it was the clerical identification and labelling of distinctive sect as 'heretical', not their *invention* of it, that justified assault upon them by those who had Weber's 'monopoly on legitimate violence': the emerging states. To Moore, Catharism was an 'alternative church with its own priesthood ... bishops and ecclesiastical organisation', the first 'potentially universal rival' to medieval Catholicism.[88] In his schema, clergy starting with St Bernard of Clairvaux and his circle *identified* a dualist sect in Languedoc and summoned the armies of the count of Toulouse and the French and English kings against it in the 1170s and in 1181. It remained the

---

82 'Le poids du contexte', in his *Hérésie*, pp. 106–41 (p. 113).

83 *Formation of a Persecuting Society*, p. 63.

84 Lobrichon, 'The chiaroscuro of heresy', pp. 80–103.

85 Zerner et al. (eds.), *Inventer l'hérésie?*

86 Chiu, 'Intellectual Origins', argues that Alain of Lille and others are not referring to *existing* heresy but to ancient dualism in their treaties against neo-Manichaens. Alain probably never even met a 'Cathar', in fact (see W. L. Wakefield and A. P. Evans (ed. and trans.), *Heresies of the High Middle Ages* (New York, 1969; rprt. 1991), p. 214).

87 C. Muessig, 'Les sermons de Jacques de Vitry sur les cathares', *CF* 31 (Toulouse, 1997), pp. 70–83.

88 Moore, *Formation of a Persecuting Society*, p. 67.

case that clerics *sought out* heresy and told rulers what corporal punishments to inflict into the 1240s and well beyond. It seems important, therefore, to stress that Moore conceptualises Catharism as a real phenomenon. Whatever its relationship to orthodoxy and however medieval authorities reacted to it, it did not originate in the textual record.

'Heresy' as heresy

The set of sources in which the sceptics have so far found heresy 'constructed' – Cluniac, Cistercian and scholastic – is rather an odd one, consisting as it does exclusively of accounts generated within the leading orthodox intellectual circles of their day. Evidence that heresy is at least partially constructed through the texts that these movements produced, and is primarily identifiable in them when contrasted with 'orthodoxy', should therefore not surprise us at all. But historians' preoccupation with likewise eradicating 'heresy', at least as a historiographical phenomenon, by perceiving it primarily textually will be unconvincing until they address two other types of sources for thirteenth-century 'heresy'.

The first of these is sources that take Christian dualism as a legitimate starting point, self-defined. These are the texts traditionally taken to be either 'Cathar'-generated or western translations of sources composed and/or used by Bogomils, such as the 'Vision of Isaiah', the 'Book of Two Principles', the 'Secret Supper' and the Cathar rituals.[89] Most of these can be dated to the late twelfth century onwards. The most serious attempt so far at deconstructing a 'Cathar' text, the recent re-examination of the Saint-Félix documents by Monique Zerner and others, has in fact rather reinforced its provenance. Sceptics will need to find significant problems with the authorship of the other texts if a good case is to be made against the existence of dualism.

The second set of sources is those by thirteenth-century 'born again' Catholics such as the Cathar-turned-inquisitor Rainier Sacconi.[90] We may expect a juxtaposition of 'orthodoxy' and 'heresy' to be at the heart of these texts, because through them a heretical ideal-type emerges. We should also consider here the tract against both Catholicism and Catharism of the Waldensian Durand of Huesca. This text, of the 1180s or 1190s, composed before he reconverted to Catholicism in 1207, explicitly attacks dualism also.[91] This is not to argue that 'heresy' is purely and simply reflected in the sources. We

---

[89] Bernard Hamilton has done most to demonstrate links between such texts. See his 'Wisdom from the East, pp. 38–60. See also Duvernoy, *Le catharisme I, passim.*

[90] Rainerius Sacconi, *Summa de Catharis et Pauperibus de Lugduno*, in *Un Traité néo-manichéen du xiiie siècle: Le Liber du duobus principiis, suivi d'un fragment de rituel cathare*, ed. A. Dondaine (Rome, 1939), pp. 64–78.

[91] Durand de Huesca, *Liber antiheresis*, ed. J. Duvernoy, *Archivum Fratrum Praedicatorum* 16 (1946), pp. 232–5.

have already observed how it could be pushed and pulled into shape in the inquisitor's record. But why would it be *invented* in the text, out of nothing?

This is not the place for a defence or otherwise of the integrity of these two sets of texts. What we shall attempt, however, is to demonstrate that the beliefs that they and scholastic texts assert were present were indeed in evidence in Quercy by *c.*1240 and are reflected in the third set of texts, inquisitorial depositions. Not only are echoes of a dualist cosmology apparently in evidence, but so are some of the heretical organisational structures that Biget and Moore consider reveal a heretical 'Church'.

Heresy, choice and agency

The Doat documents alone allow us to alter a perception of the heretical adherent that emerges from both the sociological and 'textual' approaches. In these, there is little room for individual rationality, informed choice, self-education, intellectual endeavour or originality. If it were not for the depositions we would not know how remarkable and complex individual adherents to the range of confessional choices available could be. The best illustration of this is that a purely sociological or textual approach cannot account fully for the very diverse confessional complexion of Quercy. Why did it accommodate *two* heretical sects – Catharism and Waldensianism – unless through the exercise not only of societal factors but also of informed choice? Waldensianism was another post-Gregorian heresy, in that it asked questions about clerical authority. In answer, it rejected ecclesiastical hierarchy, making no fundamental distinction between ordinary believers and its full-time practitioners. Catharism, by contrast, sought to reorder the Christian world by offering an alternative religious hierarchy to that of the Roman Church. Indeed, such a hierarchy was central to Catharism; the 'consoled' were an elect, already saved. Furthermore, it went far beyond Waldensianism in asking and answering questions about metaphysical concerns, about the nature of creation, and rejected the world as it was constructed materially. The two sects were almost entirely different, in other words: ordinary people neither answered the same profound questions about existence in the same way as each other nor responded to social issues with the same solutions.

Neither sect dominated in Quercy. In numerous depositions we shall observe the two battling it out for influence over the same audience. We shall see that many deponents made a conscious choice between them. They did not attach themselves to either Catharism or Waldensianism just because the rest of their family did. In a handful of cases, deponents told the inquisitor why they had chosen one over the other, and sometimes this is explicitly doctrinal. The evidence encourages us to consider the concept of religious dissent as information-based choice on the part of people responding consciously to what they saw and heard around them, and wanting to affect what happened to them after death. Flawed, *deeply* flawed, as they may be as accounts of what ordinary people said and believed, these sorts of documents are the closest we can come to this, and we should take the opportunity to consider the individual as well as the ideal-type where we can.

But, before exploring the inner lives of the people of Quercy further, we should understand more of the region and society within which these choices were made, beginning here with Quercy's origins.

2

Medieval Quercy

Having noted the general truisms about Occitan society and that Quercy does not always conform to them, we should not be surprised at this. While it was increasingly orientated politically and historically towards the Toulousain, as we shall see, it was geographically peripheral to Languedoc and influenced heavily by Aquitaine to the north, even to the extent that after Quercy and the Agenais were recovered from the dukes of Aquitaine in the twelfth century the administrations they had established were simply taken over.[1] But this does not mean that support for Catharism or Waldensianism would be strongest and most enduring in the south of the county, the region most obviously 'Occitan'; things were not that simple.

Quercy's Early History: Political Foundations

The first 'counts' of Quercy were a family descended from one 'Raoul', who represented royal power at Cahors from AD 823. This family retained important viscounties after Charles the Bald's ally, one 'Raimond', subsequently became count, probably in the context of Norse incursions up the Garonne. From the 870s there is little direct evidence of Carolingian control in the county. In 932 a viscount Frotard of Cahors is attested in a donation to Beaulieu, in the Limousin. Frotard was a vassal of Count Raimond-Pons of Toulouse (922–c.950) for these estates, and gave them only in his presence and with his permission. By c.960 most of Quercy was held by Count Raimond I of the neighbouring Rouergue, Marquis of Gothia. We know this from his will of 961, the most important source for tenth-century Quercy. But he too was a vassal of the count of Toulouse, Guillaume 'Taillefer' (947–1037), his cousin. Raimond of Rouergue founded the Cluniac monastery of Fons and appointed as its protector Ranulf de Cardaillac, possessor of other important allods and fiefs besides. Ranulf too was an ally of the count of Toulouse and the bishop of Cahors, holding fiefs of both.[2]

---

[1]   Taylor, 'Authority and the Cathar heresy', p. 152.
[2]   *HGL*, III, 153–5, 157–8; *HGL*, V, chartes et diplômes, no. 97, cols. 240–50; Lartigaut, *Histoire de Quercy*, pp. 88–9, 91.

Therefore, early affairs in Quercy should also be understood in terms of the relationship between Toulouse and the 'counts', later viscounts, of Turenne, in the Aquitainian Limousin. We know some of the lands that they had held in the tenth century from their donation of rights in Quercy to the Limousin abbey of Beaulieu, which they founded in the ninth. The first 'viscount' of Turenne, Bernard, descended from an archbishop of Bourges and is recorded in the late tenth century. His numerous estates in Quercy correspond to modern communes at Martel, Vayrac, Saint-Céré, Figeac and Souillac. In other words, he controlled virtually all of the northernmost reaches of the county: Limousin Quercy. Lartigaut suggests as a result that this family kept in line allodialists in the marcher lands between Aquitainian and Occitan authority.[3] Thus, authority in Quercy by the mid-tenth century was held essentially by outsiders: the viscount of Turenne, the count of Toulouse and, most power-fully, the count of Rouergue.

The death of Raimond of Rouergue in September 961 saw a shift in power away from the east of the county. His son, Raimond II, appears not to have inherited anything of great importance in Quercy because his father left the key estates to the executer of his will, Viscount Adémar of Toulouse.[4] These included Bruniquel and Monclar, castles dominating the border between Quercy and the Albigeois and the Toulousain respectively. This made Adémar one of the major allodialists in Quercy and increased the influence there of Toulouse. Furthermore, the count of Toulouse shared control of Cahors itself with a Viscount Guillaume by *c.*990.[5] In spite of the existence of other viscounts at Saint-Cirq-la-Popie, Calvignac and Brassac, Toulouse was to remain the dominant influence on Quercy as a whole until the thirteenth century.

According to the model of feudal revolution, adhered to by Lartigaut, for example, in relation to Quercy, power was usurped by castellans in *c.*1000. Certainly, that supposed symbol of the 'feudal revolution', the castle, is rarely attested before 950. Bruniquel and Saint-Céré are the earliest to be named (the lords of the latter were descended from Arlade, the brigand castellan encountered by Saint Géraud of Aurillac). References do multiply thereafter, in particular in the Lot and Dordogne valleys, so that in the eleventh century nineteen castles are recorded. They include Monclar, Saint-Geniès, Lolmie,

---

[3] *Cartulaire de l'abbaye de Beaulieu (en Limousin)*, ed. M. Deloche (Paris, 1859), nos. 184, 185; E. Flamari, *Esquisse d'histoire. Vicomté de Turenne* (Limoges, 1940), p. 9; R. Fage, *Les états de la vicomté de Turenne*, 2 vols. (Paris, 1894), I, 17; Combarieu, *Dictionnaire*, p. 55; Lartigaut, *Histoire de Quercy*, pp. 91–2. Martel (Lot) took its name from Charles Martel, who campaigned against Muslim invaders and who founded a church there: Combarieu, *Dictionnaire*, p. 152. For the relationship between the viscounts and the abbey in the eleventh century see Susan Wood's *The Proprietary Church in the Medieval West* (Oxford, 2006), pp. 324–6.

[4] On the viscounts of Toulouse see *HGL*, III, 126, 129, 157–8.

[5] *HGL*, III, 126, 129, 154–5, 157–8, 214, 379–80; *HGL*, V, chartes et diplômes, no. 97.

Montpezat (built by 1040) and Luzech (first attested in 1100). Saint-Antonin (modern Saint-Antonin-Noble-Val) also originated in this period. Some of the powerful castellans of the thirteenth century, such as the lords of Saint-Clair and of Peyrilles, are first recorded as minor knightly families in the eleventh and twelfth centuries.[6]

But even Lartigaut notes that most castles were vice-comital, tied into political networks at a higher level. Indeed, the eleventh century seems to have been characterised rather more by the emergence of new viscounts, servants of Toulouse, than new castellans *per se*, and sometimes at their expense. An example is the decline of the lords of Saint-Céré. Their rights to the profits of justice dwindled over time and were entirely absorbed by neighbouring viscounties by the thirteenth century.[7]

An exception to the rise of the viscounts at the expense of older families was the castellans of Gourdon, in the Bouriane. A fortification there in 961 was transferred by Raimond of Rouergue to one 'Aimeric' and his son, Guiraud I de Gourdon. Roger Bulit considers an Aimeric II de Gourdon, attested in 1055, to have been Guiraud's son. Aimeric II's own sons are attested in *c.*1068, and they probably included Bishop Guiraud I of Cahors (*c.*1068–*c.*1083/8).[8] We get little sense of them being subordinates to greater magnates, not even to the Turenne. They appear to have shifted for themselves after the death of Raimond of Rouergue and become independent. They would play one of the most important roles in Quercy's thirteenth-century troubles (see genealogy, p. xiv).

Quercy's Early History: Religious Life

We know much of what we do about the church of Quercy in this period again through the will of Raimond of Rouergue. He left rights and property to Figeac, Marcilhac, Saint-Théodard, Moissac and Souillac. Marcilhac was given churches, including what would become Rocamadour, by Bishop Dieudonné of Cahors in 1030. But it suffered at the hands of a family who would become significant again in the Albigensian wars: the Barasc knights of Béduer, notably Dieudonné and Pierre, sons of Giraud Barasc, under whose protection Abbot Etienne had placed the abbey. Another early foundation in *c.*1000 was Carennac, the work of the d'Aigrefeuille family, lords of Gramat and Loubressac. It was reformed by Bishop Bernard IV of Cahors (d. *c.*1068) in 1047, and the churches at Saint-Céré went to it.[9]

---

6   Lartigaut, *Histoire de Quercy*, pp. 91–2, 93, 94, 103–4, 105.
7   Lartigaut, *Histoire de Quercy*, pp. 93, 103.
8   *HGL*, III, 48–9, 158; *HGL*, V, cols. 247, 483; Bulit, *Gourdon*, pp. 48–9, 50–2.
9   Combarieu, *Dictionnaire*, pp. 49, 146, 222; Lartigaut, *Histoire de Quercy*, p. 95.

By *c.*1100 monastic life was dominated by the great abbeys to the county's north (Souillac, Marcilhac and Rocamadour), east (Figeac and Conques) and south (Saint-Théodard and Cluniac Moissac). Here we should note the influence on these of the religious of the Limousin. Some of Beaulieu's lands lay in Quercy, north of the Dordogne, and Cistercian Tulle also had lands in Quercy and claimed Rocamadour.[10] But the Aquitainian religious orientation of abbeys north of the Lot did not diminish the prestige and significance of the diocese of Cahors itself. The counts of Toulouse, as counts of Quercy, used it to make alliances with other leading families of Languedoc and openly to raise revenues. Quercinois noble families provided some of its important early bishops. Bishop Guiraud I was a lord of Gourdon.[11] But the most significant family in this respect were the lords of Cardaillac, in the east. As bishops they became lords also of Cahors, when Count Guillaume IV of Toulouse issued a charter transferring comital powers to Bishop Guiraud II de Cardaillac (*c.*1083/90–1113) and became his lord for it. This was an arrangement that would continue under his successors. The count and bishop also established canons regular in the cathedral, and the bishop awarded various estates to these and a share of the profits of the coinage the bishop already minted.[12] Guiraud appealed to Rome to reform the chapter in 1090 and seems to have acquired thirty canons and secured the adoption of the rule of St Augustine.[13] Grand ambitions which would come to typify the episcopates of the thirteenth century were already in evidence.

Political Communities in the Twelfth Century

In Chapter 1 it was noted of early medieval Quercy that its political life was increasingly influenced by its neighbour, Toulouse. This was to the extent that by 1100 there was no independent count of Cahors and Bishop Guiraud II de Cardaillac exercised comital powers in the town itself, held of Count Guillaume IV. Within Quercy, in the main, the new castellanies of the eleventh century were not independent of the count with the apparent exception of Gourdon, which would dominate the north of Quercy and whose lords would provide two bishops for the see of Cahors.

---

[10] Combarieu, *Dictionnaire*, pp. 44, 85, 90, 100, 102, 217, 202, 238, 240; Lartigaut, *Histoire de Quercy*, pp. 88–9, 93, 95–6; Lacoste, *Quercy*, II, pp. 7–9, 91; J. Bousquet, *Le Rouergue au premier moyen âge (vers 800–vers 1250)*, 2 vols. (Rodez, 1992), II, pp. 481–3, 491–2; de la Torre, Lot; Ayma, *Histoire … Cahors*, I, pp. 214, 218, 224, note 1; Woods, *The Proprietary Church*, p. 391.

[11] See Chapter 2, p. 48 above.

[12] L. d'Achery (ed.), *Spicilegium*, 2 vols. (Paris, 1723), VIII, 161; *HGL*, III, 466.

[13] *Spicilegium*, VIII, 154, 161; *HGL*, III, 197, 213–14, 466, 961; Bulit, *Gourdon*, pp. 51, 57; Lartigaut, *Histoire de Quercy*, p. 95; Lacoste, *Quercy*, II, p. 13; Combarieu, *Dictionnaire*, p. xiv.

Quercy between the Rouergue, Toulouse and Aquitaine

In 1094 Duke Guillaume IX of Aquitaine had married Philippa, daughter of Guillaume IV of Toulouse, who had died the previous year. Her claim to Toulouse was resisted by its nobles, who acknowledged instead her uncle, Raimond of Saint-Gilles, count of the Rouergue and marquis of Provence. In 1097–8 Guillaume seized Toulouse and Cahors, and also Moissac in lower Quercy, profiting from Raimond's absence on the first crusade. Subsequent decades saw both nominal and effective control of the county split between Count Bertrand of Saint-Gilles (1103–1148), Raimond's son, and the Aquitainians until, in 1123, Alphonse-Jourdain, Raimond's other son, triumphed at Toulouse.

The Aquitainians could not forget their claim, however. Henry II of England sought control of Toulouse and Quercy by right of his marriage to Eleanor, duchess of Aquitaine. He took much of the Cahorsain from Raimond V of Toulouse (1148–1194) in 1159, including Cahors. The bishop sided with him, and the lords and towns of Quercy did not always take Raimond's part either: some opposed him in the 1160s and welcomed a high-profile pilgrimage to Rocamadour on Henry's part in 1170. In 1172 the count submitted to the Aquitainians as vassal for Toulouse, but in 1188 he allied himself with various of Richard I's Aquitainian enemies, arresting allies of the duke in his lands. This prompted an attack by Richard on Quercy in which he took Moissac and sixteen castles, including Gourdon, and installed a *bailli* at Luzech even against the objections of the bishop.[14] In the context of this wider conflict, in 1191 the count of Toulouse was acknowledged as lord of Quercy by Philip Augustus, king of France, saving the royal abbeys of Figeac and Souillac (although in the former case he was granted it as a fief of the king in 1195). But by 1196 Richard had conquered most of Quercy and a truce was agreed. Count Raimond VI (1194–1222) gave Richard his daughter Jeanne in marriage. Her dowry was the neighbouring Agenais. In exchange, Richard abandoned his claim to Toulouse and restored Quercy.[15]

However, to the north of Quercy, the house of Turenne was still in its ascent. Viscount Raimond I, already minting his own coinage by the 1120s, had three legitimate offspring including Boson and Anne (sometimes called Magna, d. after 1180). Boson inherited the viscounty and Anne married Aimeric III de Gourdon (attested 1119–52). These were probably the parents of Pons I de Gourdon (attested 1152–66) and Aimeric IV de Gourdon (attested 1168–80). By *c.*1200 the viscounts held most of their quercinois seigneuries of the counts

---

[14] *IRC*, I, 36–7; *HGL*, III, 810–11; *HGL*, IV, 41, 52–3; Ayma, *Histoire ... Cahors*, I, p. 271; Lartigaut, *Histoire de Quercy*, p. 105.

[15] AD Lot, séries F. 97, no. 104; *Catalogue des actes des comtes de Toulouse: Raimond V (1149–1194)*, ed. E.-G. Léonard (Paris, 1932), no. 25 (1162/3); *HGL*, VI, 127–31, 169, 173–4; *HGL*, VII, 22–4; *HGL*, VIII, chartes lxii, col. 432; Taylor, *Heresy*, p. 148; Taylor, 'Authority and the Cathar heresy', p. 152.

of Toulouse.[16] In 1181 we find Raimond II de Turenne, Bishop Guiraud IV 'Hector' de Gourdon of Cahors (1159–1199×1202) and the abbot of Figeac instrumental in mediating a complex accord between parties claiming rights to the grange of *La Coste*.[17]

Twelfth-century documents link the bishops of Cahors to the Limousin in other ways. They witnessed activity at Beaulieu, such as a donation of 1100. In 1112 Bishop Guiraud II ruled in favour of the abbey of Tulle in the matter of disputed lands in Quercy. In the same year he donated the church of Saint-Martin-de-Bayssac to Beaulieu's Abbot Giraud.[18] In all cases, the deference and profit flowed in the direction of Aquitaine.

In part because of these external influences, but also because the county was divided by its internal geography and economic characteristics, we cannot talk of a distinctively 'quercinois' society' by 1200. Forests and high chalky plains meant that settlement was not uniform. There was easy east–west communication only along the courses of rivers. The networks of affinity, as least those we can reconstruct from the evidence, were typically local in character, especially in the sparsely settled east. In fact, it makes sense to think of Quercy as having six internal regions (Map 1). This chapter deals with the forces shaping these and the alliances and rivalries emerging in the period in which Cathars and Waldensians first infiltrated the county.

Lower Quercy

Lower Quercy corresponds roughly to modern Tarn-et-Garonne. We could even call it 'Toulousain-Quercy' in view of the economic orientation of the vital river network formed by the Tarn, Aveyron and Garonne, dominating transport between Bordeaux and Toulouse and towards the east. Castelsarrasin in particular was Toulousain in orientation and was the seat of the counts' seneschals for Quercy. Indeed, once the counts of Toulouse were assured of their immediate control of the region, even as vassals of Aquitaine, they established political structures used by their Plantagenet masters themselves, with seneschals and *baillis* at their heart, and undermined the viscounts of Quercy in the process.

For example, while the twin-viscounty of Bruniquel-Monclar had formed an essential part of the political and military control of the county from the eleventh century, Bruniquel had fallen under the influence of the viscounts

---

[16] A. Vaissière (ed.), 'Documents relatifs à l'histoire de la maison de Turenne', *Bulletin de la société scientifique, historique et archéologique de la Corrèze* 7 (1885), 310–40 (pp. 312, 330–2); Roquebert, *l'épopée*, II, pp. 110 13 and note 7; de la Chenaye-Desbois, F. A. A. et al., *Dictionnaire de la noblesse*, 3rd edn, 19 vols. (Paris, 1969; rprt. of Paris, 1863–77), IX, pp. 256–7.

[17] *CO*, nos. 200, 201, 534, 1172–3; Bulit, *Gourdon*, pp. 52–3; Lacoste, *Quercy*, II, pp. 29–30; Lartigaut, *Histoire de Quercy*, p. 92; Taylor, *Heresy*, pp. 199–200; Vaissière, 'Turenne', pp. 310, 325–6, 330–2.

[18] *Cart … Beaulieu*, p. 39; Ayma, *Histoire … Cahors*, I, pp. 254, 280.

of Albi by the 1150s, and Viscount Guillaume, probably related to Viscount Adémar III of Toulouse, had sided with the Aquitainians at key points.[19] Presumably in response, in 1176 the count took Monclar from Guillaume's son, Viscount Pons, and gave it as a fief to Arnaud de Montpezat, who seems to have been married to Pons's sister. Armand, his brother Bertrand and their brother-in-law Bertrand de Villemur – acting for his wife, who was their sister – became vassals of the count for Montpezat and Monclar, receiving them as a fief. In turn, the count received from them the town of Caylus 'in full ownership and as an allod'. This pact sealed an alliance against comital enemies: specifically named is Pons of Toulouse. This is an extremely significant charter, therefore, and in its witness list we find the names of two families of the Vaux, to the north, who were to play a role in the events with which this study is most centrally concerned: Guiraud de Gourdon-de Montcuq and Guiraud de Lolmie, close to Montcuq.[20] Nothing more is recorded about the viscounty of Bruniquel-Monclar until 1224, when it appears more as an honorific than political title, bestowed upon Count Raimond VI's brother Bertrand.[21]

Another traditional viscounty, Caussade, first noted in *c.*1006 and again in the south-east of the county, seems to have been insignificant politically after 1197,[22] even though its lords would remain vassals of the counts of Toulouse and be protected by him in the wars to come, and be very important to the development of heresy in Quercy. But from the late twelfth century it was Castelsarrasin, dominating the Garonne below its junction with the Tarn, that was the major administrative seat of Quercy for the counts of Toulouse.[23] The most significant of its seneschals was to be Pons Grimoard, a 'new man' – introduced in Chapter 1 above – who would be one of the most important people in the history of the heresy and inquisition. We know that his family were at Castelsarrasin by the late twelfth century, but they seem to have originated further north. We have records for them holding land at Lavergne and Couzou, in Limousin-Quercy, and on the Cahorsain Lot at La Fouillade (at modern Puy-l'Evêque), all of which they ceded to Obazine in 1159–60.[24] In addition, a Bernard Grimoard witnessed a charter in favour of Cistercian Obazine in 1162–3, and Pierre Grimoard one by Raimond V of Toulouse 1184.[25]

[19] *HGL*, IV, 170; Lacoste, *Quercy*, II, p. 25.
[20] *HGL*, V, chartes no. 658. See also *HGL*, IV, 170 on the viscounts of Toulouse-Bruniquel-Monclar; *HGL*, VI, 67; *HGL*, VII, 1283–5 (*c.*1284); L. Macé, *Catalogues raimondins. Actes des comtes de Toulouse, ducs de Narbonne et marquis de Provence (1112–1229)* (Toulouse, 2008), no. 156; Lartigaut, *Histoire de Quercy*, p. 93.
[21] *HGL*, IV, 171.
[22] Lartigaut, *Histoire de Quercy*, p. 92.
[23] Macé, *Catalogues raimondins*, no. 87.
[24] *CO*, nos. 146, 147, and see no. 385.
[25] *CO*, no. 160; *Catalogue ... Raimond V*, no. 107.

When Count Raimond VI of Toulouse conceded the customs of Moissac in 1197, perhaps as a reward for its loyalty in 1188, he installed a *bailli* there, Othon de Berètges.[26] But it was in terms of its religious life that Moissac was one of the region's most important towns, its abbey dominating the religious life of lower Quercy. It was tied in to clerical structures of the Toulousain as well as those of Cahors. Bishop Durand of Toulouse (1159/60–c.1171) had been a monk of Moissac, for example, and retained lands in Quercy and ties to the lords of Caussade.[27] Moissac's spiritual life was well nurtured into the twelfth century. Nonetheless, the Cathar heresy was to implant itself there by 1200, protected by the lords of Saint-Paul, a castle on the right bank of the Tarn,[28] at Caussade, as noted above, and at Castelsarassin and Montauban too.

The Vaux de Quercy

The twelfth-century Vaux, between the Lot and the Tarn and Aveyron, was typified by the *castra*, themselves typical of the Midi. In Quercy they were often founded on *pech* (a defensible natural mount, often 'puy' in place-names) or used rivers as natural fortifications. The most powerful people within them were usually their noble founders, who had seigneurial rights and usually controlled a castle integral to the *castrum*. Lartigaut observes that such lords of the Vaux were unable to become powerful independent castellans like the lords of Gourdon because of the proximity of the county of Toulouse.[29] Raimond V founded the *castrum* of Lauzerte (or *Loseler*) on land ceded for the purpose in *c.*1185 by the lords of Castanher, with whom he shared revenues from the town. He had 200 houses built there and conceded its customs immediately to attract settlers.[30] The transfer of Monclar to the lords of Montpezat and of Caylus to its new lord, possibly Raimond-Amilio de Caylus,[31] also reflects this 'hands-on' comital approach to Quercy.

We might observe, however, that the lords of Gourdon were themselves lords in the Vaux by the late twelfth century. As well as providing bishops, they were defenders of the cathedral clergy of Cahors and there was a significant overlap between their estates and those of the episcopal see, probably an outcome of the episcopates of bishops Guiraud I and IV de Gourdon. In addition, they were vassals of the count for their rights to justice in some thirty parishes, and some of these may have been in the Vaux.[32] So, whereas

---

[26] *HGL*, VIII, chartes no. 67, 441–2; *HGL*, VI, 179.

[27] *HGL*, III, 337–8.

[28] DPC, p. 231 note 331.

[29] Lartigaut, *Histoire de Quercy*, p. 93.

[30] Macé, *Catalogues raimondins*, no. 205; Lartigaut, *Histoire de Quercy*, pp. 93, 104, 105.

[31] See also Macé, *Catalogues raimondins*, commentary on nos. 205, 181.

[32] Lartigaut, *Histoire de Quercy*, p. 92; Combarieu, *Dictionnaire*, p. 53; Taylor, *Heresy*, pp. 239, 254, 256.

Lartigaut suggests that it was the proximity of Toulousain power that kept the lords of the Vaux in their place, preventing them from becoming as independently successful as the lords of Gourdon, it seems likely that the lords of Gourdon themselves were also responsible for their limited strength. Whereas Toulouse dominated Lauzerte, Monclar, Montpezat and Caylus, the other significant *castra* of the Vaux – Castelnau-Montratier, Montcuq, Montaigu, Mondenard – were aligned with Gourdon and had very different origins.

These *castra* dependent on Gourdon emerged in the twelfth century but had different origins from those of comital *castra*. Their close association with the more ancient castellany of Gourdon, and its own flourishing, suggests two possible origins. It seems possible that these new centres were established by new dynasties which had their origins in the caste of castle knights at Gourdon. The tendency in the twelfth century for castle knights to be dispersed into the countryside has been suggested for France more widely by Jean Richard and Dominique Barthélemy.[33] It seems possible that something similar may have taken place in Quercy, with knights being established as client-lords charged with fortifying and governing distant estates. One probable example is the d'Arcambal family. They first appear as castle-knights at Gourdon in the early twelfth century. We have noted that the lands of the lords of Gourdon overlapped with those of the bishops, in part because they provided bishops themselves for the see. This could account for the location of the estate of Arcambal as we find it in the later twelfth century, near Cahors. Were this the case, such lords could be expected to follow the lead of the lords of Gourdon in political and military matters in the thirteenth century. This, as we shall see, they typically did.

Castelnau-Montratier, on the other hand, was founded and governed by a secondary line of the lords of Gourdon. Because its communal archive was destroyed in 1793 it is very difficult to say much about the origins of the town before its thirteenth-century reconstruction by Ratier de Gourdon-Castelnau, from whom it took its later name.[34] Before this it was known as Castelnau-Hélène, after the founder of L'Hospitalet in *c.*1061, and perhaps also as Castelnau-des-Vaux.[35] It does seem to have been a planned and fortified *castrum* from a very early date, perhaps indeed an eleventh-century 'new castle' (there are surprisingly few of them attested in early place-names).

---

[33] J. Richard, 'Châteaux, châtelains et vassaux en Bourgogne au xie et xiie siècles', *Cahiers de civilisation médiéval* 3 (1960), pp. 433–47; D. Barthelémy, 'Castles, barons, and vavassors in the Vendôme and neighbouring regions in the eleventh and twelfth centuries', in *Cultures of Power: Lordship, Status and Process in Twelfth-Century Europe*, ed. T. N. Bisson (Philadelphia, 1995), pp. 56–68, esp. pp. 57, 67.

[34] Limayrac, *Castelnau-Montratier*, pp. 54–5.

[35] Combarieu (*Dictionnaire*, p. 115) suggests that this was to distinguish it from 'Castelnau-des-Vaux', but *cf.* Limayrac, who considers this to have been the same site: Limayrac, *Castelnau-Montratier*, pp. 53–6. On L'Hospitalet see DPC, p. 267 note 373.

The inquisition was to sit in no fewer than five *castra* of the Vaux: Montcuq, Sauveterre, Beaucaire (Lauzerte), Montpezat-de-Quercy, Almont and Castelnau-Montratier; towns that had been established by both the lords of Gourdon and the counts of Toulouse. We shall hear a good deal more about them in the following chapters. But these centres were tiny in comparison with the episcopal towns of the cahorsain Lot and urbanised lower Quercy.

The Cahorsain

Many of the towns of the Lot, as well as Cahors itself, were characterised by having the bishop as their lord. Cahors itself was a pre-eminent and precocious monetary centre. By 1188 a consulat representing the interests of the moneyers and jurists was already in existence. It is alluded to in an oath the town took to Richard the Lionheart in that year, although not directly attested until a charter of 1207.[36] There is evidence from around this time of the town beginning to assert itself by making pacts with outside parties. In 1203 Raymond of Toulouse offered protection 'to our dear and faithful townspeople and all other people'.[37] But tensions between the economic aspirations of urban elites and the hegemony of bishop-princes were to be characteristic of the identity of Cahors and towns such as Puy-l'Evêque and Cajarc in the thirteenth century. But this would be the result of the wars to come and the relative positions of the bishops and urban elites at the end of it. In spite of a flourishing economy, Cahors does not resemble twelfth-century Toulouse in terms of, for example, consular autonomy, or even in striving especially strongly towards it.

The Bouriane

The Bouriane consists of the region north of the Lot, bordered by the Agenais and Périgord to the west and to the east by the north–south communication route bisecting Quercy between Souillac and Cahors. Heavily wooded, it was the domain of the lords of Gourdon. Guiraud II de Gourdon, brother of Bishop Guiraud I of Cahors and probably the son of Aimeric II de Gourdon, left a will in 1108 on his departure to the Holy Land (where he would join forces with Raimond of Saint-Gilles) bequeathing the seigneuries of Gourdon to his wife Alpasie and son Aimeric III (d. 1152).[38] But another branch of the family appears to have dominated the town itself by 1119. In that year the castellan, Guillaume, a cousin of Aimeric III, played host to Pope Calixtus II. The papal visit resulted in a donation on 24 June that year by Guillaume and Aimeric to Abbot Pons of Cluny of a large wooded hill, 'Monmalus', there-

---

[36] Cited in Lartigaut, *Histoire de Quercy*, pp. 116–17.

[37] D118, fol. 1r–v. The original is not extant: *IRC*, no. 1.

[38] Bulit, *Gourdon*, pp. 52, 59.

after known as Mont-Saint-Jean.[39] The documents associated with this visit are worth discussing in some detail, shedding light as they do not only on the immediate material contents of the charters but also on the nature of both monastic donations and the wider society of Quercy.

Monmalus lay just below Gourdon on the road to Peyrignac, and the donation included the hamlet of Peyrignac itself and its church, which was already theoretically in Cluny's possession but which had apparently been usurped by the cathedral clergy. The monks soon established a settlement, the protection, peace and justice of which was guaranteed by the lords of Gourdon and their knights and other clients. Such men, appearing in the witness list, include the significant neighbours and associates of the lords of Gourdon in the early twelfth century. Among them is Ebrard 'le Cot', a knight of the *castrum* of Gourdon itself, and his son Arnaud. In addition, there was Giraud d'Arcambal and his brother Séguin, a family later to be found at an estate near Cahors, who were also servants at arms. We also find local families that were to be investigated by inquisitors over a century later: those of Bernard-Hugues de la Roque, Guillaume de Fénelon, Guiraud de Goulême (who were also lords of Milhac and Concorès)[40] and Reynaud de Rouffilhac; and two members of a family with origins closer to Cahors: Gausbert and Bertrand de Pestillac (Montcabrier). In a third category are people carrying the names of *castra* pertaining to the lords of Gourdon by *c.*1200 at the latest, who were, as such, possibly of cadet branches: the knights Raimond and Gausbert de Salviac, and Aimeric 'Ichier' and his brothers Rigal and Guiraud de Castelnau. A subsequent grant was then made of rights to other woods of the lords of Gourdon, witnessed in addition to the names above by Arnaud and Adémar de Salviac and Arnaud de Rouffilhac.

We learn a little more about the castle knights (*milites castri*) Ebrard and Arnaud 'le Cot' from an accompanying charter, drawn up at the same time, in which they themselves give the monks two mills with the pond to be found at the foot of the hill for their own souls, those of their family and also those of their lords Guillaume and Aimeric III de Gourdon. Furthermore, another son of Ebrard was himself given to the new house.[41] We hear no more of Ebrard and his family after this.

The lords of Gourdon and their circle were to prove central to the story of 'heresy' in its spread, toleration and persecution in Quercy. As such, I shall pay close attention to their genealogy and add significantly to the work in this area of Roger Bulit.

[39] A. Bruel (ed.), *Recueil des chartes de l'abbaye de Cluny*, 6 vols (Paris, 1876), V, no. 3937; Albe, *Les institutions*, pp. 72–5. See also Lartigaut, *Histoire de Quercy*, p. 101; Lacoste, *Quercy*, II, pp. 22–4; Bulit, *Gourdon*, pp. 54–5.

[40] Bulit, *Gourdon*, p. 92, note 1.

[41] Bruel, *Recueil … de Cluny*, no. 3938; Albe, *Les institutions*, pp. 75–6.

Guillaume de Gourdon, the donor of 1119, subsequently had a son, Bertrand, acting through charters by 1152 and until at least 1168, when he made a donation to Obazine in the same year that his cousin Aimeric IV, son of Aymeric III, confirmed other family gifts.[42] This Bertrand had a son, Guiraud, witness to no fewer than twenty-eight charters for Obazine,[43] and who – it therefore seems likely – was Abbot Guiraud II de Gourdon (1188–1204) and the same Guiraud de Gourdon-de Montcuq who witnessed the homage of the lords of Monclar to the count of Toulouse, noted above, in 1176. However, this branch of the family apparently died out with the abbot.

Aimeric III and Anne de Turenne had a son, Pons I de Gourdon (attested 1152–66), and he had a son, Fortanier I, castellan by 1172.[44] It was this branch that was most prominent at Gourdon itself by the start of the Albigensian crusade. Another son of Aimeric and Anne was Aimeric IV de Gourdon, who in 1152 confirmed his family's donations to Obazine and acted in this capacity until 1179–80.[45]

The origins of the third branch of the family, at Castelnau-Montratier, are less certain. If Bulit is correct, the common ancestor of this branch and of the others was Aimeric I. We also know of Aimeric 'Ichier' and his brothers Rigal and Guiraud de Castelnau, witnesses to the 1119 charters, and of a Gausbert I de Castelnau, who seems likely to have been the son of Izarn I of Luzech and Lucie, daughter of Viscount Odalric of Saint-Cirq.[46] There are surprisingly few places of the name 'Castelnau' attested in the region between the Dordogne and Tarn-Aveyron-Garonne,[47] and so it is wise to consider the possibility that any or all of these could have been ancestors of the lord of what would become known as Castelnau-Montratier (see below). We know that by 1200 the lords of Gourdon held most of the former viscounty of Saint-Cirq, just noted as perhaps connected to Castelnau-Montratier, the *castra* of Salviac and Montcuq, of which more will be said below, and they also had seigneurial rights at Saint-Céré, Concorès, Lavercantière, Cazals, Peyrilles,

---

[42] *CO*, no. 534; Bulit, *Gourdon*, p. 57.

[43] *CO*, nos. 260, 261, 264, 288, 290, 366, 383, 385, 389, 390, 407, 409, 410, 442, 473, 475, 478, 486, 487, 495, 516, 551, 576, 598, 605, 608, 609, 610.

[44] *CO*, no. 392 (1169–70); Combarieu and Cangardel, 'Gourdon et ses seigneurs', p. 145. Concerning Fortanier and Bertrand, Bulit notes fanciful local legends which have Fortanier killed by Richard I in defence of Gourdon, and Bertrand killing Richard I at Chalus in 1199 and being killed in turn by Richard's men: Bulit, *Gourdon*, pp. 57, 61, 62–4. Other known family members, possibly of Pons I, Aimeric IV and Bertrand de Gourdon's generation, were Bardo de Gourdon (1172–3) *CO*, no. 352, Polverellus (1170–1) *CO*, no. 325; Berengar, '*reclusus*' (1172–4) *CO*, nos. 392 (1173–4) and 393 (1172–3).

[45] *CO*, nos. 534 (1152) and 284 (1168); Bulit, *Gourdon*, pp. 53, 57.

[46] See Lacoste, *Quercy*, II, p. 13.

[47] An important one is Castelnaud on the Dordogne. Its lords were forced to give Beaulieu, of which they were secular abbots, to Cluny in 1076 (Woods, *Proprietary Church*, pp. 324–6). We shall encounter its lords in the crusading era (chapter 3).

Peyrignac, la Roque, Rouffilhac, Goulême, Milhac, Frayssinet and le Vigan, and also rights over a good half of the Causée de Gramat.[48]

Later in the century the Obazine cartulary gives us records of numerous other grand and minor families of the Bouriane. This is what shows us that the de Lavergne were related to the Grimoard family of Castelsarrasin,[49] as well as to the de la Roque, for we have an Aimeric de Lavergne de la Roque.[50] The de Lavergne were to take part in various alliances in the thirteenth century that reinforced orthodox secular solidarities in an era when the crusade elsewhere undermined them. They would apparently play no part in the heretical life of the Bouriane. The de la Roque, first mentioned in the 1119 charter above, were probably associated with either Montamel or Saint-Palavy, both in the Gourdon area. In the twelfth century we know of at least another eight family members acting as donors or witnesses at Obazine.[51] They would rise in significance as a family and, in contrast with the de Lavergne, would be implicated in heresy.

Another family that would receive a great deal of attention from inquisitors was that of the lords of the double seigneury of Goudou-Labastide. Albe considers the fief to have been established by Fortanier I de Gourdon. There was a castle at what is still known as Goudou and a fortified town known in the early documents sometimes as Labastide-Gourdon, sometimes as Labastide-Fortanier after its founder, and sometimes simply as Labastide, as, for example, in the sentence given to Gaillard de Goudou in 1241 by Pierre Seilan.[52] It was a fortified staging post and hospice between Cahors and Rocamadour, significant in its position at the eastern reaches of the seigneury that protected it, and is now called Labastide-Murat, after its more famous inhabitant.[53]

'Limousin Quercy'

The castles and estates controlled directly or indirectly by the Limousin viscounts of Turenne and the monks of Cluniac Beaulieu and Cistercian Obazine formed a sphere which we could call 'Limousin-Quercy', so extensive and established was Aquitainian influence here. It extended south of the

---

[48] *IRC*, II, no. 36; Lacoste, *Quercy*, II, p. 68; Bulit, *Gourdon*, pp. 60–1; Lartigaut, *Histoire de Quercy*, pp. 90, 92, 251; Combarieu, *Dictionnaire*, pp. 56, 184.

[49] *CO*, no. 385.

[50] *CO*, no. 178, and witness to no. 385.

[51] Hugues (*CO*, no. 585), Robert (*CO*, no. 514), Pierre (*CO*, nos. 129, 388, 405, 419, 474), Jean (*CO*, no. 387), Gerbert (*CO*, nos. 315, 551, 385), Guiraud (*CO*, no. 420), Constantine (*CO*, no. 193), Guillaume and/or Guillaume 'Chastanos' (*CO*, nos. 138, 146, 147, 160 and 245).

[52] D21, fol. 213r.

[53] Combarieu, *Dictionnaire*, pp. 94, 103. See E. Albe's work on-line at http://www.quercy. net/qmedieval/histoire/monog_albe/labastide_murat.html#Seigneurie (last accessed 6/8/09). See also DPC, p. 87, note 153, but *cf.* ibid. p. 47, note 108.

Dordogne as far as Gramat and Rocamadour, and thus abutted other major lay and monastic lordships.

As alluded to above, the influence of Obazine is essential to understanding this region, and this relationship will be discussed at length below. Otherwise, the viscounty of Brassac, roughly corresponding to modern Montvalent, was another that underwent significant changes in the twelfth century. Between the activity of Obazine and that of the viscounts of Turenne, it too was effectively dissolved. In 1165–6 Pierre de Brassac was induced to donate to Obazine lands he held at Les Alys.[54] The lords of Belcastel also claimed rights to Brassac, and Hugues de Belcastel renounced his pretension specifically to Les Alys in favour of Abbot Robert (1164–88).[55] The latter family also renounced control of the church at Mayrignac in Obazine's favour and tithes pertaining to the churches of Couzou and Bougayrou (La Cave) in 1167–8. From this process we learn that they were related to the lords of Gramat.[56] By 1190 what little remained independent was apparently held by Guillaume and Raimond de Calvinhac. They sold these to the viscounts of Turenne in that year.[57] Finally, we should not understate the influence of the bishops of Cahors in the north. Viscount Raimond I and his son Boson II performed homage to Guiraud III for Brassac and what they held at Souillac.[58]

The causses *and eastern Quercy*

I have used this term to denote the whole eastern half of the county because of its relative uniformity in confessional and political terms for our purposes. Sparsely inhabited, it was dominated by the abbey of Figeac and the castellany of Cardaillac, which provided bishops of the diocese and whose lords were the most important family to remain uncompromised by the taint of heresy in the thirteenth century.

The high chalky plains designated as *causses* were largely uninhabited in our period because of their poorer soils and severe winter climate. Plotting settlements attested by *c*.1250 on a map of Quercy reveals this absence of settlement or exploited land. Their northern formation consists firstly of the *causses* of Gramat and Martel. The plain is interrupted significantly only by the minor towns along the Célé and Lot, and then becomes the Causse de Limogne. This *causse* extends southwards as far as Caussade, which takes its name from the geology. The chalk thus divides Quercy's central longitudinal concentration of settlement – extending southwards from Gourdon through Cahors to Caussade – from the historically Rouergois-orientated east.

---

[54] CU, no. 235.
[55] CO, no. 239.
[56] CO, nos. 87, 151, 156, 202, 204, 239, 287, 344, 350, 397, 399, 532, 591, 592, 615, 689, 766.
[57] Ayma, *Histoire … Cahors*, I, pp. 270, 273–5; Combarieu, *Dictionnaire*, p. 172; Lartigaut, *Histoire de Quercy*, p. 92.
[58] Combarieu, *Dictionnaire*, p. 4.

As noted, the influence of Toulouse over the Rouergue grew and then diminished in the twelfth century. This seems a likely context for the rise of the lords of Cardaillac, who were by far the most important lords in eastern Quercy by *c.*1200. They initially rose in influence in association with Figeac. Their chapel, Saint-Thomas, pertained to Figeac from 1146, as did the nearby priory of Saint-Julien. The town itself emerged on a natural rocky outcrop, possibly on the site of an earlier fortification, on the edge of the forest of Prendignes. But its twin rectangular towers are attested only from the early thirteenth century and Lartigaut speculates that Cardaillac was originally unfortified, although this seems unlikely given the region. In 1176 Bertrand and Guillaume de Cardaillac were prominent in a gathering that aided the division of rights (*pariage*) to the town of Cayrac between Count Raimond of Toulouse and Abbot Pierre of Aurillac. Their castle at Aujols dates to the early 1100s and they had property as far west as Cahors and into the Rouergue to the east, as witnessed in their numerous donations to the commandery of La Selve between *c.*1180 to *c.*1200.[59] From its cartulary we can add flesh to the bones of a genealogy otherwise dominated by bishops.

In the donations of *Puit* in *c.*1180 and of Laroque of *c.*1200 Bertrand de Cardaillac is again attested, and he witnessed a charter of the Limousin viscount, Archambaud V of Comborn, in 1167–8. Bertrand's five brothers, Guiraud, Amblart, Raimond, Raimond Rocis and Guiraud Bonafos, were all sons of a woman called Arnauda. A Bertrand de Cardaillac, perhaps the same man, was to become commander of La Selve at some point after 1220.[60] Bertrand is also attested in the Obazine cartulary, as are the *conversus* (lay convert) Guido, a Guiraud who was perhaps Bertrand's son, a Marie and a Guiraud de Cardaillac-de Belcastel, demonstrating a link to that family also.[61] The family also had lines at Varaire, Privezac and Brengues.[62] But the de Cardaillac did not control Figeac. Its protectors were families external to Quercy, traditionally the de Caumont of the Rouergue, although Phillip Augustus took on this role directly in 1186 and entrusted it to Raimond of Toulouse in 1194/5.[63]

To conclude, we can say that the leading families in Quercy by *c.*1200 were no longer viscounts. Traditional seats such as Bruniquel-Monclar, Brassac and Caussade waned in importance and some even ceased to be acknowledged. This was in part the result of a deliberate strategy on the part of the counts

---

[59] *HGL*, VI, 67; Lartigaut, *Histoire de Quercy*, pp. 92, 104; de la Torre, *Lot*, unpaginated.

[60] *Cartulaire de la Selve: la terre, les hommes et le pouvoir en Rouergue au xiie siècle*, ed. P. Ourliac and A.-M. Magnou (Paris, 1985), nos. 4, 28, 29, 30, 39, 68, 70, 71, 98, 99, 101, 107, 108, 110, 110a, 115, 120 (and see note 1 on Bertrand), 176.

[61] *CO*, nos. 140, 158, 247, 360, 390, 689, 778, 797, 799, 841, 1174.

[62] *HGL*, III, 122; Dufour, *Cahors*, note 21; Combarieu, *Dictionnaire*, pp. 30–1, 256.

[63] AD Lot series F. 125; *HGL*, VIII, 1495. See also Bousquet, *Le Rouergue*, p. 484, notes 26–27; Lartigaut, *Histoire de Quercy*, pp. 92–3, and above p. 50.

of Toulouse – advancing new families and new kinds of political representation in the south of the region – and the Obazine–Turenne alliance in the north. The leading castellans of the eleventh century were also becoming less significant in the twelfth, as favour was bestowed on new lords of castles and *castra*. But two important exceptions are the relatively independent lords of Cardaillac and Gourdon. The shift and concentration of comital power from the Rouergue towards Toulouse made room for them, but they were not beholden to the counts of Toulouse and would not take his side in 1209. The de Cardaillac in particular were to be almost unique in Quercy as consistently enthusiastic crusaders against the lands and allies of Toulouse.

Quercy bucks a trend in terms of models for the spread of heresy also. It had a relatively vibrant orthodox religious life and close family alliances with important abbeys. Indeed, Quercy was apparently as actively and as dynamically orthodox as neighbouring Périgord, Limousin and the Rouergue, to Quercy's north and east. Even so, lower Quercy would contrast with the rest of the county in being home to heretics, both Cathar and Waldensian, by c.1200.

We should understand a little more about the nature of social relations in Quercy as a backdrop to the coming crisis. Ties between lords and vassals were such that the French invasion meant conceptual, as well as political, revolution.

Socio-political Structures and Landholding in the Twelfth Century

As alluded to above, Languedoc does not fit easily into debates concerning a collapse of public power by the early eleventh century.[64] It has long been

---

[64] On the place of southern France in this debate see the essays collected in *Fiefs et féodalité dans l'Europe méridionale (Italie, France du Midi, Péninsule Ibérique du Xe au XIIIe siècle*, ed. P. Bonnassie (Toulouse, 2002), esp. his introduction, pp. 7–21, where work on the south is contextualised within the wider debate and his defence of the concept of 'feudalism' (*féodalité*) strongly reiterated against scholarship which, in Bonnassie's view, does not take full account of the differences between the early and high Middle Ages and neglects key literature on the south. For the recent literature Bonnassie employs to support his case see, for example, that of E. Magnou-Nortier, 'La "féodalité" méridionale, a-t-elle existé? Réflexions sur quelques sources des xe, ixe et xiie siècles', in *Fiefs et féodalité dans l'Europe méridionale*, ed. P. Bonnassie (Toulouse, 2002), pp. 167–201, and F. de Gournay, 'Le fief en Rouergue (xe–xiie siècle)', in *Fiefs et féodalité dans l'Europe méridionale*, ed. P. Bonnassie (Toulouse, 2002), pp. 203–20. See also, along these lines, L. Verdon, *La terre et les hommes en Roussillon aux xiie et xiiie siècles* (Aix-en-Provence, 2001) and Hélène Débax, *La féodalité languedocienne* (Toulouse, 2003). Bonnassie is responding here primarily to work by Dominique Barthélemy, *La mutation de l'an mille, a-t-elle en lieu? Servage et chevalerie dans la France des Xe et XIe siècles* (Paris, 1997). Barthélemy can now be better appreciated in English: *The Serf, the Knight and the Historian* (Ithaca and London, 2009). This emerging consensus concerning the twelfth-century south by scholars of that region

accepted that Roman legal concepts remained intact enough in Languedoc to support the survival of the 'allod', freely held and freely transferrable land, as close to 'ownership' as we can get in the high Middle Ages, and for which neither payments nor service were owed to anyone. The Occitan fief certainly existed too. However, our understanding of socio-political structures in Languedoc should not be confused by the identification of the 'fief' with 'feudalism'.

Fiefs

As a generalisation, a cornerstone of the social fabric in the north and east of France was the understanding that services, including military service, would be rendered in exchange for the right of the fief-holder to occupy and exploit a geographically definable piece of land and the people settled on it, and often a castle. In the south, while the fief contrasted with the allod not least because homage had to be performed for it, it did not have the same military and social associations that it did north of the Dordogne. Whereas in the north society was structured around the fief, in the south the fief was simply one way in which society was structured. The difference between French and Occitan fiefs is significant because from 1209 the northern-style fief was to become the mechanism through which Occitan society would be dominated by the Albigensian crusaders.

First, although the eleventh- and twelfth-century southern fief might relate to an estate, or to part of it, it did not consist of land or property itself. Ourliac and Magnou-Nortier have observed that the performance of homage for lands themselves in the Toulousain begins only *c.*1200,[65] and the evidence points to this pattern in Quercy. Instead, the southern fief should be understood as being some, but usually not all, of the rights and revenues associated with an office, manse, settlement, church or wider territory, such as rights to

---

is also at odds with Anglophone scholarship, even on France, beginning with E. A. R. Brown, 'The tyranny of a construct: feudalism and historians of Medieval Europe', *American Historical Review* 79 (1974), pp. 1063–88, reprinted in *Debating the Middle Ages: Issues and Readings*, ed. L. K. Little and B. H. Rosenwein (Oxford, 1998), pp. 148–69 (and see the editors' introduction, pp. 107–13, for an overview of the debate to the late 1990s). See also S. Reynolds, *Fiefs and Vassals: The Medieval Evidence Reinterpreted* (Oxford, 1994). For subsequent debate in the journal *Past and Present* see especially T. N. Bisson, 'The "Feudal Revolution"', *P&P* 142 (1994), 6–42; S. White, 'Debate: The "Feudal Revolution", Comment 2', *P&P* 152 (1996), pp. 205–23; C. Wickham, 'Debate: The "Feudal Revolution", Comment 4', *P&P* 155 (1997), pp. 196–208. For myself, I think Bonnassie et al. convincing on the far south and Catalonia in the eleventh century, but find most attempts to construct a generalised picture applying to 'France' as a whole misguided. Logically, the matter is perhaps that different regions were different, but this is not exclusively the case, as demonstrated in F. L. Cheyette, 'George Duby's *Mâconnais* after fifty years: reading it then and reading it now', *Journal of Medieval History* 28 (2002), pp. 291–317.

65 *Cartulaire de la Selve*, p. 6.

taxes on transporting goods (*péage*), to tithe, to the profits of justice or to taxes on profits. The explanation, Magnou-Nortier demonstrates, lies in the origin of the southern fief in an institution of *c.*1000 called the *'fevum sive fiscum'*, in which the fief was a monetory remuneration for public officials such as viscounts.[66] It served to redistribute revenues from the nobility to their servants.[67] This is how we should understand the relationship between Count Raimond VI and his new officials Pons Grimoard, seneschal for Quercy, and Othon de Berètges, *bailli* for Moissac in *c.*1200.

Further evidence that fiefs did not imply static property as such is that we rarely find lords being dispossessed of land *itself* in an accepted legal sense: that is, by an aggrieved lord in a feudal court. Land was not withdrawn as a fief any more than allodial land could be, although both were sometimes stolen when a great prince such as the duke of Aquitaine swooped in and seized it, or when localised pacts of mutual non-aggression broke down and a petty war broke out. In these cases castles *specifically* were sometimes taken, from the 1170s at the latest, as in the case of Monclar noted above: it was seized by the count of Toulouse and a new pact was made with its new lords. We should therefore understand the capture of castles as being untypical and highly significant in terms of the political landscape until the Albigensian crusade, when it became more commonplace but also more greatly resented.

Secondly, according to Pierre Bonnassie, the southern fief had another function. Fiefs were often held of people of the same social rank, thus redistributing revenues within the private sphere among equals, leading to the concept of the *'fevum sive quartum'*, the fief as 'fourth grain' – that is, the right to a portion of the harvest.[68] This helps us to make sense of some of the complex social networks observable throughout Quercy by the thirteenth century that are not obviously hierarchical in nature. People often held fiefs of each other, being both lord and vassal for different fiefs. The relationship did not give a lord authority over a vassal except in the case of rights pertaining to the fief itself. This agrees with Ourliac and Magnou-Nortier's observation that liege homage was virtually unknown as a concept until *c.*1200.[69]

Thirdly, the territorial basis of the rights constituting the Occitan fief should not be understood as relating to a rural estate in the way we visualise for the northern fief. Hélène Débax observes that the *castrum* was at the heart of southern vassalic relationships and was the unit which we should understand as corresponding to a fief in origin. These settlements were domi-

---

[66] F. Magnou-Nortier, 'Note sur le sens du mot *fevum* en Septamanie et dans la marche d'Espagne, à la fin du xe et au début du xie siècle', *Annales du Midi* 76 (1962), 141–52. See also *Cartulaire de la Selve*, p. 5. Verdon notes the consensus on this emerging in particular from the work of Ourliac, Bonnassie and Débax, cited below: *La terre et les hommes*, p. 8.

[67] Bonnassie, *Fiefs et féodalité*, pp. 13, 19–21.

[68] Ibid., pp. 19–21.

[69] *Cartulaire de la Selve*, p. 6.

nated by knightly families, and multiple *castra* were understood as something like an 'honour' or principality.[70] In twelfth-century Quercy we have already noted several such complex family interests based around multiple *castra*. However, the large estates in Quercy seem to have constituted family allods rather than fiefs, or were a combination of the two. As with seizures and liege homage, we first find homage being demanded and performed for allods in the early thirteenth century.

Fourthly, non-nobles held fiefs. Indeed, some public offices constituted 'le ciment entre aristocratie et paysannerie'.[71] The families of both Pons Grimoard and Othon de Berètges appear not to have been noble. 'Grimoard' corresponds to neither of the two personal naming formulae through which nobility was designated,[72] while 'de Berètges' is an *apparently* noble name but one that does not relate to any known estate.[73] We should note, however, that the towns over which these 'new men' wielded the most direct authority were those of lower Quercy. These were abbatial and commercial towns, not the *castra* of the Vaux, with the exception of Montcuq from the 1220s, or the Bouriane. Very different socio-political structures governed Quercy south of the Tarn-Aveyron, therefore.

Finally, the southern fief was not essentially military. Its holder might well appear in his lord's retinue, but this was not understood as service relating to the fief and was not regulated in relation to it. Even in the case of castles, military service is not noted in the charters. As a result, whereas northern French society was a militarised society, its preparedness for large-scale warfare

---

[70] H. Débax, 'Fief et castrum: le fief dans les serments de fidélité languedociens du xie siècle', in *Fiefs et féodalité dans l'Europe méridionale (Italie, France du Midi, Péninsule Ibérique) du xe au xiiie siècle*, ed. P. Bonnassie (Toulouse, 2002), pp. 137–43, and see p. 16 in Bonnassie's introduction.

[71] Bonnassie, *Fiefs et féodalité*, p. 13.

[72] One is what we recognise as 'traditionally' seigneurial names, derived from estates, such as 'de Gourdon' or 'de Cardaillac'. C. Duhamel-Amado has shown for the southern France that these denoted the dominant, agnatic line. The second type of designation, the 'nomen-paternum' (father's name) found in the south after 1100, denotes a subordinate line taking a second name from a common ancestor, for example 'Guillelma Maurini', 'Bernardus Bonaldi' or 'Pierre Geraldi' (D21, fols. 201r, 271r and 281r): *Genèse des lignages méridionaux: l'aristocratie languedocienne du xe au xiie siècle* (Toulouse, 2001). For personal naming patterns revealing Occitan social structures, see also B. Cursente, 'The French Midi reflected in personal names, in *Personal Names Studies of Medieval Europe: Social Identity and Familial Structures*, ed. G. T. Beech et al. (Kalamazoo, 2002), pp. 87–95 (pp. 89, 92, 94); M. Bourin, 'How changes in naming reflect the evolution of familial structures in southern Europe, 950–1215', in *Personal Names Studies of Medieval Europe: Social Identity and Familial Structures*, ed. G. T. Beech et al. (Kalamazoo, 2002), pp. 3–13 (esp. p. 10; M. Bourin, 'France du Midi et France du Nord: deux systèmes anthroponymiques?' in M. Bourin et al., *L'anthroponymie. Document de l'histoire sociale des mondes méditerranéens médiévaux* (Rome, 1996).

[73] Similar examples in which nobility is assumed even without reference to an estate will be discussed below.

resulting from clearly identifiable military responsibilities, Languedoc was perhaps more accurately a *violent* society, its conflicts frequent, localised and of retribution: flaring up easily, brutal but short-lived, being unsustainable. The great powers certainly threatened each other in Languedoc and brief alliances, dominated by the Trencavel viscounts, the house of Saint-Gilles, Plantagenet claimants, the dukes of Narbonne and the Aragonese, were made. But although these rivalries were long-lasting – that between the Aquitainians and counts of Toulouse even being referred to now as The Forty-Years War[74] – actual campaigns waged by these parties before the thirteenth century were relatively few and involved small forces. Quercy was merely caught in the cross-fire between them. Again, this is an important context for the kinds of alliances made in Quercy in the Albigensian wars.

Having addressed the fief, we should return to the question of the allod in Quercy and also to that other famous feature of Occitan society, the supposedly ubiquitous and disastrous subdivision of allods at points of marriage and death resulting from the Roman legal practice of partible inheritance. We need to consider two types of allod: the *castrum* and the manse. They will be examined as physical and economic units below, but first we should consider their social and political function.

Allods

The implication of my qualification, in the case of Quercy, of Hélène Débax's suggestion that the *castra* formed the basis of the fief is that in twelfth-century Quercy all sorts of property was allodial, not only *castra* but also in the countryside. But we have also noted that the great castellans were increasing in authority, acquiring castles, establishing sub-branches and building new towns. This would seem to fly in the face of our understanding of the effects of partible inheritance on allods.

In Quercy we can explain this by suggesting that the 'allod' was sometimes rights to the profits deriving from territorial property, just as a fief was, but, unlike the fief, could also refer to the territorial property itself. How else may we understand the cession to Obazine in 1171–2 by Aimeric de la Roque of the property of Guiraud-Bernard de Ginouillac, unless we understand that Aimeric is referring to his own rights to income deriving from it, rather than to the territory itself?[75] This is sometimes more explicitly the case. In 1172–3 Hugues de la Roque ceded his rights at La Vayssière and *Garrigue-Rouge*, allods *already* donated by his brother Guiraud-Hugues.[76] Such an understanding also helps us to make sense of the simultaneous possession of the manse of Cremps in 1105 by Guillaume de Saint-Cirq, Ratier de Belfort

[74] R. Benjamin, 'A Forty Years War: Toulouse and the Plantagenets, 1156–96', *Historical Research* 61 (1988), 270–85.

[75] *CO*, no. 348.

[76] *CO*, no. 353.

and the chapter of Cahors;[77] they all held some of the rights to its produce or revenues.

This reading of the evidence leads to a different conclusion for Quercy to that of Magnou-Nortier for Languedoc more widely concerning the relationship between lay lords and the minor churches which they held. In explaining why many people could found the same church she says that lords were guardians rather than proprietors.[78] S. Woods has modified this convincingly, noting that donations in Languedoc can reflect ownership by groups of people, particularly in the case of lesser churches, explaining why many donations of the same church may be made: the group's members owned portions of its revenues individually.[79] This works for Quercy, where we have seen that other kinds of property, the 'property' (*res*) someone 'owned', was not necessarily land or buildings, or only land or buildings, but also 'things', such as rights to useage and profits.

Relevant here is that charter of 1119 of Aimeric and Guillaume de Gourdon in favour of Cluny. It is noted that, as well as the wooded hill donated outright, the monks were to have lawful access 'in all our woods' for pasturing pigs and taking wood. This grant of usufruct is a separate and distinct grant within the main charter. It has its own witness list. The charter therefore demonstrates that land might be given away in its entirety to the church, but that rights to it were something distinct from this and could be either granted or withheld.

Similarly, we have noted another donation to Cluny made at the same time by the castle-knights of Gourdon, Ebrard 'le Cot' and his son Arnaud, of two mills with the pond for monks to 'use' freely and in perpetuity. 'Use' surely implies that it is the *rights* to resources essential for the upkeep of the monks dwelling up the hill that are being granted, but that the *property* remained that of the knights. Nowhere do we see the knights relinquishing their own rights to use the mill and so on or, indeed, to charge other people for such usage. This seems to be understood in a 1120 papal confirmation of the grant by Pope Calixtus. He reiterates that the new house and all its appurtenances were to be free of any charges, and the usual threats are made against those attempting to undermine monastic liberties. It is not possession of the site of the abbey that is being confirmed in the charter but the house's exemption from charges otherwise payable.[80] We can observe the retention of rights over property donated in the case of Peyrignac in the twelfth century as well: we

[77] Combarieu, *Dictionnaire*, p. 71.

[78] E. Magnou-Nortier, *La société laïque et l'Église dans la province ecclésiastique de Narbonne (zone cispyrénéenne) de la fin du VIIIe à la fin du XIe siècle* (Toulouse, 1974), pp. 355–6, 393–4, 429–30, 445–6.

[79] Woods, *Proprietory Church*, pp. 617–21, 744, 774, and for discussion of Magnou-Nortier, *La société laïque*, pp. 308, 387, 391–2, 450, 618–20.

[80] Bruel, *Recueil … de Cluny*, no. 63.

have noted above both that the lords of Gourdon donated it to Cluny in 1119, and that in 1200 they had seigneurial rights to it.

In contrast, on the same day in 1119 an outright grant seems to have been intended in the donation by Guillaume and Pierre de Massut to the monks of possession 'in full freedom and ownership' of the manse of *La Combe* with its revenues, water and streams, and fields and wood.[81] It is explicitly the land, the rights to it *and* its associated revenues that are being donated: revenues presumably deriving not merely from sales of resources but, because this is a manse, also from rent owed by the people settled on it.

These charters show us that both land and rights to land were alienated in favour of the church or withheld from it. They allow us to understand the nature of rights associated with properties. We know that these are not assumed as being transferred with land that is donated, because they are sometimes noted separately. But relating this to allodial property when it was *not* being turned over to monks leads to the conclusion that it probably supported the allodialist in the same way as the fief supported its holder. Powerful new castellanies were growing and multiplying rather than being diminished. Whereas the church was being granted some property outright, it was surely rights to property, not property itself, that was being subdivided by lay lords in wills. This thesis is strengthened by the fact that Ourliac and Magnou-Nortier have observed something similar of rural estates in Rouergue, which also escaped the fractionalism taking place in other southern regions.[82]

Where the allod was a *castrum* this makes even more sense and is more obviously discernible. On the death of a castellan, the name of the *castrum* appears to have been retained by multiple heirs and its profits shared as a sort of basic income, although other additional estates might be acquired, perhaps through marriage, elsewhere. In other words, allods, like fiefs, formed parts of family 'honours'. Twelfth-century examples include the many branches of the lords of Saint-Céré before their domination by the viscounts of Turenne,[83] the lords of Goulême and Goulême-de Milhac and, of course, the lords of Gourdon, Gourdon de Castelnau, Gourdon de Montcuq, Gourdon de Salviac and Gourdon de Saint-Cirq. We should also observe this as a strategy of lesser nobles. Lartigaut observes that in the Obazine archive for the area around Rocamadour in the second half of the twelfth century, of 100 knightly families, sixty had a toponym, and in thirty-five cases this was the name of a parish.[84] In other words, they had come into possession of a significant holding with an administrative centre, possibly a castle. They retained rather than subdivided this, and were doing well enough to donate some of what they held to the abbey.

---

81 Bruel, *Recueil ... de Cluny*, no. 3937; Albe, *Les institutions*, pp. 72–5, 76.
82 *Cartulaire de la Selve*, pp. 13–14.
83 Lartigaut, *Histoire de Quercy*, p. 93.
84 Lartigaut, *Histoire de Quercy*, p. 94.

We should now examine the nature of the allod in terms of what it actually constituted.

The manse and the castrum

The manse, *mas-* as a prefix, as it survives in place-names, originated as a subdivision of Roman *villae* (rural estates, in whose names the suffix *-acum*, as for example in *Marcillacum*, survives only in a final *-ac* in their vernacular rendering, as in, for example, Marcillac, Souillac, Ginouillac and so on). As the essential unit of cultivation and exploitation in the countryside, we know what little we do about it from charters such as those above, describing it at the point of transfer. We lack other economic data, such as polyptychs.

The term manse appears throughout Languedoc but its history and definition vary regionally. In Quercy and the Rouergue the manse had very ancient origins as a unit of homogeneous agricultural exploitation and survived as the basic unit into the twelfth century. It did not automatically attract vicarial rights and its value related essentially to whether or not it was cultivated. For the Rouergue it has been suggested that a manse was around sixty hectares and very lightly settled, by perhaps ten people. It should be understood, therefore, as something like a hamlet and its associated land. In the donations to Le Selve a tenant was often denoted, along with the rent that they owed and any dues for pasturage, wood, fishing and so on.[85] In donations of manses in Quercy, we rarely find mention of who lived on the land.

The units of land identified for donation, settlement and organised cultivation, according to Lartigaut, mark an interim stage in the twelfth century between the isolated farmstead and nucleated settlement, perhaps helping to explain why we have so few references to rural dwellers in the twelfth century. The manse appears less frequently in the documentation into the thirteenth century in Quercy than it seems to do in Ourliac and Magnou-Nortier's Rouergue or Verdon's Rousillon.[86] During this period, in which we know that the lords of Gourdon were founding *castra* – and other *castra* appear without records of foundation but were, judging by their shape, no less 'planned' – the manse seems to have been marginalised, the rights to revenues from these fortified urban centres becoming the new defining feature of the countryside. This must have been an important stage before the northern-style fief was imposed by the crusaders and the town was understood as being held in exchange for services, rather than exploited by right. Returning to my suggestion that in Quercy we do not actually encounter *castra* as fiefs initially, rather as family allods, we can therefore observe a phase in which socio-familial complexes expanded and changed their physical and territorial infrastructure. The lords were turning rights to agricultural produce into

---

[85] *Cartulaire de la Selve*, pp. 5, 13–16, 20–1; Verdon, *La Terre*, p. 9; Lartigaut, *Histoire de Quercy*, p. 97.

[86] *Cartulaire de la Selve*, pp. 5–21; Verdon, *La terre*, pp. 66–75, 97, 106–64, 204–6.

urban revenues, such as rights to taxes on the sale of produce. This new economic dynamism would be interrupted by the northern invasion.

From allods to fiefs

A consideration of the relationship between the fief and the allod is important in understanding quercinois society before and after *c.*1200. On the one hand, the fief ranked a person below his lord in a socio-political sense. In this it was not unlike the northern fief. We can see this as an important conceptual counterpoint to possession of an allod. It is commonly said of Languedoc that the holding of land freely denoted nobility. It fixed the allodialist in at least a theoretical parity with both the free-but-impoverished peasant, on the one hand, and the count of Toulouse himself on the other. So, the fief demonstrated where someone was in the chain of command, and the allod denoted his or her legal equality with other free people, quite possibly including the fief-holder's own lord.

But, at the same time, we hear that Languedoc was a land in which social status and the ability and opportunity to display that status were paramount. This seems to contradict the 'equality' implied by the free holding of land, but Pierre Bonnassie's account of the socio-economic function of the fief resolves this. The fief was also a generous gift, and so social parity was maintained. Service was not implied by it, the land itself does not appear to change hands and, implicitly, it and a remainder of its revenues sometimes pertained still to the lord.[87] Indeed, de Vic and Vaissète and others observed that twelfth-century allodialists sometimes gave away land to receive it back as a fief in return for the protection of their new lord, and that this was a way in which the great lords developed and expanded their networks of vassals.[88] The latter observation is rather teleological, because although this *came* to be the case, explicitly, in the thirteenth century it had an external cause which de Vic and Vaissète and others missed. Bonnassie's model rings truer: the fief was a gift from which an *alliance* resulted, not subservience. In this way we can understand the gift of Caylus to Raimond VI by his new vassals for Montpezat and Monclar. As far as we know, it was not granted back to them; the fief was a counter-gift. The social function of equals holding fiefs of each other was about membership of an elite club, therefore, in which wealth was as important as freedom and in which there existed reciprocal and voluntary networks of solidarity as social glue between free people of note.[89]

---

[87] See Bonnassie, as above pp. 36–7 and Lartigaut, *Histoire de Quercy*, p. 97.

[88] *HGL*, III, 858–9.

[89] Fluidity in concepts of 'fief' and 'allod' relating to the practice of giving counter-gifts, also in the context of creating social bonds, is also noted in B. Rosenwein, *To Be a Neighbour of Saint Peter: the Social Meaning of Cluny's Property, 909–1049* (Ithaca, 1989), although in eastern, central and northern parts of France in the twelfth century understanding of what was entailed by a fief was more fixed.

But, as suggested, the thirteenth century brought about a more decisive conceptual shift in what constituted the nature of landholding. The crusade did not merely replace one lord with another, but nipped in the bud a new kind of lordship for Quercy, that which was exercised over economically productive *castra*, new settlements where knightly families could make a profit in ways they had not done a few decades previously. So the knights of Quercy lost out to the crusaders. This process, we shall see, benefited the townspeople of the new settlements instead. Like those of the more established commercial centres in lower Quercy, and like Cahors itself, they would soon be able to exact concessions in exchange for their loyalties in the wars to come: the knights lost out again.

But we should not view all of Quercy's urban centres as having the same sorts of origins, as planned and founded *castra*. Some arose from very different circumstances.

Urbanisation in its Twelfth-century Context

The origins of the *castra* of the Vaux have been discussed above, and it has been suggested that they were the result of activity in the area of the lords of Gourdon, as well as the more easily attestable influence of the counts of Toulouse. Some of Quercy's other towns were far older, ancient indeed, based on settlement in the Romano-Celtic era, although in several cases continuous settlement seems unlikely. Cahors, the most important example, will be discussed below. Saint-Sernin existed as early as the fourth century. Saint-Cirq-Lapopie was also an ancient Christian centre. The larger towns by the twelfth century were, in the main, settlements with their origins in Benedictine activity, such as Figeac and Moissac. Older medium-sized towns, such as Carennac and Catus, had their origins in clerical activity too, in the latter case emerging because of its abbey.[90] In contrast, it is impossible to tell in most cases whether the new castles of the eleventh century had settlements accompanying them until these bourgs are attested textually.[91] Certainly, many towns had their origins in political activity associated with their castles, as in the cases of those associated with the count of Toulouse and viscounts of Turenne, above. Another example is Castelsarrasin, which seems to have first been used in political affairs by Raimond V in 1162. He met there with various parties to conclude a truce in the wars with the English, as he noted in a letter to the French king.[92] We have observed the possibility that Cardai-

---

[90] Combarieu, *Dictionnaire*, pp. 223, 226; Lartigaut, *Histoire de Quercy*, p. 101–2.
[91] Lartigaut, *Histoire de Quercy*, p. 103.
[92] *HGL*, III, 833–4.

llac flourished before its castle was built, and Capdennac, too, is thought to have lacked an early seigneurial centre.[93]

In direct contrast, Gourdon is an example of the causal relationship of fortification and settlement. An eleventh-century castle on the brow of a hill, it was probably built where there was an existing *villa*. A parish church is recorded as 'below' the castle. The town grew around it and by the 1230s at the very latest there were other fortifications, because an 'upper' castle is recorded in an inquisitorial record, presumably referring to the original castle and indicating that other fortifications had been added below it. The town's suburbs grew along roads leading to other towns, such as Peyrignac, making Gourdon a communications hub. Because of this outward growth it contained several more attested small churches at an early stage: Sainte-Catherine and La Madelaine to the east and Saint-Siméon-de-la-Chapelle, a dependency of Sarlat.[94]

An example of how very varied settlements' initial focal points sometimes were is the case of the connected towns of Saint-Céré and Sainte-Spérie. The former was in origin a chapel attested in 1080, while the latter was a priory founded on the river nearby and containing St Spérie's relics. Communities grew and linked the sites, and were boosted by the resettlement of the abandoned neighbouring castle at Saint-Serenus (sometimes called Saint-Laurent-les-Tours) by knights of the viscount of Turenne. During the twelfth century these centres merged and formed a town with a market and a couple of smithies.[95]

Indeed, in the decades before 1200 more generally, economic dynamism shifted from land clearance by monks to manufacturing and trading, although the newly expanding towns maintained a close relationship with the flourishing agricultural economy that made urban life possible.[96] But, while coinage became commonplace, as was the case for Languedoc more widely, donations contained in the Obazine cartulary were expressed in pecuniary terms and are typically in *solidi* 'de Turenne' or 'de Limoges', indicating the economic as well as social influence of the north in the twelfth century.

Commercial centres: Montauban and Cahors

Towns in the south of Quercy in particular became capable of economic independence as long as the activities of the region's greatest lords did not impede this, be it in war or peace. This led to an increasing urban assertiveness and to aspirations towards greater freedom and self-management, especially in the control of taxes. This began in the commercial southern centres in the twelfth century. Montauban and Cahors are the most interesting examples.

---

[93] Lartigaut, *Histoire de Quercy*, p. 104.
[94] D21, fol. 199v; Lartigaut, *Histoire de Quercy*, pp. 103–4.
[95] Combarieu, *Dictionnaire*, pp. 222–3; Lartigaut, *Histoire de Quercy*, p. 104.
[96] Ligou, *Histoire de Montauban*, pp. 42, 43–5.

From its inception, Montauban offered economic and personal freedom from monastic lords, limited political freedom and security in a period of warfare between the counts of Toulouse and the Plantagenets. But the town also grew up in the context of the expanding economic power of the abbey of Saint-Théodard, guarded by a huge castle which served to control Toulouse–Cahors traffic. In 1144 the people of Montauriol, the settlement that had grown up around the abbey, apparently complained to Count Alphonse-Jourdain of Toulouse about the oppression they experienced at monastic hands. This, at least, was the count's justification for founding a new town for them to migrate to. He built it on the same road, to dominate the Tarn from a good defensive position. The foundation charter informed prospective migrants that anyone living in the town was free and sheltered from pursuit by outsiders. In exchange, the town would provide the count with soldiers, play host to him and his men and allow him the profits of justice, which he would also administer. Ligou identifies a significant shift in population from Montauriol to the new town in subsequent years, as well as rural–urban migration.[97]

Pope Eugenius III ordered Montauban's fortifications to be torn down, threatening interdict and excommunication. Things did not go that far, perhaps because the count took the cross and died in the Holy Land having made significant concessions to the abbey.[98] In 1149 his son, Raimond V, made a settlement with Saint-Théodard's Abbot Amiel which included half of the demesne and rights to justice, except concerning the castle, and exemptions from *péage*.[99] Subsequent clarification by Raimond VI of the division of property between the two towns favoured Montauriol's lords somewhat.[100] The counts had thus played both the radical champion of the people and the chastised prodigal son, gaining economically at both the abbey and Montauban's expense nonetheless.

But Montauban attained more political independence in 1195, receiving fuller privileges from the count in the context of military support offered against the Plantagenets. The charter transferred to ten *prud'hommes* (notables of the town) what had been comital powers, even those to justice. This allowed the families of Bertrand de Castillon and Guillaume Amiel to rise in power and wealth. The town thrived and expanded. Between 1194 and 1233 there is an astonishing lack of data for Montauban: just four charters.

97 The charter does not survive but is transcribed in part in AD Lot, F. 123 and into Montauban's 'Livre rouge' and 'Livre des serments'; *HGL*, III, 439, 731–3; Macé, *Catalogues raimondins*, nos. 47, 48; Ligou, *Histoire de Montauban*, pp. 25–7, 28, 29, 32–3, 42–3; Lartigaut, *Histoire de Quercy*, p. 96.

98 *HGL*, III, 733; Macé, *Catalogues raimondins*, no. 52.

99 J. H. Albanés (ed.), *Gallia Christiana novissima. Histoire des archévêchés, évéchês et abbayes de France*, 7 vols. (Montebéliard and Valence, 1895–1920), III, 744; *HGL*, III, 774–5; Macé, *Catalogues raimondins*, no. 57.

100 Ligou, *Histoire de Montauban*, pp. 31–2.

From this sparse evidence, however, it has been noted that, whereas the 1144 documentation deals with sales of animals, flour, salt and wine, in 1195 a significant range of manufactured goods was present. There were two mills on the Tarn and, whereas in 1144 ground flour was imported, in 1195 it was being processed locally.[101] A charter of 1170, moreover, provides evidence that there was not just a market but fairs at Montauban, perhaps even one weekly. In evidence are iron, steel, weapons, bowls and basins, salt cellars, leather, brass, wool and cloth, honey, cheese, bread, hazelnuts and almonds, all being transported by draft animals, and 'foreign' merchants too. The Tarn yields few varieties of fish, and these were being supplemented by sea fish, such as herring and eels, and even whale meat. By 1195 the markets were selling goods imported from England, Italy and Spain.[102]

Montauban was to remain firmly Toulousain in loyalty in the Albigensian crusade in defiance of Abbot Azémar of Saint-Théodard, who was technically still in charge of its churches. He would use the conflict to try to take Montauban for the abbey. We also find early evidence of the lords of La Mothe, a castle just north of Montauban, who were to be one of the most significant families in Quercy in terms of its heretical history: in 1203 at Montauban the count of Toulouse took Guillaume de La Mothe and his son Raimond under his protection, and in exchange they gave him their *borie* at Chaussous.[103]

The case of Cahors is rather different. The cathedral chapter was protected in its privileges by Rome during the twelfth century. In *c.*1100 the canons received rights to all revenue generated by the town's churches.[104] The bishop had other resources too. In 1166, for example, Pope Alexander III permitted Bishop Guiraud IV to seize 200 silver marks from 'thieving usurers' to build a bridge over the Lot, whose users would of course be taxed for the privilege.[105] This promotion of episcopal rights in the town needs to be understood in the context of the wars between Toulouse and Aquitaine, during which the issue of legitimate authority became confused. In 1159 Cahors declared for the latter party. It was then taken by the army of the French king for the count of Toulouse, and subsequently retaken by the Aquitainians.[106] Not long after this, in defiance of their bishop, the leading citizens of Cahors were brokering deals with the count of Toulouse, rival of the episcopate for authority in what was fast becoming a leading European economic centre. We have seen that in November 1203 Raymond VI made an agreement with representatives of the town that they could travel unhindered in his lands. In 1207 an accord was

---

[101] Ligou, *Histoire de Montauban*, pp. 33–4, 46–8.

[102] Ibid., pp. 35–42, 45–6.

[103] Macé, *Catalogues raimondins*, no. 317.

[104] *PL*, 151 cols. 424–5; A. Roach, *The Devil's World: Heresy and Society, 1100–1300* (Harlow, 2005), p. 20.

[105] D120, fols. 1r–2v.

[106] *HGL*, III, 810–11.

made between the towns of Toulouse and Cahors that they would compensate each other for harm done to their inhabitants by the other, with the exception of economic affairs.[107] By the time of the crusade, whatever their confessional affinities, the leading members of Cahors's elite looked to the Toulousain to protect their interests, just as the people of Montauban did. In both towns, they would disagree with their clergy over this.

Few financial records exist for Cahors before the crusade, but later documents give us a flavour of the kinds of transaction that might have taken place, such as the sale in June 1224 for forty-seven silver marks of a house by Péronne, wife of Daide Manent, and Raimonde her daughter, in their name and in that of another Daide, son of the first, to Guiraud Gros and his heirs, Pierre Ferrer and Guiraud Agarn. It was a stone house situated on one of Cahors's major thoroughfares. Its land and a wall dividing the plot from its neighbours, the children of Guiraud Elias, were sold with it. Guarantees were given by both parties 'according to the laws and customs of Cahors' (*segon los fors e las costumas de Caortz*). But this was not a straightforward sale. The house, though sold, was to continue to be held in fief of lady Guillemette, wife of Gaillard de Lard. Furthermore, the sale involved responsibility to do charitable works for the town.[108] We see, therefore, that there was no easy juxtaposition between 'commercial' and 'feudal' transactions in towns. Families such as the de Lard had been enobled through their holding of property in towns; noble lords of long-established castles made the move to towns in this period. This has been partially documented by Jean Duvernoy where non-local seigneuries are encountered in personal names in inquisition records. For example, at Moissac we encounter Raimonda de Bournac (l'Hospitalet), Raimond Delvolvé (le Boulvé) and Arnauda de Pestillac (Montcabrier). We also find émigrés from seigneuries further afield, such as Guillaume and Bertrand de Lanta (Haut-Garonne) at Moissac.[109]

Castra *and 'castelnau'*

Montauban and Cahors perhaps correlate to a more general European model of the growth of urban assertiveness in more commercial towns. But as population grew in southern France in the twelfth century, although it produced some of the most precocious western mercantile centres, other examples including Toulouse and Agen, people more typically gathered in discrete fortified settlements: those *castra* that typified rural Languedoc by the outbreak of the Albigensian Crusade.

---

[107] AD Lot, F.176 and 177; D118, fol. 3; *IRC*, no. 2; Dufour, *Cahors*, p. 21.

[108] Archives municipales de Cahors, chartes 1. The charter was formerly catalogued, and is hence sometimes cited, as Arch. com. de Cahors, *Livre nouveau*, 3, f. 190 (as in *IRC*, no. 14 and Dufour, *Cahors*, pp. 20–1).

[109] D21, fols. 285v–6r, 287r–v, 294v–5r, 297r; DPC, pp. 221, 225, 237, 241, notes 316, 322, 342, 346.

The term 'castra' was in fact somewhat ubiquitous in describing fortified sites. It was used by the chronicler Pierre des-Vaux-de-Cernay for what should really be understood as a free-standing castle,[110] while the *perfecta* Arnaude de la Mothe refered to Montauban as a *castrum*,[111] although it was more of a commercial port and not unusual in being fortified as such. Nonetheless, towns founded with military functions need to be understood as different in many senses from the growth of commercial towns. *Castra* were fortified towns within which taxes and dues could be collected, their inhabitants and economic prosperity being very immediately protected by castellans and knightly retinues.[112] By the early thirteenth century the majority of politically significant *castra* in the Vaux specifically were ruled by lords who were either part of networks of affinity ultimately focused on the lords of Gourdon or the count of Toulouse or were related to the lords of Gourdon themselves, as noted. But *castra* in general had another significance.

As Quercy underwent this process of fortification, the *castrum* supplanted the rural manse as a unit of settlement and basis of the Occitan fief, and new forms of social relationship emerged. Because rights to revenues such as taxes were granted as fiefs, there was an in-built tension between proprietors' rights and entrepreneurial profits in the context of twelfth-century economic growth. We find the emergence of patrician families in *castra* as well as more obviously 'commercial' towns. They are perhaps best understood through Jean Richard's model, noted above in the case of the origins of *castra* in the Vaux. But the model has two parts. As well as those knights dispatched into the countryside, he finds the origins of some patrician families likewise in the castle knights of the twelfth century. The Pellegri at Gourdon, of whom we shall hear more, perhaps arose in this context.

In the thirteenth century, as a result, we shall see that some *castra* would demand their own economic and finally political autonomy, alongside commercial centres such as Cahors and Montauban. But along the way some would become 'northern-style' fiefs, taken by the crusaders and given to their supporters to exploit economically in exchange for political loyalty and military service. Such economic and political tensions arguably made space for religious dissidence in the first decades of the thirteenth century. However, while the period *c.*1150 to *c.*1250 in Languedoc is characteristically seen as one in which towns were able to free themselves of seigneurial control and assert their own economic and political independence, Toulouse being the best-known example, this is only true of Quercy to some extent. It was primarily the conflicts of the thirteenth century that would make this possible.

Finally, another kind of urban transformation took place in Quercy. The turn of the thirteenth century also saw the very earliest construction in

---

[110] See the editors' appendix in PVC *History*, pp. 283–6.

[111] D23, fol. 3r.

[112] Verdon, *La Terre*, pp. 9, 60–78, 204.

Quercy of the planned, hence 'new', *castra* (giving names such as 'Castelnau') and 'reserved' or 'safe' places (giving 'Sauveterre'. However, unlike *castra* and more like bastides, these were essentially to be a product of the mid-thirteenth century onwards in the first period of regeneration after the war years, but primarily in the context of later warfare between the kings of England and France after the Treaty of Paris in 1259.[113] The lords of Gourdon were at the forefront of this movement also, in the founding of Labastide-Fortanière and the remodelling of Castelnau-Montratier.

People in the Landscape: Freedom and Servility

Before turning to this historical process in more detail we should cautiously examine the lives of ordinary people primarily engaged in agriculture and operating in a more rural setting. Lartigaut suggests that in the high Middle Ages some ninety per cent of the population of Quercy must have been involved in agriculture.[114] Beyond that, historians of Quercy find it problematic to paint an accurate picture of the human face of rural life and, as has been suggested above, it is primarily new urban settlements that are the focus of economic documentation. The cartularies contain evidence for boundaries, locations and revenues, but it is typical of land transfers in Languedoc that the records do not indicate anything about the legal status of people on the land.[115] There is consensus that most of the peasantry of Quercy were relatively free by European standards, as was the case for the south more generally,[116] but there were certainly some less-free people. In the cartulary of La Selve, which also records transactions in Quercy, we see that the lords of Cardaillac donated the manse of Laroque in *c*.1200 with people described as 'natura'. The word carried something of the sense of *colonus*, dependent on the land; not servile as such, but still less free than those described as 'feusal', or as a 'fevater', denoting someone whose servile status was not inherited and who might himself hold an allod or even a fief.[117]

But even in the case of those who were not free, there is little if any evidence for demesne organisation in the northern Languedoc.[118] The less free were not tied directly to seigneurial centres of production and the nucleated

---

113 B. and J.-J. Fénié, *Toponymie occitane* (Bordeaux, 1997), pp. 50–1. Lartigaut, *Histoire de Quercy*, p. 119. Even Sauveterre in Lower Quercy is not an example of this type of settlement, but really a castle until as late as the thirteenth century: Lartigaut, *Histoire de Quercy*, p. 101.

114 Lartigaut, *Histoire de Quercy*, p. 97.

115 Verdon, *La Terre*, p. 9.

116 Ligou, *Histoire de Montauban*, p. 42; Lartigaut, *Histoire de Quercy*, p. 117.

117 *Cartulaire de la Selve*, no. 98, and see esp. pp. 24–6 for discussion of the terminology.

118 *Cartulaire de la Selve*, p. 5.

village was not a viable feature of Quercy until the later thirteenth century.[119] Furthermore, a good many people held all or some of what they lived on as tenants. This was a perfectly common form of transaction, as free from the stain of servitude as was the allod, and in this Quercy was freer than the Rouergue.[120]

However, even in Languedoc the peasantry was being subjected to the opening up of new seigneurial structures and forms of revenue-raising, as elsewhere in Europe.[121] The *natura* of la Roque may even be evidence of this. But other evidence of diminished legal status in Quercy is harder to find. We have seen that one seigneurial innovation was the proliferation of *castra*. But seigneurial activity here involved attracting taxable settlers. It seems unlikely that increased servitude would have accompanied the activity. Quite the reverse: it is far more likely that rents and taxes on sales were what lords coveted. However, if ninety per cent of people lived off the land, but the land was typified by *castra*, it seems common sense that people living in these settlements did not make a living there, or there alone. *Castra* must have sheltered people who farmed land in the surrounding area, and this perhaps accounts in part for why we think we cannot 'find' those people. Indeed, in the 'stalls' and 'vineyards' encountered in the sentence of Raimond de Rodolos, above, and others like it, and in the many references to agricultural produce and foraged foods that we encounter through the depositions of people supporting heretics economically, we may have found some of them.

A final important feature of the economic life of Quercy was assarting. Relatively early this seems to have become an important aspect of rural life in the east of the county, bringing in particular some grassy prairie under cultivation. From the Beaulieu cartulary it has been established that there was some land clearance in the tenth century and that viticulture spread to the west of Saint-Céré in the eleventh, property sometimes being donated with its *curtis* and assarts. It was certainly the great landowners who were the initiators here. Although we have no real idea of scale, monastic settlements were not infrequently founded on virgin territory – for example, eleventh-century Labastide-du-Haut-Mont. Monastic activity, by the Cistercians and the military orders, allowed land in Quercy to be opened up and sustain more people in the twelfth century. But this feature of the expanding European economy was also typically accompanied by freer, not more servile, tenancies. People

---

[119] Lartigaut, *Histoire de Quercy*, p. 120.

[120] Ourliac and Magnou-Nortier note 'que ne possèdent pas une propriété entière – qui sera définie comme un alleu – sont placés sous le dépendence d'un mâitre': *Cartulaire de la Selve*, p. 21. They also find evidence for a group of *fevaters* whose dependency was in part related to the land they farmed but also hints at personal ties to powerful lineages (ibid.), although there is little trace of this in Quercy.

[121] Scholarship on the subject is summarised in Verdon, *La Terre*, esp. at p. 10.

on assarted land were probably liable for less than the heaviest dues owed by the free, the *quartum*: that is to say, every fourth sheaf.[122]

Orthodox Identity in the Twelfth Century

Evidence for the nature of confessional identity in Quercy in the twelfth century is limited largely to charters of donations to abbeys. Plotting the origins of people making donations on a map produces an extraordinarily dense network in the north of ties between families and their property on the one hand, and abbeys and their estates on the other. Less concentrated networks involve the cathedral clergy and leading families of the Cahors region and beyond, and likewise secular lords and Figeac. It may be that we lack some of the episcopal charters that were produced. They are rather thin on the ground for a twelfth-century see of this significance. Extant early documents for Moissac and Belleperche are fewer still, leaving us with less information about the south. But there the uneven picture of patronage and confessional identity is not necessarily incomplete. From *c.*1200 we encounter identification with dissident religious movements in lower Quercy which may account for the apparent lack of engagement on the part of the families of lower Quercy with local and more distant abbeys.

The bishop in his world

At around the turn of the century we can see the emergence of Quercy's asser-tive episcopal character. The twelfth-century bishops had had comital powers at Cahors transferred to them and acquired numerous rights and proper-ties throughout Quercy.[123] Rocamadour became a residence of the bishops of Cahors too. Albas was an episcopal palace from the point of its donation to the see by Pope Pascal II in 1106. Pascal also gave to the chapter the churches of Albas itself and Autoire and Aynac, and the revenues of Gramat, Cabr-erets, Thégra and Montdoumerc. The church at Concorès belonged to the chapter from the same year. Bishop Guillaume II de Caumont (1113–43) was the recipient of quercinois estates donated by the churches and abbeys of the Limousin.[124] We also find the bishops arbitrating some high-level disputes, for example in the case of Cayrac, not far from Moissac on the north bank

---

[122] Assarts are denoted by place-names in *-issarts, -issartons, -issatières* (Lartigaut, *Histoire de Quercy*, pp. 90, 91, 97, and esp. 98. Ourliac and Magnou-Nortier observe the process of assarting in the Rouergue starting in the twelfth century (*Cartulaire de la Selve*, pp. 17–19). See also Combarieu, *Dictionnaire*, p. 114; Ligou, *Histoire de Montauban*, p. 42.

[123] See p. 7 above.

[124] *HGL*, III, 466; Ayma, *Histoire ... Cahors*, I, 274–6; Combarieu, *Dictionnaire*, pp. 2, 8, 9, 34, 64, 106, 168, 248; Lacoste, *Quercy*, II, p. 16 and note 1, 26–7; Lartigaut, *Histoire de Quercy*, p. 95.

of the Aveyron, a crossing-point on the route to Caussade. It was contested between the count of Toulouse and the abbot of Aurillac, of whose abbey it was a dependency. In 1176 bishop Guiraud III helped them settle their differences and a *paréage* was concluded between them.[125]

Although records for the acquisition of secular fiefs by the bishops dwindle from mid-century, records for what he did hold contribute to a picture of a relatively vibrant localised religious life when contrasted with what is usually asserted about Languedoc. Even though Quercy was not unusual in western Europe by *c.*1100 in that the distribution of ecclesiastical establishments was by no means even, by the end of the century there is evidence for no fewer than 700 parishes overseen by six deacons and fourteen archpriests. Some of the towns which would later feature in the evidence for confessional choices collected by the inquisition were among those well-served enough to possess a church. Montcuq, for example, had a parish church, Saint-Hilaire, and an associated sanctuary, Saint-Privat. By the time that its environs were home to Cathar sympathisers Lauzerte had a parish church too, Nôtre-Dame, and also an archpriest residing at the foot of the hill (*pech*). The castle of Montpezat-de-Quercy had a chapel dedicated to St John the Baptist, a dependency of the church at Saint-Antonin. The chapter also had influence over the church at Beaumat, near Gourdon, an area to be infested with heresy.[126] So it cannot be said straightforwardly of Quercy that heresy emerged because there was little influence by secular clergy.

On the other hand, one result of a picture of patchy parochial organisation in the early twelfth century meant a different situation in the Bouriane. We have little evidence for ecclesiastical organisation at Gourdon itself. In *c.*1119 the first named chaplain of Gourdon, Bernuy, figures as a witness to the Mont-Saint-Jean transactions. But there was apparently no archpriest until 1215. However, this may have been because of the already significant presence of an unusual deanery, called le Vigan, a few kilometres east of Gourdon.[127] It was originally a simple community of clerks at what used to be called Carbonnac, where the village was distinguished by having three churches: Nôtre-Dame, Saint-Jean and Saint-Gal. It also celebrated a rare cult for the Midi, that of Faith, Hope, Charity and their mother Sophie. In 1083 Bishop Guiraud de Cardaillac (1083–1112) reformed it and gave it to Saint-Sernin-de-Toulouse to establish the regular life there. In 1143 the privileges and benefices of its prior, Arnaud, were placed under the protection of Bishop Guillaume de Caumont by the archbishop of Bourges. These included revenues of the church of Saint-Pierre and Saint-Sernin de Gourdon and the

[125] *HGL*, VI, 67; Ayma, *Histoire ... Cahors*, I 226–9; Lartigaut, *Histoire de Quercy*, p. 102.
[126] Lartigaut, *Histoire de Quercy*, pp. 95, 105; Combarieu, *Dictionnaire*, p. 6; de la Torre, *Lot* (unpaginated).
[127] A Raimond-Guillaume de Vigan witnessed the main charter in favour of Cluny in 1119 (p. 000 above).

majority of offerings at other churches, including the priory of Linars.[128] Indeed, by *c.*1200 the orthodox life of Gourdon appears to have been over-shadowed by the deanery. The significance of this has never been explored. In any case, a new orthodox movement was to eclipse traditional secular and Benedictine religious forms.

The Benedictine legacy

Benedictines continued to be modestly active into the twelfth century. Les Oleiras, at modern Pomarède (Cazals) was a Benedictine abbey for women founded in 1123 and a dependent of La Sauve Majeure.[129] But Quercy's abbeys could not rid themselves of lay influence, much of it hostile. We have noted the poor relationship between the counts and the monks at Saint-Théodard and at Moissac. Both struggles revealed the bishops of Cahors to have had relatively little influence in southern Quercy. In the case of Moissac, Count Alphonse-Jourdain of Toulouse restored the institution of secular abbots in 1112 and had Gausbert de Fumel elected. By 1130, however, he had recognised the illegitimacy of this institution and the rights of the regular abbot, Roger.[130] Relations were still cordial enough in 1147 when the *villa* of Escatelens and its dependencies were donated by him to the abbey,[131] but this did not mean that secular influence over the abbey had been relinquished. In 1197, when Moissac received a charter of Raimond VI, the count is acknowledged as lord of the town by virtue of his status as count of Quercy, but is also 'knight-abbot'.[132] Weak ties with their bishop were perhaps to influence the confessional choices made by the laity of lower Quercy. Ligou and others have noticed a fall in donations to Saint-Théodard in *c.*1200, and even its rights to local churches seem to have been in doubt.[133]

On the other hand, the twelfth century saw a slight strengthening of an alliance between the bishops and the Limousin abbey of Beaulieu, and thereby of the influence of the Benedictines in northern Quercy.[134] In contrast, given their prior investment in Beaulieu, the viscounts of Turenne appear not to have been as closely involved with the abbey in the twelfth century. In terms of the quercinois families too, donations to the Benedictines diminished even as the twelfth-century economy flourished. In comparison with the earlier period, fewer Benedictine foundations took place: perhaps only the pilgrim hospice

---

128   Albe, E., *Les institutions*, pp. 1–2, 4, 42–3, 52, 75; Ayma, *Histoire … Cahors*, I, 260; Lartigaut, *Histoire de Quercy*, pp. 89; Bulit, *Gourdon*, p. 51 and note 4; Combarieu, *Dictionnaire*, p. 260.
129   de la Torre, *Lot.*
130   *HGL*, III, 661, 681; *HGL*, V, nos. 403, 420; Macé, *Catalogues raimondins*, nos. 8, 15, 17.
131   Macé, *Catalogues raimondins*, no. 54.
132   Transcribed into AD Lot F. 125; *HGL*, VIII, chartes lxvii, cols. 441–2 (the charter); *HGL*, VI, 179–80 (the customs listed).
133   Ligou, *Histoire de Montauban*, p. 32.
134   Lacoste, *Quercy*, II, pp. 11–12; Combarieu, *Dictionnaire*, p. 220.

established by Hélène de Castelnau at l'Hospitalet.[135] We have noted the scarcity of churches in the Bouriane, and another was lost to the secular religious when the parish church at Alvignac, which had pertained to Carennac from 1175,[136] was subsumed by the abbey of les Fieux, founded at Alvignac in 1203 by Gerbert de Thémines. But, in general, Benedictine influence had waned in favour of the new monasticism by *c*.1200. The knightly orders began to have a presence in Quercy in the second half of the twelfth century, the commandery of la Selve being the most significant. The lords of Vayrols gave the Templars a house at Cahors, and by *c*.1160 they had houses at Durbans, Cras, Soulomès, Le Bastit-du-Causse and Sainte-Marie-de-Cahors. These were essentially established to protect pilgrim routes[137] and otherwise played a marginal role. Instead, it was the Cistercians who dominated the monastic life of Quercy in the twelfth century.

The new monasticism

Le Blanc observes that, under the abbacy of St Bernard, Cîteaux established no fewer than nine houses in Languedoc.[138] In lower Quercy the white monks were established at Belleperche (by 1143), on its border with the Toulousain at Grandselve (1144), and at La Garde-Dieu (Mirabel), near Caussade, a daughter house of Fontmourlhes-Saint-Martin-le-Désarnut (Lavercantière).[139] La Garde-Dieu was visited by Count Raimond of Toulouse and Viscount Raimond II of Turenne in 1181, and endowed with lands originally given to the count by the abbot of Aurillac.[140] The count returned in 1194 and granted it further privileges.[141] In 1163 the viscounts of Bruniquel established Saint-Marcel at nearby Septfonds, and in 1175 it became a daughter house of Cadouin.[142] Yet this area was soon to be a significant seat of heresy, in spite of the white monks. It may be, however, that it was they who drew the attention of the crusaders of 1209 to the Caussade region in 1209, as we shall see in Chapter 3.

We should understand the implantation of the Cistercians in lower Quercy as a contrast with the counts' relationship with the Benedictines. Grandselve was affiliated to Cadouin, in Périgord, but was Toulousain-orientated, being

135 AD Lot F. 365; Combarieu, *Dictionnaire*, p. 142; Lacoste, *Quercy*, II, pp. 11, 13–14, 15.
136 Combarieu, *Dictionnaire*, pp. 49, 146, 222; Lartigaut, *Histoire de Quercy*, p. 95.
137 J. Juillet, *Templiers et Hospitaliers en Quercy: les commanderies et prieurés sur le chemin de Notre-Dame de Rocamadour* (Grenoble, 1999), p. 79.
138 G. Leblanc, 'L'abbaye nouvelle près de Gourdon', *Mémoires de la société archéologique du Midi de la France* 27 (1961), 49–75, at 51.
139 Lartigaut, *Histoire de Quercy*, p. 97.
140 *HGL*, VI, 100; Lartigaut, *Histoire de Quercy*, p. 97.
141 *HGL*, VI, 162.
142 Lartigaut, *Histoire de Quercy*, p. 96; Lacoste, *Quercy*, II, pp. 33–4; B. Wildhaber, 'Catalogue des établissents cisterciens de Languedoc aux xiiie et xive siècles', *CF* 21 (Toulouse, 1986), pp. 21–44 (p. 34).

patronised by Count Alphonse-Jourdain even before its absorption by Cîteaux, and afterwards by Raimond V. In 1157 the latter relinquished secular rights there.[143] But the religious crisis to come would sever the Toulousain ties, as we shall see in Chapter 3. Belleperche was founded between 1130 and 1140 by the lords of Arcambal for Géraud de Sales, and they remained important donors. The family were themselves allies of the count of Toulouse.[144] Indeed, the counts embraced the movement in Quercy, Raimond V giving Belleperche rights and lands in the Toulousain by 1164, including free passage on the Garonne.[145] In the early 1200s its abbot would argue that the count and his son were not supporters of heresy,[146] and the relationship between the abbey and the count was still good during the crusade.[147] But the Arcambal themselves would fall foul of clerical authority in several contexts; donations to the abbey would crash by 1210 to a fraction of what they were in the 1180s;[148] and Belleperche would be entered by men sought by inquisitors, their heretical character only a thinly veiled secret within the house.

Outside lower Quercy Cîteaux had no houses as such in the twelfth century, but its daughter double house, Obazine-Coyreux, founded in the Limousin between c.1134 and 1140, pressed upon Rocamadour from c.1147, even as Tulle and Beaulieu fought over the pilgrimage centre; and, as we shall see, by 1164 it too was in conflict with Tulle directly. Obazine was to shape social responses to the new monastic order in the north of Quercy, drawing donations toward itself. Most of its granges were in northern Quercy, including in the region of Rocamadour, and we have records of several dozen donations made by families of the Bouriane.[149] We shall use its cartulary to learn more

[143] *HGL*, VIII, 697–8 (no. 192); Macé, *Catalogues raimondins*, nos. 14, 68, 102, 119, 462, 527; B. Barrière, 'Les abbayes issues de l'érémitisme', *CF* 21 (Toulouse, 1986), pp. 71–105 (pp. 101–2); M. Mousnier, 'Grandselve et la société de son temps', *CF* 21 (Toulouse, 1986), pp. 108, 124.

[144] The father and son, both called Montarsin d'Arcambal, received the *borie* of Saint-Porquier from Count Alphonse-Jourdain, probably before Belleperche became Cistercian, but in 1174 the family gave up the fief to the count, who donated it to the abbey: Macé, *Catalogues raimondins*, nos. 40, 143; *GC*, XIII, 259; *HGL*, III, 747, 749; A. Bondéelle-Souchier, *Bibliothèques cisterciennes dans la France médiéval* (Paris, 1991), pp. 25–6. For detailed references see also M. Mousnier, 'Implantations monastiques et encadrement des populations en Gascogne Toulousaine dans la première moitié du xii siècle', in *Crises et réformes dans l'Église, de la réforme grégorienne à la préréforme: Actes du 115e Congrès national des sociétés savantes, Section d'histoire médiévale et de philologie, Avignon, 1990* (Paris, 1991), unpaginated.

[145] *Catalogue … Raimond V*, no. 101 (a confirmation of 1182); Macé, *Catalogues raimondins*, no. 105; *HGL*, III, 848, 749; *HGL*, V, no. dxlv.

[146] Kienzle, *Cistercians, Heresy and Crusade*, p. 215.

[147] Macé, *Catalogues raimondins*, no. 428.

[148] J.-L. Biget, 'L'art cistercien dans le Midi toulousain', *CF* 21 (Toulouse, 1986), pp. 313–70 (p. 325).

[149] *CO*, pp. 9–10, 22–5. In one of the earliest donations, in 1138–59 Bernarde de la Coste made a donation approved of by three sons, Guiraud, Bernard and Adémar (*CO*, no. 8).

about families investigated in the 1240s, including relatively minor knightly clans as well as great barons.

We can construct several modest case studies of devotional affiliation to Obazine, in some cases concerning otherwise almost obscure families such as the de Vayssière. They donated lands in transactions that were clearly very meaningful for them. In 1169–70, at Le Vigan, Guiraud-Hugues de Vayssière and his son Hugues renounced their rights on some of the abbey's lands in exchange for Hugues's mother's eventual entrance to Coyroux. These turn out to have been lands they had previously purchased *from* Obazine. We also learn that Hugues had previously quarrelled with Abbot Robert, perhaps concerning these rights or lands, because some of the transactions involve their reconciliation.[150]

Another example is that of the lords of what is modern Saint-Michel-des-Bannières. Pierre-Arnaud and his brother Guillaume surrendered their patrimony in exchange for their mother's entry to Coyroux and 200 *solidi* on the occasion of Pierre-Arnaud's departure for Jerusalem in 1170–1. Their kinsman Guiraud had already given land at nearby la Rivière to ensure the entry of his two sisters Saura and Dulcia. This was done with the approval of his brothers Guillaume and Raoul.[151]

It is worth noting two things about these donations and other case studies that support them. Firstly, Obazine was intent on securing lands and/or rights to lands in the Bouriane quite strategically, to the extent that it would choose to buy or sell rather than simply wait for donations. Indeed, we should suspect that the monks suggested what might be donated also! In the case of the de Vayssière, Obazine presumably profited in both senses, to the extent that it is tempting even to speculate that the donation was anticipated when the sale to the family was first made. Secondly, the evidence does not confirm the accepted picture of female religiosity in Languedoc: that women had no outlet in the monastic life in the twelfth century. The evidence in fact conforms more to a model asserted by de Vic and Vaissète and others, in a rare non-narrative excursus in their history-telling, suggesting that in Quercy it was commonplace for families to make donations with a view to the entrance of a female family member to double houses,[152] even though there were few female or double-houses locally.

A further example highlights the very strategic way in which Obazine was seeking and aquiring property. The Obazine cartulary produces evidence for many relatively minor estates, none of which is more fascinating than Couzou. Between *c.*1160 and *c.*1174 it was surely ceded entirely to the abbey

---

[150] *CO*, nos. 62, 73, 97, 166, 189, 203, 208, 219, 223, 288 (the reconciliation with abbot Robert), 209, 290, 291, 353, 534, 571, 592. Raimond de Vayssière had already made a donation in 1168–9, witnessed by Guiraud de Gourdon (*CO*, no. 264).

[151] *CO*, nos. 329, 331.

[152] *HGL*, III, 859. Unfortunately they do not furnish us with examples of their own.

in a complex series of minor transactions. We have seen the Grimoard family ceding rights to it above and, likewise, the Belcastel-Gramat family gave up the tithe. The brothers Bernard-Raimond and Rigaud de Baussac were perhaps proportionately too generous to the abbey in their donation of 1167–8, because we hear little else from them in the cartulary. Gerbert de Thémines, his wife Guiraude and their son renounced their claim to Couzou in 1168–9. Rights to it had already been surrendered by Guillaume de Lavergne in 1159–60 when, a decade later, the brothers Gerbert and Aimeric de Lavergne did likewise. Hugues d'Aulanès and his brothers Guiraud, Hélie, Bernard and Guillaume ceded rights to Couzou and other manses in 1171, and their home itself was a grange of Couzou. Also generous, or heavily pressured, were Pierre 'de Montagern' and Pierre-Amaury de Mandeville.[153] All of this provides good evidence that rights to land were both more measurable and valuable than land itself. So many families and members of families had claims to this estate that these cannot possibly relate to physical divisions of property, but instead to the profits of that property.

However, the influence of Obazine in Quercy was quite localised. Even when families living a distance from the Limousin made donations they were often of property or rights of more use to the abbey, owing to proximity, than they were to themselves. The Grimoards of Castelsarrasin gave up their northern connections when they relinquished their rights at Couzou. The lords of Cardaillac were not great patrons of Obazine, although Guiraud and his wife Marie were donors in 1160–1,[154] but they too ceded possession at Couzou, for example in the case of Guiraud, his wife Marie and their son Bernard in 1172–3.[155] From the Vaux, Jeanne de Lacoste and her sons ceded their rights to Saint-Palavy in 1163–4.[156]

Patronage of Obazine by the lords of Gourdon was especially extensive, as indicated above. Furthermore, its second and fourth abbots, Guiraud I (1159–64) and Guiraud II (1188–1204), were of the family. In 1159–60 Anne, wife of Aimeric III de Gourdon, donated to it the manse of *Coirez*.[157] In 1165–6 Pons de Gourdon, probably their son, donated all of his rights to *Cramazel lo Vell* and other estates to serve as his mother's dowry for Coyroux.[158] And in 1168 Aimeric IV de Gourdon confirmed these and other family donations, perhaps after Pons's death.[159] The temporal and spiritual concerns of the family overlapped: Bertrand I de Gourdon and Abbot Guiraud I de Gourdon assented as

---

[153] *CO*, nos. 158, 187, 253, 258, 386.
[154] *CO*, no. 140.
[155] *CO*, no. 360.
[156] *CO*, no. 179.
[157] *CO*, no. 195.
[158] *CO*, no. 200. At the same time he witnessed the cession of rights at the same estate by Arnaud de Fenelor (*CO*, no. 202).
[159] *CO*, no. 284. This was confirmed by Viscount Raimond III in 1202–3 (no. 1247).

witnesses and social superiors to the donations by the lords Vayssière noted above.[160]

In another example, the lords of la Roque, a family who were also to feature in inquisitorial records for the 1240s, donated property and rights in 1160, 1163–4 and 1172–4. They were Aimeric, Guiraud-Hugues, Guiraud-Amiel and Roger de la Roque; the brothers Adémar and 'G.'; the brothers Guitard and Guiraud, their mother Béatrice and Guiraud's wife Alaiz; Bernard-Hugues de la Roque and his son Hugues; Gausbert, son of Jeanne; and Bernard de Laroque-de Mareuil and Amaury de la Roque-de Lavergne. The property in question included some in the Limousin, making this another family with influence in Aquitaine.[161] They also donated rights at Le Vigan to Obazine, as witnessed by Bishop Guiraud IV.[162]

In Limousin-Quercy the knights of Arques (Strenquels),[163] a stone's throw from the Dordogne, produced a monk of the abbey in 1170–1, Pierre-Ramnulf, who gave *La Claustra* to Abbot Robert (1164–88) probably in 1169–70, buying out his brothers Arnaud and Raimond for 200 *solidi* in order to do so.[164] Family members are frequently attested in the second half of the century, as witnesses as well as donors, often several of them present at the same time.[165] Aside from being of localised prosopographical interest, this family and others like them, for whom we have extensive data in the cartulary, played little part in the coming changes, the crusade and inquisition troubling themselves little with Limousin-Quercy. But some provide evidence for wider political changes and devotional affinities that were to be significant in the Albigensian wars and beyond.

One of these changes was that the influence of Beaulieu and Tulle in Quercy was being eclipsed by the Cistercians, in northern as well as lower Quercy. We can see this in the evidence for an estate in which the knights of Arques had a stake and one over which Obazine and Tulle vied for influence in the second half of the century: Saint-Michel-de-Bannières. Tulle probably still held the church itself, but Obazine was ceded the patrimony of Saint-Michel by its lords Pierre-Arnaud and Guillaume in c.1170, and Raimond d'Arques

---

[160] *CO*, nos. 264, 288.
[161] *CO*, nos. 148, 152, 178, 192, 286, 338, 348, 352, 358, 361–363.
[162] *CO*, no. 353.
[163] The identification of Arques (canton of Vayrac) is Barrière's. The knights are referred to collectively in *CO*, no. 292.
[164] *CO*, no. 328, and see no. 292.
[165] They are Guillaume, Archambaud, Arnaud, Guiraud, Pierre, Rodulfus (probably two men of that name), Pierre d'Arques-de Floirac, Pierre-Austorgus and Raimond, who ceded rights at Saint-Michel-de-Bannières: *CO*, nos. 37, 81, 91, 100, 129, 130, 131, 132, 134, 137, 156, 161, 173, 186, 194, 207, 246, 281, 292, 304, 328, 331, 349, 370, 371, 470, 567, 587, 694, 798, 384, 1202.

ceded his rights there around the same time.[166] When, in 1204, Guitard and Guillaume de Saint-Michel were in dispute with Beaulieu over property at *Fondial*, Abbot Guiraud II de Gourdon acted as judge, demonstrating the abbey's influence by this date.[167]

Indeed, by *c.*1200 the dominant partnership in the north was that between the Cistercians and the related houses of Gourdon and Turenne, as we might imagine from the many connections between the three parties already noted. In the second half of the century the viscounts appear to have shifted not only their patronage but their political and economic interests decisively into the new movement. They sold land in Quercy to Obazine, as we have seen. Daughter houses and granges otherwise founded on their lands north of the Dordogne included Saint-Palavy. To the south it had La Dame, Les Alys, Bonnecoste near Calès, Calès itself and Carlucet. Because of the location of many of Obazine's granges on these estates, these too fell, or remained, under both the influence and protection of the viscounts.[168] In fact, by the end of the century the house of Turenne had tied up all the tangled threads of its legacy of Benedictine loyalty. Their lingering dispute with Tulle concerning Rocamadour was settled in 1190, when Viscount Raimond III performed homage to the abbot of Beaulieu, an act witnessed by Guiraud II de Gourdon-de Salviac.[169] But the viscount went on pilgrimage in 1190–1 and neatly left to Obazine all he held at Beaulieu and the rights to other lands in the Limousin for which he owed the abbot homage.[170] Obazine thus shaped the political landscape as it reshaped its socio-geography. It is quite possible, therefore, that the influence of the Cistercians was something that kept heretical influence in Quercy at bay for as long as it was contained.

The lords of Quercy beyond lower Quercy would come to accept the presence of heretics in the 1220s and in some cases engage with and protect them. I shall argue that they needed a reason other than the 'appeal' of heresy to do this, not least because the 'appeal' of the Cistercians had already proved powerful and transformative in a way it had apparently not elsewhere in Languedoc. The success of religious dissidence in Quercy was due to its toleration by lay lords, not to the power of heretical messages, although there is evidence for that as well, as we shall see. The experiences of its lay lords in the early decades of the thirteenth century would prove crucial.

---

[166] *CO*, pp. 24–5 and nos. 329, 331, and Lartigaut, *Histoire de Quercy*, pp. 96–7; and see above, pp. 000–00.
[167] *Cart … Beaulieu*, no. 37.
[168] *CO*, p. 22.
[169] *Cart … Beaulieu*, no. 194.
[170] *CO*, supplt. no. 1239.

3

War and its Aftermath

Many southern-French nobles and townspeople took to what was being defined as 'heresy', adhering to new beliefs and devotional practices in the twelfth century, while possibly not fully understanding or minding the doctrinal distinctiveness of the different 'christianities'. This distinction was, however, at the heart of a crisis in Rome, in abbeys such as Cîteaux and in the Paris schools as they grappled in their own way with 'heresy' of various types in the twelfth century.[1] So it is possible to describe two parallel processes taking place by c.1180. On the one hand there was an attraction on a large scale to popular new sects at a grass-roots level and, in the case of Catharism, some level of belief in a new meta-narrative for creation and the nature of human existence. On the other, a process of doctrinal 'tightening up' was taking place as clergy established for themselves what was and was not orthodox belief and practice, and codified how to deal with dissent in legislation such as *Ad abolendam*.

Ad abolendam names the Cathar sect and the Waldensians (or the 'Poor of Lyons'), among others, but its most detailed condemnations relate to traits clergy attributed specifically to dualists. So while it condemns preaching without license and commentary on the sacraments by those so proscribed it refers to *consolati* ('the consoled'), or *credentes*, or *perfecti*, terms almost only ever used about dualists. It refers to the structural hierarchy specific to Cathars; to the believer and follower who would be consoled at death, and the 'perfected' heretic, who had been consoled. The bull gives bishops the responsibility to seek out heresy by sending deputies into every community once a year to speak to three reliable witnesses. It makes clear the kinds of punishments appropriate to the crime, including handing over the recalcitrant to the secular arm. It also requires oaths through which lay authorities were answerable to bishops and archbishops, in case they undermined this process, and condemns those allowing heresy to flourish, who were to be barred from public office.

A key question to address, then, is the extent to which confessional adherence formed the basis of partisan support in the traumatic events of the

---

[1]   For the most recent survey of 'heresy' in western Europe that can be called comprehensive, see Lambert, *Medieval Heresy*. See esp. pp. 52–96 for the twelfth century.

twenty years to follow. It is quite possible that, in the minds of many, there was no need to make a distinction between religious forms or to choose one over the other before *c*.1184. But if by that time the ordinary laity did not understand the illegality of dualist doctrine or the implications of preaching it – or even preaching something doctrinally 'orthodox' without license in the case of the Waldensians – their social betters, people such as the count of Toulouse and the viscount of Turenne, certainly did, as was evident in their activity at Toulouse and Lavaur in 1178 and 1181. It is impossible to imagine that by *c*.1190 there was not widespread collective lay knowledge that the various religious forms were legally fundamental and oppositional in the eyes of secular authorities, whether or not people wanted to make such a distinction themselves. Heresy had crept in and was in the hearts of the populace before it was called 'heresy', but this does not mean that military action against those preaching novel doctrines and their protectors in 1209 took Languedoc by surprise.

However, the above generalisations do not apply as well to Quercy as they do to the Cathar heartlands, except for lower Quercy, where we know from depositions in Doat 21 and 22 that there were Cathars by *c*.1200. Elsewhere, the county was largely free of doctrinal dissidence until well into the crusade. Heresy did not migrate northwards as a result of proximity to heretical neighbours, as though through some irresistible magnetic pull or ideological 'seepage'. Indeed, in the Agenais, where Catharism had been present for decades in towns of the Lot, by 1209 it had not even spread upstream into the Vaux, in spite of the river being an otherwise important communications artery. Furthermore, while there were Cathars and Waldensians in lower Quercy by 1209, they had no significant presence downstream in the towns of the Agenais Garonne, and this was in spite of the many similarities and ties between the towns of the 'pays de la moyenne Garonne', as they are known. Unlikely as it seems, Catharism did not even cross the Garonne into Gascony.[2]

Of course, this is not to suggest that no heretics travelled along and across the rivers and roads of the northern Languedoc. The point is that their ideas could not gain purchase unless conditions were right. For example, we know of strong links between the heretical communities of Villemur in the Toulousain and lower Quercy. The necessary conditions in that case relate to a shared political and urban culture, the relative indifference of Raimond VI towards the heresy even at Castelsarrasin, the seat of his seneschal, the weak position of secular clergy and lay resentment of the monks in the towns of lower Quercy. I suggest that town elites and *castra* lords made conscious decisions about whether or not to tolerate the new movements, very possibly already present in their towns and, to some extent, 'testing the water' (I am

---

[2]   For the location of Catharism by 1209 in the towns of the northern Languedoc, see Taylor, *Heresy*, pp. 1, 144, 154, 170–80, 185–6, 231.

not arguing that they were 'invited' in). They did this in the context always of the wider socio-political networks within which they operated. These decisions were crucial in the transmission or restriction of heresy. Heresy did not just 'happen', it had to be *allowed* to take root in a community by those dominating it. But, as we shall see, this did not necessarily indicate the confessional preference of such lords or elites themselves.

What would change quercinois society to the extent that it was willing to risk the fate of the Agenais and Languedoc more widely was the experience of crusade from 1209. Not only did the wars fail to destroy the Cathar heresy in Languedoc; they gave it new life in Quercy.

The Albigensian Crusade in the Languedoc

The Albigensian crusade of 1209–29, discussed in this section in terms of its course in Languedoc more widely, was not the inevitable result of the extent to which Catharism had taken root in Languedoc.[3] In some senses it was a last resort, and even then it was not what its architect, Pope Innocent III, had envisaged. As we have seen, it was widely held among orthodox clergy that the southern French church was ill-equipped to address Catharism and to break the bonds attaching the laity to it. In 1204 the pope had sent Cistercians to preach in the Midi, but these were no more effective than their brother the legate Henri de Marcy had been in the twelfth century.[4] But the failure also of Dominic Guzman and his fellow preachers genuinely surprised the pope. Like the heretics, they led the simple life and preached in the vernacular. So Rome determined to undermine political support for heresy by excommunicating local rulers who were *fautores* ('favourers' or 'patrons'; singular: *fautor*) of Catharism, thereby allowing lords more loyal to Rome to replace them. Even as he made arrangements for the crusade, the pope envisaged that such loyal lords would be local. Crucially, in many cases, this was not to be.

What triggered the crusade specifically was the murder of the papal legate Pierre de Castelnau on 14 January 1208 on – it was asserted but never proved – the orders of Count Raimond VI of Toulouse.[5] Pope Innocent failed to rouse the enthusiasm of John of England and Philip Augustus, however. They were mired in conflicts of their own and unwilling to undertake an attack

---

[3] See Barber, *The Cathars*, pp. 120–40, for discussion of the relationship between crusading and the extirpation of heresy.

[4] On preaching in the crusade period see B. M. Kienzle, 'Hélinand de Froidmont et la prédication cistercienne dans le Midi (1145–1229)', *CF* 31 (Toulouse, 1997), pp. 37–67, and Muessig, 'Les sermons de Jacques de Vitry', pp. 70–83. See also Mousnier, 'Grandselve', pp. 119–21; Lambert, *Medieval Heresy*, p. 93.

[5] Certainly this was Pierre des-Vaux-de-Cernay's interpretation of events: PVC *History*, pp. 31–4.

on Raimond VI, who in any case was John's vassal and married to his niece, and was Philip's nephew by marriage. But by 1208 Philip was happy for a crusade involving French warriors to be launched without him, although the Anglo-Toulousain alliance was solid.

Once the crusade was inevitable, without kings, it was to monks that the pope entrusted the military endeavour.[6] In June 1209 Arnaud Amaury, abbot of Cîteaux, led an army consisting essentially of northern French knights and nobles down the Rhône. But the excommunicate Raimond VI wisely made his peace with the pope and joined the crusade himself, promising to confront those who sheltered heretics. The army was deployed instead against his enemy, Raimond-Roger Trencavel, viscount of Béziers, whose town was destroyed and the townsfolk, 'heretical' or otherwise, massacred.

The Trencavel lands fell in 1209–11, and out of these campaigns Simon de Montfort, a lord of the Île-de-France, emerged as the crusade's new leader. He secured a second excommunication of Raimond VI in 1211, and by 1212 most of the count's lands had fallen too. By this stage it was even clearer that it was not only protectors of heresy who were considered legitimate targets for the crusade, but anyone controlling a castle or town that the crusaders might want, strategically or otherwise. In 1213 King Peter of Aragon, lord of some of Languedoc's nobles and *faidits*,[7] became so outraged that he intervened in favour of the southerners. His army was defeated at Muret in September and he was killed. A series of rebellions took place in 1214, in which lords of Quercy would play an important role, but de Montfort was recognised as count of Toulouse by the French crown and confirmed in this at the Fourth Lateran Council of 1215. Even the still-unconquered towns of Toulouse and Montauban were deemed to be his. Worse, Raimond VI's son, also called Raimond, was to be denied his Toulousain patrimony, even though no case could be made that he favoured heretics himself.

Unsurprisingly, the south rebelled against this decision, initially successfully, and between 1216 and 1225 the crusade was effectively ground down, especially after de Montfort was killed in 1218. No leader fit to replace him could be found, but Languedoc was exhausted and too traumatised by the war to continue resistance to northern armies, which by this point were properly supported by the French crown. Raimond VI died in August 1222 and, although the young Raimond had reoccupied much of his patrimony by March 1224, it was the French who had the resources to come out on top. In June 1226 King Louis VIII marched his army southwards down the Rhône, just as the crusade of 1209 had done. There was only minor resistance. Even though the crusaders lost Castelsarrasin in 1228 (discussed below), the young Raimond VII sued for peace. In Paris in April 1229 an agreement was reached

---

6   For the course of the crusade with reference to the northern Languedoc, see *HGL*, VI, 632–7, 641; Taylor, *Heresy*, pp. 148–9, 215–20.

7   Knights dispossessed of their castles, in this case by the crusaders.

with Louis IX. Raimond lost almost everything to the east of the Toulousain but retained the title 'count of Toulouse', the Toulousain itself and also the Agenais and Quercy. But he would have to make heavy reparations to the Church, demilitarise his lands by destroying castles and town walls and vow to seek out and punish heretics. He was also induced to betroth his daughter Jeanne to Alphonse of Poitiers, the king's brother. So the lands of Toulouse, including Quercy, would ultimately be lost to the crown if Raimond died with no male heir, which he did in 1249. His patrimony passed ultimately to Philip III of France when Jeanne and Alphonse both died in 1271.

Quercy Divided, 1209–1229

The leading lords of Quercy did not hesitate or waver in deciding which side to support and, led by their bishop, they saw action in the Agenais in 1209 even before the main crusader army had reached Languedoc. Only Guillaume de Tudela tells us about this campaign.[8]

The Agenais–Quercy campaign, May–June 1209

Just after 21 July, when the crusaders crossed the Hérault and entered the Trencavel lands, a smaller force arrived from the Agenais to meet it. The crusading force had been raised a month earlier. With it were the archbishop of Bordeaux and the bishops of Agen, Bazas, Limoges and Cahors, the latter being Guillaume IV de Cardaillac (1208–34/5). At its head was Count Gui of Auvergne. But it was apparently Viscount Raimond III of Turenne who had raised most of it. He had been invited very specifically to involve himself in the crusade from the outset; William of Tudela tells us that Rome had commissioned Arnaud Amaury with recruitment from the Limousin.[9]

'[A]ll of Quercy' came with the viscount, we are told.[10] Those named are Bertrand de Gourdon and his kinsman Ratier de Castelnau-Montratier, and the bishop's nephew Bertrand II de Cardaillac. The force perhaps also included Pierre de Saint-Pierre, an episcopal vassal since 1200 for tithes at Saint-Germain-de-Bel-Air and Saint-Nazaire-le-Vieux, who had at least promised help to the bishop in the crusade.[11] In supporting the crusaders, Bishop Guillaume was defying his lord Raymond VI, to whom he had performed homage for his secular powers at Cahors. But canon twenty-seven of the Third Lateran Council (1179) allowed a vassal to renounce his oath to a

---

8   *Chanson*, I, 38–45; Taylor, *Heresy*, pp. 190–1; Taylor, 'Authority and the Cathar heresy',
    pp. 159–60.
9   *Chanson*, I, 38–45.
10 *Chanson*, I, 40–41.
11 Combarieu, *Dictionnaire*, p. 231.

protector of heretics. The bishop was not unusual among his colleagues in doing this, and the viscount too held fiefs in Quercy of the count.

Then the poet tells us what this army had been doing for the past month. It had first attacked Puylaroque, in south-eastern Quercy, close to Montpezat and Caussade, and then must have traversed the county and entered the Agenais, probably via the Lot, attacking Gontaud and Tonneins and besieging Casseneuil.[12] Pierre des-Vaux-de-Cernay was later to describe the latter town as 'one of the most important and long-established seats of heresy'. For once, the chronicler was right in making such an expansive claim.[13] But the siege was raised when Gui of Auvergne argued with the archbishop, apparently about Gui's rights to the town.

The poet admits to being confused as to how this led to the abandoning of the siege. The campaign was in part a civil and internecine war. The crusade's Agenais targets were towns controlled by other members of Bishop Arnaud de Rovinha's family, in particular his brother Hugues, lord of Casseneuil. But we cannot convincingly interpret the attack simply as the settling of a family feud. Too many resources were put into it for that, and it does not help us weave the non-Agenais parties into the picture. However, it seems improbable that Bishop Arnaud had not excommunicated his brother for sheltering heretics in order to allow for the town to be seized. Possibly, there-fore, Count Gui had assumed that the seigneurie of the town would be his as the crusade's military leader, while Bishop Arnaud might understandably have considered it to be his. If the archbishop was forced to intervene and was unsuccessful, this might have led both parties to lose interest in the siege. It has to be stressed, as the chroniclers note and as would be appreciated in 1214 also, that Casseneuil was a difficult town to take.

Many heretics were burned in this early campaign, we are then told. The poet was struck that even women who refused to recant were executed. This is unlikely to have been at Casseneuil, which had not fallen. The reference may therefore refer to the entire expedition. Then the poet tells us that the army was joined by the bishop of Le Puy, arriving from the Ardèche via Saint-Antonin and Caussade, having extracted what sounds like protection money from their inhabitants. Finally, he says that the inhabitants of Vill-emur 'suffered a sad blow'.[14] The alarm had been raised there by a boy who had come to tell the town that the army was about to abandon Casseneuil. The townspeople burned their houses and fled in terror, probably during

---

[12] The poet deals with Puylaroque in the same few lines as the Agenais towns, in spite of its great distance, giving the surely false impression that the destruction of all took place in a very short period of time.

[13] PVC *History*, p. 233. On Casseneuil see Taylor, *Heresy*, pp. esp. 165, 179–82, 188, 190–1, 231–2.

[14] *Chanson*, I, 42. Translation is *Song*, p. 18. On Villemur see Taylor, *Heresy*, pp. 178–80.

the night of 21/22 June,[15] presumably thinking that Villemur would be the crusade's next target. But why their escape made this a 'sad blow' is not clear. Guillaume de Tudela is baffled again, and only happy once he concludes 'I shall tell you no more about that army',[16] and returns to discussion of the main force, by now at Montpellier.

Historians have likewise had difficulty interpreting the campaign from its brief but confusing narrative.[17] Contextual problems partially explain our discomfort. To begin with, it was very premature. The muster of the main army was not until 24 June, at Lyon. Raimond VI was in the process of making his peace with the pope in May 1209. Although absolution was not granted until 18 June, and he took the cross only on 22 June, he had been offering his surrender insistently since January under almost any conditions the pope may have cared to name. As Guillaume de Tudela tells us immediately before discussing the Agenais campaign, the count was already hurrying to meet the crusaders and join them.[18] It seems impossible, therefore, that the Quercy crusaders were unaware of his desire for reconciliation. The same goes for Quercy's clerics. One of those chosen by the count to travel to Rome that winter for the very purpose of pleading his cause was the abbot of Saint-Théodard. This was a strategically sound move in theory. In practice, however, the abbot would conspire against him.[19] The monks of that abbey were the count's enemies, as we have seen. But until his election as abbot of Cîteaux in 1201, Arnaud Amaury had been abbot of Grandselve. His links with the abbey, and therefore his knowledge of affairs in the north-west of Languedoc, were never severed.[20] In other words, the Cistercians too had abandoned the count.

It is possible, however, that these crusaders were planning anyway to muster early and await the main army. Just as the pope and the legates would prove unwilling to call the crusade off once they heard that Raimond VI had surrendered, and would thus attack the Trencavel lands,[21] perhaps the quercinois lords had to find an alternative outlet for their violence once they had heard that the count wanted to surrender. In this case Hugues de Rovinha was a substitute target in the way that the viscount of Béziers would soon

---

15 *Song*, p. 18 n. 5; *Chanson* I 42–4.

16 *Chanson*, I, 44. Translation is *Song*, p. 18.

17 Myself included: Taylor, *Heresy*, pp. 190–91.

18 *Chanson*, I, 38–9.

19 Ligou, *Histoire de Montauban*, p. 32. A good overview of the process leading up to Raimond VI taking the cross is that of Jonathan Sumption: *Albigensian Crusade*, pp. 79–85. He notes that the count made had choices in the men whom he entrusted to represent him in Rome (ibid., p. 82). The abbot certainly fits this category. He was the count's enemy and would later conspire more openly with the crusaders.

20 PVC *History*, p. 24. Mousnier stresses the on-going involvement of Grandselve in the crusade: 'Grandselve', pp. 119, 121–4.

21 Sumption, *Albigensian Crusade*, p. 82.

be. A vassal of the count, as a notorious *fautor* of heresy, he would have to be dispossessed.

Another factor to consider is that, irrespective of Raimond VI's attitude to the spread of heresy, the lords of Gourdon were already his rivals in terms of secular dominance in the Vaux de Quercy, as discussed in Chapter 2. In 1209, therefore, the lords of Gourdon took the side of Rome and France against their own overlord, throwing off his authority as an excommunicated *fautor* of heresy. This seems even more likely when we consider the activity of their ally, the viscount of Turenne. Although the viscount too held most of his quercinois seigneuries of Raimond VI, he could straightforwardly defect in the comfort of the knowledge that the count was excommunicate.

Yet none of this helps us to account for the interest of the lords of Quercy in the Agenais specifically. It is not possible to identify ties that might shed light on their enthusiasm, familial or seigneurial, for example. Instead, a more straightforward approach seems to make sense. Given what we know of pre-crusade orthodoxy in Quercy, not least on the part of the de Gourdon and de Cardaillac, and given that there were certainly many heretics in the Agenais towns of the Lot, perhaps these knights straightforwardly followed their religious conviction, their bishop and their powerful neighbour the viscount into a war of faith. These were just the kind of local champions of the Roman church that the pope wanted in control, after all. In terms of the counts of Auvergne, they had been ceded rights in the county of Rodez by Raimond VI as recently as 1208 and 1209,[22] but I can establish no links between the Auvergne and the Agenais.

The attack of Saint-Antonin is difficult to account for in the same way, however. Pierre des Vaux-de-Cernay later called its lord, Viscount Adémar-Jourdain, 'an evil and depraved knight',[23] and he would be attacked again. This is poor evidence of heretical activity, but it seems possible that he was a genuine political obstacle to cleansing lower Quercy more generally of its heretics: they can only have operated with his tacit approval.

However, we do have a little circumstantial evidence to help us make sense of the targeting of Puylaroque, Caussade and Saint-Antonin. We should recall that in 1181 Count Raimond V and the Viscount Raimond II of Turenne were at the Cistercian house of La Garde-Dieu, close to these *castra*, forging an alliance with its monks. This was surely in the context of their 'crusade' against the recalcitrant heretics at Lavaur, in the Albigeois, that same year. With its close ties to the Albigeois, the Caussade area was an important focus for Cathar activity in the early thirteenth century.[24] It was very possibly the monks at La Garde-Dieu who drew the viscount's attention to this in *c*.1209.

---

[22] Macé, *Catalogues raimondins*, nos. 364, 371, 372. The viscounts of Turenne and Limoges had witnessed the former charter, at Martel.

[23] PVC *History*, p. 152.

[24] Albe, *L'hérésie ... en Quercy*, pp. 9–10, 15, 40.

The crusade in lower Quercy, 1211–1212

In summer 1211, the year after Raimond VI was excommunicated for a second time, the *castrum* of Caylus in Quercy was torched by crusaders. Pierre des-Vaux-de-Cernay is clear that its possession by the count was what warranted this.[25] The destruction probably just refers to the castle, because the inhabitants of the *castrum* itself are described as having been subdued but as subsequently rebelling, and in May 1212 Baudouin of Toulouse recovered the town for the crusade.[26] In this period de Montfort also secured the Quercy–Albi border by finally taking Saint-Antonin from Viscount Adémar-Jourdain. First he attacked it, in 1211, and then besieged it in May 1212 when the viscount refused to surrender. Surrender was later arranged and, as at Caylus, the townspeople were allowed to go free so that the *castrum* would remain populated, and the viscount was locked up at Carcassonne.[27] The castle of Viscount Pons of Toulouse was seized in 1212 as well.[28]

Abbot Raimond du Proët of Moissac was in the crusaders' camp in spring 1211. He was Raimond VI's rival for secular control in the town, an issue resolved only nominally by 1210. Its inhabitants showed their support for the count by expelling the abbot in early 1212, and he was imprisoned at Montauban.[29] So, having subdued the Caussade region and Caylus, the crusade found its excuse to attack the Tarn-Aveyron-Garonne. On 6 August 1212 it entered the Vaux from the Agenais via Montcuq, which had been abandoned by its then *bailli*, Guiraud de Montfabès. The *castrum* was given to Baudouin of Toulouse, count Raimond's northern-raised half-brother, and a fervent crusader.[30]

Just as Montcuq was strategically important in terms of access to the Agenais, the towns of lower Quercy dominated communications between Cahors and the Toulousain, and also Toulouse and Bordeaux, via the Agenais, on the Garonne. In contrast with the towns on the Agenais Garonne in the same period, they did contain significant heretical communities.[31] Castelsarrasin and Montauban were strengthened by capable allies of the counts of Toulouse and Foix, but Moissac was less well defended by its hired garrison.

---

[25] PVC *History*, p. 126; Lartigaut, *Histoire de Quercy*, p. 105. Not much is recorded about Caylus between the count establishing Raimond-Amilio there in or shortly after 1176 (see above, Chapter 2, p. 52) and 1211.

[26] PVC *History*, pp. 154–5.

[27] PVC *History*, pp. 140, 152–53.

[28] HGL, VI, 386. He had been an enemy of the count of Toulouse (see chapter 2) but whether some reconciliation had taken place, making him a comital ally, I do not know.

[29] AD Tarn-et-Garonne, C 541; PL 206, 806 (the abbot's incarceration); Macé, *Catalogues raimondins*, no. 390 and see no. 396; HGL, VIII, 160, 611–12; Taylor, *Heresy*, pp. 194–5, 196.

[30] PVC *History*, pp. 154–5; PVC *Histoire*, p. 127; Taylor, *Heresy*, p. 191; Lartigaut, *Histoire de Quercy*, p. 105.

[31] For discussion of this feature of the Agenais, see Taylor, 'Authority and the Cathar heresy', p. 165.

The army reached it on 14 August 1211. To begin with the town was able to repel offensives, but it became demoralised after soldiers from Montauban were captured by Baudouin of Toulouse and his new quercinois allies, Armand de Mondenard and Hugues de Breil. The captured were held prisoner in the besiegers' camp, which only had to sit tight and await the arrival of northern reinforcements. Worse, the garrison at Castelsarrasin deserted and the town surrendered, so, when Moissac was offered its safety if it surrendered its *routiers*, the townspeople opened the gates on 8 September and a French sergeant was stationed there.[32] On 14 September the abbot returned, acknowledging de Montfort as his lord in secular matters.[33] Although a siege of Montauban could not be attempted so late in the season, Toulousain influence in lower Quercy was seriously compromised.

The crusaders had made other allies in Quercy in this period. The bishop transferred his homage for Cahors to Simon de Montfort on 20 June 1211,[34] and the crusaders of 1209 did likewise in August 1212, at Cahors itself.[35] Raimond de Salvagnac, a merchant of Cahors, took the cross in 1211 and became de Montfort's banker,[36] and in 1212 the crusaders were joined by Arnaud de Montaigu, probably a vassal of the lords of Gourdon, who was given Biron, a conquered castle in Périgord in July 1212.[37] The viscount of Monclar also renounced his loyalty to Toulouse, as others before him had, the significance of which has been discussed in Chapter 2, and joined forces with Baudouin of Toulouse.[38] Thus the last remaining viscounty in Quercy slipped from Toulousain control into the hands of the crusade.

In 1213, as a result, the security of Quercy could be taken for granted and political and military affairs focused again on the central southern counties of Languedoc. But, even after the attempt to bring a solution resulted in the death of Pierre of Aragon, the region as a whole would rebel further. This was in no small part the result of some remarkable events in Quercy.

---

[32] *Chanson*, I, 261–77; PVC *History*, pp. 161–5 (the chronicler almost lost his life during the siege: p. 163). See also Taylor, *Heresy*, p. 196; Sumption, *Albigensian Crusade*, pp. 151–3; Roquebert, *L'épopée*, I, pp. 477–81, and see II, 122.

[33] AD Lot F. 125; HGL, VIII, 621; Taylor, *Heresy*, p. 196.

[34] D122, fol. 3r; Albe, *L'hérésie ... en Quercy*, p. 2.

[35] According to William of Tudela they sent their bishop to the siege of Toulouse to arrange this (*Chanson*, I, 202–3), but they were following an order from de Montfort himself according to Pierre des Vaux-de-Cernay: PVC *History*, pp. 125–7; PVC *Histoire*, p. 101 and note 4.

[36] PVC *History*, pp. xxxi and 116 note 40; *Chanson*, I, 72, 174; HGL, III, *preuves* no. 205; Dufour, *Cahors*, p. 11.

[37] *Chanson*, I, 256–61; PVC *Histoire*, pp. 113, 132; Taylor, *Heresy*, pp. 195, 239; Taylor, 'Authority and the Cathar heresy', pp. 176–7.

[38] *Chanson*, I, 176; Roquebert, *L'épopée*, I, 480, 503.

Resistance in the Vaux, 1214

On the evening of 17 February 1214 Baudouin of Toulouse went to bed in the *castrum* of Lolmie, whose castellans had performed homage to him as the new lord of Montcuq. In nearby houses the crusader Guillaume de Contres and a French sergeant called Simon were sleeping. They were the new masters of Castelsarrasin and Moissac respectively. The treacherous knights of Lolmie locked the oblivious Baudouin in his room. They had previously sent word to Mondenard, seven kilometres away, where knights and mercenaries were garrisoned by Bertrand de Mondenard, kinsman of the crusader Armand de Mondenard, and to Ratier de Castelnau-Montratier who, Pierre des-Vaux-Cernay tells us, was considered a friend by Baudouin, but who had switched sides. They were told that Baudouin would be secured and that they could come and take him with no trouble, if they so wished.[39]

The chief lord of Lolmie raced to meet Ratier and the mercenaries and handed over the key. He then questioned the townspeople to discover where the rest of Baudouin's companions were billeted and had these detained, while Ratier seized the bemused Baudouin and killed or put to flight the members of his entourage. They took Baudouin to Montcuq, to the delight of what were thoroughly evil townspeople, according the Pierre des-Vaux-de-Cernay, and tried to force him to dismiss the garrison by starving him for two days and refusing to let him take Holy Communion. He refused, but the terrified defenders surrendered anyway and were hung. Baudouin was then taken to Montauban and was met there by his brother Raimond VI, who had him strung up from a walnut tree. The rebellion soon spread to Moissac, its French master now dead. The townspeople handed the town to Raimond VI and its garrison was forced to retreat to its castle.[40]

The lords of Castelnau and Mondenard, and with them the towns of Montcuq and Moissac, were therefore the first powers to rebel in 1214. They triggered insurrection elsewhere in Languedoc, the *volte-face* reviving morale after the death in the previous year of Pierre of Aragon.[41] We hear that men of Quercy were involved in attacking the crusaders throughout Languedoc in the months leading up to the Fourth Lateran.[42] Montcuq itself was rewarded with concessions when the count formally asserted his possession of all that Baudouin had held, including Caylus and Bruniquel, sometime after March 1214.[43]

---

[39] PVC *History*, pp. 223 and note 30, 114, 232; Taylor, *Heresy*, p. 239.

[40] PVC *History*, pp. 224, 225, 226–7; William of Puylaurens, *Chronicle*, chapter 22, pp. 50–1; *Chanson*, I, 276; Albe, *L'hérésie ... en Quercy*, p. 4.

[41] PVC *History*, p. 199; *RHF*, XIX, 210; Roquebert, *L'épopée*, II, pp. 199 and 278; Taylor, *Heresy*, p. 197.

[42] PVC *History*, pp. 225–30 (p. 230).

[43] Macé, *Catalogues raimondins*, no. 410.

In July 1214 the legate Robert de Courçon issued a charter granting to de Montfort rights to the conquered lands of the Agenais, Quercy, Albigeois and the county of Rodez 'in perpetuity' (*in perpetuum*).[44] This he did in spite of a general peace placed upon Languedoc by the pope in anticipation of the Fourth Lateran Council. A force moved from Carcassonne to Quercy via Morlhon in the Rouergue, which they destroyed. Pierre des-Vaux-de-Cernay tells us that they found seven Waldensians there and burned them gleefully. Then the campaign in Quercy was launched, and for the first time we hear its people described generically as opposed to the crusade, specifically as enemies of the faith. In the first two weeks of June the *castrum* of the 'evil traitor' Ratier de Castelnau was destroyed along with other castles nearby and Mondenard. The lords of neither castle were taken, however; they had fled to Casseneuil in the Agenais which the crusaders of 1209 – that is to say, including Ratier de Castelnau – had attacked unsuccessfully. From the Vaux, via Montcuq, the crusade followed them. Hugues de Rovinha's *castrum* fell in late August.[45]

While finding refuge at Casseneuil, Ratier de Castelnau, and thereby the family of the lords of Gourdon, would have encountered Cathars as allies probably for the first time. Indeed, the events of 1213–14 must have alienated the clan more generally. It was one of the worst examples of the crusaders' policy of imposing foreign lords even on orthodox southern fiefs. What justified the possession of Montcuq by Baudouin of Toulouse rather than quercinois crusaders? We know that the lords of Gourdon had a claim to it and held property there already.[46] The significance of this cannot be overstated.

The Périgord campaign, 1214

In late August 1214, after Casseneuil itself had fallen, de Montfort decided to attack a stretch of the Dordogne in southern Périgord. Aspects of this campaign are difficult to interpret, but it was crucial for questions of authority and loyalty in Quercy itself. Information had apparently reached the crusade that castles along the river harboured enemies of the faith: heretics and *routiers*.[47] The accusation about mercinaries was accurate, although this did not mark the area out as unusual, but there is no evidence of heresy in Périgord.

First, the crusaders destroyed the castle of a robber chief, Gaillard de Beynac.[48] When they reached the castles of Domme, Montfort and Castelnaud they found them deserted, their lords having fled out of fear of the army that had crushed Casseneuil, according to the chronicler. The army

---

[44] *Catalogue des actes de Simon et d'Amaury de Montfort*, ed. A. Molinier (Paris, 1874), p. 85.

[45] PVC *History*, pp. 165, 232–7; Taylor, *Heresy*, p. 194.

[46] Taylor, *Heresy*, p. 239, and see below, p. 000.

[47] PVC *Histoire*, pp. 198–9; Taylor, *Heresy*, pp. 194, 197.

[48] PVC *History*, p. 238–9.

destroyed Domme, Beynac and Montfort and occupied Castelnaud.[49] Pierre des Vaux-de-Cernay insists that the attack was because the castellans were notoriously barbarous.[50] But they had not taken the man who appears to have been the real target of this campaign, the *routier* chief Bernard de Cazenac, who possessed Domme and who was married to Hélis, the lady of Montfort and Castelnaud. De Cazenac seems no worse than other *routiers* to the historian. Furthermore, he had supported the French king against John of England in their wars which, if anything, should have inclined the crusaders towards him.[51] So how can we account for this attack?

According to the chronicler, stories vilifying de Cazenac and his wife reached the crusaders in around 18 June, at Casseneuil.[52] Viscount Raimond III of Turenne, who had first become de Montfort's vassal in 1211,[53] was in the camp at this point. He had performed homage to de Montfort on 14 June[54] and was still with the army when the castles of the Dordogne were taken. In September 1214 he was invested with the captured castles.[55] It seems highly likely that it was he who had induced the crusaders to campaign in the Dordogne: he had a legal claim to both Montfort and Castelnaud, should de Cazenac be dispossesed. This was because in 1185 Viscount Raimond II had been granted overlordship of Castelnaud by Raimond V of Toulouse, of whom he then held it. The viscount was in turn owed homage for it from the castellans themselves, Matfré and Bernard de Castelnaud. The latter knight was the father of Hélis de Montfort's mother, also called Hélis, whom the viscount married.[56] Viscount Raimond III was their son and in 1214 became Count Raimond VI's vassal for Castelnaud, which he had inherited from his

49 PVC *History*, pp. 236, 238–9, and see PVC *Hystoria*, II, p. 228 note 5; Taylor, *Heresy*, p. 197; HGL, VI, 448–51.

50 PVC *Histoire*, p. 238; Taylor, *Heresy*, p. 197–8; C. Taylor, 'Innocent III, King John and the Albigensian Crusade (1209–1216)', in *Pope Innocent III and his World*, ed. J. C. Moore (London, 1999), pp. 205–27 (pp. 213–14).

51 PVC *Hystoria*, p. 228 note 5; Taylor, *Heresy*, p. 198.

52 He says that news of enemies of the peace being harboured in the castles of the Dordogne arrived 'after these events', i.e. the siege of Casseneuil: PVC *History*, p. 337.

53 Vaissière, 'Turenne', pp. 310, 325–6.

54 AD Lot F. 125; D75, fols. 51r–52r.

55 Molinier, *Actes*, pp. 82, 88, 89a, 288; D75, fols. 55r–56v; Taylor, *Heresy*, p. 199. See also Roquebert, *L'épopée*, I, pp. 239–40 and II, pp. 110–13 and note 7; de la Chenaye-Desbois, *Dictionnaire*, XIX, pp. 256–7.

56 Roger of Howden calls Raimond II of Turenne 'Raimond of Castelnau' in 1178: *Chronica magistri Rogeri de Houedene*, ed. W. Stubbs, 2 vols. (London, 1868–71), II, pp. 150–55. Raimond II was also the vassal of the count of Toulouse for the viscounty of Brassac, near Castres, and for Salignac (now in southern Périgord), confirmed in 1203/4. Macé, *Catalogues raimondins*, nos. 204, 332. In 1236 Viscount Raimond IV would do homage for these possessions to Raimond VII of Toulouse saying that his predecessors had held them of the count's predecessors: Vaissière, 'Turenne', pp. 310–12, 325–6; Roquebert, *L'épopée*, II, pp. 294, 350; T. Pataki, 'Hommages rendus aux vicomtes de Turenne (1163–1304)', *BSEL* 109 (1988), pp. 111–12, no. 2; Macé, *Catalogues raimondins*, no. 205. The knights of

mother.[57] So, it seems that in 1214 he was asserting his inherited rights to the castle, possibly because de Cazenac had refused to performed homage to him as his wife's father had.

But it is not *entirely* certain that the viscount of 1214 was Raimond III, viscount from 1190/1. It probably was, as is usually supposed, not least because Pierre des-Vaux-de-Cernay identifies him as the younger Hélis's brother, although it could possibly have been Raimond IV.[58] But the real problem with this episode is that it seems surprising that *either* viscount could have wielded such influence over the crusaders in 1214, because in 1213 the viscount of Turenne had gone over to the southern party with King Pierre of Aragon and fought with him at Muret.[59] He would have had to have been very contrite in 1214 to win de Montfort's trust. He would switch sides again, in 1217–18, to fight alongside de Cazenac himself as a southern partisan (see below). In addition, it seems unlikely that de Cazenac's loyalty was really to his family all along in 1214, because in September he made an unsuccessful attempt to recover Castelnaud[60] and in the same month the viscount performed homage once again to de Montfort.[61]

The lords of Gourdon were also involved in events concerning Castelnaud. Guillaume de Gourdon-de-Salviac, nephew of Bertrand I de Gourdon, the crusader, apparently also married a Hélis de Montfort. Her identification as a daughter of a viscount Raimond of Turenne,[62] makes it most likely that the younger Hélis was married twice. This is, therefore, another way in which the lords of Gourdon and the viscounts of Turenne were related, and it also implies that at some point Guillaume was lord of Montfort and Castelnau.

After the Périgord campaign de Montfort moved to Figeac. He had been given judicial rights over it by the king in place of the rights of its protector, the count of Toulouse.[63] The abbot of Figeac leased him the castle of Peyrusse

Castelnaud themselves were possibly descendants of the lords of 'Castelnau' who were secular abbots of Beaulieu, for which see Woods, *The Proprietary Church*, pp. 324–6.

[57] Vaissière, 'Turenne', pp. 312, 330–2.

[58] PVC *History*, p. 238. C. Higounet found evidence suggesting that Raimond III may have died in 1212: C. Higounet, *Le conté de Comminges des ses origines à son annexion à la Couronne*, 2 vols (Toulouse/Paris, 1949), I, p. 149. The significance of this is perhaps over-stated in Taylor, *Heresy*, pp. 199–200.

[59] He may even have changed sides before this. In 1211 and 1212 he was one of the southern parties named by the monks of Grandselve as despoiling its properties: Mousnier, 'Grandselve', p. 122.

[60] Although he would take it in 1215: PVC *History*, p. 253; J. J. Escande, *Histoire de Périgord*, 2nd edn (Sarlat, 1955), pp. 95–6; Taylor, *Heresy*, p. 212.

[61] AD Lot F. 125.

[62] HGL, VI, 558.

[63] PVC *History*, p. 239; HGL, VI, 449. The history of Rodez and the Rouergue in the context of the Albigensian crusade and inquisition has yet to be thoroughly explored. Count Henri of Rodez was forced to submit to the crusaders in 1214, in spite of stressing weak links with Toulouse and stronger association with the Plantagenet dukes of Aquitaine,

in Rouergue for ten silver marks annually and transferred to him two estates which pertained to Figeac, but which had formerly been held of its abbot by Raimond of Toulouse. They were Capdenac (which de Montfort had in any case seized) and Lentillac-Saint-Blaise. In October he was acknowledged by the lords of Capdenac as their suzerain, as witnessed by the bishop. In April 1215 he received the homage of Bishop Guillaume of Cahors for Pestillac and that of Bernard de Cardaillac for some of his castles, including Larnagol.[64]

On the eve of the Fourth Lateran Council, therefore, the crusaders held lower Quercy except for Montauban, had subdued and taken control of those castellanies in central Quercy which had opposed them, had the loyalty of the Cardaillac-Benedictine sphere to the east of the county and still had the co-operation of the lords of Gourdon, with the exception of Ratier de Castelnau.

Supporting Toulouse, 1217–18

Once news of the outcome of the Fourth Lateran Council reached Languedoc southerners began planning to resist it by force. Lords of Quercy were involved in action once more from September 1217, when Raimond VI re-entered Toulouse and proceeded to hold out for what would be a protracted siege. With him in the town were the defector Dorde Barasc, lord of Béduer and Lissac, near Figeac, who had been forced to submit and destroy his own castle by de Montfort in 1214 as he had set about crushing the rebellion in Quercy.[65]

Bernard de Cazenac set about raising the army in Quercy and Péri-gord that included Raimond de Turenne and Arnaud de Montaigu. It also contained Bernard de Montaigu, Guillaume Barasc, Araimfré de Montpezat, Bertrand de Pestillac, Hugues de Lamothe, Ratier de Caussade and the lords of Gourdon, Ratier de Castelnau and Bertrand de Gourdon. The latter was taking up the southern cause for the first time and this shift in allegiance would prove transformative for the Bouriane. On 13 January 1218 the pope wrote to several lords of Quercy criticising their support for Toulouse.[66] De Cazenac entered the city to relieve it around Easter time, nonetheless.[67]

and he had to perform homage to Amaury de Montfort in 1219: PVC *Histoire*, p. 315; Bousquet, *Le Rouergue au premier Moyen Age*, I, pp. 107–8. This allowed him to retain his county, if only as a fief, and to attract among other advantages the protection of the papacy in 1217, and at the great siege of Toulouse he was in the crusaders' camp: ibid., p. 108. However, his son Hugues IV was a southern partisan and excommunicated after the murder of the inquisitors at Avignonet in 1242: ibid., pp. 108–9.

[64] AD Lot F. 125; Combarieu, *Dictionnaire*, p. 129; HGL, VI, 449, 454–5.

[65] *Catalogue des actes de Simon et d'Amaury de Montfort*, ed. A. Molinier (Paris, 1874), p. 8; *Chanson*, III, 303 note 6; PVC *History*, pp. 230–2; PVC *Histoire*, pp. 197–8; HGL VI, 447, 451; HGL VIII, 653–5. See also Taylor, *Heresy*, p. 197; Roquebert, *L'épopée*, II, pp. 269–76, 287.

[66] *Chanson*, II, 296–9 and III, 308–11; RHF, XIX, 648 (transcribed in AD Lot F. 125); Taylor, *Heresy*, p. 216.

[67] *Chanson*, III, 60–1, 138–41, 302–3, 308–13; Taylor, *Heresy*, p. 216; Roquebert, *L'épopée*, III, 275; Barrère, *Histoire*, I, 363.

Submission to France, 1219–29

Even though the siege of Toulouse had collapsed after the death of Simon de Montfort, his son Amaury was able to secure Moissac and much of lower Quercy.[68] But he was not able to crush the wider rebellion. In the 1220s the crown was forced to become more and more involved. In February 1223, and again in the context of the Peace, the bishop of Cahors performed homage to Louis VIII rather than to the count for his town.[69] But the count still controlled a good deal of Quercy. He then regained the county, oaths to crusader lords and the crown by quercinois inhabitants notwithstanding, except for Cahors, which the bishop was to hold. However, he was forced to destroy fortifications at Montcuq, Moissac and Montauban in 1229, he had to suffer an episcopal *bailli* at Montcuq, Pierre Martis, and saw many seigneurial rights over Montauban restored to the abbey.[70] But he had gained Peyrusse, which Abbot Guillaume of Figeac had held and still coveted,[71] and had won back Castelsarrasin, in 1228.[72] The wars had allowed him to use castles in Quercy in securing important alliances in Languedoc. Even Bertrand de Cardaillac did homage to him in 1229.[73] The fifth Viscount Raimond of Turenne held Martel, Creysse and Saint-Céré independently by the end of the crusade, but in 1232 and 1236 would do homage to Raimond VII for them.[74]

However, the lords of Quercy themselves appear to have been far less engaged with the conflict in its later stages than they had been in the previous few years. Hugues de Lamothe of Montauban was in a force that defeated crusaders at Baziège in early 1219.[75] A third siege of Toulouse took place from 17 June to 1 August 1219, and the anonymous continuator of the *Chanson* (whose narrative breaks off during his account of it) tells us that lords of Quercy who were present among the defenders were Hugues de Lamothe of Montauban and Dorde and Arnaud Barasc, all of whom had joined his party during the siege of Toulouse.[76] But Hugues and the count's other quercinois ally Araimfré de Montpezat were among those massacred at Marmande in the Agenais at the end of its siege of 1218–19.[77] Otherwise, the sources for Quercy are relatively quiet until the 'peace' of 1229.

[68] Taylor, *Heresy*, p. 217.
[69] Archives municipales de Montauban, *Te igitur*, fol. 31; *IRC* 1, nos. 19, 20.
[70] *IRC*, p. 26; Macé, *Catalogues raimondins*, no. 519; Ligou, *Histoire de Montauban*, p. 32.
[71] Bousquet, *Le Rouergue*, p. 484.
[72] He had restored rights of péage at Castelsarrasin to an otherwise unknown Raimond de Varage in the previous year: Macé, *Catalogues raimondins*, no. 543.
[73] D143, fol. 101. See also AD Lot. F 123 (summary only).
[74] Lartigaut, *Histoire de Quercy*, p. 117.
[75] *Chanson*, III, 236–51, 262–5; Taylor, *Heresy*, p. 217.
[76] *Chanson*, III, 302–17; Taylor, *Heresy*, p. 216.
[77] *Chanson*, III, 256–7, 282–91; Taylor, *Heresy*, pp. 217–19.

The Confederation of Rocamadour, 1233

Secular documentation for the period after 1229 in Quercy – and there is a good deal of it – throws up a vast amount of prosopographical data, including information about individuals and groups of people who appear in the crusader narratives and who would fall foul of the inquisition. We have evidence of a civil war at Cahors, and are able to establish a picture of the domination of the Bouriane by the lords of Gourdon and their client families, and to an extent this applies to the Vaux as well. Firstly, we should explore a peace league of 1233 that became known as the Confederation of Rocamadour.[78]

After the crusade the land was said to have been plagued by unemployed mercenaries. The confederation was an organisation established against them. In spite of its own rhetoric, the crusade had not cleared the region of such people. Their employment by both sides in the conflict undoubtedly imperilled the ordinary people of Quercy, and matters were worse when *routiers* were under-employed, as was the case after the Peace of 1229. The Confederation was established to deal with this problem but also to address the detection and elimination of heretical subversion with a focus on religious houses, necessitated by their apparent infiltration by Cathars, about which more will be said.

The Confederation undertook an eight-year programme to bring peace and holy order to the region. What it *actually* did is not recorded, but the charter is a useful document nonetheless. It is a snapshot of who 'counted' in orthodox Quercy in the years between the crusade and the inquisition. Its architects were Bertrand de Gourdon, Viscount Raimond IV of Turenne, Gausbert de Castelnau,[79] the abbots of Tulle and of Figeac and the bishop of Cahors. The knights Aymeric, Gaillard and Hugues de la Roque and their men also signed, as did Gaillard and Raimond d'Assier and their men, Dorde and Guillaume de Bouyssou, and the unnamed knights and men of Thémines, Camboulit, Corn, Lavergne, Anglars, Lentilhac and Sénaillac. Also assenting were the lords and men of the towns of Faycelles, Saint-Cirque, la Capelle-Bagnac, Felzins and Bio, and the men of the towns of Issepts, Fons and Livernon. The consuls of Cardaillac signed, as did those of Figeac and Cahors, saving the rights of their lords the abbot and Cahors.[80]

That the lords of Cardaillac themselves are not recorded is inexplicable

---

[78] Archives municipales de Cahors, AA 1; Bulit, *Gourdon*, p. 65; Lartigaut, *Histoire de Quercy*, p. 110.

[79] Although, as noted earlier, it is sometimes difficult to distinguish between Castelnau-Montratier and Castelnaud, possession of this 'Castelnaud' by Raimond of Turenne makes the latter castle possible.

[80] The accord also involved several lords of Rouergue and the Auvergne. This must be a different Hugues de la Mothe because the other died at Muret in 1919 (above, p. 100).

and surprising. It is also interesting to note that many of these towns and lords had not distinguished themselves during the crusade in any sense that we know of, yet they were significant enough to be invited to take part in the accord. We should keep in mind, therefore, that the towns and people dominating the sources for the crusade did not entirely dominate the county. Between the towns and castles with whose stories we are most familiar, many others are attested only in less spectacular circumstances, such as in this charter and in monastic donations and other property transfers. We can also observe from the document that the assent of townspeople was valued. In most cases they are present with their knightly lords and have no independent collective identity, but we know that there were in evidence by this time consuls at Cahors, Figeac and Cardaillac.[81]

In fact, the period between the later stages of the crusade and the conclusion of the inquests in Quercy in the mid-1240s was of crucial importance in terms of the relationships between towns and their lords. Those emerging as leading centres in the first half of the thirteenth century were the monastic towns of Moissac and Figeac, the commercial towns of Montauban and Cahors, and the *castrum* of Gourdon. Gourdon and Moissac did not prosper to the same extent as Montauban, Cahors and Figeac,[82] and although Figeac was emerging as a financial centre as well as a monastic one[83] it was nowhere near as significant in this respect as Cahors, already of international renown. If anything, Cahors prospered because of the wars. In this it contrasts with the economic malaise and even destruction of resources experienced in more minor towns. These in the twelfth century had begun to generate their own artisanal industries, weaving being significant,[84] but they had been harmed by decades of warfare. The articles of the Confederation's charter can therefore be read from the point of view of the people of Quercy's towns as much as those of the religious and secular lords. One reading of it is as a partnership between towns, on the one hand, and the landed and religious elite on the other. Another is of an alliance between, on the one hand, clergy, nobles and the *castra* they dominated, and on the other, ambitious town consulates and other urban elites striving towards consular status. Most strikingly, it is also an accord between enemies in the crusade.

Towards Urban Autonomy

Indeed, in the face of violence and insecurity, the war decades were also those in which the first charters granting limited autonomy to towns began

---

[81] See above, Chapter 2, pp. 55, 103.

[82] Lartigaut, *Histoire de Quercy*, p. 111.

[83] It was home to Cahorsin merchants from the twelfth century, and merchants from Figeac are recorded at Marseille and Montpellier: Lartigaut, *Histoire de Quercy*, pp. 115–16.

[84] Lartigaut, *Histoire de Quercy*, p. 118.

to be issued. Montauban had had certain privileges since its foundation, as we have seen in Chapter 2, but in 1221 it was rewarded by the count for its loyalty in the wars, receiving exemptions and other concessions.[85] In the same year Moissac had its customs recognised by the count and was promised protection in exchange for its continued help.[86] To the north, Martel received its charter of customs in 1218/19; Rocamadour did so in 1223, and won a second charter in 1235, Labastide-Fortanier (now Labastide-Murat, after its more famous son) received its in 1238; and Capdenac in 1243. Montcuq also received its seal in 1243, and at Figeac the process took place in stages from 1245 to 1254. In what would be one of the most obvious examples of urban liberties following from a weakening of seigneurial authority, Gourdon received its freedom in 1243.[87] It would follow a wider pattern for the northern Languedoc for its lords to have to make concessions to the town in exchange for its loyalty in this period.

In the sphere of the lords of Gourdon
The lords giving away significant rights of self-government to their town in 1243[88] were a new generation and not the crusaders. They were Fortanier II de Gourdon-de Saint-Cirq, son of Bertrand, Aimeric II de Gourdon-Castelnau, and Guillaume de Gourdon-de-Salviac. Fortanier II was by this time the principal lord of the castle. His several children included Pons, Marsebelie (or Sibylle) and Hugues de la Roque-de-Gourdon.[89] He was probably the brother of Pons de Gourdon-de-Belcastel.[90] Aimeric II was the son of Ratier de Castelnau, by then dead. He was also co-lord of La Fontade and Saint-Romain, a couple of kilometres south-east and south-west of Gourdon respectively, and lord of Lavercantière and Peyrilles, near which he had established the

---

85 AD Tarn-et-Garonne, AA1, fol. 4v; Macé, *Catalogues raimondins*, nos. 444, 445.
86 Macé, *Catalogues raimondins*, nos. 475, 477, 478, 486. We learn that two of its consuls were Guiraud Peitavy and Raimond de Jean, whose families would be investigated by Pierre Seilan.
87 For colour reproductions of these charters see the marvellous teaching aid devised by the archivists at Cahors: H. Duthu-Latour et al., *Les Villes du Quercy au moyen âge: consulats-économie-société, 1250–1350* (Cahors, 2003), p. 21.
88 AD Lot E. ter 21. It is often stated that the customs of Gourdon were conceded in February 1244, for example in the Archives municipales de Gourdon, charter AA2, published in *BSEL* 6 (1880). There is a *vidimus* of 1269 also of a charter of 1244. However, in the dating system used in much local documentation in our period the year began on March 25, the Feast of the Annunciation. The charter was thus conceded in February 1243 CE: Duthu-Latour, *Les Villes du Quercy*, p. 21; Bulit, *Gourdon*, pp. 67 note 168, 69, 70, 72–6, 78; Dufour, *Cahors*, p. 32; Combarieu, *Dictionnaire*, p. 104; R. Latouche, *Archives de Tarn-et-Garonne* (Montauban, 1920), p. 13.
89 Lacoste, *Quercy*, II, p. 202; Bulit, *Gourdon*, pp. 69, 70; Albe, *Les institutions*, p. 78.
90 Bulit, *Gourdon*, p. 78.

Grandmontines at Déganazès with his wife Amagne in 1235.[91] Thirdly, Guillaume de Gourdon-de Salviac, a nephew of Bertrand, was to play a crucial role in the fortunes of this generation of the family. In 1241–2 he did homage to Raimond VI for his castle and all he held in Quercy and Périgord,[92] and, as we have seen, was apparently married to Hélis de Montfort at some point.

Gourdon had begun to assert itself economically in the twelfth century. Clozier notes that a Barthélemy de la Rive exported wine to London, for instance.[93] In the charter conceded by the three lords, the economic well-being of the town, or of its *prudhommes* at any rate, was to be the responsibility of four consuls assisted by two officials nominated by the lords of the town. The consuls, furthermore, should work in the interests of both the town and its lords, and the lords would support and defend the townspeople and traders in the town. Traditional legal penalties and the lords' rights to the profits of justice were enshrined. There is no mention of heresy or attempt of any sort to regulate religious affairs in the charter. Lords and the consuls took oaths of mutual support. In this sense the charter stands in stark contrast with the wars that raged in Cahors and Cajarc concerning the same sorts of rights and obligations.

Cahors, Cajarc and the bishop

The most significant quercinois town by far in terms of a conflict of interests between urban notables and their lord is Cahors. The events of the crusade did not damage it in spite of heretical activity, admittedly low-level, and in part because most of it was held by the bishop directly. It was presumably also because the destruction of one of western Europe's leading financial centres profited no one.

Cahors' commercial opportunities originated in the popularity of the trade route between Montpellier and the Atlantic and the influence of Italian lenders attracted to the town. Cahors also saw demographic growth and an expansion in mercantile activity even in the war years.[94] The former was possibly the result of the arrival of refugees from the war-torn Languedoc, which is little documented. Indeed, the town's history as a centre of international financial significance, as traditionally told, lacks sufficient engagement with the impact of the war on whose fringes it lay.[95] In fact, Cahors pros-

---

91 Lacoste, *Quercy*, II, p. 243; Bulit, *Gourdon*, pp. 70, 78. Lartigaut attributes the foundation to a Pons II de Gourdon: *Histoire*, p. 121. The de Peyrilles-de-Rivière properties included the castle of Fages, in the commune of Peyrilles, held of the lords of Gourdon and mentioned in a treaty between Phillip Augustus and Richard the Lionheart: DPC, notes 117, 118; Combarieu, *Dictionnaire*, p. 185.

92 AD Lot, F. 123; Lacoste, *Quercy*, II, p. 253; Bulit, *Gourdon*, p. 71.

93 P. Wolff, 'Le problème des Cahorsins', *Annales du Midi* 62 (1950), p. 234.

94 Ibid., pp. 229–38; C. Wyffles, 'Les Cahorsins en Flandre au xiie siècle', *Annales du Midi* 103 (1991), pp. 307–21; Lartigaut, *Histoire de Quercy*, pp. 111–12, 114–16.

95 Dufour at least contextualises political developments at Cahors within the wider events

pered hugely by financing the crusade. We have seen that one of its bankers, Raimond de Salvagnac, raised money for Simon de Montfort and acted as his treasurer, and he was with him in Paris in 1211.[96] In a similar context, the crown issued documents ensuring safe passage to a Raimond d'Arcambal.[97] It is in this sense that we must surely understand a letter written to the townspeople by Philip Augustus in April 1214 urging them, rather vaguely, not to allow into the town anyone likely to cause them harm:[98] the crusaders needed the cash to keep flowing. Thus the usurers – 'Cahorsins', as they were known in international circles and by those in debt to them, their activity illegal but conspicuous and tolerated by all – supported their bishop's party in the context of the crusade. In other senses, too, town and bishop had shared economic interests. For example, they were of one mind in matters such as enforcing control of traffic along the Lot, another of the keys to the town's success.[99]

But the decades preceding the eventual recognition of the customs of Cahors by the bishop in 1260, in particular the 1230s and 1240s, have been described by Albe as a period of nothing less than civil war between the bishop and the consuls.[100] It all began with debts accrued in war-time. We should recall from Chapter 2 that there are relatively few acquisitions recorded for the bishop in the decades prior to 1200 and so their financial situation was perhaps an issue before the wars. Whatever the case, raising armies from 1209 onwards had not been a cheap business for Bishop Guillaume de Cardaillac. For political support he bound himself ever more tightly to de Montfort, performing homage for his seigneurial rights to the new count of Toulouse first in 1211,[101] even though the crusade posed no real threat to Cahors. But, economically, he needed the co-operation of the town more than of the crusade's commander, so 1211 also saw the first of a series of concessions to it.

In exchange for promises in that year to leave the town's coinage to the consuls, he was loaned 10,000 *solidi*.[102] As early as 1214 Cahors's families were able to take advantage of the bishop's debts even to the extent of assuming the trappings of nobility. Bishop Guillaume ceded land in the modern canton of Catus to Bertrand Jean, for example, on which he founded the town of 'Joanis' (modern Les Junies) and the family became known as 'de Jean', as though after the estate.[103] In 1217 the bishop began to sell back to families

of the crusade, if only in the sense of providing a narrative structure for the events to follow: *Cahors*, pp. 8–15.

96 DPC, pp. 56–59; *IRC*, nos. 3, 8–9 and note 2.
97 *IRC*, no. 10 note 2.
98 Arch. mun. de Cahors, *Livre noir*, fol. 18; *IRC*, no. 7.
99 Lartigaut, *Histoire de Quercy*, pp. 110–11, 112.
100 *IRC*, no. 32 and commentary.
101 D122, fols. 3r–4v.
102 D118, fols. 7r–8r; D119, fol. 7. See also AD Lot, F. 176; *IRC*, nos. 5, 6, 10.
103 Combarieu, *Dictionnaire*, 112.

of Cahors property the cathedral had bought from previous generations.[104] In 1219 he was forced to allow the consuls free traffic between Cahors and Fumel for as long as it suited them.[105] He agreed a further concession in 1220, stipulating that neither party would make appeals to the pope against the other.[106] In 1224 he sold to the consuls the right to mint coins for six years for 6,000 cahorsin *solidi*.[107] But the lenders began refusing him the credit to pay off old debts, and in 1226 he liquidised assets at Luzech and Puy-l'Evêque which he had seized during the crusade.[108] In 1230 he was allowed to borrow 200 silver marks from the consuls to pay off the notorious Lombard lender known as 'Juvénal', who was based at Cahors, and also to make a donation to Dominican revenues with a loan from Raimond d'Arcambal. For this he acknowledged a debt to the consuls of another twenty silver marks as interest,[109] and concessions concerning consular rights to administer justice were wrung from him.[110]

The bankrupt crusader-bishop died in February 1234, but this did not wipe out episcopal debts. After the brief episcopacy of Pons Antéjac, Bishop Guiraud Barasc-Béduer (1237–50), formerly the archpriest of Salviac,[111] went on the ideological offensive. In 1237/8 he and the chapter made an agreement with some of the ordinary people, artisans and *minores* ('the lesser people'), against the *maiores* (literally, 'the greater') – that is to say, against the merchants, jurists and usurers who controlled the consulate. It was what Dufour terms 'a sort of holy league', according to which they would help each other to defend the town and preserve its property and liberty: its fourteen articles include action against heretics and the defenders of heresy.[112] We have to read 'against the grain' here. There is little evidence that the consuls were associated with 'heretics' in the sense of religious dissenters (even though many of them came from families with branches elsewhere that did, as the inquisitors would soon demonstrate). Rather, the charter is legitimist in the secular as well as the confessional sphere. It also tells us implicitly that the consuls did not speak for *all* of the laypeople of Cahors.[113]

---

104 Arch. mun. de Cahors, AA 1, transcribed, in D118, fols. 9r–12r, and in A.D. Lot F. 176.
105 Arch. mun. de Cahors, HH 1.
106 A.D. Lot, F. 176; D118, fols. 19r–20v.
107 Arch. mun. de Cahors, DD 1; D118, fols. 21r–23r.
108 Dufour, *Cahors*, 17; Combarieu, *Dictionnaire*, pp. 17 and 194–5. Humbert de Luzech was an episcopal servant (*IRC*, 26 n. 2).
109 Arch. mun. de Cahors, CC 50, and see DD 2; D118, fols. 30r–32r.
110 D118, fols. 33r–59r; Dufour, *Cahors*, p. 20.
111 E. Sol, *L'église de Cahors sous les Carolingiens et Capétiens* (Paris, 1938), pp. 123–4; Leblanc, 'L'Abbaye-Nouvelle', p. 50.
112 Paris, Bibliothèque nationale de France, Ms Lat. 5219, no. 4 (heresy at article 10), noted and transcribed in *IRC*, no. 29 and D118, fols. 60r–63r. See also Dufour, *Cahors*, p. 25; Lartigaut, *Histoire de Quercy*, pp. 116–17.
113 Other evidence for apparently 'minor' people can be found in a June 1224 charter of

It seems to have been this pact that precipitated the civil war, because the bishop's powerful creditors began to call in his debts more assertively. Arnaud Béraldy, a businessman of a powerful family which had allied with the crusade, and who was now a consul, pursued him for 350 marks owed by his predecessor.[114] The bishop was unable to pay in full and had no other credit. He was forced to pledge rights at Luzech, Puy-L'Evêque, Bélaye, Mont-pezat and *Eglaudières*, and to alienate the fiefs of Pradines and Cessac into the bargain, the former probably to the benefit of the de Jean and Béraldy families also.[115] Now the bloodshed began, the bishop's servants being attacked while about their work. We hear about it because Pope Innocent IV entrusted the bishop of Albi with investigating the affair.[116]

In the documentation of this civil strife we find the names of all the leading families of Cahors, and Albe was the first to note that many of them are represented in the inquisition records of 1241-5.[117] For example, in an inter-ventionist royal missive of 1246 we find mention of the de Jean (Bertrand, Hélie and Pierre), Raimond d'Arcambal, Pierre Donadieu, Raimond de Lard, Imbert de Castelnau, Donadieu de la Garrigue and Pierre de La Mothe.[118] The consuls of Cahors were excommunicated to a man by the bishop on 31 March 1248 and the town's churchmen forbidden from having anything to do with them. Through this documentation we learn the names of their twelve leaders: Imbert de Castelnau, Raimond d'Arcambal and both Pierre and Bertrand de Jean again, and three more men with kin who had associated with heretics elsewhere in Quercy: Bernard Faure, Gausbert de Salviac, and Pierre de Gourdon. The charges included physical violence against episcopal servants including Guillaume Austorg.[119]

What we have at Cahors is an extreme version of the struggle in many towns for increased self-governance against a secular lord, in this case a

---

sale of house: Arch. mun. de Cahors, chartes 1. Of the seventeen people named, only Pierre Donadieu and Benoît de Jean are of families noted in other sources for Cahors.

[114] De Béraldy was an ally of Simon de Montfort: Combarieu, *Dictionnaire*, p. 76; Dufour, *Cahors*, pp. 25, 104. Pierre Béral(dy), also consul of Cahors in the 1230s, is one of P. Wolff's famous Cahorsins in London in 1250 ('Le problème', p. 231 note 15).

[115] A.D. Lot, J. 634. Lartigaut notes that both families had rights to the castellany of Pradines from as early as 1228 and were to form a formidable force at both Cahors and Pradines: J. Lartigaut, 'Le testament d'une grande bourgeoise de Cahors, Sébélie de Jean, veuve d'Arnaud Béral (1286)', *BSEL* 113 (1992), pp. 103–24 (esp. pp. 104–5, 112). See also Lartigaut, *Histoire de Quercy*, p. 110. Dufour notes that the merchant's family did homage to the bishops for Cessac for some time thereafter (*Cahors*, pp. 25–6). In 1236 Bishop Pons was able to purchase rights to Bélaye (Lartigaut, *Histoire de Quercy*, p. 111).

[116] D119, fol. 202; *IRC*, nos. 31, 34, 35.

[117] *IRC*, no. 38.

[118] A. Teulet et al. (eds.), *Layettes du trésor des chartes*, 5 vols. (Paris, 1863–1909), J. 1029, no. 8; *IRC*, no. 35.

[119] *IRC*, no. 37, and at p. 6 note 2.

bishop. As in other towns, this apparently political struggle was really about rights to profits. But whereas most of Languedoc paid a huge economic price for engagement in the wars, the pious warfare of the bishop of Cahors and the essentially neutral stance of his town not only saved it from the economic disaster but afforded it the opportunity to lend money for interest and use the resulting debts to exact political and economic concessions. We should there-fore look a little more into the motivations of the townspeople themselves.

As suggested in Chapter 2 above, aspirations towards self-governance were really a feature of Cahors only after the crusade. Dufour's assertion is that the customs were recognised long before they were first written down in 1260, but he pushes the evidence too far in reading an understanding of shared seigneurial and urban authority into sources such as King Phillip's letter of April 1219, which is directed, vaguely, to bishop and citizens (*episcopo et burgensibus*).[120] It was perfectly commonplace for townspeople to be recog-nised as distinct from the bishop or cathedral chapter in an address to a town. But it is admittedly less common for secular charters to consider people *other* than the urban elite, as in the address of 1203 by Raimond VI to 'our beloved and faithful citizens and all other men' ('dilectos et fideles nostros burgenses et omnes alios homines') of Cahors.[121] Here we see a hint that the two groups of lay people, the *minores* and *maiores*, might have had different interests and outlooks in some situations (though implicitly not here), but not that they operated according to unwritten customs.

However, there is evidence that the customs were acknowledged *infor-mally* by 1224. As we saw in Chapter 2, Na Péronne and her daughter Na Raimonde agreed the sale of their house according to the law code and customs of Cahors. And when a large bell in the cathedral tower broke in the 1220s a dispute arose as to the responsibility for mending it: did it pertain to the bishop and the chapter, or to the town? Both parties wanted to pay for the repairs, thereby confirming rights to the fabric of the church. The way ownership of the bell was expressed was in terms of who had been ringing it *customarily*. Albe suggests that the incident, although seemingly trivial, no doubt reflected other, underlying tensions. But when Moissac was besieged in 1212, according to Pierre des Vaux-de-Cernay, 'to show their contempt for God and our army, [the townspeople] rang the bells in the church … every hour of every day as if celebrating a festival':[122] in *themselves*, it seems, bells could be a source of tension.[123]

In 1229 the legate Romanus reported on his inquiry into the matter at Cahors. Three citizens, including Raimond d'Arcambal, had been interviewed

---

[120] Arch. mun. de Cahors, *Livre noir*, p. xviii; Dufour, *Cahors*, pp. 20–1.

[121] D118, fol. 1r–v.

[122] PVC *History*, p. 162.

[123] See J. H. Arnold, *Belief and Unbelief in Medieval Europe* (London, 2005), p. 111, on the concept of community ownership of the fabric of churches.

and swore that they had rung the bell during the six years before it broke. It was concluded by the legate on 30 December that there was indeed precedent here and that the people could continue to ring the bell; however, the bell belonged to the cathedral.[124] That crucial year for the war-torn Languedoc, 1229, was therefore also a low point in the relationship between the people of Cahors and its ecclesiastical hierarchy. By that time, in the later stages of the war, the consuls had also found themselves in a position to make regional alliances rather more threatening to the bishops' authority than previously. By October 1225 they had appealed to Raimond of Toulouse to support them against the bishop, and the count responded sympathetically to *dilectos nostros consuls*.[125] In 1227 they negotiated terms for trade and safe passage with the viscount of Turenne, and did likewise with the consuls of Figeac in 1232.[126]

But for all the tension between the secular and religious spheres, Cahors did not become anything like a significant arena for heresy. Again we see that there is no automatic relationship between towns – even thriving commercial centres with unpopular lords – and heresy. There are only a handful of references to heresy in the town, and some of these relate to heretics brought from elsewhere to be imprisoned (see Chapters 4–6). In all probability, the heretics were made unwelcome in the town by the consuls as much as by the bishop, and this undermines further the concept of 'heretical families', because the consuls were part of far wider familial networks, some tainted with heresy, as we shall see.

On the other hand, we should not overstate actual antipathy towards heresy or a generalised enthusiasm at Cahors for crusading. Over late August–early September 1214 the unpopular papal legate Robert de Courçon tried to make his way northwards from the siege of Casseneuil via Cahors. The townspeople refused him access. We know this because Pope Innocent addressed them concerning their action.[127] They offered the clever defence that they had not intended to insult the legate at all. Their objective had been to ward off the counts of Toulouse and Foix because, while fighting in the northern Languedoc recently, their armies had killed seventy-two inhabitants of Cahors who had been beyond the town walls, and had taken others prisoner. The people of Cahors argued that they feared bringing the wrath of

---

124 Arch. mun. de Cahors, FF 2; D118, fols. 26r–v, 28r–29v. Mention is made of the documentation in AD Lot, F. 176 and see *IRC*, nos. 19, 20, 21.i. See also Dufour, *Cahors*, pp. 22–3.

125 D118, fols. 24r–25r and AD Lot, F. 176 (copies of lost original); *HGL*, III, 21 and VI, 593; *IRC*, no. 16; Dufour, *Cahors*, p. 21.

126 Arch. mun. de Cahors, BB1; Dufour, *Cahors*, pp. 15–17, 23 and see below.

127 Arch. mun. de Cahors, AA 58; D118, fol. 13r; *HGL*, III, 264; Dufour, *Cahors*, pp. 23–4. In *IRC*, nos. 8, 11, Albe gives the date as 1216, as does the wrapping on AA 58. If this was indeed the date of the pope's response, de Montfort had already retaliated by burning down the gates in question and demanding 1500 *livres Tournois* as compensation to the crusaders: D118, fol. 13r.

their southern neighbours upon themselves again by offering hospitality to the legate. To plead their case two notables, Bertrand de Bégous and Raimond de Ratier, went to Rome in 1216–17. We should remember also, although the lawyers did not note it, that Philip Augustus had written to the town in April 1214 telling it not to allow in anyone they suspected could do them harm. We can only speculate as to whether a deliberate mis-reading of this instruction was used as justification.

Finally, the lay elite of Cahors was part of that orthodox ideological alliance that was the Confederation of Rocamadour. The consuls who signed the accord for their town included Raimond d'Arcambal, Pierre Béraldy, Pierre de Vayrac, Arnaud Berenger, Bernard Faure, René Delpech, Pierre Mauri and a Hugues de La Mothe: eight out of twelve signatories, each belonging to a family that would be investigated and have members condemned by the inquisitors. It appears, in contrast, that none of the families of the seven consuls of Figeac were investigated.

The history of the town of Cajarc also involved conflict with the bishop over the same sorts of issues. A charter was granted verbally at some point in the late 1240s, possible 1249, when the town's seal was also first acknowledged. It is the background to this that concerns us. Cajarc had once pertained to the cathedral chapter and then to the viscounts of Saint-Cirq, but by *c.*1240 Bishop Guiraud had the dominant influence there, as bishop and also as a member of a family with rights in the town, along with his co-lords for Cajarc, the lords of Cardaillac and Balaguier.[128]

But while Géraud was the town's lord and bishop on the one hand, he was also paying off to it debts accrued during the crusade by Bishop Guillaume de Cardaillac. Furthermore, in borrowing money earlier in the 1240s the bishop promised the recognition of Cajarc's customs and privileges,[129] but neither had been forthcoming. The papacy intervened on the bishop's side, humbling the town in the process, and the bishop pardoned most of the inhabitants in 1248, supported by his nephew, Arnaud Barasc.[130] But this was not before a distinction had been made between his personal rights as a member of the Barasc family and the rights of the cathedral and chapter.[131] The concessions at Cajarc were therefore made in the context of outright

---

128   *Charte … Cajarc*, ed. Combarieu, pp. 5, 6–7, 11; Lartigaut, *Histoire de Quercy*, p. 111. More work could be done on the politics within this town in the 1240s, specifically the internal dispute among the townspeople resolved in 1249. See *Charte … Cajarc*, pièces justificatives no. 6 and Duthu-Latour, *Les Villes du Quercy*, p. 21.

129   *Charte … Cajarc*, pp. 9–10 and pièces justificatives no. 2; Dufour, *Cahors*, pp. 15–17, 25. Dufour argues that customs for Cajarc probably also already existed and that this was an extension and confirmation of these, with which Combarieu disagrees (*Charte … Cajarc*, p. 5). The earliest extant version of Cajarc's customs dates to 1256 (Dufour, *Cahors*, p. 25 note 3).

130   *Charte … Cajarc*, pp. 7–8, 10 and pièces justificatives no. 5.

131   Ibid., pp. 7–8, 10 and note 4; Lartigaut, *Histoire de Quercy*, p. 111.

rebellion by townspeople. By *c.*1245, as Dufour observes, the bishop was far more a bishop than a lord, of any town.[132]

Inquisition

Orthodox and heterodox religiosity by the 1230s

In comparison with the political and economic life of Quercy, for which there is a large amount of suitable documentation, it is more difficult to gain an impression of the social impact of the crusade. Yet we must consider the war as a possible cause of the spread of heresy nonetheless, using what evidence we have. Peter Biller has noted that by *c.*1266 in Languedoc there was resentment when women and the infirm were forced by priests to travel long distances to attend mass in times of war. The Waldensian rejection of all violence was widely known about and must have resonated all the more strongly during the crusade.[133] And we do know that the fall of castles and towns sheltering heretics in the crusade forced migrations, as did the cleansing of the region that was a condition of the Peace of 1229. The war also enabled Bishop Guillaume to seize Luzech in 1226 because its castellan, Amalvin, was said to be sheltering heretics.[134] This, too, may have caused heretical suspects to flee, perhaps to Sauveterre; in the 1240s Rixende de Luzech was discovered at Sauveterre to have eaten frequently with heretics,[135] and Guiraude *del Rieu* of Luzech left her marriage to become a *perfecta*.[136]

But, again, we should note that Quercy cannot be seen as essentially 'heretical' in this period. Anger and fear of war produced various responses. At the same time as Catharism and Waldensianism were infiltrating new communities orthodox religious houses continued to be patronised and founded well into the thirteenth century, even by families who also contained heretical adherents. However, there was certainly less enthusiastic support for the monastic life than there had been. We have noted the falling-off of donations to Belleperche in the twelfth and very early thirteenth centuries in Chapter 2. Only two donations and two acquisitions were made in the abbey's favour between 1211 and 1220.[137] Nonetheless, the Cistercians, specifically Obazine, continued to dominate the religious life of northern Quercy.[138] But the other orders grew also. A Benedictine house, La Daurade,

---

[132] Dufour, *Cahors*, pp. 20, 27–8, 30.
[133] Biller, 'Medieval Waldensian abhorrence of killing', pp. 90, 91–2, 92; Ames, *Righteous Persecution* pp. 187–8
[134] Combarieu, *Dictionnaire*, p. 148.
[135] D21, fol. 227r.
[136] D21, fol. 190r.
[137] Biget, 'L'art cistercien', p. 325.
[138] CO, supplt. no. 1297.

was established at Cahors in the early thirteenth century.[139] Grandmontine Déganazès established daughter houses: Francou in lower Quercy and Petit-Grandmont at Cahors.[140] The military orders continued to have a presence in Quercy in the crusade years as before, although they were still essentially orientated towards protecting pilgrims, notably in eastern Quercy, rather than crusading. In lower Quercy they came also to possess Lacapelle-Livron (La Cabane de Monson).[141]

Most notably, however, 1221–41 saw a rapid rise in the number of mendicant houses. Dossat argues that, in spite of the large numbers of Waldensians at Montauban, the Fransiscans and Poor Clares were welcomed too, attracting more popular devotion than did Saint-Théodard. Franciscans were also established at Cahors, by Christophe de Romagne in 1226, and at Figeac, Gourdon, Martel, Montcuq, Moissac and Montauban, by Guillaume Amiel in the last case, where his relatives the Carbonnel family figure prominently among their donors. The Dominicans thrived at Cahors from *c.*1226 in a convent founded by Pierre Seilan, the future inquisitor, and with another property donated in the same year by Raimond Bénech. There were also friars at Cabessut, a suburb of Cahors, established by the Béraldy family, and they were at nearby Saint-Géry from 1227. The de Jean and Donadieu families of Cahors were also associated with friars.[142] But in the rest of the diocese the Dominicans would have little impact until the 1250s, after the inquisition.[143]

We should also note the possible influence of the Poor Catholics in Quercy. We saw in Chapter 2 that some of them originated in the northern Languedoc, where the Waldensians, whom they hoped to convert, were flourishing. There is no direct evidence for this in Quercy. In any case, the group still posed problems for the southern French clergy. Compromises had been made as part of bringing the Poor Catholics into the universal fold. The pope had exempted them from being compelled to go to war against other Christians and from taking oaths. This, the ordinary prelates in the region felt, gave them an air of moral superiority. Some of these insisted that the Poor Catho-

---

139 Lartigaut, *Histoire de Quercy*, pp. 112–13.
140 Ibid., p. 121.
141 Ibid.
142 Albe, *L'hérésie ... en Quercy*, p. 6.
143 Dossat, 'De Vaudès à Saint-François', pp. 403–13; Y. Dossat, 'Opposition des anciens ordres à l'installation des mendients', *CF* 8 (Toulouse, 1973), pp. 277, 279; F.-R. Durieux, 'Approches de l'histoire franciscaine du Languedoc au xiiie siècle', *CF* 8 (Toulouse, 1973), pp. 79–100 (p. 83); H. Dedieu, 'Quelques traces de religion populaire autour des Frères Mineurs de la Province d'Aquitaine', *CF* 11 (Toulouse, 1976), pp. 229–49; C. Ribaucourt, 'Les mendiants du Midi d'après la cartographie de l'"enquête"', *CF* 8 (Toulouse, 1973), pp. 25–33 (pp. 30–1). Pierre Seilan also helped to establish the Dominicans at Toulouse: M.-H. Vicaire, 'La province dominicaine de Provence, 1215–1295', *CF* 8 (Toulouse, 1973), p. 72; Lartigaut, 'Le testament', p. 110 and *Histoire de Quercy*, p. 113; Albe, *Les institutions*, pp. 91–2.

lics still considered judicial execution a mortal sin. The pope suggested to the new movement that they might prove their orthodoxy by compliance with these local clergy and working closely with preachers whose orthodoxy was certain when preaching against heretics.[144]

The inquisitors in Quercy

The Peace of Paris decreed that heretics be banished by secular authorities. An organised flight from Toulouse took place as early as Easter 1229,[145] and from Gourdon also, as we shall see. Furthermore, all males over fourteen years of age and females over twelve were sworn to reveal the whereabouts of heretics, and public officials were sworn to deliver them. This portion of the legislation links the Peace directly to inquisition. In the same year we see the start of practices with which the inquisition would become synonymous.[146] An inquest at Toulouse heard the evidence of the *perfectus* Guillaume Solier and a handful of other people. This yielded the names of numerous suspects, but in general attempts to engage all Christians pro-actively to bring about the revelation of the identities and whereabouts of the majority of *perfecti* failed. Further intervention was required and it came from indigenous authorities and from Rome, confident in the ability of the mendicants. It produced inquisition. Indeed, the inquest at Toulouse may be seen as one of the first steps: the nature and source of the evidence against the defendants had been concealed by the papal legate in order to protect the witnesses. Soon *inquisitio hereticae pravitatis* (inquisition of heretical wickedness) was being initiated by bishops too, and it was not a great leap from this for Rome to involve highly trained Dominicans in inquisitorial activity.

But at the same time the Roman inquisition was a coming-together of ancient and twelfth- and early thirteenth century legislation against heresy, and the punishment of heresy 'by the secular arm' was already well established. Furthermore, in this early phase of inquisition, there was no great difference in terms of the techniques of, or rules governing, inquests by bishops or friars. Until the bull *Ad extirpanda* (1252) bishops had a good deal of authority over the Dominicans, and inquisition was an extension of their own

---

144 Cameron, *Waldenses*, p. 53.
145 Guillaume Pelhisson, *Chronique*, p. 13; D21, fol. 199r.
146 The inquisitorial process in the region under discussion has been very thoroughly examined in the works used in this summary. For published sources see C. Douais (ed.), *Documents pour servir à l'histoire de l'Inquisition dans le Languedoc* (Paris, 1900; rprt. 1977), esp. pp. vi–xxii, cxliv–clxvi, ccx–ccxxiii; Teulet, *Layettes*, III, 3877; HGL, VI, 57–8; HGL, VII, *ordonnances* 419; HGL, VIII, 1313–4 and as cited; Guillaume Pelhisson, *Chronique*, esp. pp. 13–42. For analysis, see Dossat, 'Une figure d'inquisiteur: Bernard de Caux', and 'L'inquisiteur Bernard de Caux' as cited; Lea, *Inquisition*; Hamilton, *Medieval Inquisition*; Albe, *L'Hérésie ... en Quercy*; Duvernoy, *Le catharisme II*, pp. 267–73, 353–5 and DPC, pp. 19–27; Passerat, 'Cathares', esp. pp. 152–5; Barber, *The Cathars*, pp. 144–64; Y. Dossat, 'La repression de l'hérésie par les évêques', CF 6 (Toulouse, 1971), pp. 217–51.

investigative obligations. Inquisitors could not, for example, award sentences of death or life imprisonment without reference to the diocese, and could be suspended from their duties and even excommunicated by bishops.[147]

But the Dominican inquisition in our period became specialist to the extent that even in its earliest phase it was 'a chain of tribunals … perpetually manned by those who had no other work to attend'.[148] They benefited from the bureaucratic advances making possible more systematic investigation, note-taking and record keeping. As we shall see, these extensive trial records were not created to be filed away having served their purpose. They were working documents and remained active and accessible, their contents a threat hanging over both the convicted and the acquitted for the remainder of their lives. Thus the records themselves were the target of violence at times, for example at Narbonne in 1235 and 1248, when they were destroyed.[149] Ultimately, this operational specialism and the increased autonomy for which the Dominicans strived led to conflict. It is in the context of a charged atmosphere of tension between the friars, with the backing of Rome, and the secular authority of bishops and the count of Toulouse that we should understand the operations of inquisitors in Quercy.

Pierre Seilan and Guillaume Arnaud were probably named inquisitors for the dioceses of Cahors and Toulouse by the pope in 1231 because they were natives of the region.[150] They instigated an inquest based at Cahors from 1233 to 1239, as recorded by Guillaume Pelhisson, and Pierre Seilan's fellow Dominican Pons de Mons became prior of the house they then established at Cahors for such operations.[151] But if their roots in the region were intended to make their presence and authority more palatable, this failed. When Othon de Berètges, the count's *bailli* for Moissac and Montcuq, was tried in 1244, we learn from his testimony that he had been instructed to obstruct the inquisitors in the previous decade. He was to dispute their judicial authority publicly and forbid anyone convicted from accepting their penance on the orders of

---

147 But *cf.* Christine Caldwell Ames, who stresses that although *inquisitio hereticae pravitatis* had twelfth-century origins it was never implemented fervently until the 1230s: *Righteous Persecution*, pp. 2–3, 229.

148 Lea, *Inquisition*, p. 116.

149 Ames, *Righteous Persecution*, p. 48.

150 Pierre Seilan came from an important Toulousain family but was prior of the Dominican convent at Limoges, which he founded, until 1233, and then prior of the convent of Toulouse (1235–7). Jörg Feuchter is the authority on him: 'Le pouvoir de l'inquisition', and 'Pierre Sellan, un viellard expérimenté', in *Les inquisiteurs. Portraits de défenseurs de la foi en Languedon (xiiie–xive siècles)*, ed. L. Albaret (toulouse, 2001), pp. 41–55 and 'Pierre Sellan. Le pouvoir de l'inquisition à travers ses peines. Le cas de Montauban (1241)', in *Inquisition et pouvir*, ed. G. Audisio (Aix-en-Provence, 2003), pp. 235–55. See also Lartigaut, *Histoire de Quercy*, p. 113.

151 *Chronique de Guillaume Pelhisson*, pp. 25, 70–1 and note 57, 92–3.

Raimond VII himself, who was even supported in this by the bishop of Agen, with whom the count established his own inquest in 1243.[152]

But in no sense does this imply that the count was in the slightest way sympathetic to heresy. In 1233/4, for example, extensive statutes against heresy and against the protectors of heretics were set down by his court.[153] They included that confiscations were to be carried out with respect to the property of those who failed to aid the church if called upon in apprehending heretics. But Raimond VII wanted an inquest that he could control, and he could not control the Dominicans. The pope, eager to keep the peace as well as to eradicate heresy, removed Pierre Seilan from the Toulousain in 1235 and confined him to operations in Quercy, and between 1238 and 1241 Rome suspended the inquests entirely, again at comital insistence.[154] In 1243 the count initiated inquisition of his own in the dioceses of Agen and Cahors, staffed by clergy of his choosing, to the satisfaction and with the support of Bishop Arnaud IV de Galard of Agen.[155] The comital inquisition continued into the second half of the decade.[156] Bishop Arnaud supported Raymond's objections to Bernard de Caux, and the inquisition as a whole was removed from the control of the mendicants by Innocent IV in 1248 and put under that of Bishop Guillaume II of Agen.[157]

Even so, before 1238 and after 1241 the Roman inquisition would impact dramatically on Quercy. The generalisation 'that the episcopate at large looked with disfavour on these new functions and activities of the upstart Mendicants there can be no doubt'[158] surely applied to Bishop Guiraud Barasc-Béduer also. But there is relatively little evidence of the successful prosecution of heresy in Quercy *except* under the Dominicans. In explaining this, we must again consider the weakened political power of the bishops resulting from their financial woes. At the same time as they were being forced to make concessions to towns such as Cajarc they were expected to pay inquisitors' expenses and build and maintain prisons for heretics while having very little influence in the way they were used. While they were supposed to profit from the seizure of heretical property, such as the Baussan house at Cahors,

---

152 D22, fols. 45v–46.

153 *HGL*, VIII, 963–70.

154 *Spicilegium*, IV, 265.

155 D31, fol. 40r–v; *HGL*, VI, 737–8; *HGL*, VIII, 1088–9.

156 *HGL*, VIII, 1240–1. For discussion of this in the context of the strategy of Pope Innocent IV in dealing with tensions between the bishop of Agen and the inquisitors see Roquebert, *Les Cathares*, pp. 182–5, 169, 182–6, 196–7, 205–7.

157 *Spicilegium*, VI, 265; Y. Dossat is the authority on Bernard de Caux: Dossat, 'Une figure d'inquisiteur: Bernard de Caux', pp. 253–72 (pp. 266–8), and 'L'inquisiteur Bernard de Caux et l'Agenais', pp. 75–79 (p. 75). The exact reason for the pope's acquiescence in 1238 is not known but it seems most probable that he feared an alliance between Raimond VI and the Emperor Frederick II (Hamilton, *Medieval Inquisition*, p. 62).

158 Lea, *Inquisition*, p. 101.

this was in practice offset by Bishop Guiraud having to sell off property at Cajarc in 1243 to meet the debts left by Bishop Guillaume.[159]

The Quercy inquests: an overview

We now turn to the work of these inquisitors in the diocese of Cahors. Pierre Seilan travelled from a base, Cahors, to smaller settlements where heretical enclaves might lie. His work for which we have most records is the book of sentences resulting from the 1241–2 activity of this peripatetic court at Gourdon, Montcuq, Sauveterre, Beaucaire (Lauzerte), Montauban, Moissac, Montpezat, Almont and Castelnau-Montratier. Chapter 4 explores the content of these inquests. His inquest was followed in 1243 by one at Puylaroque by the inquisitor known as Brother Ferrer.

The next significant records relating to Quercy derive from the 1243–5 inquisition of Bernard de Caux and Jean de Saint-Pierre held at Agen, where material relating to Quercy was abundant. Significantly, their investigations included an inquest into the murder of the inquisitors Guillaume Arnaud and Etienne de Saint-Thibéry and their retinue at Avignonet on 28 May 1242. We should read the evidence taken from 1243 onwards alongside the activity of royal commissioners following the murders. The latter obtained oaths of loyalty from southern towns and lords, which in Quercy were the town of Montauban (from the knights and the *bailli*) the lords of Corbarieu to its south, Roquefort, the consuls, knights and nobles of Cahuzac, the consuls of Montaigu, Guillaume de Gourdon-de Salviac, Bertrand and Hugues de Cardaillac, Guillaume and Dorde Barasc, and the towns of Capdenac, Caylus, Lauzerte, Montcuq, Moissac, Peyrusse and Castelsarrassin.[160] Given the role of some of these towns and lords in the wars, and the findings of Pierre Seilan at the time, these were very appropriate parties for the crown and clergy to want to bind to themselves legally. A second important context to the Quercy inquests is that many of the inquests of 1243–4 were held during the famous siege of Montségur, a southern stronghold in the Pyrenees, the fate of which concerned the whole of Languedoc.

The instructions these Dominican inquisitors received from Rome are contained in edicts of Gregory IX and Honorius III by the 1240s, and appear in inquisitors' handbooks by 1248.[161] The first stage of inquest was an advance warning that inquisitors were arriving. People were summoned by their

---

159 *Charte … Cajarc*, pp. 9, 36–7 (pièces justificatives no. 2, a copy of Arch. mun. de Cajarc no. 98).

160 Teulet, *Layettes*, II, no. 3087 (at 309a–b), no. 3088 (at 309b), no. 5065 (at 503b); *HGL*, VI, 754–5; *HGL*, VIII, 1118–1120.

161 The most significant early texts are ones deriving from Raimond de Penafort's sentences of 1241–2: C. Douais (ed.), 'Saint Raymond de Peñafort et les hérétiques: Directoire à l'usage des inquisiteurs aragonais, 1242', *Le moyen âge* 12 (1899), 305–25; and Bernard de Caux and Jean de St-Pierre's *Processus inquisitionis* of 1248–9: A. Tardif, 'Document pour l'histoire du *processus per inquisitionem* et de l'*inquisitio heretice pravitatis*', *Nouvelle revue*

priest and the inquisitor addressed them, indicating their obligation to come to him with anything they knew, or even their suspicions, within twelve days or face excommunication should their silence later prove misguided. Even if someone merely differed from other people in terms of lifestyle or morality, this might be an indication of deviance in doctrinal areas. The practice of absolute secrecy about the content of the proceedings became institutionalised. Testimony was heard only by the inquisitors and two other men not connected to the deponents. Usually they were two other Dominicans.

In terms of what was considered a crime, Duvernoy describes an important tension in the 1230s between what lay people and clerics believed the responsibility of the former to have been. The attitude of the laity, he says, was that when they expelled heretics in 1229 they had played their part in helping their count keep his side of the agreement made in Paris. But the implication of this from the Dominican perspective was that they had happily tolerated heretics *before* 1229. He suggests that the laity did not accept that this should be punishable in itself, let alone imply that they had shared the beliefs of heretics. But the clergy considered passive tolerance a crime just like participation or belief in heresy. It was denounceable, renounceable and punishable with varying degrees of severity. Therefore, evidence concerning even very low-level activity was sought every bit as eagerly by the inquisitors as the unmasking of major heresiarchs. The most minor crimes of those only slipping into heresy were important.[162] From 1243 at the latest, even seeing a *perfectus* or *perfecta* without reporting it made you culpable.[163]

Like other victims of inquisition, people in Quercy were accused and investigated on the basis of rumours about them (*fama*) as much as demonstrable fact, because the secret nature of accusation meant that 'evidence' was not necessarily verifiable. Furthermore, the evidence of 'lesser types' not usually allowed to give evidence in court was allowed if, and only if, it counted against the accused. Faced with all this, the accused was likely to confess and recant within the period of grace, receiving a sentence less severe than they otherwise might, in particular if they were forthcoming with regard to other people. But woe betide them if they were successfully accused again. Such people faced the stake, with the comfort only of the sacraments before execution if they repented again at the last. And the inquisition ruined a victim and even his family in the civil sphere too. The Fourth Lateran Council

historique de droit français et étranger 7 (1983), 669–78. Most recently on early inquisitors' manuals see Ames, *Righteous Persecution*, pp. 148–9, 245 note 45.

[162] On this see Arnold, *Inquisition and Power*, pp. 88–11 and discussion in Ames, *Righteous Persecution*, p. 9.

[163] Council of Narbonne (1243 or 1244), canon 29, in J. D. Mansi (ed.), *Concilia*, introduction and 53 vols. (originally *Sacrorum conciliorum nova et amplissima collectio*, 53 vols. (Florence, 1759–1927)) (rprt. Graz, 1960–61), p. 23 (incorrectly dated to 1235). See Duvernoy in Guillaume Pelhisson, *Chronique* pp. 15–16 and note 27.

had decreed that anyone aiding heretics lost many civil rights if they were not reconciled to the Church within a year. These were rights to hold public office, vote, make a will and inherit property. By 1239, the property of a guilty person was to be confiscated entirely, and their heirs disinherited and unable to take public office themselves for two generations.

But although many features of inquisition were already in place by the 1240s, when systematic operations began in Quercy, many of the things we think we know about 'the' inquisition were not yet true and would not be so until after the activity in Quercy ended. In fact, early inquests had a relatively 'light touch'. It may seem an unlikely thing to say of an inquisitor but, in considering the long history of inquisition, Lea is probably justified in calling Pierre Seilan 'one of the most moderate of inquisitors'.[164] Imprisonment or confiscation of goods was not yet common, although partly because special-ised prisons had not yet been built in Quercy (although we shall see that the walls of Cahors could serve as a prison). Whipping was not carried out in Quercy itself either.[165] We also have examples of even relapsed *credentes* being spared the stake (see Chapter 4). By far the most common penance Pierre Seilan awarded was pilgrimage, although not infrequently to distant places, even Constantinople and the Holy Land.[166] Lea argues that, although it is not made explicit in most sentences involving pilgrimage, flogging on arrival at the penitent's destination was so commonplace as to be assumed routine.[167] Pilgrimages were often made barefoot too. So this penance should not be considered a non-corporal punishment, and of course had to be undertaken at the penitent's own expense. But it was *relatively* compassionate, supposed to benefit as well as chastise.

As well as pilgrimages, the other penalty found in a huge proportion of Pierre Seilan's sentences was the instruction to support a pauper for a year. His enthusiasm in this area may relate to the discrediting of levying simple fines as punishment. In 1237 Pons Grimoard, Raimond VI's seneschal for Quercy since 1234,[168] was fined ten *livres* (pounds), but this practice had laid the Dominicans open to accusations of self-interest and was ruled out by

---

[164] Lea, *Inquisition*, p. 219.

[165] DPC, pp. 17, 21 note 34.

[166] He apparently did this in the face of papal opposition, because in 1242–3 this punish-ment was forbidden, the pope fearing the influence of the heretics on Christians over-seas. Nonetheless, the practice picked up in the late 1240s and persisted into the early 1250s: Lea, *Inquisition*, pp. 220–1. Systematic work on what we could call 'the implica-tion of inquisitorial sentences' is so far lacking. Feuchter has noted the opportunities for Montauban: 'Le pouvoir de l'inquisition'.

[167] Lea, *Inquisition*, pp. 218–19. The councils of Tarragona (1242), Narbonne (1244) and Béziers (1246) explicitly order flagellation as a punishment for heretics. On flagella-tion as an appropriate punishment see also Ames, *Righteous Persecution*, pp. 150, 155–7, 173–4.

[168] D22, fols. 39r–40r.

the Council of Narbonne in 1244. In 1244 the Dominicans at Cahors forbade inquisitors from receiving gifts as well. Lea suggests that Seilan was one of those unhappy with the process, and that his other penances were a form of commutation of fines.

However, of the sentence we most closely associate with the medieval inquisition, burning at the stake, we find little evidence in the inquests of the 1240s, even though this was allowed. In fact, even the relapse into heretical belief by one who had previously renounced their error did not lead automatically to relaxation to the secular arm, as it would later do, in spite of this being the spirit of the papal bull *Excommunicamus* (1229). It was only those too stubborn to renounce heresy on this second occasion who faced death. And *Excommunicamus* also established that those who had renounced heretical belief only through fear of death should have their death sentence commuted to life imprisonment.[169] It was not the goal of the early inquisitors to kill heretics, in other words, to the extent that the 1244 Council of Narbonne sought an end to such compassion.[170]

It was in fact *Ad extirpanda* of 1252 that marked the shift towards what came to typify inquisition as we think of it. It made torture legal practice for the first time and insisted that *all* heretics and relapsed converts be burned.[171] The 1240s were only at the very start of what became the process of mass public condemnations and the *auto de fé*. The logic of the accused not knowing who had given evidence against them or what this evidence was is that false testimony and conspiracies against a witness by their neighbours were viable. But the best-known examples of this are fourteenth-century in date.[172] Nonetheless, the impact of inquisition on communities was enormous and its presence, and even the threat of its presence, drove, as Malcolm Barber puts it, 'a wedge into the façade of community solidarity so that the loyalties and fears which held it together could be undermined'.[173] We shall now look at such communities and their inherent tensions and solidarities in Quercy.

---

[169] This was reinforced locally by the Council of Toulouse in the same year with the added proscription that they should be imprisoned in such a way that they could not communicate heresy to others (Lea, *Inquisition*, p. 239).

[170] It was not even the case, at least until the Council of Béziers (1246), that everyone evading the 'Period of Grace' was imprisoned as they should have been, because of the lack of prisons. People in Languedoc were being spared punishment because they had dependent family or were infirm or old: Ames, *Righteous Persecution*, pp. 184–5; Lea, *Inquisition*, pp. 239–40.

[171] Lea, *Inquisition*, p. 88.

[172] As in Lea, *Inquisition*, pp. 194–6.

[173] Barber, *The Cathars*, p. 148.

4

'Heretical' Quercy:
The Evidence Gathered by *c.*1245

In this chapter the depositional evidence as it relates to significant individuals and families is outlined. In reading this kind of evidence alongside evidence for monastic, town, military and other secular and regular activity such as that addressed in Chapters 2 and 3, we see certain individuals and families emerge as more significant than others in both socio-political and 'heretical' circles. This helps us further in reconstructing those networks of political and confessional affinity that shaped Quercy between *c.*1209 and the mid-1240s, an aspect of quercinois life that will analysed in Chapter 6. A wealth of more incidental data emerges also from the depositions relating to what we could call the 'social life of heresy', and also evidence that helps us to explore competing belief systems and interactions between them. The data the depositions and sentences reveal is detailed and prosopographical in nature. They have never received the treatment they deserve in this sense, except in some cases in the work of Edmunde Albe. This approach will be built on in Chapters 5–7 and the evidence related both to what we have learned about Quercy in previous chapters and to further evidence for the social and political life of Quercy.

Guillaume Arnaud and Pierre Seilan's First Inquests

Cahors (1233), Moissac (1234) and Montauban (1236)

We have no direct evidence of prosecutions until those enacted by Guilluame Arnaud in the mid-1230s[1] and there we do not have registers and records as we do for the work of Pierre Seilan and Bernard de Caux. Most of the evidence for the earliest phase of the inquisition as it relates to Quercy comes from Guillaume Pelhisson, from references to it in later inquests and from a

---

[1] Dufour asserts that the first condemnation for heresy that we know of in Quercy after the Peace of Paris was that of three brothers of the Massip family of Cahors, as early as 1231. The Dominicans apparently seized a large town house from them and gave it to the bishop. We know of this because in 1245 Bishop Guiraud de Barasc-Béduer handed it over to Arnaud Béraldy, his creditor (even so, he still owed him eighty-five marks): Dufour, *Cahors*, pp. 25–6. The basis of Dufor's claim is not clear.

few urban charters. Even so the evidence is very revealing exactly because it is so multi-faceted: we can read about 'heresy' as part of the narrative of urban life that was addressed in Chapter 3. For example, Guillaume Pelhisson tells us that several bodies were exhumed by Guillaume Arnaud and Pierre Seilan at Cahors in 1234. However, the corpse of a man called Imbert de Castelnau was dug up and removed by his son before the inquisitors got to it. Duvernoy, in his edition of Guillaume Pelhisson, uses *Te igitur to* identify both the father and son as usurers at Cahors.[2] We have seen that an Imbert de Castelnau would also be the subject of an investigation into the civil war at Cahors in 1246 and again in 1248. He could perhaps have been the son in question. Another suspect, Raimond de Brouelles, fled to Rome before he could be taken, apparently drowning himself in the Tiber.[3]

Pierre Seilan was to operate extensively in Quercy in his own right, but in the 1230s appears to have been Guillaume Arnaud's apprentice and assistant. When restricted specifically to operations in Quercy from 1235, at the count's request Guillaume Pelhisson and Pons de Mons accompanied Seilan. In this way inquisitors were 'trained up' on the job.[4]

We can usefully read other charter evidence against an inquisitorial background in the 1230s, such as a 1235 confirmation by the consuls of Cahors of the recent gift of a house by Guillaume Baussa to his wife Bernarde de Durfort. Albe notes that this demonstrates the growth in influence of the consuls over civil affairs, but also that what was probably taking place was the transfer of property into another's name, to prevent its confiscation, by someone who was expecting to be investigated by inquisitors. We can therefore note the probable involvement of the consuls in a process of collusion designed to deny the clergy property pertaining to a condemned person. Based on other evidence for Cahors, it seems unlikely that they were colluding in aiding heretical activity any more directly. It was probably a substantial property though, given the efforts of Bernarde's family in recovering possession of it, which they did in 1242. Her nephew Guillaume de Durfort, whose family were lords of Lauzerte (see Chapter 2 above), was awarded the house in exchange for fifty *livres*, which the bishop again paid to his creditors. Guillaume Baussa was indeed condemned by Guillaume Arnaud to spend several years in the Holy Land. In the event, however, Bernarde was found guilty too, and had to undertake several pilgrimages of her own. The couple's penances were complete by 1255, attested in an act of Bishop Barthélemy of Cahors,

---

2   Guillaume Pelhisson, *Chronique*, pp. 56–7; Combarieu and Lacombe, *Te Igitur*, p. 228. See also *HGL*, VI, 688.
3   Guillaume Pelhisson, *Chronique*, pp. 56–7, and see pp. 91–3; Passerat, 'Cathares en Bas-Quercy', pp. 149–65 (p. 153).
4   Guillaume Pelhisson, *Chronique*, pp. 70–1.

and Bernarde was finally allowed to own the house and other possessions again.[5]

When the news of this inquest at Montauban reached Moissac, more implicated people fled. The de la Garde family, this time Raimond and Pierre as well as Jean, were denounced for having visited the Cathar deacon Bernard de Lamothe when he and fellow *perfecti* were at houses at Moissac and at the home of Falquet, *perfectus* and lord of the nearby castle of Saint-Paul on the Tarn.[6] But at the same time the count of Toulouse was attempting to forbid inquisitors from passing sentences on the living, as we learn from the later deposition of Othon de Berètges. Othon forbade people from accepting punishments, at his master's instruction, because the Dominicans could not produce written evidence of their judicial competence. So the count, who had passed legislation allowing for the confiscation of the property of those who sheltered heretics, now threatened to seize the property of those who co-operated with inquisitors by accepting penances.[7]

In early 1236 Pierre Seilan and Guillaume Arnaud were at Montauban. The reason for this perhaps relates to earlier activity by two otherwise unknown friars – Guillaume de la Cordelle and Guillaume de Beauvais – which had resulted in the confessions and penances of two inhabitants of the town.[8] Crucially, these inquisitors also secured the confession of Pons Grimoard. After this, in April 1236, Guillaume Arnaud was moved to Carcassonne.[9]

Cathar communities remained active in lower Quercy, which we know from evidence from the 1240s. But this was a society now under great strain. Key *perfecti* and protectors of heretics had been identified and many had been eliminated as a threat. However significant the Cathar community at Cahors had in fact been, it appears to have collapsed entirely, its legacy being about rights to confiscated property rather than confessional affiliation. The geography of heresy extended to central and even northern Quercy. Although inquisitors in Quercy had not paid it any attention that we know of, this had taken place in the 1220s, because Pierre Seilan's register makes several references to the great flight of 1229 and to events taking place before it.

Pierre Seilan's inquest

We now turn to evidence for some of the more interesting and significant individuals and families in Quercy, and others still will be discussed in Chapter 5.

---

5   Arch. mun. de Cahors, chartes 26, 30, 52.
6   Guillaume Pelhisson, *Chronique*, p. 57 note 34, and see below.
7   D22, fols. 45v–6r.
8   As would be attested in 1241: D21, fol. 234r (sentence of Jean Fournier-Faure) mentions Guillaume de la Cordelle, and D21, fol. 242r–v (that of Bernard Raimond) mentions Guillaume de Beauvais.
9   Guillaume Pelhisson, *Chronique*, pp. 70–1, 90–3; Albe, *L'hérésie ... en Quercy*, p. 7.

The records do not appear consecutively in the manuscript, but are addressed in chronological order here. We also encounter examples of the formulae and other evidence discussed in the abstract in Chapter 1. Detailed analysis of the data, however, is reserved for Chapters 5 and 6.

Montauban and Moissac (2–9 May 1241)
It has been observed that the sociology of heresy at Montauban is not easy to understand.[10] This may be because it is traditionally envisaged by the historian through the testimony of its famous daughter, the *perfecta* Arnaude de Lamothe. Arnaude's is one of the most tragic and sympathetic case studies of the Cathar life. On the run since the flight of 1229, she was finally apprehended and on 13 and 31 August 1243 at Puylaroque she confessed her crimes to the inquisitor Brother Ferrer.[11] But her testimony is not the most useful for understanding Montauban itself, because she had not lived there since before the crusade but in a house of *perfectae* in Villemur, into which the *perfectus* Bernard de la Mothe, possibly her uncle,[12] had introduced her. Arnaude, her sister Péronne and their mother, Austorgue, received the *consolamentum* there, and it is about Villemur that her testimony about her early heretical activity is most centrally concerned. Furthermore, her testimony is in response to events all the way up to 1243 and cannot be read in isolation from the impact of the inquest of 1241. Indeed, it was from this that much was learned about her, her uncle and the rest of her extensive family. This may even be the reason that her own account is less concerned with Montauban, because a great deal was already known. Arnaude would attest merely that at Montauban her family often had the good men in the home, and that she had adored them when she was young. There is no evidence that the 1241 inquest led directly to her capture, but having been betrayed by her terrified siblings must have had some impact on what she told and how willingly she told it to Brother Ferrer. Indeed, Pierre Seilan's register demonstrates that the de la Mothe family was large and central to the heretical life of Montauban itself and that the Dominicans knew a good deal about Arnaude before she was taken. This evidence, in Doat 21, has been under-exploited.

The de la Mothe family were probably lords of modern Lamothe-Capdeville, just north of Montauban, on the Aveyron.[13] They were allies of the count of Toulouse by c.1203 and we have noted that Hugues de le Mothe fought in

---

10 Ligou, *Histoire de Montauban*, p. 40.
11 D23, fols. 2v–49v, esp. 2v–5v. She has been studied most extensively and recently in Lambert, *The Cathars*, pp. 74–5, 77, 80, 132, 137–8, 144, 150, 153, 169–70.
12 It has been suggested by E. Griffe that he may have originally been from Moissac, although I am not sure what the evidence is for this (*Le Languedoc cathare ... 1209–29*, pp. 175–7). For his activity elsewhere in Languedoc see ibid., pp. 163, 165, 181, 184, 187, 204; Roquebert, *L'épopée*, I, p. 241 and IV, pp. 113–14; Duvernoy, *Le catharisme I*, pp. 261–2.
13 Taylor, *Heresy*, pp. 181–2, 253.

the defence of Toulouse in the crusade. Arnaude and Péronne's father was also called Bernard, but Austorgue figures more centrally than he in the evidence. The couple had at least seven other children: Dulcia, Hugues, Na Mauraude, Bertrand, Aremand, Guillaume-Bernard and Raimond. Most had a good deal of regular contact with *perfecti* at Montauban and contributed towards supporting them economically. Bertrand had visited his mother and sisters at Lavaur when they were on the run.[14] Raimond had too, remaining with them overnight and eating with them.[15] Hugues had also visited the three women,[16] as had Na Maurade, although she did not bow to her mother's pressure to become a *perfecta* as well.[17] The point of this for the inquisitor was that after the Peace of Paris the siblings had not only failed to inform the authorities that their mother and sisters were at Lavaur, or anywhere else, but had gone out of their way to be with them and protect them. Dulcia, on the other hand, had not visited them and confessed to more passive involvement.[18] But she nonetheless saw Bernard de la Mothe and his *socius* Guillaume Solier[19] and other *perfecti* at the Montauban house of the *perfecta* Jeanne d'Avignon – of whom more will be said – where she heard them preach. She had also adored heretics and given them bread, wine and fruit, and she considered heretics to be good men. But not all of the siblings were Cathars *credentes*. Guillaume-Bernard attended heretical preaching with his mother as a child, and had considered *perfecti* good men. But he apparently stated that he now considered their teaching blasphemous and that he did not believe them.[20]

Another Bernard de Lamothe was the husband of Na de la Garrigue.[21] Other family members were Arnaude de la Garrigue, who had called both Waldensian and Cathar doctors when her niece and husband had been ill, and Serena, married to Raimond de la Garrigue, who had seen and listened to *perfecti*.[22] 'La Garrigue' may well refer to la Garrigue de Caussade in south-eastern Quercy. At Montauban we find two other people connected to Caussade. Bertrande de Caussade had accompanied a *perfecta* to certain houses and often eaten with her,[23] and Bernard Teissier of Caussade admitted that he and his wife Stéphanie had had *perfecti* of both sexes stay with them.[24]

---

[14] D21, fols. 278v–9r.
[15] D21, fol. 251r–v.
[16] D21, fol. 280v.
[17] D21, fols. 276v–7r. On Dulcia and Mauraude see also Feuchter, 'Le pouvoir de l'Inquisition', pp. 242–3.
[18] D21, fol. 277r–v.
[19] It is unusual for *socii* to be named in the Doat manuscripts.
[20] D21, fol. 233r–v.
[21] D21, fol. 249v and see below.
[22] D21, fol. 270v in both cases.
[23] D21, fol. 252r.
[24] D21, fols. 268v–9r.

Across the Tarn from Montauban lay the suburb and fishing port of Sapiac.[25] There are probably only two references to its lords in lay documentation, and they are relatively insignificant at that.[26] But we can nonetheless say a fair amount of them by 1241 using Doat 21. We discover that they had involvement with both Cathars and Waldensians. Arnaud de Sapiac senior and his wife adored, sheltered and fed *perfecti*. Believers attended ceremonies at their house, and he housed the *perfecta* Jeanne d'Avignon and her *socia* in one of his properties for a year.[27] Guillemette de Sapiac received Jeanne and her companions and adored them many times. She had met and adored so many heretics that she did not know the number – which is another formulaic expression typical of Doat 21 – and had continued doing so in spite of being reconciled with the Catholic faith by the bishop of Cahors. She had even seen Guillaume Abit, Cathar bishop of the Carcassès in 1226, and his *socius*.[28] Arnaud's son Arnaud admitted accompanying heretics on journeys often.[29] Other members of the family considered both Cathars and Waldensians good men. They were Fauresse,[30] Bernard,[31] Na Babilonia (wife of Bon de Sapiac),[32] and Rom de Sapiac.[33] Rom was unusual in his family because of his far stronger adhererence to the Waldensian sect. When his son and wife were ill, they were consulted. This was not unusual even in 'Cathar' families, as we shall see, but when his son died it was the former sect which comforted him: the son was not consoled, in other words, although many others in this family may well have been.[34] Finally, Faïs de Sapiac, by contrast, declared that she did not believe in either the Cathar or Waldensian faiths. Nonetheless, she had seen heretics who she believed to have given a sick woman the *consolamentum*. Thye woman subsequently died on the road to Villemur. Faïs had also heard *perfecti* preach, had often given wine and bread to Waldensians and received them, and had also consulted them when sick.[35]

The river was vital to both the economy and heretical life of the Montauban area. In the deposition of Hugues 'du Port' we hear that he ran a hostel in

---

[25] Now the area between the river and the railway station.

[26] Guiraud de Sapiac witnessed the homage of Bernard-Guillaume de Cos to Raimond V in 1168 (Macé, *Catalogues raimondins*, no. 117), and in 1218 Jourdain de Sapiac was given Villemade as payment for a debt owed originally by Raimond V (*HGL*, VIII, no. 192; D169, fol. 199r; Macé, *Catalogues raimondins*, no. 461).

[27] D21, fol. 230v.

[28] D21, fols. 240v–1r; DPC, 144–5 note 28; Taylor, *Heresy*, p. 237. Guillemette escaped execution, however, although her punishment was extensive, involving pilgrimages to six centres and wearing a cross for seven years in Rome.

[29] D21, fol. 255r–v.

[30] D21, fols. 240v–1r.

[31] D21, fol. 252v.

[32] D21, fol. 272r–v.

[33] D21, fol. 266v.

[34] D21, fol. 266v.

[35] D21, fol. 268r–v.

which *perfecti* resided for six months, and also had a house just down-river at Corbarieu, on the route to Villemur, where he received them.[36] This is the first reference we have to what was an important ritual site for the *perfecti*.

We know something of three generations of the de Coutes family, Waldensian adherents, through the eyes of its women. Domina Coutes listened to them preaching on Easter Sunday, confessed her sins to one and received a penance from him, and consulted them in case of illness, as well as committing the usual heretical crimes associated with this sect. But she had eaten cherries with *perfectae*.[37] Next interviewed was her daughter, Géraude, who had called in Waldensian doctors many times to her sick son, giving them food as payment. She too heard them preach on Easter Sunday, at the de Coutes house in fact, and had led them to other houses to preach. We also hear that she was sent food by *perfecti*, which she ate.[38]

Three of the de Castillon of Montauban had had contact only with Cathars. Jean had patronised them in various ways, including bringing an eel to *perfectae*, who gave him a belt and a purse.[39] Raimond Bernard de Coutes said he had discussed dying 'in their hands' and, like Hugues du Port, ran an inn at which they stayed.[40] Arnaud had eaten in the same house as Cathars, one where he was living, but had taken part in Waldensian religious activity and consulted them about illness.[41] Pierre had likewise consulted them and heard both Waldensians and Cathars preach.[42] Bernarde, Bernard's wife, had had contact only with Waldensians, she said, and was an adherent of that sect.[43]

Other families of Montauban that we encountered in previous chapters include the lords of Lolmie. Those of the Vaux were murderers of Baudouin of Toulouse in 1214. But at Montauban in the 1240s, Jean de Lolmie insisted that he had already confessed to Archbishop Arnaud of Narbonne his extensive involvement.[44] Here we find a relapsed *credens* escaping the maximum punishment available to the inquisitor. The final deposition of interest at Montauban is that of Guillaume Maffré-de Reilon, who admitted eating with Pierre Guilhem 'condamnato'.[45] We do not hear in which faith the latter was 'condemned', but it seems likely that the Pierre Guilhem who appears nine depositions later, and who had often Waldensians in his father's house, might be the son of that heretic.[46] And another Guillaume Maffré associated with

---

[36] D21, fol. 265r–v.
[37] D21, fols. 241v–2r.
[38] D21, fol. 242r.
[39] D21, fol. 259r–v.
[40] D21, fols. 259v–60r.
[41] D21, fols. 253v–4r.
[42] D21, fol. 252r.
[43] D21, fol. 243v.
[44] D21, fol. 240v.
[45] D21, fol. 236v.
[46] D21, fol. 238r.

Waldensians and had been treated by their doctors.[47] Finally we have two families which will be dealt with in detail in Chapter 5: seven members of the Carbonnel family were investigated, and a family of significance at Castel-sarrasin, the Mazeler, was represented at Montauban by Etienne Mazeler, a Waldensian adherent.[48]

Turning to Moissac, we see that, as well as undermining the prescriptions of 1229 on behalf of the count, as we have seen, the comital *bailli* for the town in the 1230s, Othon de Berètges, had protected the infamous *perfectus* Raimond Imbert.[49] We have noted that Moissac was also heavily influenced by the lords of the castle of Saint-Paul, on the Tarn. From Pons Grimoard's initial deposition of 1234 we learn that Vigouroux de la Bacone had been in a meeting at the de Saint-Paul home in c.1204.[50] Before this inquest many of Moissac's *perfecti* had fled, including Jean Cristofals and Falquet de Saint-Paul, who went to Italy, as we noted earlier. Nonetheless, in Ascension week 1241 the inquisitors still managed to convict ninety-nine people.[51] Falquet's wife, the *credens* Na Aurimonde, lady of Moissac, admitted to having heard the preaching of the heresiarch Vigouroux de la Bacone, to considering Cathars good people and their faith a good one, to adoring them also, and to having provided for them extensively.[52] The sentence of their son, Raimond, follows soon after her record. He saw heretics at the family home many times and had adored them.[53] A woman called Ricarde, the wet nurse of another of Falquet's sons, Hugues, had adored heretics too many times to count and considered them good people and had faith in them.[54] Another woman, Bitorte, notes that Falquet gave her mother's cape to heretics according to her wishes, presumably when she died.[55] Guiraud Guallard had led Vigouroux de la Bacone and his unnamed *socius* to the same house in c.1231, where he saw Falquet de Saint-Paul and his two sons Hugo and Bartholemew adore the heretics.[56]

We have seen that in the 1230s three lords of la Garde, Raimond, Pierre and Jean, had been investigated. In 1241 Raimond de la Garde, perhaps the same, had once considered all Cisterciens and other religious to be the real heretics.[57] Among his other crimes, he had seen Cathars in his brother's house and had hidden some in his cellar, possibly the same refuge in which

---

[47] D21, fol. 236v.
[48] D21, fol. 260r–v; DPC, pp. 178–9.
[49] D23, fol. 167v.
[50] Doat 22, fol. 36r–v.
[51] D21, fols. 282v–306r.
[52] D21, fol. 290r v.
[53] D21, fol. 290v.
[54] D21, fols. 295v–6r.
[55] D21, fol. 294r–v.
[56] Doat 22, fol. 18v.
[57] D21, fol. 304v.

Guillaume Augier saw two of them.[58] The deposition of Pierre's wife, Ricarde, is the first in the Moissac record. She is said to have admitted seeing heretics and listening to them preach.[59] Lombarde, wife of Jean, who was still alive at Montségur in 1241, admitted extensive involvement including having them in her house.[60]

We should also note a branch of the de la Mothe at Moissac. Na Gassac and her husband Arnaud de Lamothe were heavily implicated in Cathar activity.[61] Finally, we should note of Moissac that only two people are recorded as having seen Waldensians, and yet, intriguingly, the evidence of the two deponents concerned appears to reveal very extensive Waldensian activity indeed. Arnaud Faure, son of Stephen Faure, had received them a good thirty times, he said, and saw them in his father's house, had eaten with them, including bread blessed by them, and given them money.[62] Guillaume de Bérens of Moissac remembered seeing when he was a child up to thirty Waldensians at one time in a house.[63] The scale of the Waldensian presence indicated in these two depositions only indicates that even such a vast inquest was not thorough.

Gourdon (1–24 December 1241)

That heresy had deeply influenced the Bouriane by the 1240s is evident from the passing of 131 sentences at Gourdon.[64] The very first is that of Huguette, wife of Raimond Guiraud. She admitted to having received *perfecti*, going to their house, adoring them many times and giving them 'of her goods' (another frequently recurring phrase in the register). She admitted to listening to them preach many times.[65] Here the *audivit* describing her response to the preaching demonstrates that their words had had an impact on this woman. Indeed, the heretics became so much a part of her life that she assisted them at her husband's *consolamentum*, a crime that was very common. Pierre Seilan sent her on pilgrimages to as far away as Santiago-de-Compostella and Canterbury and sentenced her to wear a cross on her clothes for one year and to support a pauper for as long as she lived. Huguette's sentence is worth noting in full because, aside from supporting a pauper, it was a punishment which became one of the models used at Gourdon: 'Idem quod Huga excepto paupere' follows many depositions. With an intriguing circularity, making it quite difficult to establish patterns concerning the order in which

---

[58] D21, fols. 286v–7r.

[59] D21, fol. 282v.

[60] D21, fol. 288r; Guillaume Pelhisson, *Chronique*, pp. 56–9; DPC, pp. 12, 226–7.

[61] D21, fol. 305r–v.

[62] D21, fol. 296r.

[63] D21, fol. 285v.

[64] D21, fols. 185r–213v. See also Albe, *L'hérésie … en Quercy*, pp. 12–39.

[65] D21, fol. 185r–v.

witnesses were called or interviewed, the sentence of Huguette's own son, Raoul Giraudou, is the penultimate recorded at Gourdon. He had listened to *perfecti* preach and accompanied them while travelling.[66]

In one of the most evocative depositions, Guillaume Ricart outlines a lifetime of devotion to the *perfecti*. He routinely heard them preach and adored them, far more times than he could remember, and took part in some of the most intimate ceremonies binding *credentes* to the sect, such as the monthly *apparellamentum* at which *perfecti* ritually recognised members of the sect's hierarchy, and he recalled receiving the kiss of peace.[67] Among the most interesting gifts received from heretics were the scissors they gave him, while he had supplied them with a cloak, a shirt, a tunic and grain. He had led Waldesians to them in order that the sects could hold a debate; he was their agent (*depositarius*) and had led them to safety in 1229. He believed that Cathars were good men, and when he died, he wanted it to be in their hands.[68]

Turning to the lords of Gourdon themselves, we find there is a good deal to say. Not only were they key figures in the political life of Quercy, they also played one of the most important roles in the success and protection of the *perfecti*. Bertrand was effectively forced to concede that there had been an established heretical centre in his town with his knowledge. He admitted to receiving *perfecti* at his home within the *castrum*, where he listened to their 'blasphemies', knowing them to be heretics. But in the case of two, Vigouroux de la Bacone and Barthélemy de Carcassonne, he had spoken with them, almost certainly in 1223, but sent them away. Vigouroux was well known in Quercy, but in the case of Barthélemy Bertrand said that he had not known that he was a heretic at the time, only discovering this later.[69] This was not an insignificant encounter but a central episode, not just for Quercy but for Catharism more widely, as we shall see.

Bertrand's son Fortanier appears to have been a more active Cathar sympathiser. He is recorded as thinking them good men, listening to them preach very many times and adoring them; he could not recall how many times. Indeed, whenever he saw them he adored them. He had received seven *livres* of Cahors for accompanying them on a journey, perhaps in 1229. He had housed them in the upper castle at Gourdon, 'adored' them, given them money and grain, eaten with them and received their gifts.[70]

Other nobles of the Bouriane feature in the Gourdon register. Several of the lords of Goudou were implicated. Gaillard de Goudou received *perfecti* at his

---

[66] D21, fols. 200v, 213v.
[67] Duvernoy, *Le catharisme I*, 204, 211.
[68] D21, fol. 208v.
[69] D21, fol. 186r–v. The two were together in Quercy in that year, in the context of a schism within the Cathar community: Taylor, *Heresy*, p. 228, and see Chapter 7 below.
[70] D21, fols. 199v–200r.

house at Labastide and ate with them.[71] Pierre-Guillaume de Goudou[72] and Arnaud 'Rectus' de Goudou[73] were condemned to undertake several pilgrimages.

The lords of Fages de Peyrilles were vassals of the lords of Gourdon and mentioned in a treaty between Philip Augustus and Richard the Lionheart.[74] Hugues de Fages-de Peyrilles had seen heretics, heard them preach and accompanied them.[75] His confession is followed by that of Raimond de Peyrilles.[76] Duvernoy suggests that the lords of Rivière were also lords of Peyrilles. Guiraude had received *perfecti* and given them food[77] and Bernarde had likewise supported them,[78] although Jeanne admitted only to having seen them.[79]

Among the lords of Goulême, lords also of Milhac and Concorès, was one of the few *perfecti* named in the Gourdon documentation, Raoul 'scabiosus', noted above. His widow Raimonde is recorded as admitting to having assisted at his *consolamentum*. She had also hosted heretics and often adored them and listened to them preach, and had continued to do so after her husband's death.[80] Another Raimonde, wife of Guillaume de Goulême, had received and fed a Waldensian believing him to be a good man.[81] Their castle was perhaps taken from its chief lord in the wars, because Guiraud de Goulême is 'son of a faidit' (*filius faiditi*)[82] and Raimonde's husband Guillaume is 'brother of a faidit' (*fratris faiditi*).[83] Gaillarde patronised the Waldensian Pierre de Vals.[84] Péronne, who had many times heard heretics preach, was another widow of a lord of Goulême.[85] Aladaïs de Goulême admitted to having 'seen' Pierre de Vals on three occasions and considered him a good man.[86] Guillemette, wife of Aimeric de Goulême-de Milhac, had consulted him over an illness.[87] In all, nine members of this family were sentenced in 1241.

---

71   D21, fols. 193r, 213r.
72   D21, fols. 195v, 197v–8r.
73   D21, fols. 195v, 197r; DPC, pp. 52–3 (where Duvernoy identifies Arnaud 'Cedus' as Arnaud Rectus), pp. 56–7.
74   Combarieu, *Dictionnaire*, p. 185.
75   D21, fols. 195r, 205r, 213r; DPC, pp. 52–3 and notes 117–18, pp. 72–3, 86–7.
76   D21, fols. 205r, 210r.
77   D21, fols. 153r, 205v–206r.
78   D21, fols. 193v, 208r–v.
79   D21, fols. 194r, 207r.
80   D21, fol. 200v–1r.
81   D21, fol. 206v.
82   D21, fols. 191v, 213v.
83   D21, fols. 193v–4r.
84   D21, fols. 206v–207r.
85   D21, fol. 189r–v.
86   D21, fol. 211v.
87   D21, fol. 213r.

A branch of the de Goulême family was lords of Milhac by the 1240s.[88] Pierre de Goulême-de Milhac was punished for heeding and helping Cathars.[89] Guillemette, wife of Aimeric de Goulême-de Milhac, had associated with both sects.[90] Pierre de Goulème-de Milhac had seen heretics and received things from them for helping them.[91] Jean de Pech-de Milhac adored *perfecti*, listened to them preach and guided them on journeys.[92]

Aside from Raimonde, three other people are recorded as having assisted in the *consolamentum* of Raoul de Goulême: Guillaume de Montgaillard and his wife Agnès,[93] and Bertrand de Lascroa.[94] Lascroa, or Lestroa, modern Bouscot, was a hideout north of Gourdon, according to Duvernoy. Bertrand had seen many *perfecti* and heard them preach, exchanging the kiss of peace with them, going to them one Christmas Eve, giving them flour and assisting also at the *consolamentum* of Guillaume Moulinier. He considered the *perfecti* good men, had adored them many times and had eaten with them.[95] Raimond de Lascroa had also listened to them, had given them goods and accompanied them on a journey.[96]

One *credens* emerging as central to the heretical life of the region, and who received one of the heaviest sentences, was En Roques. From the testimony of Bertrand de Lascroa and Bernard de Latour[97] we learn that Guillaume Moulinier's *consolamentum* had taken place at his house, and that he held money for the heretics. En Roques himself made one of the fuller, or fullest recorded, testimonies in this collection. He believed in the heretics' faith fully and had associated with Cathars for a long time. Heretical meetings were held at his house. He had assisted at two *consolamenta* aside from the one in his house. In fact he could not even remember all of the heretics he had met nor how many times he had eaten with them, listened to them and so on, because it was so many. He had also assisted in the flight of 1229, and when he died he intended to be consoled. He was expelled from Languedoc to spend three years at Constantinople.[98] His wife Ricarde was also punished, although comparatively lightly considering her apparently established position as 'hostess of heretics' (*receptatrix hereticorum*) and intention likewise to be consoled on her deathbed.[99]

---

88 Bulit, *Gourdon*, p. 92 n. 1.
89 D21, fols. 193r, 212r.
90 D21, fols. 192v, 204v, 212v–13r.
91 D21, fols. 192v, 212r.
92 D21, fol. 191r.
93 D21, fols. 188r–v, 211r, identified in DPC, pp. 36–7, 82–3 note 147.
94 D21, fol. 188r; DPC, p 35 and note 80.
95 D21, fols. 210v–11r.
96 D21, fols. 191v, 210r.
97 D21, fols. 187v–188r.
98 D21, fols. 198v–199r.
99 D21, fols. 195v–6r, 197v–8r.

But we know that at Gourdon there was tolerance of difference rather than rigid adherence to a particular system, because Waldensians are very much in evidence in the record, to the extent that they seem as ubiquitous as Cathars at Gourdon and in the castles and *castra* of the Bouriane. Most striking is the number of witnesses who noted their involvement with the Waldensian doctor Pierre de Vals. Pierre de las Oleiras (modern Les Oulières near Pomarède) had accompanied him on a journey and given him four loaves.[100] It was he whom Bertrand Auriol considered to be a good man, although he also knew the *perfectus* Touzet de Noguès. Bernard Bonald considered that Waldensians such as Pierre had more to recommend them than Cathars. Guillaume Ichier had seen Pierre at Puy on the Lot.[101] Women among the lords of Braulens (modern Braulès) apparently patronised him specifically: Bertrande de Braulens had received him in her home to cure her sick son[102] and Guillemette, wife of Guiraud de Braulens, had seen him on many occasions and believed him to be a good man.[103] More will be said about the attitude of women toward this heretic in Chapter 5.

Some other deponents at Gourdon admitted only to interaction with Waldensians. Raimonde de Goulême had received and fed a Waldensian, believing him to be a good man;[104] Arnaud-Guillaume de la Vigue had likewise seen them regularly and listened to them preach;[105] Guillemette and Bernarde de Laribe both listened to Waldensians preach and gave them goods, receiving pilgrimages to le Puy and Saint-Gilles;[106] and, again, Waldensians alone were revered by Guiraude and Bernarde, both wives of men named Raimond de Rouffilhac.[107]

Significantly, we have members of families of Cahors at Gourdon. The de Jean were represented at Gourdon by Péronne and her husband Raimond, she having given *perfecti* wine, bread and nuts, although she favoured Waldensians more, it would seem.[108] The wife of Pons d'Arcambal, of another family with powerful members at Cahors, had received Cathars twice in her home, sent them wine and broad beans, listened to them preach and adored them around seven times.[109] Pons himself was condemned to wear a cross for five years and to undertake pilgrimages.[110]

---

[100] D21, fol. 189r.
[101] D21, fol. 186v.
[102] D21, fol. 189r. Duvernoy transcribes what I'm sure is 'Bertranda' as 'Bertrandus': DPC, p. 36. Peter Biller concurs with me on this.
[103] D21, fol. 203v.
[104] D21, fol. 206v.
[105] D21, fol. 190v.
[106] D21, fol. 190r–v.
[107] D21, fols. 192v, 211v.
[108] D21, fols. 194v, 203v.
[109] D21, fol. 189r; DPC, p. 36–7 note 85.
[110] D21, fol. 192r.

Montcuq, Sauveterre, Beaucaire, Montpezat, Almont, Castelnau-Montratier (10 February–24 March 1242)[111]

At various points in Lent 1242[112] the inquest operated in the Vaux. The evidence of Bertrand de La Roque-de-Montcuq is among the most significant, not just for Montcuq but for Quercy, and this will be discussed in Chapter 5. We also have a Sibille de Montcuq, who had seen plenty of heretics in many places. She had adored them and brought people to see them.[113] Several witnesses refer to an important *credens*, a woman called Guillemassa.[114] Another very significant *credens* of Montcuq was the priest François, of whom the inquisitors noted specifically that he had not come forward in the period of grace. He admitted having assisted in a disputation between Waldensians and Cathars. He believed the former sect to be good, but it was Cathars he seems to have favoured. He had escorted Vigouroux de la Bacone and his *socius* to the mass of Lacoste. While they remained there he gave them bread, fruit and a 'new cooking pot' (i.e. one that had never contained meat) and supported them using his own money. He delivered a book and silver from Vigouroux to Guillaume Baussa, the *credens* of Cahors. He also greeted Vigouroux on behalf of 'a certain woman' and exchanged other greetings with Vigouroux. He sent heretics a blanket and sheets. He considered the *perfecti* good men, but he had also heard Waldensians preach in the castle of Montcuq.[115]

The Montcuq environs contained numerous minor estates and several of their families were found to be involved in the heresy when Pierre Seilan arrived. The family of Saint-Geniès had been among the most important *credentes*: Gaillard, Bernard, Bertrand and his widow Na Finas, and Guillaume, lord of the manse at Laborda, between Montcuq and Saint-Geniès, and his wife Na Marquèse.[116] Bernard possibly had legal powers, perhaps under Othon de Berètges, *bailli* for both Moissac and Montcuq, because it is recorded that had seen and spoken with *perfecti* and could have captured them, had he wished to, but that he had not wanted to.[117]

We have lords of other towns at Montcuq too. Three lords of Montaigu were tried; Pierre,[118] Raimond[119] and Bernard, of whom we hear through the deposition of his wife Na Sauris.[120] Finally, Bertrand de Gourdon-de Montcuq

---

111 For convictions in central Quercy see also Albe, *L'hérésie ... en Quercy*, p. 16.
112 See DPC, p. 91 note 155 for the dating.
113 D21, fol. 219v.
114 D21, fol. 219r, 223r, 224r, 225r–v, and see 226v–7r.
115 D21, fol. 219v–220r.
116 D21, fol. 214r, 221v–2r, 226r; DPC, p. 91 note 159.
117 D21, fol. 226r.
118 D21, fol. 215r.
119 D21, fol. 216v.
120 D21, fol. 222v.

was tried and he said he had seen heretics many times, heard them preach, given them two *solidi* and received and delivered letters on their behalf.[121]

Modern Sauveterre is a tiny hamlet perched on a hill west of Castelnau-Montratier. It yielded only five sentences. Its lord was Guiraud de Gourdon-de Sauveterre-de Mondenard (see the genealogy p. xiv). He admitted extensive contact with *perfecti* and received one of the heaviest sentences, a penance of three years in Constantinople. He admitted to listening to them preach, adoring them, assisting in a *consolamentum* and receiving the kiss of peace. He had fed and sheltered them on his manse and believed them to be good men. He had received them on the order of one 'Illamada', which Duvernoy suggests could perhaps be a rendering of Guillemassa, the *credens* of Montcuq.[122] This suggestion is supported by the fact that Pierre Cadel of Montcuq said that he was ordered to lead heretics from Montcuq to Sauveterre by Guillemassa.[123] Another connection between the two *castra* is that Raimond de la Raimondière of Sauveterre said that he had seen heretics preach publicly at Montcuq.[124]

Seven people were then convicted at Beaucaire, a hilltop hamlet a short distance from the fortified *Loseler*, modern Lauzerte, founded by the count of Toulouse, as noted. Its deponents were closely involved in the Cathar heresy, and to some extent with Waldensianism. Beaucaire was influenced heavily by the heretical lords of Caussade, who seem to have been its principal lords. Beaucaire's deponents provide important evidence about heresy which will be drawn on in Chapter 5, but also tell us about the lords of Caussade, who were also lords, or at least patrons, of Beaucaire. This connection was the main focus of the 1242 enquiry. We hear that an important *credens*, Eustache, had sent Guillaume, *perfectus* lord of Caussade, greetings via an intermediary whom we have already encountered: François, the priest of Montcuq. Eustache had gone to find another *perfectus* himself, one who had commanded him to do so, and spent five days with him, eating with him, staying in the same house as him, listening to his preaching, adoring him and accepting from him twenty *solidi*.[125] Guillaume, the miller of Beaucaire, said that when women came to his mill and said 'God and St Martin have given us a good mill', he replied that it was holy Guillaume who had made a good

---

121 D21, fols. 215v–16r. He was sent to Le Puy, Saint-Gilles, Santiago, Saint-Denis and Canterbury. It is unclear why Duvernoy interprets 'B.' as Bernard rather than Bertrand, which is also abbreviated to 'B.' in the register and is a Gourdon family name.

122 D21, fols. 226v–7r; DPC, p. 118–19 and note 218; Dossat, 'L'inquisiteur Bernard de Caux', p. 75; Albe, *L'hérésie ... en Quercy*, p. 15. There was an important *perfectus* also called Guiraud de Gourdon, but this Gourdon was in the locality of Caraman (Haute-Garonne), of which he was Cathar deacon: Duvernoy, *Le catharisme II*, 231.

123 D21, fol. 224r.

124 D21, fol. 227r.

125 D21, fol. 228r.

mill, surely meaning Guillaume de Caussade.[126] Pierre 'V.' (perhaps Vidien) de Valtauren said that Jauffré de Caussade had sent him to his brother, Guillaume de Caussade, to call him to Beaucaire. The witness found Guillaume at Montcuq, but he was not able to come as requested.[127]

Pierre Seilan next convicted twenty-two people at Montpezat. Since the Peace of 1229 Bertrand de Montpezat[128] and Guirauda, wife of Pierre-Arnaud de Montpezat,[129] had often heard Cathars preach. Pierre de Montpezat, a boatman, had transported heretics to Moissac and Agen in his boat.[130] Two other families in particular played a significant role: the Cabanoles and the family of En Gorse. Barthélemy de Cabanoles 'saw' *perfecti*, as did Guillaume de Cabanoles, in c.1221. Domestique de Cabanoles received *perfecti* in her house and gave them around thirty *solidi* and goods including an eel pie and wine.[131] En Gorses himself received heretics in his house and heard a debate between *perfecti* and Waldensians.[132] His daughter, another Domestique, saw *perfecti* in her father's house.[133] Another daughter saw *perfecti* and listened to them preach.[134] En Gorse's wife Marthe had called for her *perfecta* aunt, Huguette, when she was ill, in case she died, and the aunt had summoned *perfecti* to administer the *consolamentum* (Marthe had presumably lapsed from the perfected state on recovering from the illness). We hear more about the eel pie too: Marthe had been responsible for conveying it to the heretics on behalf of Domestique, and she gave them presents of her own as well.[135]

Pierre de Bruelh perhaps had some jurisdiction at Montpezat. He admitted that that he had met and spoken with *perfecti*, including some on the road to Belfort. He could have arrested them, but did not, and let them go.[136] Huguette, wife of Arnaud Pellegri, perhaps of the Gourdon Pellegris, was also convicted.[137] A member of the seigneurial family of Saint-Jean-de-Mazerac (Puylaroque) was also investigated at Montpezat. She was the *perfecta* Raimonde de Mazerac, prioress of the Augustinian house of Lativia (La Lécune). She had been a *perfecta* for four or five years. Important 'surplus' evidence escapes the formulaic in her case. Pierre Seilan recorded not only the *answers* to questions that would have revealed the Docetist heresy, but that Raimonda herself asked the inquisitors whether the Blessed Virgin had

---

[126] D21, fol. 227v.
[127] D21, fol. 228.
[128] D21, fol. 306r.
[129] D21, fol. 306v.
[130] D21, fol. 239v.
[131] D21, fol. 306v.
[132] D21, fol. 308v.
[133] D21, fols. 307v–8r.
[134] D21, fol. 308r.
[135] D21, fol. 307r–v.
[136] D21, fol. 308v.
[137] D21, fol. 308r.

suffered giving birth like other women, and whether she had suckled Jesus bodily. The scribe then records that they had found in their records depositions of others who had given evidence against this *perfecta*.[138] We do not know who these witnesses were, although Arnaude de la Mothe would testify against her in 1243 (see below).

The inquisitor then travelled to Almont, modern Réalville, between Caussade and Montauban. There, the priest Arnaud de la Roque admitted seeing *perfecti* in a vineyard. He ate pears with them and read their book. He was defrocked and sent to Santiago and Rome with a letter from the inquisitor as his punishment.[139] None of the other records for Almont are as evocative, but we learn of a few significant families and connections. A landowner, Etienne Sobressen, saw two *perfecti* leaving his property at Mas del Pech.[140] Of the lords of del Pech, Hugues had escorted *perfecti* for money,[141] although Gausbert had simply happened upon four or five of them in his house and not reported it.[142] Pierre d'Aussac, near Montpezat, saw many *perfecti* and had them in his house.[143] It is also worth noting that four members of Bishop Pons d'Antéjac's family were convicted: Gaillard,[144] Guillaume,[145] Gausbert[146] and Hugues.[147] We also find that Bernarde de Rou had been a *perfecta* for seven years.[148]

The last inquest, at Castelnau-Montratier, yielded eleven convictions. Among the most interesting activity there was that of heretical doctors. Guillaume de la Mothe, quite possibly of the Montauban family, was helped through an illness by a *perfectus*.[149] Petronilla de Fabrica had them cure her son and then her husband, and, perhaps in payment, did work for them. One of the most extensively implicated *credentes* was a woman, Bigordane. She knew two *perfectae* to whom she gave cloth to make bandages. She heard them preach and adored them every time she saw them, and took them fish and wine on someone else's orders. She also received two men one night who seemed to be pilgrims. When they left in the morning they told her they

138 D21, fol. 307r. Albe identified the abbey as Lécune but had read Lativia as 'Latinia'. Duvernoy follows him with regard to the abbey but correctly reads 'Lativia', so the interpretation is safe (Albe, *L'hérésie ... en Quercy*, p. 16; DPC, pp. 13, 256–7).
139 D21, fol. 310r.
140 D21, fol. 310r–v; DPC, p. 261 note 369.
141 D21, fol. 309r.
142 D21, fol. 309r.
143 D21, fol. 309r.
144 D21, fol. 309v.
145 D21, fol. 309v.
146 D21, fol. 310r.
147 D21, fol. 310r.
148 D21, fol. 309v.
149 D21, fol. 311r.

were *perfecti*. Finally, she would defend the heretics when people spoke evil of them and, as many other people had told Pierre Seilan, she loved them.[150]

Brother Ferrer's Inquest of 1243 at Puylaroque, on Montauban and Moissac: Arnaude de Lamothe

Three depositions stand out from Brother Ferrer's register in relation to Quercy. Arnaude de Lamothe's is the best known. On 13 and 31 August 1243, at Puylaroque, she confessed her crimes to the inquisitor.[151] She was already damned. Her family had given Pierre Seilan enough evidence to condem her, but worse was that she had relapsed into the heretical life after being reconverted.[152] There was little cause to hold back and her detailed account is one of the most important we have for understanding Catharism in the era of its persecution. Some of its most moving content concerns the terrible month Arnaude and her *perfecta* sister Péronne spent in an underground hide-out in a wood, where Péronne died and Arnaude buried her with the help of three *credentes*. She also recalled her life at Villemur and how, when the crusaders struck camp in 1209, the then Cathar deacon of Villemur evacuated the *perfecti* of the town into the Albigeois.[153] This is the same episode that Guillaume de Tudela recalled in his *Chanson*.

As noted, relatively little of Arnaude's evidence concerns Montauban, although what does so often echoes elements of the depositions of 1241–2. She recalled of Bernard de Lamothe that in *c.*1214 he was at Montauban with his *socius* Guillaume Solier and family members.[154] Also, he was at Jeanne d'Avignon's house, where Arnaude and Péronne were, along with their siblings Dulcia and Mauraude.[155] She refers also to her brothers Aremand[156] and Raimond[157] and mentions the *perfectus* Touzet de Noguès, and also that the six women of Linars were 'heretics wearing the habits of nuns' (*haereticae sub habitu monialium*).[158]

Guillaume Donadieu de Mazerac

We learn more about Quercy, in particular the south-east, from the deponent known to the inquisitors as Guillaume d'Elves and also Guillaume Donadieu

---

[150] D21, fols. 310r–12v.
[151] D23, fols. 2v–49v.
[152] D23, fols. 6v–7r.
[153] D23, fols. 2v–5v.
[154] D23, fol. 7r.
[155] D23, fol. 7r.
[156] D23, fol. 4r.
[157] D23, fol. 7v.
[158] D23, fols. 7v–8r.

de Mazerac.[159] As such, we can connect him to the seigneurie of Mazerac and thereby to the heretical prioress Raimonde de Mazerac of Lativia, although he himself was a knight of Caussade. He confessed little concerning himself and said that he had in any case already confessed to Pierre Seilan at Cahors and to Bernard de Caux, and had been absolved.[160] We learn that he had had the heretic Hugues de Maorte and his *socius* at his own house at Mazerac, and led them to his brother Pierre's. There there were members of the Belfort family, encountered by Pierre Seilan at Beaucaire, including Ratier and Bernard, and Bernarde and Arnaude de la Garrigue.[161] His most important testimony concerns the lords of Caussade. He saw Pierre de Caussade at Najac (Aveyron), when his own brother, the *perfectus* Grimal Donadieu, was present,[162] and at another time saw the heresiarch Guillaume de Caussade himself there.[163]

The Latin translation of Guillaume's deposition describes the seigneurie at Caussade as an honour containing several manses. Some were used as hideouts. Thus, at the manse of Lautardia he saw the *perfectus* Bernard Carbonnel and the heresiarch Sicard de Lunel, who would later be reconciled with Catholicism.[164] At another manse, La Garrigue-de-Caussade, he saw heretics including Guillaume de Caussade with Bernard de la Garrigue and Etienne de la Garrigue-de Najac.[165] At the manse of la Pradelle he saw the heretics Arnaud de la Pradelle and his family, Guiraud, Arnaud and the latter's son Raimond, and also Bernard de la Garde, knight of Montalzat. Guillaume's brother Pierre was at the heart of a heretical network linking Caussade with Cahors, holding a great deal of silver on behalf of the heretics and moving money around for them, which involved the witness in communications between Guillaume de Caussade and the heretics of Cahors.[166]

Raimond Jean d'Abia[167]

The third key witness in Doat 23 is Raimond Jean d'Abia. He discusses Villemur for the most part, but from there he escorted heretics throughout lower Quercy. At Moissac, he was with them at Pierre Escudier's home, where he

---

[159] D23, fols. 209r–17v. This deposition has been edited by Yves Dossat, 'Les cathares', pp. 290–8.

[160] D23, fol. 217r.

[161] D23, fol. 210v; DCBC, 58 note 9.

[162] D23, fol. 209v.

[163] D23, fol. 211r. He also notes also a Guiraud de Caussade: D23, fol. 215v.

[164] D23, fol. 215v.

[165] D23, fol. 214r.

[166] D23, fols. 216v–17r.

[167] Peter Biller has suggested to me that 'Abia' may be Latin 'Albia', i.e. Albi, with the Doat scribe omitting the 'l'. I think it is more likely to be Albias, lying between Caussade and Montauban.

met the brothers Raimond and Pierre Escudier.[168] The brothers went also to the Saint-Paul home when the heretics were received there, as were Raimond and Pierre de la Garde.[169] He noted that the lady of Moissac, probably meaning Na Aurimonde, de Saint-Paul's wife, adored heretics along with her daughter Ondrada and Ondrada's two sons.[170] He was with a party from Villemur at Jeanne d'Avignon's house at Montauban, and from him we learn that she had a son, Bon.[171] At Castelsarrasin the group stayed at Etienne Sanche's home, where he saw Raimond Campeiran, and also saw Jean and Guillaume Faure de Pechermer and their mother and sister adore heretics. Then the party went to the Faure home at Pechhermer, itself a suburb on the road to Moissac and of whose principal family we shall hear a good deal more. They stayed there for four days. There he met Bernard de Cazenac, the *faidit* of Périgord noted in Chapter 3. De Cazenac did not adore heretics, though. This was in c.1228.[172] We shall learn more about this meeting later.

Bernard de Caux's inquests November 1243–March 1244

Bernard de Caux was the chief inquisitor for the diocese of Cahors and Agen from 1243. At these towns between 23 November 1243 and 18 May 1244 he heard evidence relating to lower Quercy, mostly from deponents of Castelsarrasin.[173] The depositions in Doat 22 contrast with Pierre Seilan's register in that they all focus on the same few families, the scope being far narrower than that of Doat 21. It seems that he aimed in large part at exposing the crimes of a key political network involving servants of the count of Toulouse, a very different focus from that of Pierre Seilan. The witnesses implicate each other over and over again.

In some cases, the inquisitors were looking for evidence about the assassination of inquisitors in 1242, discussed in Chapter 3. Bernard called certain witnesses specifically in this context and asked different questions of them. For this reason, Doat 22 does not always follow the formulaic pattern discernable in Doat 21 ('Did you see heretics?' 'Did you adore them?' and so on), although in several cases these sort of questions were certainly asked. Below is evidence extracted from the depositions concerning individuals' place in socio-political networks and in events in previous decades, and their atti-

---

[168] D23, fol. 263r.

[169] D23, fol. 264r.

[170] D23, fol. 266r.

[171] D23, fol. 262r.

[172] D23, fol. 264v.

[173] The depositions as set down in Doat 22 are not ordered chronologically. I have presented them in the order in which they were made. See also Duvernoy's introduction to DCBC, 2, although I disagree with some of his dates.

tudes to heretics (in almost all cases Cathars, there being little if any evidence of Waldensians at Castelsarrasin).

Bernarde Targuier (30 November 1243)

The first person to be interrogated, on 30 November 1243, was Bernarde Targuier.[174] She admitted that she had at one time been a *perfecta* herself, but had been reconciled to the Roman faith by Bishop Fulk of Toulouse. She had then married Pons Gran, deceased by 1243, and since she had been reconciled she had not seen any heretics, she claimed, except Bernard de La Mothe, who returned money she had lent him. But, prior to this, she told the inquisitor, around thirty years previously, she had seen him and his *socius* at the house of Guillaume Faure de Pechermer. Another time she had also seen Guillaume Faure and Arnaud de Bressols with the same two *perfecti*. Furthermore, her sister Guillemette was a *perfecta*, and she and Bernarde had lived at Villemur in a house for *perfectae* run by Unaude Calvera. She had then lived at Corbarieu for four months and met the knights Bernard de Lunel and Raimond Bernard, who had come to venerate Bernard de La Mothe. Indeed, when people, powerful or humble, heard mass at Corbarieu, afterwards they came straight on to listen to the *perfectus* preach, she said. Finally, she added that she and her *socia* Unaude had seen Guillemette, wife of Guillaume Faure d'Agre, and Huguette, wife of Raimond Faure d'Agre, at the house of Guillaume Faure de Pechermer. The house at Corbarieu was the home of Bernarde Targuier of Castelsarrasin for four months once she became a heretic.[175]

Guillaume Faure de Pechhermer (30 November und 7 December 1243)

The Faure family, of the Castelsarrasin suburb of Pechermer, were by 1243 a mixture of heretics, *credentes* and people who claimed, or were claimed by others, to adhere only to the Roman faith. Guillaume Faure was interrogated on 30 November 1243 and again on 7 December, and gives us a very detailed understanding of elite life at Castelsarrasin.[176] Both his parents had been consoled before death, as were other other family members, and many more had a good deal of contact with the Cathar hierarchy. His brother was Arnaud Faure, whom he admitted to having seen at the home of the heretic Raimond Grimoard with other *perfecti*. He understood that Arnaud had become a heretic himself, along with his uncle Benoît and the latter's son Etienne. Guillaume was married to Bernarde, daughter of Guillaume Arnaud, a *routier*. Her husband declared her to be free of the stain of heresy. She did not love the heretics, he said, and had rebuked him over his involvement with them.[177] Likewise his sister Guillemette had no time for them. However,

---

[174]   D22, fols. 1r–3r.
[175]   D22, fols. 2v, 3r.
[176]   D22, fols. 3r–9v, 9v–10r.
[177]   D22, fol. 9v, but *cf.* the testimony of Guiraud Guallard: D22, fol. 27r.

he had seen another sister, Guiraude, at a heretical gathering at the house of Pons Grimoard.

Guillaume ran a hostel.[178] It is not clear whether this was for *perfecti* specifically, but he had had the heretics Bernard de Lamothe, Guillaume Solier, Guillaume Salamon, Vigouroux de la Bacone, Pons Guilabert, Hugues Pradier and Vital Grimoard stay there. Coming to see such *perfecti* were *credentes* including Pons Grimoard, Aimeric de Bressols, Arnaud Mazeler, Raimond de Serra, Jourdain de Berètges, Arnaud Pagan, Guillaume Audebert, Na Compta and Raimond Rauc and his wife.

Guillaume himself had often adored heretics, asked them for blessings and so on. He had held their beliefs since he could tell good from evil. However, he said that had made his confession to the inquisitor Guillaume Arnaud at Castelsarrasin in the 1230s, and had nothing to do with the heretics since then; he had not seen them, protected them, led them, fed them or received them at home. He had not even heard about any heretics, except that in *c.*1240 he had helped the heretic Sernin at harvest time. Also, the heretic Raimond Imbert had stayed at his hostel in *c.*1239. He had received a 100 *livres* fine for allowing him to escape. 'In fact' – we can almost hear him admitting what he could no longer deny – he '*had*, in fact, associated with heretics' since the confession. Furthermore, only two years earlier he had helped Arnaud Serdan and his would-be *socius*, because they wanted to become heretics, to journey to Pons Guilhabert and his *socius*, who were at the home of Arnaud Mazaler, implicitly to that end.

But he wanted to clarify something, he said. Here again we can almost hear the deponent's voice, because the scribe has not edited for brevity. The account is further compelling because in this instance the deponent did know some of what other witnesses had said about him. Someone had said that he had sent letters to the heretics at Montségur, but he denied this. What had happened, he said, was that he had sent a letter to Raimond de Campendu[179] in the diocese of Carcassonne. But the latter was not to be found at home, because he was at the siege of Montségur. The messenger's name was Arnaud de Bazas and the notary was Etienne de Laudegria, he said. We can almost hear him add, 'You can ask them. They'll tell you the same thing.' Nonetheless, he was sentenced to perpetual imprisonment or exile, to be determined later.

Not only did the inquisitors want Guillaume Faure to admit his own and his family's sins, they wanted him to incriminate his neighbours specifically. There were key families and family members in whom the inquisitor was most interested; the Faures themselves, the Grimoards (Pons, Guillaume, Na Pros and the *perfectus* Raimond), the de Broccolo (Bertrand, Aimeric, Arnaud

---

[178] D22, fol. 6v.
[179] Identified by Duvernoy: DCBC, pp. 19–20, note 29.

and Arnaude), the Audeberts (Guillaume), the Berètges (Jourdain, Othon and Na Berètges), the Mazalers (Arnaud and his sons Etienne and Guillaume), the Rauc (Arnaud, Rainaud, Raimond and Raimond's wife), the de Cavalsauts (Pons the *perfectus*, Jean, who was the husband of Na Pros de Grimoard, and the *perfecti* Guillaume and Bernard), the *perfectus* Raimond Imbert, the Sanches (the *perfectus* Etienne and Raimonde), the Campeirans (Fort and Raimond), the Pagans (Jean, Arnaud and his wife Pétronille), Na Compta and Raimond and Arnaude de Serra.

Elements of this record appear straightforward, because of the formulae by which it is structured: a claim by the witness to have seen certain people with heretics; where (the houses or property of other suspects being of particular interest to the inquisitor, perhaps because it might lead to the conviction of other family members who were suspects, and also because their houses could be seized to cover inquisitors' expenses); and what they had done with the heretics. Typical of the record is that a witness said that in *c.*1220, at Raimond de Campeiran's house, he saw Vigoroux de la Bacone, Bernard de Lamothe and their *socii*, and with them were Rainaud Rauc, Arnaud Pagan and Raimond and Fort de Campairan. Likewise, he saw Raimond Grimoard at Arnaud Pagan's house, with the heretics Pons de Cavelsaut and Bernard de Lamothe and their *socii*. They were debating with two priests. Guillaume himself and Arnaud and Pétronille Pagan were assisting them.

Similar evidence served to condemn his neighbours the Grimoards and Sanches. Pons Grimoard, he claimed, had witnessed the *consolamentum* of Etienne Sanche at Castelsarrasin, as had Guillaume Grimoard, who was perhaps Pons's uncle, and Pierre Grimoard, perhaps his cousin, and others. It was around twenty years ago, he said. He himself had helped Sernin and another *perfectus*, Pons, prepare for the ritual. Etienne's wife Raimonde was there too. But both Guillaume himself and Raimonde were ejected from the room when the ceremony actually took place. He also saw Sernin and Pons at the home of Na Pros de Cavelsaut. They were administering the *consolamentum* to Arnaude, widow of Bertrand de Bressols. He implicated the Campeirans too, admitting to having seen Vigouroux de la Bacone and Bernard de la Mothe and their *socii* in *c.*1220 at the house of Raimond de Campairan. With them were Rainaud Rauc, Arnaud Pagan and Raimond and Fort Campeiran, all listening to them preaching.

One of the most significant confessions he made – indeed, it seems to have been the main reason he was called back in to see the inquisitors on 7 December 1243,[180] because it is the very first item addressed – was that he had taken part in a meeting in his own house between Bernard de Lamothe, Pons Grimoard and Bernard de Cazenac 'of the diocese of Périgord, to whom the count gave Castelsarrasin', and they all listened to the heretic preach. This is

---

180   D22, fol. 9r; DCBC, p. 23.

our second reference to this meeting, first recalled by Raimond Jean d'Abia in 1243. Pons Grimoard's own would be a third.

Pons Grimoard (22 January–8 February 1244)

Pons Grimoard,[181] seneschal for the count, recalled, as Raimond Jean had, that this meeting took place in about 1228, and, as both the latter and Guillaume Faure had, that it took place in the Faure house. Also there were Bernard de Lamothe and his *socius*. With them were Guillaume Faure, Aimeric de Bressols, Raimond-Guillaume de Berètges, Hugues de Cavelsaut. Pons admitted that he heard the heretics preach several times and he adored them. He contradicts Raimond Jean d'Abia's evidence though. According to him, it was not only de Cazenac who did not adore the heretics. He did not recall any of those present doing so.[182] Whether or not he wanted to protect other people in the town through his testimony that no one adored the heretics in 1228, as the highest-ranking deponent in Quercy the inquisitors constructed a chronology for him, one of political and religious dissent with the witness entirely at their mercy.

To begin with, Pons's letter of absolution of 29 March 1236 was proof that he understood fully the implications of a lapse back into heretical adherence. By his own testimony and that of others in the 1240s, he had indeed continued in the heresy, as we shall see. The power of the documentation thus enabled the friars not only to punish but to exert a great hold over him, perhaps to further manipulate him by creating some distance between him and the communal solidarity which led this powerful individual to protect other people.

The first use the inquisitors made of him was to investigate the earliest heretical activity that those living in the 1240s remembered. Thus the first incident he discusses in his deposition was when he saw two *perfecti*, Pierre Baudouy and his *socius*, in his uncle Raimond Grimoard's house at Castelsarrasin in *c.*1204. This is an extremely early recollection and is one of the few accounts we have of Catharism in Quercy before the wrath of Rome fell upon it. It is followed by several more accounts of activity 'at the same time'.[183] He saw 'at the same house' the heretic Raimond Aimeric and his *socius* with Raimond Grimoard and with them the de Cavelsauts (Hugues and Jean, brothers, Hugues's wife Bertrande, and Na Prous de Cavelsaut, who was Jean's wife), the Faures (Raimond and Bertrand, who were the brothers of Guillaume Faure, and Arnaud, father Guillaume de Castillon), Pons's own brother Vital, the brothers Bernard and Pierre Audebert, Arnaud Pagan and Raimond de Bressols, the uncle of Aimeric de Bressols. All of these

---

181   D22, fols. 32v–39v (22/1/1244), 38v–40r (1237, letter of pentitence), 40r–42v (8/2/1244); DCBC, pp. 52–61, 62–5; *HGL*, VIII, 1016.
182   D22, fol. 35r; DCBC, p. 5.
183   D22, fol. 34r.

people listened to the *perfecti* preach. At the end of this account Pons admits himself to having adored heretics in that house many times, genuflecting and requesting to be blessed, and states that all of the men above, but not the women, did likewise at various times.

Can we trust Pons to have remembered accurately who was at which meeting in *c.*1204? He was still young then, because he tells us that he was treated by a heretical doctor around thirty-five years earlier in a room in his mother's house,[184] rather than at his own. Is this not rather a list of everyone he knew to be *credentes* of Castelsarrasin before the crusade? Certainly, Pons seems to have been induced to start at the beginning and state who was involved with the heresy as far back as he could remember, and in fact *c.*1204 marked the start of his own belief in the heresy, as he noted later in his deposition.

Then he recalled events at another significant time for Quercy, *c.*1214, or 'about thirty years ago', when *politically* dissident Quercy had first emerged. He saw heretics he could not name in Arnaud Faure's house. He saw *perfecti* often at that house, in fact, and also adored them there. Also in *c.*1214 his uncle Raimond Grimoard was hereticated at Corbarieu. Pons, Guillaume Faure, Bertrand de Saint-André and Hugues and Jean de Cavelsaut were there, and knew full well that he was going to be consoled. Pons himself did not attend the actual ceremony, though.

Otherwise, from his lengthy statements we can draw up a list of people implicated in the heresy by him most extensively. They include Hugues, Jean de Cavelsaut, Bertrande and Na Prous de Cavelsaut;[185] Raimond, Bertrand, Arnaud, Vital and Guillaume Faure; Bernard and Pierre Audebert; Rostanh and Raimond de Bressols, and Aimeric de Bressols and his cousin; Etienne Sanche and his wife Raimonde; Raimond-Guillaume and Jourdain de Berètges; Etienne and Arnaud Mazaler and Arnaud's wife Guiraude; and Raimond de Serra, Rainaud Rauc, Arnaud Pagan, Arnaud de la Mothe, Jean de la Garde, Guillaume de Castillon, Arnaud Calvera,[186] Bernarde (the wife of Pons Gran) and Guillaume Raimond, 'doctor of the heretics' (*medicus hereticorum*), of whom more will be said. Of these, Etienne Sanche, Hugues de Cavelsaut, Raimond de Bressols and Arnaud Calvera he heard had been consoled, presumably at death.

He then discussed the crime for which he had previously been convicted and which had resulted in his abjuration of heresy and letter of penitence. In *c.*1234, when he was the seneschal of the diocese of Cahors for the count of

---

[184] D22, fol. 40v.

[185] The *credens* Matfré de Paulhac of Villemur would note a 'B. de Cavelsaut' and his *socius* as heretics (D22, fols. 58v–9r).

[186] Someone of this name witnessed the 1203 charter of Raimond VI in favour of the people of Cahors: *IRC*, I, no. 1. We have noted the *perfecta* Unaude de Calvera who ran a house for women at Villemur.

Toulouse, he saw Guillaume de Caussade and his *socius* in the home of Pierre de Belfort at Lauzerte.[187] While he himself had been asleep in bed, Pierre had woken him and showed him the heretics. When he asked Guillaume de Caussade where he had appeared from, he said he had been in the tower when Pons had arrived; hiding, in other words. From this we learn that the heretical lord of Beaucaire had allies in neighbouring Lauzerte also. But Pons neglected to capture the heretics, and at the end of the depositions he admits that he did wrong in this period, when he was seneschal for the diocese, after the peace was made between the count and the Church and in which he was supposed to be pursuing heretics and *credentes* by nature of his office, not least because he had sworn to do so in the period when the peace was signed.

Pons insisted that he had stopped believing in the heretics when he confessed to Guillaume Arnaud. He had had nothing to do with them since. Neither had he ever recommended their beliefs to anyone. He had told only the truth to Guillaume Arnaud, and he had never forbidden anyone from telling the truth about themself or anyone else to the inquisitors, implicitly since that reconciliation. Pons Grimoard states explicitly that he never spoke of heretics to his mother or to his nephews Pierre and Etienne, and he never heard them speak about heretics or love them.[188] In 1243 his penance of 1236 had been completed, and Bernard de Caux and Pons de Mons accepted that he knew that he had done wrong as seneschal for Quercy after the Peace of 1229: that it had been his duty to seize heretics, not allow them to go free as he had Guillaume de Caussade. He should have arrested them, he admitted, and arrested Pierre de Belfort likewise. He freely abjured heresy again and was freed of excommunication. He was instructed to appear at Cahors before the following Sunday, 21 February 1244,[189] and add to his confession anything he wanted to, and to carry with him the original letters from the bishop of Cahors. Implicitly, this second appearance was for sentencing. We have no record of it. However, others had testified against him and he had knowledge of heresy at Castelsarrasin since the 1230s and had done nothing about it.

Guillaume Féraut (25 January 1244)

After the depositions of Guillaume Faure and Pons Grimoard, Guillaume Féraut's deposition of 25 Jan 1244 is brief.[190] However, it tells us a good deal indirectly. He said that he had had nothing to do with heretics himself. What he was induced to do, it would seem, was to add even more to the evidence condemning Guillaume Faure; the deponent said that at Jean de Toulouse's house he had heard Guillaume Faure say to the deponent's own nephew, who was ill, that Christ was the *bailli* of God and had volunteered to be his

---

[187] D22, fols. 37r, 42r; Duvernoy, *Le catharisme II*, pp. 264, 284–5.

[188] D22, fol. 41r–v.

[189] DCBC, p. 66 note 19.

[190] D22, fols. 25v–27r.

son, along with other unorthodox ideas which will be addressed in Chapter 6, and other evidence from this witness condemning Guillaume Faure. This was about ten years previously, and no one else had heard it, just the sick son and the deponent.

After condemning Guillaume Faure the deponent then positioned himself more firmly within a set of people who may or may not have existed, those who supported the inquisitors and were prepared to say so to other people; Pierre de Quissac had said to him that he supported the penance awarded to Guillaume Faure de Pechermer, the exile overseas or whatever it would be.[191] Had he been asked directly about Pierre? We cannot know. But he himself had committed that most minor of crimes: not reporting Guillaume Faure's error earlier, and so mentioning at this point that he had been the inquisitors' apologist cannot have hurt.

Jean Vital (26 January 1244)

The deposition of Jean Vital,[192] son of Vital Ortola, is also relatively brief but significant, and again Gullaume Faure is one of its main subjects, as is the murders at Avignonet in 1242. The deponent told Bernard de Caux that shortly after the crime the *perfectus* Etienne Mazeler arrived in Castelsarrasin, having travelled from Moissac. Guillaume Audebert and Guillaume Faure and others were celebrating the recent turn of events. Guillaume Audebert said to the heretic, 'Do you want to hear some good *coblas* or *sirventès* [lyrics or satirical songs]?'. The heretic declared that he would, and so Audebert sang that Brother Guillaume Arnaud 'Cogot es escogotatz et pesseiatz'. Catherine Léglu interprets this imagery as meaning that the 'proud' inquisitor had been 'brought low with an axe' and was a 'humiliated laughing stock'. Etienne Mazaler apparently agreed with Guillaume Audebert, approving of the lyrics and adding 'cocula carta es trencada'. This possibly means that the record (i.e. of confessions and penances) was destroyed, although Léglu makes the case based on the grammar that the inquisitor himself was metaphorically the destroyed charter.[193] Guillaume Faure apparently also later said 'Come here, you other masked, rabid Catholics. We have been blind but now we have our sight back, and we shall have it much longer than you will.'[194]

---

191 Duvernoy notes here that Pierre Seilan had been undermined in imposing long pilgrimages overseas, and that they were being replaced by periods in prison, sometimes perpetual (DCBC, p. 41 note 3).

192 D22, fols. 10v–13r.

193 D22, fol. 11r–v. See P. Bec, *Nouvelle anthologie de la lyrique occitane du moyen âge*, 2nd edn (Poitiers, 1970), pp. 122–3; Duvernoy, *Le catharisme II*, p. 281; Y. Dossat, 'Le massacre d'Avignonet', CF 6 (Toulouse, 1971), pp. 343–58; C. Léglu, 'Vernacular poems and inquisitors in Languedoc and Champagne, c.1242–1249', *Viator* 33 (2002), pp. 117–132 (pp. 119–21). I am grateful to Catherine for her correspondence relating to this deposition.

194 D22, fol. 11v.

We must remember that some of these *credentes* had good reason to cele-brate, because the murdered Guillaume Arnaud had first wrung confessions from them in the 1230s. Jean apparently also reported hearing Pierre de Quissac say that 'he gave nothing for all the masses sung at Cahors, and if the inquisitors ordered him to go there, he'd go the other way, and that no one cared as much as an egg about excommunication, because the Church's authority was groundless'.[195]

Jean implicated Guillaume Faure and Guillaume Audebert in events in the mid-1220s also, stating that they were openly in the house of the heretic Bernard Audebert, uncle of the latter, at Castelsarrasin. But he had not adored any heretics there himself. He had also seen the *perfectus* Hugues de Cavel-saut in his home at Castelsarrasin, again operating openly, and with him were Guillaume Faure de Pechhermer and Arnaud and Rostanh de Bres-sols. Guillaume Audebert in particular, he asserted, of whom much else had been written, had also made some very extreme statements about the nature of creation, which will be discussed here in Chapter 5. But personally, he insisted, he had nothing to do with heretics.

Guiraud Guallard (28 January–22 March 1244)

Guiraud Guallard had also already given evidence to Guillaume Arnaud but he was called by Bernard de Caux several times, on 28 January, 22 February, 8 March and 22 March 1244, to make and confirm statements. Guiraud confessed to having withheld evidence about Vital Grimoard and the de Bressols family in the 1230s.[196] But before he again abjured heresy in front of the inquisitors he gave numerous accounts that condemned his fellow minor nobles.[197] Implicated most heavily were Pons Grimoard and his wife Arnaude, Pons's father Vital, and his uncles Raimond-Bernard Grimoard and Raimond Grimoard, the *perfectus*. Also incriminated were Othon de Berètges and his wife Na Berètges, and from their family Raimond-Guillaume and Raimond. Then there were Guillaume, Vital and Aimeric de Bressols and Na Pros de Bressols and her son Arnaud and his wife Grazide. Also listed were Etienne and Raimonde Sanche. Likewise the de Cavelsaut: Jean and Na Pros (daughter of Raimond Grimoard), Hugues, Bertrande (daughter of Hugues and Bertrande de Malause), Pons and Bernard (*perfecti*) and Raimonde (*perfecta* and daughter of Na Pros). Of another leading family implicated, the Targuier, were Guillaume, who he notes was the brother of Etienne Mazeler junior, Guillaume's daughter Bernarde, who had been a *perfecta* and was the widow of Pons Gran, and their two sons, one of them called Guillaume, apparently both in England. In addition, he mentions Etienne Mazeler, senior and junior; Petrona de Cahors, the widow of Gausbert de Gascobat; Guillaume and Na

[195] D22, fols. 11r–12v.
[196] D22, fol. 18r; Taylor, 'Authority and the Cathar heresy', p. 145.
[197] D22, fols. 13v–25v.

Arnaude de Calvera; Raimond de Serra, his wife Aurimonde and the two *perfectae* Raimonde and Arnaude de Serra; Falquet de St-Paul of Moissac and his sons Hugues and Bartholemew; and finally Guillaume Audebert.

The following is typical of the kinds of circumstances in which he noted that people of Castelsarrasin were involved. In about 1220, he said, Bernard de Lamothe was at Vital Grimoard's house with Raimond de Serra, Raimond Grimoard, Raimond-Bernard Grimoard and Johannes de Cavelsaut. In about 1230 he had seen Vigouroux de la Bacone and Bernard de Lamothe in the home of Arnaud de Bressols, along with Pons Grimoard and his father Vital, Raimond-Guillaume, Othon de Berètges, Guillaume Audebert, Etienne 'the scribe' and Guillaume, Vital and Aimeric de Bressols. All of them, including the witness but with the exceptions of Pons Grimoard and Othon de Berètges, had adored the heretics. Around the same time he saw Vigouroux de la Bacone and his *socius* at the port at Moissac with Guillaume-Raimond de Berètges, Guillaume Faure de Pechhermer, Arnaud Pagan and Vital Grimoard. He noted that Arnaude Grimoard alone did not adore heretics.

Pierre de Noye (25 × 29 February 1244)

Somewhere between 25 and 29 February 1244 Pierre de Noye confessed,[198] and he admitted at the outset to having had the heretics Pons Guilabert and Sernin in his house for seven nights. Na Compta had venerated them there, as had Jean de Toulouse and others, who had led the heretics there in the first place. Pierre had then led the heretics to Moissac, to Pons d'Ax. Pierre also implicated Guillaume Faure, in whose house he encountered Bernard de Lamothe, Guillaume Solier, Saturninus, Pons d'Airoux and Pons Guilabert, all heretics, and with the Jean de Toulouse again, Na Relis and Guillaume Faure himself. He likewise betrayed Rainaud Rauc, Arnaud Pagan and his wife Pétronille, and Hugues de Cavalsaut, but he stated that his own wife Raimonde did not love the heretics and had not adored them.

Most of what he reported, he said, had taken place twenty or more years ago – that is, during the crusade. But we learn a little of life during the siege of Castelsarrasin. He had the knights Bernard de Durfort-de Saverdun, Guilhabert de Pechauriol and Bernard de Ribière lodge with him. They had all adored heretics. He had believed teachings of the *perfecti* himself for six years but had then rejected them, because they taught that if one did not die in their faith they could not be saved. He had had nothing to do with them for ten years: since before Guillame Arnaud's inquisition, in other words.

Pérégrine Gasc (29 February 1244)

Pérégrine,[199] wife of Guillaume Gasc, was a one-time servant to Eleanor of Aragon, daughter of King Pierre of Aragon and wife of Raimond VI of

---

[198] D22, fols. 27r–29v.
[199] D22, fol. 30r–v.

Toulouse. She made her deposition on 29 February 1244. Little of her evidence concerns Quercy and it is not certain that she was from Castelsarrasin. But she had encountered Waldensians at Moissac, at the home of Pierre Ortola, now deceased, in c.1224. She had never listened to them preach though, she said, and she had never had anything to do with the *perfecti*.

Arnaud de Corbarieu (10 March 1244)
Interviewed on 10 March 1244 was Arnaud de Corbarieu, *domicellus* (young knight) and *consanguineus* (kinsman) of Bertrand de Corbarieu.[200] The latter was implicitly lord of Combarieu. As we shall see, the place was central to Cathar operations in lower Quercy. But Arnaud himself does not tell us much about it. He lived at Villemur. However, he did say that he had had observed three men who he discovered later to have been Waldensians on a hill called *Malrazenc* between Saint-Nauphary and Corbarieu with Bernard del Pech and Raimond de Lavaur. He had also seen the Waldensian Toulza de Lavaur labouring on the walls of the church of Saint-Nauphary, but he had not had any contact with him.

Arnaude Grimoard (10 × 14 March 1244)
Possibly interviewed next, although the date and outcome are uncertain, was Arnaude Grimoard, Pons Grimoard's wife.[201] Pons and also Guiraud Guallard had said that she did not associate with heretics, as we have seen. But other people had evidently contradicted them. When asked if she would like to defend herself against evidence given about her in this inquest, she said she wanted to think about it. Asked again later, when she had composed herself, she said the same. So the inquisitor gave her a time limit of a month to think about it. She was to reappear on 12 March 1244, and we do not know the outcome.

Na Berètges (14 March 1244)
When interviewed on 14 March 1244, Na Berètges, the wife of Pierre Grimoard senior, had more to say.[202] She attested that she had seen the heretics Vigouroux de la Bacone and his *socius*, and Othon de Barètges and many other people with them. But she did not adore them herself, even though many did, and she did not see Othon himself, Arnaude, wife of Raimond de Barètges, or Arnaude, wife of Pons Grimoard, adore them. But they did all listen to the heretics preach, herself included. When asked whether Vigouroux had asked her, Othon and the others who had not adored him to do so, she said no, he had not. But here we learn something interesting about inquisition record-keeping. She was asked whether she had known that Guillaume

Arnaud came as inquisitor to Castelsarrasin. She said yes, and that she had in fact confessed to him and his fellow inquisitor that she and others had seen heretics, adored them and listened to their preaching. She had admitted so truthfully, she said. But evidently the inquisitors had no record of her in the 1230s, which she explained by saying that her confession had not been written down because the inquisitor had not wanted to do so. Whether she was telling the truth or not we cannot know, but this was a strategy worth pursuing.

Othon de Berètges (17 March 1244)

Considering the extent of evidence against him, Na Berètges's brother Othon, the *bailli* of Moissac and Montcuq, was not required to give an especially lengthy statement on 17 March 1244 because he straightforwardly admitted most of it.[203] The first and last thing he did was to implicate Guillaume Faure. He said that the latter had invited him to his house and there he saw many people with the *perfecti* Vigouroux de la Bacone and Touzet de Noguès, who were preaching.[204] In the audience too were Pons Grimoard senior and Etienne the scribe. Everyone listened to the heretics, but no one adored them. He concluded that he had often heard Guillaume Faure praise the sect of the heretics.

Othon, in fact, failed to arrest the heresiarch Vigouroux twice. He confessed to having seen him at Arnaud de Bressols's house also, with his *socius*. He also saw there Arnaude and Pons Grimoard and Na Berètges, his own sister. There were lots of others there too, but no one adored the heretics. He was asked whether he had found the women there or whether they had led him there, but said he could not remember; he had not gone there to see heretics, in fact, but simply to give a horse to Arnaud (another deponent strategy which will be discussed in Chapter 6). Next he associated several men of Castelsarrasin with Bernarde de Lamothe, describing a meeting between them all on the bank of the Garonne. They were Arnaud de Bressols, Grimoard de Castillon, Pierre Béraldy, Guillaume Brugole, Pierre Hugues, Arnaud Pagan and Vital de Bressols. All the above, he said, he had already confessed to the friars but he said that he had not given evidence under oath because, as his sister had claimed, they had not wanted to take his deposition.

When they had given him a penance it was in fact for other crimes committed at Moissac during the time when he had been *bailli*. It was then that he had instructed the people, on the count's own orders, he claimed, that they should not accept penances from the inquisitors or he would arrest them and seize their goods. He was to tell them that this was because the inquisitors did not have the authority to judge them, nor could they produce letters

---

[203] D22, fols. 44v–6r.
[204] D22 online, 69 correction (a). Duvernoy notes that Touzet is 'Joset' in the register of Pierre Seilan.

showing that they did. Asked whether he had had written authorisation for this from the count, he said he did not remember. He was then asked whether he wanted to defend himself against evidence given by other witnesses. He said he wanted a day to think it over. He was given until the feast of the Annunciation to make up his mind and to recall whether he had indeed had written instructions from the count. Again, we do not know the outcome.

Raimond de Roudoules (22 March 1244)
From Raimond de Roudoles,[205] interviewed on 22 March 1244, the inquisitor apparently got evidence condemning only Aimeric de Na Regina, as observed above (she had apparently said that God was not born of the Virgin but only appeared to have done so, and that God was not present in the mass). He admitted that although he had himself repeated this, about the Mass and the Virgin, in Arnaud de Bressols's vineyard and at Guillaume Centoulh's stall on the road to Castelsarrasin, he had not actually believed it himself.

Raimond Centoulh (March 1244)
Finally, a kinsman of this Guillaume Centoulh, Raimond Centoulh, was interviewed.[206] He gave evidence against the wife of Arnaud Bos de Gontaud, of the Agenais, who repeated other doctrinal errors. She had told the deponent that she believed what the heretics taught, certainly, because 'wiser people than you and I believe it'.

In Chapter 5 we shall discuss some of the more incidental content of these depositions, details indicating that inquisitors were interested in recording not only that someone had believed in, encountered or aided Cathars and Waldensians, but also the ways in which such involvement in heresy might manifest itself.

---

[205] D22, fol. 31r–v.
[206] D22, fols. 31v–32v (exact date uncertain); DCBC, pp. 50–1.

5

Heresy: A Social and Cultural Life

Here we begin to piece together an impression of the impact of the Cathar and Waldensian heresies on everyday life in Quercy. To begin with we look into the question of the relationship between the family and heresy, examining some families in detail and drawing on the full range of evidence we have for them in order to suggest the scope and scale of heretical adherence in the sorts of families that played a part in Quercy's political and religious development by *c*.1240. First we observe some further families at relatively close quarters. They are interesting in terms of the devotional and secular networks of which they were part. They are not necessarily typical of some of the wider patterns describing heresy, the individual and the family in Quercy. Those will be explored later.

The Sectarian and the Family

Some 'heretical families'

The Pellegri are interesting for several reasons. Duvernoy identifies them as notables of Gourdon. They were already growing in significance in our period and Bulit describes how they continued to grow in importance in Gourdon right into the fourteenth century.[1] They seem to be among those families that had risen from more humble status, like the Grimoards; non-noble but significant nonetheless. They are also part of a set of only four families represented in Doat 21 by two or more people, of which all deponents admitted contact with the same sect and only that sect.

We know of four Pellegri at Gourdon in 1241–2, Pierre, Galtier, Guillaume and Raimond, and they were *credentes* of the Cathars. Pierre said that he had lost count of the number of times he had adored the heretics. He is unusual for Quercy in referring to the monthly ceremonial *apparellamentum*, at which he assisted twice, and he also served at two *consolamenta*. He had also given Cathars goods and had hosted them, including in his home at Gourdon.[2] Pierre was a highly significant *credens*, therefore. Galtier had also seen them

---

[1] DPC, pp. 32–3 and notes 72, 76, 84–5; Bulit, *Gourdon*, I, pp. 149–50, 159, 173, 192.
[2] D21, fol. 187r. On the ritual see Duvernoy, *Le catharisme II*, pp. 203–8.

frequently and often heard them preaching. He had been their messenger, brought them six *solidi* once, assisted at a *consolamentum* and is one of only a small set of deponents who refer to having received the heretics' 'kiss of peace'.[3] Guillaume gave them two small tunics and had eaten bread blessed by them, let them spend part of a night at his house, listened to them preach often and in various homes, and adored them many times.[4] Raimond had seen them often and adored them, held money and a book for them and was given a pair of gloves. He was sent to Constantinople for two years.[5] The Pellegri had a branch at Montpezat as well, where Huguette, wife of Arnaud Pellegri of Montpezat, was convicted for associating with *perfecti*.[6] They were Cathar partisans as a family. But they were unusual in this. Most families were associated with both sects, thereby undermining the concept of the 'Cathar family'.

The eight people of Montauban with the family name Foulcaut appeared before the inquisitors and confessed to frequent contact, spiritual and economic, with Cathars and Waldensians. Na Foulcaut had often encountered, adored and listened to the preaching of Cathars.[7] Etienne Foulcaut had had *perfecti* in his house and been involved in money-lending in this context.[8] Na Assaga, his wife, associated with Waldensians.[9] The family are untypical, however, because they had several members who were associated with *both* sects (an issue to which we shall return). Arnaud Foulcaut had listened to *perfecti* preach about the New Testament, entertained them in his house and performed services for them. He had also had Waldensians in his house to treat his brother Pierre-Raimond's illness, which Pierre-Raimond himself confirmed. They received the same sentence, two years at Constantinople.[10] Gaillarde, Arnaud's husband had said about Waldensians, but was likewise also close to the *perfecti* she and her husband also hosted.[11] Their daughter Poncia, wife of Durand Abit, had done just as her mother,[12] as had another daughter, Raimonde, except that she had never adored the *perfecti*.[13]

Like the Foulcault, the Carbonnel family of Montauban were involved with Cathars, Waldensians and sometimes both. There are no other families within which as many individuals appear to have admitted encounters with

---

3   D21, fol. 197v.
4   D21, fols. 186v–187r.
5   D21, fols. 192r–v, 211v.
6   D21, fol. 308r.
7   D21, fols. 271v–2r.
8   D21, fol. 267v.
9   D21, fols. 272v–3r.
10 D21, fol. 245r–v (Arnaud) and 245v (Pierre Raimond). I am heavily indebted to Peter Biller and John Arnold for their help in interpreting fol. 245r–v, *cf.* DPC, p. 153 note 258.
11 D21, fols. 245v–6r.
12 D21, fol. 272r.
13 D21, fols. 271v–2r.

both sects as the Carbonnel. In Chapter 4 we saw that in 1243 Guillaume Donadieu de Mazerac spoke of a *perfectus* called Bernard Carbonnel. But he was not referred to by the seven members of the Carbonnel family interviewed in 1241–2. However, Pierre Carbonnel senior admitted to eating and sleeping alongside Cathars. He had also given food and wine to Waldensians a very specific fifty times. He presumably meant lots of times; we can almost see him shrugging his shoulders when asked to be specific, with 'I do not know. Maybe fifty.' As well as listening to Waldensians preach he assisted them at their ritual supper and gave them meat and drink in his house.[14] This time we almost hear Pierre Seilan's voice: 'What did you feed them? Was it meat? ... ah, Waldensians then'.

The involvement of Pierre's kinsman Jacques Carbonnel included assisting at a disputation between Cathars and Waldensians.[15] More will be said about debates between the sects below. Guillaume Carbonnel had once been on a boat with *perfecti*, he admitted, but had had Waldensians in a house belonging to himself and a brother.[16] Na Carbonnel had seen many Waldensians and given them food in her youth without knowing they were heretics, but she had also seen a *perfectus*.[17] Guillemette, wife of Pierre Carbonnel, had had Waldensians preaching in her house and moved otherwise in their confessional circle.[18] Raimond Carbonnel gave Waldensians four pennies.[19] Gausbert Carbonnel had seen *perfecti* and *perfectae*, helping them once in finding someone they were looking for.[20]

It should be noted, however, that much of the activity above is low-level and sometimes pragmatic and circumstantial, and that substantial engagement with both sects by one person is rare. In other words, the overwhelming majority of individuals in Quercy are recorded as having involvement with *either* Cathars *or* Waldensians, but not both. In the case of the Carbonnel, four out of seven members are recorded as associating with both sects, but Guillemette, Raimond and Gausbert Carbonnel are more typical of individuals in Quercy, where we find that individuals, not families, were sectarian. In contrast with the observations of Anne Brenon and others for Languedoc more widely that heresy rather 'ran in the family', families in Quercy did not identify as a group with any specific set of beliefs. This will be returned to and demonstrated in a quantitative sense shortly. Furthermore, the Carbonnel did not only mix with both sects but were also great patrons of the Francis-

---

14 D21, fols. 255v–6r.
15 D21, fol. 234r–v.
16 D21, fol. 254v.
17 D21, fol. 269v.
18 D21, fol. 244r.
19 D21, fol. 234r.
20 D21, fols. 254v–5r.

cans at Montauban.[21] However, their relatives the Amiel family, who actually founded the convent, do not appear in documentation for heresy at all. 'Heretical' activity was not necessarily the central devotional concern of families with heretical members, in other words.

The de Jean family, originating in the Cahorsain, contained one member, Péronne of Gourdon, who mixed with both sects, although favouring Waldensians more, having sheltered Pierre de Vals for eight days and done likewise for a Waldensian woman called Guiraude.[22] She is the only example of mixed adherence. Péronne and her husband Raimond de Jean had given Cathars wine, bread and nuts. They had a branch at Montauban, where Arnaud de Jean-Davy was a Waldensian adherent.[23] But we have also noted their rise at Cahors at the expense of the episcopacy, beginning in 1214 when Bishop Guillaume ceded the land on which they founded Les Juniès, and that from 1237/8 they were openly at war with their bishop. However, even though the bishop numbered the de Jean among other rebellious families he called 'heretics' in his legitimist alliance with the ordinary people (*minores*), discussed in Chapter 3, there is no evidence that they actually supported either of the two sects at Cahors itself. Furthermore, they are notable also as patrons of friars at Cahors from 1226, just as the de Carbonnel were at Montauban. This 'new money' family was resident in three of the most important towns in Quercy, therefore, but opposing very different aspects of ecclesiastical hegemony in each. This family was as much shaped by urban as by confessional identity.

In Chapter 2 we encountered the de la Roque family. They first emerged as knights of Gourdon in the early twelfth century and by the time of the Albigensian crusade had acquired estates also in the Limousin, and operated in alliance with Obazine. Aimeric, Gaillard and Hugues de la Roque signed the 1233 peace charter, like the de Jean, and Hugues, Pons and Hernando were among those signing an oath of loyalty to the crown in 1243 on behalf of Montauban.[24] So we see that their 'orthodox' interests spanned Quercy. Nonetheless, the family were infamously associated with Catharism rather than Catholicism by the 1240s, because along with the de Goulême they protected the priory of women at Linars who were in fact *perfectae*. The failure of Linars' thirteenth-century protectors is a great contrast to their earlier, extensive role in promoting orthodox religiosity and co-operating with the bishop in 1233. Furthermore, three members were convicted concerning Catharism at Gourdon. Of these, En Roques himself was an extremely prominent *credens* (he and his wife Ricarde were discussed in Chapter 4). Also at Gourdon, Adémar

---

21 See above, pp. 000–00.
22 D21, fols. 194v, 203v.
23 D21, fol. 282r.
24 Teulet, *Layettes*, II, 501 (no. 3056), 502a–b (no. 3059).

de la Roque-de Villeneuve attested that his mother had been consoled and that he himself had had extensive devotional contact with the Cathar sect.[25]

Doat 21 also informs us of a branch of the family at Montcuq, where Jean de la Roque had admitted to minor offences committed while young.[26] Bertrand de la Roque-de Montcuq had been involved more seriously. He saw and adored heretics in the house of Arnaud de Primes (this is one of a very few records of Montcuq *credentes* implicating each other). He was a key member of two of the most important heretical networks extending beyond Montcuq, involving the lords of Caussade and the Cathar heresiarch Vigouroux de la Bacone.[27] Bertrand had received in his house the *perfecti* Guillaume de Caussade and his brother Guiraud, and had sent heretics to Vigouroux, probably to Castelmoron, downstream from Montcuq, where we know that he had a house.[28] Furthermore, Bertrand saw Vigouroux at Moissac and was asked by him to escort him somewhere, and he saw other *perfecti* at Vaillac, in the Gourdon area. Bertrand also confessed 'to everything that had been said against him at Mercuès' and other places (although we have no record of what these accusations were). In Chapter 4 we also noted that Arnaud de la Roque, a priest of Almont, associated with *perfecti*.[29] We have a Pierre Raimond de la Roque in 'P. R. Boca' of Montauban (if Duvernoy is correct that this could be rendered 'Roca').[30] More certainly, at Montauban Guiraude de la Roque admitted listening to Waldensians preach, probably in the house of Bernarde Mela.[31] So, here we have a family straddling towns but with a relatively uniform confessional make-up, the latter admission being the only evidence that associates it with Waldensians. So, on one level, the de la Roque again seem like a 'Cathar family' by the 1240s. But they also undermine the traditional understanding of why individuals or families took to heresy: the de la Roque certainly did not emerge out of any monastic malaise.

Like the de la Roque, the d'Arcambal were investigated in both episcopal and inquisitorial courts. Arcambal is just west of Cahors and in the early twelfth century the family provided knights at Gourdon and founded the abbey of Belleperche, as noted above. During the Albigensian crusade Raimond d'Arcambal served de Montfort as a messenger, and he was a signatory to the Rocamadour charter in 1233. We have also noted that the family was among the bishop's creditors and involved in the civil strife at Cahors, and that Raimond would be excommunicated. That was the branch at Cahors. At Gourdon, the d'Arcambal were at odds with the clergy in a different way.

---

25 D21, fols. 192r, 205v.
26 D21, fol. 22v.
27 D21, fols. 219r–v, 226v; DPC, pp. 100–1 and note 186, 116–17.
28 D21, fol. 219r–v; Taylor, *Heresy*, pp. 28–9, 232.
29 D21, fol. 310r.
30 D21, fols. 231v–2r; DPC, pp. 128–9 and note c.
31 D21, fol. 273r.

Pons d'Arcambal[32] and his wife Hélie[33] were punished for having received Cathars in their home. Pons could not remember how many times he had adored them and eaten food blessed by them.[34] Hélie had listened to them preach and adored them around seven times, she is recorded as having said.[35] Finally, Gautier d'Arcambal of Montauban was sent to Constantinople for five years because of very extensive involvement with Cathars, believing in salvation through them and hosting a debate between the heretical sects in his home.[36]

Among Montauban's consuls in *c*.1241, the family names Lartigue, Cos and Antéjac are most heavily represented, none of them with heretical members. We know a little about the latter. A member of this family, lords of modern Saint-Martin d'Antéjac, provided Cahors with its bishop in 1236–7, as we have seen. In other words, Montauban was a town in which notable families might be entirely 'orthodox'. Yet this generalisation can be applied to the Antéjac family only at Cahors and Montauban. When the inquisition visited Almont in 1242, the *castrum* closest to the Antéjac castle, no fewer than four of the mere twenty-three people convicted were of this family.[37] Again, heretical activity did not run in the family, but is best understood as a characteristic of a certain family in a certain town.

This best describes the de la Mothe also, whose members, Jörg Feuchter notes, all disappear from the consulate of Montauban in 1241.[38] Surely ranking highest in the hierarchy of families most closely associated with Catharism, by the 1240s they operated in various secular devotional contexts in different places. Guillaume de la Mothe was prior of the abbey of Saint-Pierre-des-Cuisines in 1213, when he arbitrated in a dispute at the abbey of Moissac.[39] Possibly the same Guillaume witnessed an accord between Raimond of Toulouse and the abbot of Montauban in 1231.[40] He was possibly also the 'G.' de la Mothe who witnessed a donation to Lizac, a dependency of Moissac, in 1202,[41] although a 'Guiraud' de la Mothe had witnessed a donation of revenues to the house in 1170.[42] We saw that a Hugues de la Mothe rode with Bernard de Cazenac in 1217, so he was subversive if not necessarily

---

32 D21, fols. 192r, 202v.
33 D21, fol. 189r.
34 D21, fol. 215r.
35 D21, fol. 189r.
36 D21, fols. 195v, 196v–7r.
37 D21, fols. 226v–7v.
38 Feuchter, 'Le pouvoir de l'inquisition'.
39 AD Tarn-et-Garonne, G. liasse 662. Documents in this bundle are not individually catalogued.
40 Teulet, *Layettes*, II, 223b, no. 2159.
41 AD Tarn-et-Garonne, G. liasse 662.
42 AD Tarn-et-Garonne, G. liasse 692.

'heretical'. He may even have been the Hugues de la Mothe who signed for the town of Cahors in 1233. These events took place during the period in which the family contained at least four *perfecti*. So even the de la Mothe, with a minimum of four *perfecti* and many *credentes*, was neither a 'Cathar family' nor even 'heretical'.

So, some families appear to have reacted in the matter of heresy differently in different towns. Two points emerge from this. Firstly, some families were neither 'heretical' nor 'orthodox', and we should stress this point because the nature of the record must hide others. In *c.*1240 we essentially have records that 'notice' heretical activity. It was what the inquisitor was looking for, after all. His record privileges those that were associated with heresy, even those who merely 'saw' heretics and did not report it. While it seems likely that there were very few people in any given town who had never even 'seen' a heretic – when they were evidently ubiquitous in the towns in question by *c.*1240 – in most places we also have no comparable accounts of the 'ordinary' activity and belief that guilty people might, in addition, have been engaged in. There is every possibility that in some families members engaged in orthodox activity that was as heartfelt and genuine as any other religious form, although families that *demonstrably* straddle both the 'orthodox' and 'heretical' spheres are relatively few. In itself this is an apparent indication of declining orthodox religiosity, as we have noted, and also the result of us having relatively few documents that throw light on secular orthodox activity. But there are some families involved in both spheres, for example the Carbonnel, de Jean, de la Roque, d'Arcambal, de la Mothe and Antéjac.

Secondly, as suggested, a family's confessional complexion could vary greatly from town to town but could equally be mixed within a single town, as, for example, in the cases of the Foucault, Carbonnel, de Jean and de la Roque. We should also note that families with members at Cahors were only engaged in orthodox activity there. In the first place, heretical activity was more likely to be noticed in towns which were full of the staff of the cathedral clergy. Secondly, as I hope to demonstrate in the case of Quercy, heresy could only really take root where lords of towns allowed it to, which could not take place in episcopal towns. Otherwise, 'heresy' as uncovered in 1241–2 in the northern Languedoc had apparently existed alongside a relatively vibrant and apparently ubiquitous Catholicism. Even though the legitimacy of some clerical manifestations may have been contested, such as episcopal power in the town of Cahors and undoubtedly that of Pierre Seilan, open and overt anti-clericalism was apparently not the norm.

Now we return to the limitation of models in which the 'heretical' individual is shaped by the family unit.

The significance of heresy in the family

Table 1 represents Jean Duvernoy's statistics using Pierre Seilan's register for individuals recorded as adhering to Catharism and Waldensianism at

Montauban and Gourdon,[43] the two most significant towns in Quercy in terms of heretical activity, and in fact the only two from which the sample size is big enough for us to observe quantitative patterns.

Table 1. Duvernoy's statistics for individuals adhering to Catharism and Waldensianism at Montauban and Gourdon.

	Cathar	*% of total*	*Waldensian*	*% of total*	*Mixed*	*% of total*
Montauban (246 people)	81	32.9	130	52.8	35	14.2
Gourdon (131 people)	87	66.4	30	22.9	14	10.6

These figures indicate that, with the notable exception of Peter Biller, historians have understated the scale and significance of the Waldensian presence, particularly in the south of the county, where far more deponents were found guilty of association with Waldensians than with Cathars. But they also demonstrate that, given this high profile for Waldensians, a remarkably small percentage of deponents admitted to or were found guilty of contact with *both* sects.

This is significant in addressing a historiographical view noted in Chapter 1, that the specifics of heresy were not what mattered to the adherent, and that heresy had more of a sociological function, binding individuals to an otherwise arbitrarily constructed 'community', fulfilling vague 'needs' not fully met by the Catholic clergy. Sociological explanations for 'heresy' suggest a vast grey area where the orthodoxies of the Catholic polemicists and the dualist metanarrative overlapped and were thus obscured. As suggested, this cannot be demonstrated because we do not have 'negative depositions' or otherwise routinely recorded accounts of non-criminal belief and activity of deponents that we would need to explore this model.

However, in Quercy we *can* compare two confessional affiliations and gauge the extent of the overlap, because we have quantitative data for both Cathar and Waldensian adherence. Using this, we find the very opposite of a grey area or passive 'overlapping'. We find that beliefs were contested and weighed up against each other, and that individuals selected between them. This rather suggests that they may have done the same in the case of orthodox teachings.

My own figures for 'mixed' contact from the same data as Duvernoy's are in fact a little higher: 17% at Montauban and 16% at Gourdon. This indicates that Duvernoy has read evidence for some individuals more confidently than

---

[43] DPC, p. 25.

I have in allying them with one sect or another. This is not an exact science. The statistics for Montauban have already been revised once by Duvernoy since 1990, and Feuchter agrees with his 246 but finds the inquest of 1241–2 in its entirety to contain the names of 647 deponents, compared with Duvernoy's 622.[44]

The discrepancy between Duvernoy's figures and my own is also because in some cases adherents of one sect appear to have had a merely pragmatic relationship with another. At Beaucaire, for example, Guillaume de Saint-Michel believed Waldensians to be good men and believed what they said, considering himself *credens Valdensium*, and had given them shoes, but he had also had financial dealings with Cathars.[45] Such contact indicates tolerance and familiarity with both sects but not faith or even serious consideration of both. It seems likely that Duvernoy has categorised Guillaume as associated only with Waldensians. However, for their own purposes the inquisitors considered them as associating with both sects. In order to be as generous as possible to the 'grey area' school in challenging it, I have done likewise in allocating them to categories.

Certainly, Duvernoy's statistics for Cathar-only adherence must include such deponents as Ricarde, married to Etienne Gautier, who sheltered *perfecti* as well as listening to them, sending them grain, bread and wine and believing them to be 'the best people in the World'. She had simply 'seen' a Waldensian.[46] Duvernoy probably also included as an adherent of only one sect Pierre Bacou of Montauban, one of the Waldensians' most active and devoted followers, who only once encountered Cathars and then in the context of aiding the Waldensians in a debate with them.[47] He has a counterpart, Gautier d'Arcambal of Gourdon, who encountered Waldensians only in a dispute in his own house in which he was supporting the Cathars, in whose hands he wished to die.[48] Ricarde, Pierre and Gautier were real partisans, in other words. But inquisitors considered them guilty of associating with *both* sects – 'seeing' heretics without reporting them being a crime in itself – and I have likewise categorised their association as 'mixed'. Yet, even stretching the definition of the 'mixed' category to include such cases, the figure still remains low, well below one-in-five. If devotional alternatives thrived with little distinction being made between confessional forms in the minds of the

---

[44] J. Duvernoy, 'Les origines du movement vaudois', *Heresis* 13/14 (1990), pp. 173–98 (pp. 188–9); Feuchter, 'Le pouvoir de l'inquisition', p. 239 (Montauban) and 'Pierre Sellan', p. 51 (Quercy more widely).

[45] D21, fol. 225r–v. This is a very rare example of the term *credens* being used to describe a Waldensian adherent.

[46] D21, fols. 194v, 203v.

[47] D21, fol. 231r–v.

[48] D21, fols. 195v, 196v–7r.

laity, we should expect to find far more depositions indicating at least *some* contact with *both* sects than we do.

Furthermore, we have an indication in some instances of *why* it was that some people selected one heretical form over the other, evidence that by 1241 people chose consciously and deliberately between them on the basis of what they taught. Thus we may suggest that they also distinguished between 'heresy' and 'orthodoxy' more clearly than some historiographical models suggest. This evidence will be discussed in Chapter 6. But first we need to address statistically another historiographical suggestion, that confessional adherence was not chosen but 'ran in families'.

The pattern of individual sectarianism that we have noted is even more striking when we consider it in relation to the evidence for the heretical preferences of whole families. Far from being the source of heretical identity, families appear pluralist in confessional identity, even though their constituent members were not (Table 2).

Table 2. Percentage of families[49] associated with one or both sects at Montauban and Gourdon.

	Cathar	% of total	Waldensian	% of total	Mixed	% of total
Montauban (34 families)	5	14.7	7	20.6	22	64.7
Gourdon (24 families)	8	33.3	2	8.3	14	58.3

We can see that the proportion of families with 'mixed' adherence is far higher than it was for individuals. In the fifty-eight cases where we have depositional and other evidence for two or more members of a quercinois family in the period from *c*.1200 to 1242, only in twenty-two did all deponents admit contact with the same sect and only that sect. Furthermore, within this set we have twenty-five families represented by three or more people. Of these, only in four did all members admit to involvement with the same sect as each other. They are the de Gourdon (Cathars),[50] the Sabatier (Waldensians),[51] the de Fages-de-Peyrilles (Cathars) and the Pellegri (Cathars).[52]

The 'Cathar family', supposedly a characteristic of Languedoc, is scarcely to be found in Quercy. While Brenon asserts for the Toulousain that '(o)ne was born a Cathar just as one's neighbour might be born a Catholic – the family's religious options were this conditioning, even if this did not rule out the

---

[49] As represented by more than one member in the same town.
[50] References throughout.
[51] D21, fol. 240r.
[52] D21, fols. 186v–187r, 192r–v, 197r, 211v.

possibility of later divergence', and sees as typical 'whole families entering the Cathar church *en bloc*, or virtually so',[53] in Quercy confessional distinctions did not matter as much within families as they did to their component individuals. Even in the *perfecta* Jeanne d'Avignon's family, Arnaud d'Avignon and Raimonde his wife called a Waldensian doctor to see their son and had Waldensians in Jeanne's own house at other times, considering them to be good people. Indeed, Raimonde's deposition does not even mention 'heretics'.[54] Like others, she had strong confessional preferences. Such people are most typical of people constituting members of 'heretical' families, and such families typically contained people with a range of devotional preferences.

In another example, Guillaume Guiraud senior[55] and his *credens* son, also called Guillaume,[56] had had *perfecti* in their home. They were taken there by the son, who had been sent to seek out other *credentes* to attend them. But they were merely 'found there' by the father, who does not seem to have been involved further in the heresy except that he borrowed money from *perfecti* – fifty *solidi* – and had listened to their preaching. The father had only been a patron of the Waldensians, as had another Guillaume Guiraud, son of Hugues Guiraud, who mentioned only that sect, Waldensian doctors having treated his illness in exchange for goods,[57] another family member, Etienne.[58]

Another example of confessional ambivalence is that of the de Goulême, lords also of Milhac and Concorès, who were tried at Gourdon. In spite of having produced the infamous *perfectus* Raoul 'the scabby', and allowing the abbey under their protection and that of the de la Roque at Linars to become infested by *perfectae*,[59] of the nine members sentenced in 1241, Gaillarde, Aladaïs and Guillemette (wife of Aimeric de Goulême-de Milhac) consulted and patronised an infamous Waldensian, Pierre de Vals.[60] Raimonde, Gaillarde and Pierre were likewise committed to his sect.[61] Indeed, of those tried, only Guiraud and Na Péronne were Cathar adherents.[62] As in the case of Jeanne d'Avignon, even *perfecti* did not always succeed in 'converting' their family *en masse*.

These and most families were apparently relaxed or ambivalent about confessional allegiance. However, if there are very few specifically 'Cathar' or 'Waldensian' families, there are plenty that seemed 'heretical' to the inquisi-

---

53 Brenon, 'Catharism in the family', pp. 296, 301.
54 D21, fol. 254v.
55 D21, fols. 229v–30r.
56 D21, fol. 230r.
57 D21, fol. 230r.
58 D21, fol. 230r.
59 D23, fols. 7v–8r.
60 D21, fols. 206v–207r, 211v, 213r.
61 D21, fols. 192v, 193v, 193v–4r, 206v, 212v.
62 D21, fols. 188v–9r, 191v–4r, 213v.

tors, with several members heavily involved in doctrinal dissent and activity or supporting or concealing it.

An important case study is the Bonald family of Gourdon. Bernard Bonald had met both Pierre de Vals – and through this contact had believed it wrong to take oaths – and the *perfectus* Touzet de Noguès. He had had the latter in his house, but disputed what he said and personally recommended the Waldensian sect.[63] So how had he been close enough to Touzet to host him and yet not be an adherent? Very possibly it was through Guillaume Bonald, an entirely convinced Cathar adherent, both fervent and educated, who had actively embraced both the form and the content of their teachings. He had read the gospels in the vernacular many times, been present and assisted at ceremonies and been involved in gift exchanges with them, and he had also introduced people to them. Yet he too had contact with Waldensians. The structure of his deposition implies that they were perhaps the first sect he was attracted to.[64] Far from doctrine being unimportant to the Bonalds, it was fundamental and life-changing, but they did not follow each other into a vaguely defined 'heresy'; they were committed sectarians.

The Inquisitors' Interest in Men, Women and Children

Having explored some of the evidence in a prosopographical sense, we can turn to addressing the evidence thematically, identifying the generalities in which the inquisitors were interested in terms of questions they seem to have asked and the evidence they chose to record.

Gendered categories

Notable in Bernard de Caux's register is evidence that questions were asked about women as a 'type' of *credens* and in relation to male defendants. Often they are described as 'X, wife of Y', as in the case of Poncia, wife of the very active Waldensian adherent Pierre Bacou,[65] and Ricarde, wife of Etienne Gautier, who was far more active in the heresy than her husband.[66] Likewise, women are often 'X daughter of Z' , as in the case of a *perfecta*, Raimonde, recorded as being the daughter of Guillaume de Saint-Vim and as having been in her father's house with Unaude, another *perfecta*, described as the daughter of En Troga. We can almost hear the inquisitorial staff's 'Their fathers should be ashamed of them!'

These women do not appear, on the face of it, to have been accorded the kind of independent legal and social status that historians assert for women

---

[63] D21, fol. 201r.
[64] D21, fol. 187r–v.
[65] D21, fols. 248v–49r.
[66] D21, fols. 194v, 203v.

in Languedoc. However, this was a record made by outsiders, and so it is quite possible that the inquisitors imposed this form of identification, in part to understand the structure of particular families. Furthermore, if inquisitors were interested in women as part of families, men too are sometimes also described as being someone's son, nephew, and so on.

However, inquisitors were sometimes interested in the *activity* of women as distinct from that of men, often soliciting answers that 'grouped' women. Guiraud Gaillard was induced to talk about the *perfecta* Raimonde de Cavelsaut and her *socia*, and his sister, Na Raials, who wanted to return to the heresy. He also implicated Na Pros de Cavalsaut, mother of Raimonde, saying that he saw the *perfecta* in her house. Several of the other women there adored the heretic: Na Pros herself, Petrona Marigote and Na Hélis. One of the latest accounts of these women together is at the meeting with Vigouroux de la Bacone in 1228 or the early 1230s.[67] We hear that Petrona de Cahors and Na Pros de Cavelsaut had the *perfecta* Raimonde de Cahors in their homes at Castelsarrasin, and they awaited Aurimonde de Serra who was consoled in *c*.1240 by the *perfectus* Guillaume Bernard.[68] In the final item of Guillaume Faure's deposition he gives an account of a heretical meeting, listing *credentes* present. He appears to have been asked to identify first the men, whose names appear as a list, and then the woman, because the record adds 'Item, he saw there his own sister Guiraude, and (Na) Compta and (Na) Pros de Cavelsaut'.[69]

In terms of what it was that the women recorded actually *did*, female *credentes* do not emerge as having had a specifically gendered relationship with heretics. It may be that we read too much into 'women only' meetings even by observing them; there are many meetings at which only men are recorded, and women hosted mixed and all-male meetings. Na Pros de Cavelsaut, among other women, did so,[70] and Na Pana de Guia had *perfecti* disputing with Waldensians in her house.[71] Indeed, in terms of hosting *perfecti* women could be very prominent. Arnaud Bertrand saw Waldensians as well as Cathars at the house of Guillemassa of Montcuq.[72] Her servant, Alazaïs, had seen as many as twenty heretics there many times, and she had prepared and served them food.[73]

Women appear to have had a particular fondness for the Waldensian doctor Pierre de Vals, mentioning him far more than men do. At Gourdon,

---

[67] D22, fol. 19r–v.

[68] D22, fols. 17r–v. 17v and 25r.

[69] D22, fol. 10r.

[70] D22, fols. 7v, 17r–v, 17v, 20r, 24v, 28v.

[71] D21, fol. 194v, 203v.

[72] D21, fol. 225r–v. Guillaume-Bernard d'En Arces' is the first reference to her: D21, fol. 223r.

[73] D21, fol. 224r.

Péronne, wife of Raimond de Jean, told the inquisition that she had sheltered him for eight days and given him food and other goods.[74] Guillemette,
wife of Gausbert Gaut, heard him preach and sent him a flask of wine.[75]
We have noted that Bertranda and Guillemette de Braulès encountered him
several times and believed him to be a good man.[76] Gaillarde de Goulême
also patronised Pierre,[77] as did Aladaïs de Goulême[78] and Guillemette, wife
of Aimeric de Goulême-de Milhac, who had consulted him over an illness.[79]
But Na Guia's adulation has the ring of a special fondness. She 'loved him
like an angel from God'.[80]

Of the two sexes it does seem to have been the case that it was primarily
men who accompanied heretics on their journeys, although we do know that
a *ductrix* (female 'leader', in the sense of chaperone) of heretics, Hartemanda
de Balenx, did so along the Lot between the Agenais and Quercy.[81] But otherwise men and women were responsible for hosting, feeding and sheltering
heretics, holding meetings and debates in their houses, being consoled and
cured by them and assisting Cathars in their ceremonies. Indeed, it is important to note that, while *perfectae* were not allowed to perform *consolamenta*
except in direst need, there is no evidence that women were not welcome
at the ceremony. They often played an assisting role. Raimonde, widow of
Raoul de Goulême, was one of several women who assisted at her husband's
consolamentum. But women need not be relatives to play a role. Guillemette
de Bouloc assisted in the ritual performed for an unnamed man she may not
even have known. But none of this is to suggest that Cathars were gender-
blind when it came to their supporters any more than inquisitors were.
Cathar loathing of pregnancy was misogynistic. Guillemette had once been
encouraged to adore heretics by a woman but in practice was not allowed
to because she was pregnant. This had not undermined her faith in them
though; she had later adored many of them and had eventually assisted at
the *consolamentum* of a sick man.[82]

In terms of the *perfectae* of Quercy themselves, we can note that their lives
were different from those of Cathar men in three respects; we do not hear
of them performing *consolamenta* in Quercy; they did not preach outdoors
or 'publicly' as far as we can see; and they are very often noted as living
in single-sex houses. However, we should not over-stress the divergence of
these patterns. When it comes to evidence for the *consolamenta*, it is a striking

---

74 D21, fols. 194v, 203v.
75 D21, fol. 212v.
76 D21, fol. 203v.
77 D21, fols. 206v–207r.
78 D21, fol. 211v.
79 D21, fol. 213r.
80 D21, fols. 194v, 203v.
81 D21, fols. 216r, 219v; Taylor, 'Authority and the Cathar heresy', p. 166.
82 D21, fol. 296r–v.

fact of the Quercy evidence that it is rarely clear exactly who *did* perform the ceremony. Typically we are told who was consoled, but not the heretics undertaking this. Sometimes it can be deduced from the names of *perfecti* listed as being present, but female *perfectae* are sometimes listed too. This is not to suggest that women did perform it, rather to note that inquisitors do not seem particularly interested in collecting examples of which *perfecti* did so. As such, I do not think that the Quercy evidence can be used as evidence that the ritual was a male preserve either. We know that in direst need – for example, at Montségur in 1244, when the dead and dying were literally piling up – women did perform this sacrament, and so we should keep the possibility open that at some point during the crusade this may also have happened.

Some flexibility towards the evidence is needed in terms of public preaching also. It would not be safe to assume that women spoke in the outdoor and public meetings, with their voices being silenced by the non-gender specific *'perfecti'*. Likewise, to imagine a *perfecta* speaking up in a debate with a priest or a Waldensian is appealing, but there is no evidence for it. But much depends what we consider 'public' preaching. Some form of preaching – that is to say, the communication of teachings – surely formed an important part of all-female meetings. We shall see in the case of the heretical hostess Guillemassa that even female *credentes* taught errors to other people, so *perfectae* surely did. Indeed, we have at least one reference to people hearing *perfectae* preach in the case of Jeanne d'Avignon (below). But these were not sealed meetings in the sense that men kept away from them. Sometimes it is through the testimony of men who 'saw' these gatherings that we know about them in the first place. But male Cathars do seem to have had a more visible presence, and also to have travelled more, almost always with their *socii*. They are more often described as 'arriving' in places and being encountered 'on the road'. In contrast, women are most often encountered in houses.

In terms of domestic arrangements, male and female Cathars usually lived differently. Residences for *perfectae* were of four types. Raimonde de Cavelsaut remained living in her parents' home after being consoled, which we do not have examples of in the case of men. In other types of arrangement women lived separately from men. Sometimes *perfectae* lived with female *credentes*. Pros de Cavelsaut's house, for example, was used as a covert residence for *perfectae*, and her servant Passiona and friends worked in their service.[83] We have evidence for houses exclusively run by Cathar women: rural monastic houses that had been taken over by them, and houses established in the midst of urban communities, like those we know of at Villemur in which the de la Mothe women of Montauban and the Targuiers of Castelsarrasin were raised

---

[83] D22, fols. 7v, 17r–v, 17v, 20r, 24v, 28v.

as *perfectae*.[84] Certainly, Cathar men separated from their wives, and in this context we can perhaps understand a curious reference. Guillaume Faure de Pechermer said that the socially prominent *perfecti* Guillaume de Cavelsaut and Raimond Grimoard of Castelsarrasin both had wives at Gontaud (Lot-et-Garonne), perhaps meaning that women sometimes lived together as deserted wives, but not as *perfectae*.

At Montauban itself we have evidence for two houses run by a particularly well-attested *perfecta*, Jeanne d'Avignon. She was given her house by Arnaud de Sapiac, at his own admission and for which she rewarded him. From Arnaude de la Mothe we hear that this was before 1226.[85] But Gausbert Sicard de Courande provided her with another residence and told Pierre Seilan that it had been in some way consecrated.[86] He claimed that for his generosity he was sent twenty *solidi* and his wife was sent wine. He also bought provisions for the women.[87] It was probably at one of these houses that Pierre de la Pomarède was employed for three weeks.[88] Benoît 'the joker' (*joculator*) of Montauban worked in Jeanne's vineyard and once spied Bernard de la Mothe and others *perfecti* there.[89] Raimonde Salinier often sold Jeanne bread, bought other food for her, had her pray for her and heard her preach.[90] In her own home Guillemette de Sapiac adored Jeanne and her *sociae* many times.[91] Na Maraude and Dulcia de Lamothe also mention her.[92] Jeanne herself was reconciled with the orthodox faith after 1229.[93]

Where we have a record of the fact that Péronne, wife of Raimond de Jean, told the inquisition at Gourdon that she had sheltered a Waldensian woman, Guiraude,[94] this is extremely unusual, in that the Waldensian is named. We have hardly any named Waldensians in Quercy at all, Pierre de Vals being the only other example. But we do also have the odd reference to *houses* of Waldensian women, specifically ones let to them by Na Algartz at Montcuq and Bernarde Fabrissa at Beaucaire,[95] as well as to Waldensian houses more generally, such as one at Montauban.[96] But groups of women may have been

---

[84] See Taylor, *Heresy*, pp. 181–2, 233.

[85] D21, fol. 230v; D23, fol. 7r; DPC, pp. 126–7 note 232.

[86] It was 'hereticata ... pro hereticis mulieribus': D21, fol. 231r; DPC, pp. 126–7 note 233. On this supposed ritual, see p. 000 below.

[87] D21, fol. 231r.

[88] D22, fols. 260v–1r.

[89] D21, fols. 266v–7r.

[90] D21, fols. 240r–1r; Taylor, *Heresy*, p. 237.

[91] D21, fols. 240v–1r; Taylor, *Heresy*, p. 237.

[92] D21, fols. 276v, 277r.

[93] D23, fol. 262r; DPC, p. 127 note 232.

[94] D21, fols. 194v, 203v.

[95] D21, fols. 219r, 228r–v, and see Biller, 'The preaching of Waldensian sisters', pp. 134–7, 155, 156.

[96] D21, fol. 242r.

hidden by the non-gender specific 'Valdenses' in the way that groups of *perfectae* were not.[97]

Childhood

In most cases, we do not know at what stage people were hereticated, so the extent of the phenomenon of childhood *consolamenta* is unclear, and even more so the extent to which children were involved in the choice to devote their lives to the sect. Arnaude and Péronne de la Mothe, as we know, were separated from their siblings as children and went to live in Villemur, and there were consoled. We do not gain an impression of how Arnaude felt about this process or exactly how old they were. But Pétronille de Pierre-Etienne, also of Montauban, said that she was consoled at around twelve years old, and had believed in the Cathar faith at that age.[98] Sicard de Lunel had told the inquisition that Gausbert de Cours's daughter, Bertrande, expressed her wish to become a *perfecta* and left her home with himself and other *perfecti*, and that she did this with her father's blessing and with money she might otherwise have received as a dowry. The father's involvement and the un-married status of Bernarde do give the impression that she was young herself.[99]

There was a point before which children were not expected to participate in sectarian activity, or it was recognised that it was not appropriate to involve them, as is implied also in the objections of dualists and other 'heretics' to infant baptism: Guiraud Gaillard observed that on one occasion Etienne Sanche and his wife Raimonde had adored heretics, but that their little girl was too small to do so.[100] In a very touching story, but one that hints that unconsenting children might become involved with heresy in any case, Guillemette de Sapiac stated that she had been raised by her *perfecta* aunt who had dressed her up in a little heretic outfit for a couple of years, even though Guillemette does not appear to have received the *consolamentum*.[101] We also have evidence of juvenile education in heresy. Jacques Carbonnel, we hear, attended Waldensian schools and read with them aged about twelve. He also assisted at their Maundy Thursday ritual celebration of the Last Supper.[102]

Other children were put into the service of the heretics. Jean del Pradel of Montauban said that when he was about ten years old he took bread, fruit and other food to *perfecti*.[103] Hugues du Port had taken bread to Waldensians on his mother's behalf many times as a child, and he had lived with them at

---

[97] Biller, 'Preaching', pp. 129–30, 130.

[98] D21, fol. 244v.

[99] See above, p. 000.

[100] D22, fol. 15r.

[101] D21, fols. 240v–1r; DPC, pp. 144–5 note 248.

[102] D21, fol. 234r–v.

[103] D21, fols. 251v–2r.

Saint-Antonin for two months too.[104] Raimond Ache had spent five days with heretics as a child and ran errands for them, including for his mother after she became a *perfecta*, buying food with money she sent him.[105] Gaillard d'En Arces was only around twelve when he accompanied travelling heretics with Hartemanda de Balenx.[106] Raimond Hugues acted as a Waldensian's guide when he was about ten years old and remained devoted to the sect, through which 'one could be saved'.[107] It was apparently in the context of running errands for heretics that most childhood exposure to the two sects took place, although deponents perhaps felt it the most innocent way to admit their early heretical activity, attempting to downplay its significance.

Economic Life and Well-being

Brief though the records in Doat 21 are, they give us a good deal of information about many other types of economic activity engaged in by heretics and their believers. Like orthodox renouncers, the Cathar *perfecti* did not own personal property but held what they had collectively. Evidence for the nature of this commonwealth most often refers to practicalities, to food and clothing. But this need not imply near-destitution or constant begging. While, unlike monks, Cathars and Waldensians did not amass country estates and objects of beauty, we have seen that they nonetheless owned and rented property in towns, and we shall observe further evidence that they – in particular the *perfecti* – received, held and borrowed money and paid for services.

Where did these resources come from? Unlike their Cistercian neighbours, they did not invest in farming, in other forms of production or in commerce. In spite of references to them weaving in other regions, in Quercy they did not even weave their own cloth; Raimond 'the weaver',[108] Guiraude, wife of Bernard Manhe,[109] and a Cahorsin weaver of Moissac apparently did that.[110] The Cathar treasury can in fact be accounted for by confessions of which the following are very typical: Pierre de Lanes gave *perfectae* a gift of five *solidi*;[111] Bernard Estève gave twelve *denari* (pennies) to some of them, and to another three *solidi* to buy shoes;[112] Raimond Allègre lent them money.[113] In other words, they do not seem to have generated income and were not

---

104 D21, fol. 256r–v.
105 D21, fol. 289r–v; DPC, pp. 226–9.
106 D21, fol. 219v; DPC, pp. 106–7.
107 D21, fol. 255r; DPC, pp. 168–9.
108 D21, fols 244v–5r
109 D21, fol. 291r.
110 D21, fol. 291r.
111 D21, fol. 231r.
112 D21, fol. 290r.
113 D21 fol. 214r.

self-supporting through their own activity, but were economically dependent on their supporters, including absorbing whatever property initiates brought with them into the movement. Even where we find Cathars handing over money it takes the form of loans and payments for services. Whereas Waldensians received money likewise from supporters, they also worked, most notably as doctors, as we shall see, and Arnaud de Corbarieu had seen Touzet de Noguès labouring on the walls of the church of Saint-Nauphary, probably at Lavaur itself (in the Albigeois).[114]

A Cathar's work in Quercy seems to have been essentially ritualistic. So while, unlike clergy, they did not demand taxes or dues such as tithe – and it has been suggested that they were popular with landowners because of this – neither were they simple and undemanding. We could even call Cathars 'high maintenance', not least from the 1230s, when the inquisitors began to show interest in even minor humanitarian and Christian support such as giving them food and shelter, which became enough to condemn a person. There is therefore an irony in sentences such as that of Ricarde, wife of to Etienne Galtier, who had sheltered *perfecti* and sent them grain, bread and wine. She was told to wear a cross and to 'support a pauper for a year'. Here we encounter what we might call the concept of the 'deserving poor' on Pierre Seilan's part. He knew full well that she *had* been supporting people heavily dependent on charity: Cathars.[115]

So, while there is no evidence whatsoever for Cathars possessing anything even approaching the amount of wealth and material resources amassed by the secular and regular clergy in Languedoc – had they done so they would surely have paid their way rather than solicit minor, sometimes humiliatingly small gifts – they were not as unlike Catholic clergy in this sense as they appear. Indeed, we might speculate that their treasury was perhaps larger than those of the new orders – the Franciscans and Dominicans – when these first emerged and before they became Rome's secret police. Furthermore, while it is true that the gifts they received were often indeed so minor that there was certainly an understanding that 'no gift was too small', we should note that gifts even of a handful of nuts had more than an economic role. They acknowledged and strengthened existing devotional solidarities.

We now turn to the vast amount of data we have for the exact nature of these economic relationship between heretics and their supporters.

Money: give and take
We have many accounts of financial transactions, and they hint at quite complex economic structures binding people together. Heretics received money, but we have seen that they gave as well, rewarding and encouraging

---

[114] He calls him 'Toulza of Lavaur' but this is probably the same person; Pierre Seilan and Bernard de Caux's staff have recorded his name differently.
[115] D21, fols. 194v, 203v.

their supporters. Financial patronage sometimes reflected the social status of the giver and reinforced existing hierachies. Pons Grimoard said that he once sent money to Guillaume Faure to pay for a meal for *perfecti*, including Bernard de Lamothe, at the Faure home.[116] Guillaume Faure was a well-connected and significant man, as we have seen, but he was the seneschal's inferior. Pons was expressing his 'largesse' in his statement, just as he was when he said that he often sent money – totalling about thirty cahorsin *solidis* – to heretics via Rainaud Rauc and even via Guillaume Faure himself.[117]

Cathars also made money out of performing *consolamenta*. Marthe, wife of En Gorses at Montpezat, paid explicitly for hers. To one *perfectus* she paid ten cahorsin *solidi*, and to the other five.[118] But such transactions did not always go smoothly. Hugues du Port of Montauban told that heretics involved him in trying to force money out of the dying Raimond de Bruelh 'because he had received the body of Christ'. It seems that Raimond had been consoled but had not paid the *perfecti* at that time, and had then received extreme unction and determined not to pay up all.[119]

We also have significant evidence for bequests being made to each sect. Na Aurimonde of Moissac, the wife of the *perfectus* Falquet de Saint-Paul, gave goods from a dead woman to *perfecti*: a 'camel' (*de camello*) hat, a cloak, a tunic, an undergarment, a belt and a pen-knife. The deceased had in fact charged a priest with sharing them out among the recipients. In addition, she passed on twenty *solidi* bequeathed by someone else.[120] Bertrand de Lascroa assisted at the *consolamentum* of Guillaume Moulinier and recalled that the latter had left 100 *solidi* to the *perfecti*, which the deponent took to En Roques, who in turn passed it on to them.[121] Bitorte of Moissac noted that Falquet de Saint-Paul gave her mother's cape to other *perfecti* according to her wishes, presumably when she too died.[122]

People also left Waldensians goods and money.[123] At Montauban, Raimond Carbonnel's brother Jacques had pressed him into leaving them 200 *solidi* in his will.[124] Sibille de Lagarde's mother had ordained before she died that her daughter should pass on some of her belongings to them.[125] But, unlike in the case of Cathars, there is no connection made between this payment and any ceremony. We should perhaps revisit Pierre de Noye's objection to

---

116 D22, fol. 37r.
117 D22, fol. 37r.
118 D21, fol. 307r–v.
119 D21, fol. 265r–v; DPC, p. 187 note 280.
120 D21, fol. 290r–v; DPC, pp. 228–31 and note 330
121 D21, fol. 188r; DPC, p. 35 and note 80.
122 D21, fol. 294r–v.
123 For example at D21, fols. 234r, 275v; Biller, '*Thesaurus Absconditus*', p. 102.
124 D21, fol. 234r–v.
125 D21, fol. 224r; DPC, pp. 110–11.

the self-proclaimed monopoly of the Cathars on saving people[126] and ask whether this too might have something to do with attitudes to money. We have also noted that Sicard de Lunel took Bertrande de Cours's dowry from her father when he admitted her to the sect, and should ask whether this was the case also for young, otherwise marriageable initiates such as Arnaude and Péronne de la Mothe.

But the flow of money was not all one way; sympathisers and non-sympathisers made money out of Cathars too, mainly through selling them things. We have several examples of people renting houses to them, exploiting their need for shelter but at the same time tying themselves to the heretics. Pétronille de la Fargue admitted at Castelnau-Montratier that she and her husband had let a house to *perfecti*, but she had also fed them in return for their attending to her sick son, another kind of economic relationship entirely. Bernarde Faure of Beaucaire rented a house to Waldensians for a year. They exhorted her not to swear or kill, and she believed them to be good people and often gave them food and wine. In other words, just because these women were landladies of heretics does not mean that their relationship was solely about business. Maybe they would have let them have these houses rent-free if they could have afforded it, as might have Na Algars du Villar, who rented her house out to female Waldensians for a stay of two years, but likewise gave them goods and believed them to be good women,[127] and Bernard de Lasmartres, who rented them a house and listened to them preaching.[128]

Food, goods and their meaning
Food was at the heart of heretical networks, sometimes bringing colour into otherwise formulaic accounts. Bernard Guiraud, son of Stephen Guiraud, was exiled for one year to Constantinople for listening to preaching, for adoring heretics, for believing them to be good men and in salvation through their faith ... and for eating their strawberries![129] Gausbert de Clusel took fruit to heretics from a *perfecta* and sent wine to them by donkey in two saddlebags.[130] Other people sent to Cathars food which included fish (and specifically eels, an eel pie and a sea bass),[131] fruit (and specifically pears, cherries, strawberries and grapes),[132] vegetables (and specifically, leeks, broad beans and spring onions),[133] wine in various containers,[134] oil (and specifically bay

---

126 See above, pp. 000–00.
127 D21, fol. 219r. See also Biller, *Waldenses*, p. 100.
128 D21, fol. 221v.
129 D21, fols. 290v–1r.
130 D21, fols. 293r–4r; DPC, pp. 233–4 and note 336.
131 D21, fols. 259r, 299v–300r, 304v–5r, 302r, 306v, 307r–v.
132 D21, fols. 220v, 241v–2r, 298r–v, 301r, 304v–5r.
133 D21, fols. 194r, 202v–203r.
134 D21, fols. 298r–v, 301r, 305r, 306v.

tree oil),[135] vinegar,[136] wheat,[137] pies[138] and, very commonly, bread.[139] Pierre Seilan was particularly interested in recollections of people giving Waldensians meat and cheese.[140] Cathars would not touch these foodstuffs, so these details told the inquisitor which sect of heretics the believer was involved with: he wanted to know this regardless of whether the *credens* was centrally aware of or interested in the reason behind *perfecti* 'pickiness'.

We also have references to vessels for cooking and consuming food: to *patellas*, which Duvernoy suggests is a type of casserole pot used at Moissac, and to bowls and cups.[141] The significance here again concerns the uncompromising dietary needs of the *perfecti*. Such utensils had to be new or reserved only for them. Even accidental consumption of the products of coition would condemn the heretic to reincarnation in the physical realm. Having a *perfectus* round to dinner or feeding one in the family meant cooking for someone with a dietary regime so strict that they would not touch food prepared for them, with however much love and care and desire to please, if it had been contaminated by meat products, perhaps by having been stored or cooked in a pot that had previously contained them, however well it had been cleaned. This is why François the clerk had had to send them a 'new cooking-pot' (*olla nova*) – in other words, an untainted one – on the orders of Guillemassa.[142] Thus, the renouncers set themselves apart from those less pure not so much through abstaining – whereby they might have made cheap and undemanding guests – but by costing time and money and causing inconvenience and, increasingly, danger to the host into the bargain. Furthermore, the diligent host, for his or her part, was by implication less-than-pure, indeed tainted.

Clothes and stitched goods feature almost as prominently as food does in the depositions. Peter Biller notes the making of sandals for Waldensians as a feature of heretical life in Quercy, as at Montauban, Gourdon and Montcuq.[143] There seems to have been market enough for two dealers in other stitched leather goods at Moissac; both Pons Limousy and Hélie the mercer sold *perfecti* belts and purses, also believing them to be good men and adoring them.[144] At Gourdon, Etienne de la Combe hosted *perfecti* but mended shoes for Waldensians.[145] People made other goods specifically for heretics: Raimond

---

135 D21, fols. 240v, 301r.
136 D21, fol. 306v.
137 D21, fols. 299r, 307v.
138 D21, fol. 214r.
139 D21, e.g. fols. 299v, 301r, 302r.
140 For example, D21, fols. 237r–v, 247v.
141 D21, fol. 301r; DPC, pp. 246–7 note 357.
142 D21, fol. 219v. The translation of *olla nova* is Duvernoy's: DPC, p. 103.
143 D21, fols. 203r, 215r, 261v; Biller, 'Thesaurus Absconditus', p. 101.
144 D21, fols. 286v, 294r.
145 D21, fol. 203r.

the weaver, for example, made cloth for *perfecti*.[146] Na Aurimonde of Moissac, noted above, seems to have been a kind of bursar for Cathars, procuring for them four pairs of gloves, four linen hats and Egyptian cotton. She also gave gloves from herself and gifts from consoled people.[147] Guillaume Pellegri of Gourdon gave *perfecti* two little tunics.[148] Such accounts are surely under-used by social historians and at the same time force the historian of heresy to consider fully the material as well as the spiritual life of heresy, as Andrew Roach has done so successfully.

Services rendered

Heretics also gave goods themselves, usually as payment for services rendered. Raimond Pellegri held money for them and was given a pair of gloves.[149] Bernard de Sapiac had been asked to carry a message to a third party and had been given a cape for this presumably dangerous work.[150] Arnaud de Primes received Cathars in his home at Montcuq and was given wheat in return.[151] Arnaud 'Rectus' de Goudou shaved a *perfectus* and was given a cap.[152]

We also encounter people who seem to have worked for heretics on a formal and ongoing basis. This is the impression we get of Benoît's work in Jeanne d'Avignon's vineyard, noted above.[153] Several were more specifically servants in a domestic capacity. Guillaume de Réjac had spent five days as a servant to *perfecti*.[154] Algée of Montauban served for four days in a house of *perfecti* at Villemur, to which she had accompanied a sick man to receive the *consolamentum*.[155] Guillemette Maury of Montauban had been the servant of a *perfecta* for five years.[156] Being paid did not preclude being an adherent of the sect, because Guillemette had also adored them around nine times,[157] but genuine adherence to the sect being served was most common in the case of Waldensians. A woman called Cahorsine had been the domestic of a Waldensian for three years, but although she had eaten with them only 'as a servant' – that is to say, not in a ritual context – she had indeed had faith in

---

146 D21, fols. 244v–5r.
147 D22, fol. 290r–v; DPC, pp. 228–31 and note 330.
148 D21, fols. 186v–187r.
149 D21, fols. 192r–v, 211v.
150 D21, fol. 252v.
151 D22, fol. 214r–v.
152 D21, fol. 195v, 197r; DPC, pp. 52–3 (where Duvernoy identifies Arnaud 'Cedus' as Arnaud Rectus), pp. 56–7.
153 D21, fols. 266v–7r.
154 D21, fol. 285v.
155 D21, fol. 278r–v.
156 D21, fol. 271r.
157 D21, fol. 271r.

them.[158] Arnaud Sarrailher had worked for them in a formal arrangement too, but also believed them to be good people with a good faith.[159]

Doctors and patients

One of the most important functions of heretics of both sects was, naturally, to give comfort and succour to their believers in times of crisis such as physical illness. It is likely that their success or otherwise in this capacity affected the way that they were viewed by non-believers and potential converts also. But heretics did not only comfort the dying and, in the case of Cathars, secure them in the afterlife. Both sects had members who attempted to cure the sick as well. It was Waldensians in particular who were renowned as doctors.[160]

This was evidently central to their success in Quercy. Bernard Tessendier, for example, had taken his brother Raimond to a Waldensian when sick, as Raimond himself confirmed, and was an adherent of this sect in particular.[161] Huguette Maury of Montauban had been treated by a Waldensian during an illness, perhaps the heretic to whom she gave cheese and oil.[162] Arnaud-Bernard de Rouzet admitted that a Waldensian woman had washed his head, possibly treating an infection or infestation.[163] Raimond Gastaud of Montauban consulted a Waldensian doctor many times for his illness.[164] Guillemette Faidit, wife of Pons Faucaire, had Waldensians treat her sick son.[165] Her relative Gaucelme Faidit also had them treat a sick child several times, although she had also helped a sick man to Villemur, where he was consoled.[166] Pons de de la Jonquière of Montauban even spoke of a Waldensian hospital, which he had visited often.[167] Guillaume Géraud, son of Hugues Géraud, had Waldensian doctors treat his illness in exchange for goods,[168] as did another family member, Etienne.[169] We have noted that several women called in the most famous Waldensian in Quercy, Pierre de Vals. He was also

---

[158] D21, fols. 263v–4r.

[159] D21, fol. 266r.

[160] Biller, 'Curate infirmos', pp. 49–67. On Cathar doctors see also Walter Wakefield, 'Heretics as physicians in the Thirteenth Century', *Speculum* 57 (1982), pp. 328–31; Arnold, *Inquisition and Power*, pp. 135–6; Pegg, *Corruption of Angels*, pp. 106–7.

[161] D21 fols. 271v (Bernard), 280v (Raimond).

[162] D21, fol. 247v.

[163] D21, fols. 214v–15r; DPC, pp. 92–3 note 162 (modern Rouget). Duvernoy may have confused this witness with the *credens* Bernard Arnaud (DPC, pp. 90–1 and D21, fol. 214r).

[164] D21, fols. 261v–2r.

[165] D21, fol. 269v.

[166] D21, fol. 275r–v.

[167] D21, fol. 249r–v.

[168] D21, fol. 230r.

[169] D21, fol. 230r.

summoned by Pierre de la Chapelle when his wife was sick, visiting twice and charging twenty pennies.[170]

In short, Waldensian doctors were so renowned that even fervent Cathar adherents appear to have had no hesitation in calling on their services, there being a total of fourteen individuals in Doat 21 who saw both sects but saw Waldensians *only* in a medical context. Jean Touzet received the *consolamentum* at Villemur, yet he consulted Waldensian doctors when ill and believed them to be good men.[171] Raimond Touzet likewise consulted them when he injured his hand, although it was again Cathars to whom he related in ritual terms.[172] The same can be said of Guillemette, wife of Aimeric de Goulême-de-Milhac.[173] Géraude, daughter of Na Courtes, called them in to treat her sick son, but accepted presents from *perfecti*.[174] A woman called Algée served and adored Cathars and had extensive involvement in their day-to-day life, but when she became ill it was to Waldensians that she turned.[175] Pragmatism was shown in this matter, in other words. Furthermore, some people's *only* recorded heretical contact was in this context, as in the case of Bernarde Roux of Gourdon, who called in Pierre de Vals when her son was sick, when she gave him food, and called for his help for other illnesses besides.[176]

Of course, not all doctors were fully fledged sectarians but simply performed their professional duties. From the confession of Arnaud, a doctor of Montauban, we learn about the treatment of maladies and injuries more generally. He had made a ligature for a *perfectus*'s broken leg, given them ointments and sold them ginger. For such things he was prescribed two years at Constantinople for his spiritual health.[177] Guillaume Faure believed the mother of Vital Sabatier the surgeon to have been a *perfecta*, but there is no suggestion that the doctor was an adherent himself.

We also have a few references concerning the physical health of heretics themselves, specifically Cathars. We have encountered Raoul 'the scabby'. Benoît 'the joker' helped a *perfecta* visit *perfecti* at the leper-house at *Courtinal*.[178] Furthermore, we know of a doctor who appears to have specifically treated heretics and to have been a *perfectus* himself. Pons Grimoard refers to such a man, Guillaume Raimond. He came with his *socius* to treat Pons over the course of eight or nine days, making a cast, for which Pons later paid. The

---

170   D21, fol. 203v.
171   D21, fols. 232v–3r.
172   D21, fols. 233v–4r.
173   D21, fol. 213r.
174   D21, fols. 241v–2r; DPC, pp. 144–5.
175   D21 fol. 278r–v; DPC, pp. 206–7.
176   D21, fols. 194v, 204v.
177   D21, fols. 256v–7r.
178   D21, fols. 266v–7r.

doctor himself eventually died at the home of Arnaud Pagan.[179] Duvernoy identifies him rather as Guillaume-Bernard d'Airoux, a more widely known doctor-*perfectus*.[180] Pons seems to have attempted to protect him from the inquisitors.[181]

We also have examples of Cathars themselves performing medical functions, specifically at Castelnau-Montratier, as in the case of Pétronille de la Fargue; Guillaume de la Mothe, quite possibly of the Montauban family, was helped through an illness by a *perfectus* there also.[182] But we must remember in the case of Cathars that they were intending to care for the body in life and also to secure the safe passage of the soul at the point of death, after which they were indifferent to the state or fate of the corporal vessel that had carried it. When a sick person came to the *perfecti* it was a win–win situation for the sect.

Thriving and Hiding

In the many accounts of people helping heretics in their travels and having heretics stay with them it is not always easy to determine whether this was in the sense of taking part in a vibrant alternative culture in which peripatetic heretics undertook preaching tours and performed rituals as part of winning converts and constructing heretical solidarities, or whether heretics were drawing on solidarities *already* established by being moved around secretly and being hidden by supporters.

Houses and hideouts: leading and fleeing
Bertrand de Valette's deposition gives us more information about such networks of safety and solidarity. He and his men guarded some *perfecti* for almost a year on several manses near Moissac and other locations, and helped them travel to each other between hiding places. For this, he received 200 *solidi* from them.[183] Bernard de Lasalle-de Malaveilhe found Cathars in his house but let them stay and then took them to Saint-Médard's wood, near Moissac.[184] Benoît of Montauban led a *perfectus* to some underground passages at Villemur.[185] However, the major event to consider in terms of managing travel is the flight from Gourdon at Easter 1229, when it had

---

179 D22, fols. 35v, 40v. The account in fact states that the doctor did *not* give Pons a cast, but this makes little sense. Duvernoy is probably right in thinking that the scribe inserted 'non' accidentally (DCBC, pp. 62–3 note a).

180 DCBC, pp. 55–6 and note 6.

181 D22, fol. 42r.

182 D21, fol. 311r.

183 D21, fol. 285r–v.

184 D21, fol. 284r–v.

185 D21, fols. 266v–7r.

become clear that Raimond of Toulouse would be true to his word and would aid the church in seeking out and persecuting heretics.[186] Numerous men admitted to having taken part in helping the *perfecti* make this exodus, including Guillaume Ricart,[187] Pierre de Las Oleiras,[188] Guillaume d'Eysses[189] and En Roques.[190]

Other accounts seem to relate to a situation in which Cathars were operating more openly. Among other things, Gausbert de Clusel accompanied some to *Clamade* and others from Moissac to Piac and had them preach to him *en route*.[191] Hugues Jauffré's wife Jauffrette and her sister Raimonde had heretics in their house at Moissac for three months,[192] but we do not know the circumstances. Hugues himself was also involved in leading heretics throughout the region, receiving thirty cahorsin *solidi* for this on one occasion and seventy *solidi* when he had accommodated some at his house.[193] But again, we cannot establish the context. Raimond de Montaigu seemed to have organised their itinerary for a time, because the language used implies he was both escorting them and making arrangements for them. He was 'with them' when they preached in one house (i.e. he did not just 'hear them'), and led them to another house, perhaps where he had arranged for them to be received.[194] Again, we cannot know the circumstances simply from Pierre Seilan's record. However, Raimond de Castelnau claimed that when he took *perfecti* in his boat from Moissac to Toulouse he did not know them to be heretics at first, although when he discovered this he took them anyway.[195] This probably indicates that this took place after 1229, when they discarded their distinctive clothing in order to prevent easy detection.

Likewise, of the many references to heretics travelling or being encountered beyond Quercy, it is difficult to know whether they were where they wanted or where they had to be. Pons Gran and Bernarde Targuier had two sons who were in England by 1243, perhaps working, perhaps having fled, or perhaps on pilgrimage to Canterbury, where many of the condemned of 1241 were sent.[196] A wealthy local man, Boussoulens, received heretics including

---

[186] D21, fols. 189r, 199r, 201v; Duvernoy, *Le Catharisme II*, p. 268; Lambert, *The Cathars*, p. 137.

[187] D21, fol. 208v.

[188] D21, fols. 188v–191r.

[189] D21, fol. 201v.

[190] D21, fols. 198v–9r.

[191] D21, fols. 293r–4r; DPC, pp. 233–4 and note 336.

[192] D21, fol. 300v.

[193] D21, fol. 297v.

[194] D21, fol. 216v.

[195] D21, fol. 286r–v.

[196] D22, fol. 15v.

Guilabert de Castres and his *socius* at Montauban, according to his wife Raimonde, but he also had a house on Majorca where she often saw *perfecti*.[197]

Whatever the circumstances of the heretics, we have many accounts of them using the river networks of the region along with other travellers. Raimond Delvolvé (le Boulvé) was someone who arranged such transport within Quercy.[198] They were ferried to and from the Agenais by boatmen from Moissac.[199] Raimond Gautier confirms the heretical traffic between the towns of lower and the northern Toulousain, admitting to transporting *perfecti* in his boat from Montauban and Moissac and Villemur.[200] Heretics used the roads too, of course. Pierre Bernard had transported a *perfecta* on his donkey, receiving eleven pennies for this.[201]

Contacts and communications

Turning to the nature and scope of heretical contacts and communications, as opposed to their logistics, many journeys were of course routine trips between towns and heretics' and *credentes'* homes in Quercy. We have noted contacts between Sauveterre and Montcuq that were facilitated by the *credens* Guillemassa in Chapter 4. Similar trips meant that Guillaume Faure de Pechermer was also perfectly familiar with the community at Moissac. In the home of Falquet de Saint-Paul he saw the heretics Pons Dairos and Sernin.[202] Before 1228, he had seen Pons Pellicier, Arnaud del Vic, Etienne Raimond and Jean de la Garde listening to *perfecti* preach.[203] Further afield, Jean Touzet of Montauban attended a heretication at Rabestens (Tarn).[204] His relative Durand Touzet of Montauban had been to see heretics at Lavaur (also Tarn) with another of their supporters, probably Bertrand de la Mothe, and had seen heretics at his mother's house.[205]

Contacts and communications with heretics in the neighbouring Agenais were well established.[206] The community at Montcuq was central to this network because of its location. We find there people connected with the Monflanquin area of the Agenais, most significantly Hartemanda de Balenx, who escorted heretics within and to and from the Agenais with Gaillard d'En Arces and Etienne de Na Raimonde of Montcuq.[207] One of the most important people in terms of contacts between heretics of the Agenais, Quercy and

---

[197] D21, fol. 262r; DPC, pp. 180–1.
[198] D21, fol. 287r–v.
[199] Taylor, *Heresy*, p. 232.
[200] D21, fol. 246r–v.
[201] D21, fol. 218v.
[202] D22, fol. 6r.
[203] D22, fols. 4v–5r.
[204] D21, fol. 232v.
[205] D21, fol. 279r.
[206] Taylor, *Heresy*, pp. 225–60, *passim*.
[207] D21, fols. 216r, 222v, 226r. For her identification see also DPC, pp. 95, 107, 115.

further afield must have been Durand Vairet, also tried at Montcuq. He had been at Martel, where he saw heretics, the only reference we have to heresy in Limousin-Quercy. He had also been with Barthélemy de Carcassonne for two days at Laure (Aude) in the company of around seventy *perfecti* who held a banquet. He was therefore probably involved in the context of a schism that took place in Cathar circles in 1223;[208] and, as well as admitting to the more usual crimes, he had even been involved in seeking advice concerning getting a heretic set free.[209] Guillaume Barrère, the deponent whose sentence follows that of Durand Vairet, had also been involved in the Aude network. As part of very extensive activity he had led heretics from Montolieu (Aude again) to Toulouse, supporting them financially *en route*.[210] As such, we are confronted by *credentes* in Quercy who were tapped into networks in Languedoc more widely, and we should not consider them marginal to the heretical 'private life' of the region.

We now turn to the evidence in the Doat documents for what we, as opposed to the inquisitor, would consider heretical activity itself; that is to say, ritual and other devotional practice.

---

[208] Hamilton, 'The Cathar council of Saint Félix', pp. 26–8, 42, 47, 51–3; Taylor, *Heresy*, pp. 226–8.

[209] D21, fols. 220r–21r.

[210] D21, fol. 221r–v.

6

Heresy and What it Meant

Deponent Strategies in the Face of Inquisition

It is important to think of inquisition as a diachronic process rather than an institution. Doat manuscripts 21–23 are not evidence of three inquests abstracted from space and time, in no particular order, but are part of an unfolding narrative, each influencing the next. So, when reading the depositions in Doat 21, for example, we must remember that they were made in the knowledge of what had taken place in the inquests of the 1230s. Although the 1230s seem obscurer and dimmer to us, this is only because of the nature of the record. As we have noted, only indirect evidence survives of events such as the mass burning at Moissac, Pons Grimoard's trial, the pre-empting of a trial likely to dispossess the Baussa family at Cahors and so on. These wounds were fresh and surely significant in influencing what people volunteered and concealed from 1241 onwards.

For example, several witnesses were already 'on thin ice', most notably the officials Pons Grimoard and Othon de Berètges and the knight Guillaume Guallard, who had been investigated in the 1230s by Guillaume Arnaud and Pierre Seilan. Others claimed that they had previously been absolved for crimes attributed to them by the inquisitors of the 1240s. At Castelnau-Montratier Pétronne de Prestes claimed that although she had sinned she had been absolved by the archdeacon on the orders of the bishop. But she was nonetheless given a harsh penalty for her involvement with Waldensians – pilgrimages to le Puy, Saint-Gilles, Santiago, Saint-Denis and Canterbury. So the record was perhaps to hand and the sins that she claimed had been forgiven had not been.[1] Similarly, Pétronille de Pierre-Etienne of Montauban claimed that Bishop Fulk of Toulouse had absolved her. We know that she must have claimed to have undergone a penance for her crimes, because the scribe noted that this claim needed to be verified.[2] Such instances reveal the significance of the record to both witness and inquisitor.

The results of the 1241–2 inquest also surely shaped responses to Brother Ferrer and Bernard de Caux in 1243–4. Arnaude de la Mothe would have been

---

[1] D21, fols. 310v–11r.
[2] D21, fol. 244v.

aware that most of her family had already implicated her and her sister and mother, as well as condemning themselves out of their own mouths. Similarly, witnesses from Montauban were aware in 1243–4 of the evidence that was given there in 1241. The presence of the family and political networks that we have identified throughout Quercy in previous chapters surely implies that each inquest must have created ripples fanning out far beyond the town in which it took place.

We have suggested some of the strategies that deponents seem to have employed to help them negotiate the path between their past and future via the inquisitor's court, such as seeking to minimise the significance of contact with heretics by stressing the young – and therefore innocent – age at which it took place. There follow here observations on further strategies deponents employed in Quercy, and how specific people might attempt to influence the process with respect to themselves and to their family, friends, neighbours and wider community.[3] Certain key defensive stances emerge, the first of which was to find ways to minimise the significance of one's involvement with the heresy in relation to that of other people.

'It's not me you should be questioning'

During the extensive deposition made in 1243 by Jean Vital in front of Bernard de Caux, he apparently stated that he had heard Etienne Mazeler say that it had been a great sin to burn a house at Moissac where two heretics had been arrested. It was an even greater sin than if 'the house of the best religion in the world' (*domus melioris religionis de mundo*) were to burn.[4] According to the same witness, Pierre de Quissac had said that he 'gave nothing for all the masses sung at Cahors, and if the inquisitors ordered him to go there, he'd go the other way' and that 'no one cared as much as an egg about excommunication, because the Church's authority was groundless'.[5] He further attested that Guillaume Faure called the inquisitors masked and rabid Catholics, and made threats concerning them.[6]

A couple of things are going on here in terms of the relationship between people in Quercy and the inquisitors. The first is a glimpse of what some of the laity thought about the authority of the Dominicans; they disputed their legitimacy. In this they shared the sentiments of the count of Toulouse himself. But this was what was apparently said *about* the inquisitors, not to them. It probably did represent the attitudes of many, but was bluster rather than a willingness to confront the Dominicans. It did the fearless braggers no good when it reached the court via a third party such as Jean Vital. In the

---

[3] Given, *Inquisition*, pp. 2–4 and esp. pp. 93–165.
[4] D22, fol. 12r. 'Religion' here denotes monasticism, and the phrase means the best monastery or convent in the world.
[5] D22, fols. 11v–12r.
[6] D22, fol. 11v.

long run, as a strategy for challenging the power of the Dominicans, it was worse than saying nothing at all.

The second is the desperate attempts of Jean Vital himself to extricate himself from a harsh sentence by revealing as much as he possibly could about the crimes of others. He insisted that he had had nothing to do with the heretics. Nonetheless, he had been concealing evidence, including evidence of support for the recent murder of the inquisitors at Avignonet on the parts of Etienne Mazeler, Guillaume Audebert and Guillaume Faure, who had clearly trusted Jean's loyalty to the extent that they were celebrating the event in his presence.

Jean's strategy is not difficult to discern. He was offering extensive and reliable insider evidence that would allow the conviction of dozens of *credentes*. Of course he was hoping for leniency in sentencing. Although we have no record of his sentence there is nothing else in the Doat documentation to lead us to believe that individuals negotiated their situation in this way at all successfully.

Another, similar, strategy was to admit involvement to some extent but no further, significantly less far than other people had gone: other people closer to the Cathar 'inner circle', in other words. Taking part in heretical ceremonies implicated a defendant most seriously. Accordingly, *credentes* frequently claimed to have been excluded from the ritual *consolamentum*. We have noted examples of this in Chapter 5. Guiraud Guallard tried to protect himself by recounting a series of events that he said took place in *c*.1230. Bernard de Lamothe and his *socius* were in Arnaud de Bressols's stable, attending Hugues de Cavelsaut, who was ill. Guillaume Imbert and his wife Malebouche were there also. The *credentes* all attended to the heretics and adored them. But after five days, Guiraud saw the doors closed. According to what Guillaume Imbert and Malebouche told him, the heretics had then consoled the dying man. Guiraud believed this to be the case.[7] The date is significant here. In the 1230s Guiraud had been reconciled with the Catholic faith by Guillaume Arnaud on the assumption that all his sins had been confessed. But this further sin only came out now, and it was therefore important to stress that his contact was routine and to play down the significance of his own part in the heretication. The closed door implies that he had not been trusted enough to know that it was taking place; at least, it implies this in Guiraud's account of the incident.

Guillaume Faure: 'stitched up'

When exploring who said what about whom to the inquisitor, speculating *why* they said it is irresistible. We have to be careful here. We have the testimony of people who were themselves in very deep trouble. Their evidence

---

[7]   D22, fol. 14r.

reflects a reality very specific to them and not necessarily reflective of those informal structures and knowledge that dominated life in a given town before the inquisitors arrived. We cannot reconstruct social relationships from the evidence: this is no Montaillou. Having said this, it would be a shame not to interrogate the evidence at all in this sense.

I have suggested elsewhere that because Castelsarrasin submitted to crusader authority in 1212 it did not suffer the destruction and deprivation experienced in some towns in Languedoc, and that a relative light touch in terms of its administration under the crusaders allowed for the survival of the heresy in private homes. Furthermore, the town was governed from *c*.1234 by a member of the most important family in heretical terms, Pons Grimoard. This is significant. The Grimoards both dominated and governed a town that had fared relatively well out of the crusade and the Peace of 1229 in comparison with some of its neighbours, and had carried the honour of having been liberated from French rule by an alliance of quercinois nobles in collaboration with Bernard de Cazenac a year before. We have noted a good deal of information about the Grimoards and their relatives in Doat 22. The father of the *seneschal* Pons Grimoard was Vital and his mother was Arnaude. Vital became a *perfectus*, as did his brother Raimond, at Corbarieu in 1213, and their brother Pierre was consoled on his death-bed. Well-attended heretical meetings were held in family homes from as early as 1204. Furthermore, Pierre had formed a marriage alliance with what was the second most significant family in political terms, the de Berètges, important because Othon de Barètges was Raimond VII's *bailli* at Moissac and Montcuq.[8] Both Othon and Na Barètges were active and committed *credentes*. Another important match was that between Pons's cousin, Pros, and Jean de Cavelsaut, whose family also contained many *credentes* and the *perfecti* Arnaud, Guillaume, Pons and Hugues, and Pros and Johannes's own daughter, Raimonde, hereticated by *c*.1218. These three inter-related families formed the political elite at Castelsarrasin and were at the heart of heretical elites also. When leading heresiarchs and *perfecti* such as Bernard de Lamothe, Vigouroux de la Bacone and a *perfecta* of Villemur called Unaude were at Castelsarrasin, they were most often found in the company and under the protection of these families.

Although depositions give only glimpses of complex phenomena such as social interaction and family politics, while working on these families I have come to view the Grimoard-de Barètges-de Cavelsaut as something of a faction within the elite at Castelsarrasin, rather than simply comprising the elite. They seem essentially distinct from another circle dominated by another wealthy but non-noble family, that of Guillaume Faure de Pechermer. As I have suggested, it is dangerous to infer too much about pre-existing

---

8   Other family members noted in D22 are Raimond-Guillaume, Guillaume-Raimond, Raimond and his wife Unauda, and Jordan.

communal tensions from evidence given about other people to the inquisitor. Nonetheless, Guillaume Faure fared very badly owing to the evidence of important witnesses in the Grimoard faction. Several people cast him in a central role as a heavily implicated *credens* in evidence given to both Brother Ferrer and Bernard de Caux. The evidence of Pons Grimoard and Othon de Berètges features significantly here, as does that of Bernarde Targuier, Jean Vital, Guillaume Féraut, Pierre de Quissac and Raimond Jean d'Abia.

Pons Grimoard in particular stresses the Faure involvement in heretical activity. Sometimes Guillaume Faure is cast as more prominent than Pons, attending the *consolamentum* of Raimond Grimoard, for example, which Pons himself did not witness. Guillaume certainly had enemies in Pierre de Quissac and Guillaume Féraut; the latter, as we have seen, attested that he had heard the former say that he supported whatever penance would be awarded to Guillaume Faure.[9] Pierre was perhaps trying to defend Guillaume Féraut here as much as he was informing on Guillaume Faure, because Jean Vital had attested that Guillaume Féraut had said that he would defy the inquisitors. But Guillaume Faure, the fall-guy, was already Guillaume Féraut's enemy: it was Féraut who had reported him as having called Christ God's *bailli* and not his son. Furthermore, Guillaume Féraut also said that he had found a letter on the road when travelling a short distance behind Guillaume Faure. It was addressed to *perfecti*, he said, and added that he had given it to Bernard de Caux. The witness had gone out of his way to implicate Guillaume Faure, therefore, and we shall encounter more of what he said about him below.

From a series of depositions we gain the impression that Guillaume Faure had enemies everywhere. Pierre de Noye associates him with Bernard de Lamothe, Guillaume Solier, Sernin, Pons d'Airos and Pons Guilabert, all heretics of repute beyond Quercy, whom he adored; Guiraud Gaillard and Pierre de Noye also associate him with leading *perfecti*; Jean Vital has him celebrating the murders at Avignonet; and the first and last events recalled by Othon de Bèretges attested to Guillaume Faure's deep involvement with Cathars. We should note that Guillaume Faure's deposition was only the second to be made in Bernard de Caux's court, and so the evidence given against him may have resulted directly from the vast amount of evidence he gave against others. It may be that Pons Grimoard became aware of what had passed between him and the inquisitor in 1243, and that this gave him much to ponder over Christmas that year before he himself was summoned. However, Bernarde Targuier's testimony was the very first to be heard, and she too marked him out as an active *credens*, believing what the heretics taught and actively supporting them, and particularly associates him with

---

[9] Pilgrimages overseas were being replaced by prison sentences (DCBC, p. 41 note 3).

Bernard de la Mothe. In fact, she began by testifying to his heretical activity thirty years earlier.

None of this is to say that Guillaume Faure did not do or say the things attributed to him, but it is the case that other deponents do appear to have rather gone out of their way to point to this. He perhaps had more of an ally in Guiraud Guallard, whose account features a good deal more evidence condemning the Grimoards than the Faures. Nonetheless, all those in contact with him were at risk. For example, through his wife, Guillaume was related to the Audebert family. Jean Vital positions both Guillaume Faure and Guillaume Audebert very centrally in his damning account of the reception at Castelsarrasin of the news of the murders at Avignonet in 1242, and also in events in the 1220s. Any society subjected to the kinds of stresses produced by inquisition, which historians observe as turning neighbour against neighbour, family against family and individuals against their own kin, will show these tensions at some point. At Castelsarrasin, they are revealed nowhere more obviously than in a general cutting adrift of Guillaume Faure from communal solidarities.

We now turn to another more generalised form of defence, having the wool pulled over one's own eyes by heretical 'wolves in sheep's clothing'.

'It was not my fault'

The defence of not knowing heretics to be heretics on meeting them was a common one at Moissac in particular. Perhaps the *credentes* there had discussed it as a strategy. Raimonde, wife of Pons Pellipier, for one, did not know heretics were heretics until her husband spoke to them, she said.[10] Bernard de Tournac had let four heretics into his house before he recognised them as such.[11] This form of accidental contact on the part of people tried at Moissac was most common where they had transported heretics. Raimond de Loc said that he had transported *perfecti* three times, to Villemur, Montauban and Agen, not knowing at first that they were heretics, but knowing they were when accepting payment.[12] Isarn the 'bridge-keeper' and Bernard 'the sailor' were sentenced together, which is unusual. They had taken three *perfecti* by boat from Moissac to Tonneins, in the Agenais. They said that they did not know that their passengers were heretics until they arrived at La Pointe, where the Tarn and Garonne meet, but knew for the rest of the journey.[13] Guillaume de Lanta helped some to the river before he realised they were heretics, but crossed the water with them anyway.[14] Raimond de Castelnau took *perfecti* from Moissac to Toulouse in his boat. Like the others, he said that he

---

[10] D21, fol. 287v.
[11] D21, fol. 286v.
[12] D21, fol. 305r.
[13] D21, fol. 293r.
[14] D21, fols. 285v–6r.

did not know them to be heretics at first, but, on discovering it, he took them anyway.[15] Astoundingly, Pierre-Bernard Sabatier had apparently escorted a heretic all the way to Italy but did not know he was a *perfectus* until they got there![16] Pierre Seilan was far from impressed, because none of these 'innocent' encounters had been reported earlier. In other words, deponents were claiming that they had been tricked, or at least misled, but on discovering the truth had not acted upon it. By this admission they condemned themselves: Raimonde, Raimond de Loc Raimond, Isarn, Bernard, Guillaume and Pierre-Raimond were all sent to Le Puy, Saint-Gilles and Santiago-de-Compostella, and Bernard to Santiago. The inquisitor was similarly unimpressed with Na Coutes of Montauban. We have heard that she admitted eating cherries with *perfectae*, but to this admission she apparently added that she had heard since then that they had been reconciled with the Church, as though that would in some way mitigate in her favour, which it did not.

Sometimes, 'it was not my fault' means, more sinisterly, that a deponent claimed to have been threatened by others into not reporting heresy or, more immediately, not co-operating with the inquisitors. Gaillard de Goudou admitted that he had promised not to betray other believers. This promise, which he appears to have kept, as well as his reception of heretics at La Bastide, earned him a sojourn for a year at Constantinople.[17] We do not know whether pressure had been put upon him to make this promise, but in some cases it was. Guiraud Guallard said that after he had abjured heresy with the help of Guillaume Arnaud he had had nothing to do with heretics. But he knew a good deal about the activity of others, with the result that only eight days before Bernard de Caux questioned him he was warned 'in peril of his eyes' to say nothing by Vital, Grazide and Aimeric de Bressols, and Na Pros de Bressols had sent her son Arnaud to warn him to say nothing about her. Nonetheless, he told Bernard de Caux that he had seen her with *perfectae* in the home of Arnaud de Bressols.[18] This is one of the few *direct* insights we get into relationships between quercinois individuals in a community being put under pressure by the inquisition, and we shall observe more indirect evidence of this below. Perhaps less menacing was what Garcias de Bonafous of Montauban had told people considering giving evidence against others. He apparently told Pierre Seilan that he had told people many times that no one could be saved except through the *perfecti*, and that if someone said to him that they were going to tell the inquisitors what they knew in the period of grace he told them that if they would speak to the good men *instead*, then they could be saved.[19]

---

[15]   D21 fol. 286v.
[16]   D21, fols. 287v–8r.
[17]   D21, fols. 193r, 213r.
[18]   D22, fol. 18r.
[19]   D21, fols. 305v–6r.

One rule for some…?

We do not know what sentences were passed in the case of the deponents dealt with in Doat 22 because no book of sentences such as Pierre Seilan's survives in relation to that inquest. This is a shame, because a further point concerning sentencing should be made, and it would be useful if we had a record of Bernard de Caux's sentences to help shed light on this.

The fact is that some of those who were clearly 'guilty' in Doat 21 appear to have escaped punishment. There are six of them: Pierre and Galtier Pellegri of Gourdon, Na Aurimonde de Saint-Paul of Moissac,[20] the clerk François of Montcuq[21] and Bertrand[22] and Fortanier[23] de Gourdon. That no sentences are recorded for them is strange. Doat 21 is clearly a record of sentences, after all. Certainly the apparent lack of sentencing cannot be accidental. The coincidence of two lords of Gourdon and two members of the Pellegri being among only six people to escape is too unlikely. So what, if anything, characterised this group?

We have already encountered these deponents in Chapters 4 and 5. Na Aurimonde, the lady of Moissac, had been the wife of *perfectus* Falquet de Saint-Paul and remained at the heart of lay activity involving Cathars. Along with their brothers Guillaume and Raimond, Pierre and Galtier Pellegri seem to be among those families that had risen from a more humble status; non-noble, but notable, and conspicuously so in terms of heretical activity. François the clerk associated with Waldensians and Cathars, including Vigouroux de la Bacone, Guillaume de Caussade, Guillaume Baussan and the important *credens* Guillemassa. The lords of Gourdon were extensively implicated, as we have seen: Bertrand in having tolerated and protected heretics and Fortanier in actual engagement with Catharism.

In short, these people were among the most significant protectors of heretics, and one reason that they were so important to heretics was their status. What these people who escaped sentencing had in common was that they were all part of the noble and urban elite. They were well-connected and well-resourced and operated as such in both the secular and heretical spheres. Na Aurimonde's family was the most powerful at Moissac. The Pellegri were a family in its ascent in an increasingly commercialised Gourdon. The clerk is a partial exception, in that we do not know where he fitted in socially, at Montcuq or elsewhere, but his extensive involvement implies that he was well-connected and no impoverished country cleric. He was certainly educated and moved in the highest heretical circles. The lords of Gourdon were the highest-ranking and most influential nobles not only of Gourdon,

---

[20] D21, fol. 290r–v.
[21] D21, fols. 219v–20r.
[22] D21, fol. 186r–v.
[23] D21, fol. 199v.

and not only of those tried in Quercy, but in any context in Quercy. In Chapter 7 we shall examine further this curious business.

We now turn to evidence that, among a range of orthodox and unorthodox beliefs, dualism had some resonance in Quercy with the laity and even with some of the Catholic religious too. It is essential to understanding events at a macro level that they took place because there was a very real threat to orthodox social order.

Debating the Cosmos

My contention is that many people engaged with ideas about the nature of creation and made decisions for themselves about which ones they found convincing. Some of these notions may have had origins in other times and places. Central to building up networks of solidarity within which heretics could thrive and hide was the influencing of ordinary people to consider Cathars and Waldensians to be 'good men'. And central to *that* was education and the testing out of ideas.

Learning and reading

Both sects emerge from the sources as being considered more literate than most people. Waldensians read with believers and also lent them books.[24] From Doat 21 we also discover that they ran schools.[25] Pierre Seilan's register contains far more reference to literacy among Cathar adherents, however,[26] and Biller notes that Cathars specifically were thought of as 'bookish' by ordinary people.[27] Accordingly, at Gourdon we have a reference to a book kept by Raimond Pellegri, who is discussed above, from which 'anyone who wanted to would read'.[28] At Almont, the priest Arnaud de la Roque admitted reading a book belonging to heretics, with whom he also ate pears.[29] Guillaume Bonald admitted taking part in ceremonies and reading Cathar books.[30] Raimond de Peyrilles had knowingly read a heretical book.[31] Guillaume de Barbe had led to a port on the river someone whom he had heard reading a book on the Apocalypse in heretical company.[32] Pierre Estève of Montauban had, among

---

[24] D21, fols. 234v, 274r; P. Biller, 'Topos and reality of the heretic as *illiteratus*', in his *Medieval Waldensians* (Woodbridge, 2001), pp. 169–90, p. 176.

[25] D21, fol. 234r–v.

[26] D21, fols. 187r–v, 87v, 196r, 196v, 201r, 202r, 203r, 206r, 210r, 211v, 215v, 220r, 221v, 229r, 257v, 298r, 300v, 301r, 301v, 303v. Also as identified in Biller, 'Topos and reality', p. 176 notes 49, 50.

[27] Biller, 'Topos and reality', p. 177.

[28] D21, fol. 211v.

[29] D21, fol. 310r.

[30] D21, fols. 187r–v, 201r.

[31] D21 fol. 188r–v.

[32] D21, fol. 300r–v.

the usual things, heard a reading from a heretical book.[33] Sicard de Lunel said that the *perfectus* Grimal Donadieu took him to a cave on the right bank of the Lot at Vers where Cathar books were hidden, and still were, he thought, by 1255 (they could ask P. Pouzazil where they were, Sicard suggested). In addition, he 'saw and handled' the Old and New Testament, one book called the *Book of the Prophets*, and three others.[34] Other people kept books safe for heretics. Guillaume de Burc had held heretical texts for Cathars for eight days or so.[35] Guillaume Barrère had received a heretical book which someone had sent him.[36] Pierre de Cassagnoles was instructed at Gourdon to wear a cross and visit holy places in part as penance for reading and keeping safe heretical books.[37] But believers did not necessarily *read* these books. As with Brian Stock's 'textual communities', a person did not have to be able to read to take part in text-based discussions,[38] especially when what was read aloud was read in the vernacular, as we know some Cathar books were and which many of those mentioned must have been.

Notions about the physical and metaphysical
So, what was it that people in Quercy reported as having read and having heard preached by heretics? We have encountered the formulaic questions used by inquisitors to establish what was, to them, a distinct set of beliefs, which if admitted to branded the suspect *credens haereticorum*. We have observed the near-ubiquitous formulaic question–answer methodology of Doat 21 used by the inquisitor to establish which sect a deponent had been influenced by and how deeply within its belief system they had immersed themselves. I have also suggested that, even though we know that depositions and sentences were structured according to this formula, it does not mean that their content was necessarily entirely imposed from the outside. Where the testimony given by deponents is both reminiscent of dualist belief but at the same time not as straightforward as 's/he believed that God did not make visible things, that Christ was not born of the virgin' and so on, we have real grounds for taking seriously the possibility that they may in fact have conceded these 'dualist' traits, because they are recorded as having said not only thus but more, things that the formulaic question did not accommodate. Where *only* non-formulaic material is noted, we should come to a similar conclusion.

To recapitulate the formulaic words used by the people who admitted contact with what the inquisitors called 'heretics' – some apparently said that

---

[33] D21, fols. 297v–8r.
[34] See also Blaquiere and Dossat, 'Les cathares au jour le jour', p. 263.
[35] D21, fols. 228v–9r.
[36] D21, fol. 221r–v.
[37] D21, fols. 194r, 202v–203r.
[38] B. Stock, *The Implications of Literacy: Written language and Models of Interpretation in the Eleventh and Twelfth Centuries* (Princeton, 1983), pp. 92–240 *passim*.

indeed they believed that God did not make the visible world, that marriage and baptism availed nothing, that the consecrated host was not the body of Christ and that there is no resurrection of the dead. Of the most important people, Guillaume Faure de Pechermer had come to believe through his contact with Cathars.[39] Pons Grimoard, for one, admitted the same.[40] Guillaume-Bernard d'En Arces also said he had believed, from time to time, that God did not make visible things and that one could not know a woman without sin. He also expressed the belief that the body of Christ was not the body of Christ. He learned these errors from Guillemassa, he said.[41]

There was a similar formula identifying deponents with Waldensians.[42] In terms of heretical activity, the inquisitor would establish what food a deponent had taken heretics, in order to distinguish between the two sects. The inquisitor would also ask whether the person being questioned had eaten bread blessed by Waldensians or had taken part in the Waldensian Maundy Thursday supper. In terms of belief, a heretic was anyone who considered it wrong to kill or swear oaths, believed something different about what was holy and what was a sin, and therefore inhabited a different mental and ethical universe from the inquisitors, in which Waldensians had more authority than priests in identifying what would save a person and what would condemn them. At Montcuq a woman called Blanche had sought out and listened to many Waldensians preach. She believed them to be good men, eating bread blessed by them, and believing that no one should swear or kill.[43] Guillaume de Caveroque had been ideologically influenced by this sect, having had dealings with them at work (leading Duvernoy to suggest that he was a clerk). As a result he became a follower, believing not only that they were good people but also that one should neither kill nor swear oaths, as they taught him. Indeed, he had already defended them against friars on the matter of whether one should kill.[44] Géraude de Roquefort, tried at Montcuq, likewise believed after them that it was wrong to swear and kill, and the inquisition clearly connected this to her belief in the Waldensians as good men.[45] There are dozens of such accounts, the only substantial difference being that not everyone had taken part in the suppers.

But what is really problematic about such accounts is not only whether deponents had believed and done these things – although there are so many examples that it seems impossible that many had not – so much as what

---

[39] D22, fol. 5r–v.

[40] D22, fols. 37v–8r.

[41] D22, fol. 223r.

[42] On inquisitorial formulae for Waldensians and what the historian should make of it, see Biller, 'Goodbye to Waldensianism?', p. 19.

[43] D21, fol. 214v.

[44] D21, fol. 216v.

[45] D21, fols. 216v–7r.

else they believed. Did they simply believe what was told to them by 'good men' because they liked the 'good men' better than priests, or did they bring questions and opinions about the 'truth' of Christianity into the discourse themselves? In the case of people convicted of believing the Cathar heresy, some did, and many were willing to inform on other *credentes* in this context.

Raimond Centolh, for example, supposedly said that he heard the wife of Arnaud Bos de Gontaud say at market time that the devil made man from clay, and asked God to put the soul in the man. God said to the devil 'He will be stronger than you or I if he is made of clay, so make him from silt'. The Devil did, and God said 'This is good. Indeed, he is neither strong nor weak', and he then put the soul in the man.[46]

Jean Vital observed that Guillaume Audebert had said

> You want to know the truth about the world below and that above? I tell you that one day when the Lord was preaching to his people in heaven, a messenger came from Earth and said to him that if he did not send someone quickly, he would lose the world. So the lord sent Lucibel into the world at once, and accepted him as his brother, and after this Lucibel wanted to have some of what was above and some of what was below for his inheritance, but the lord did not want this. On account of this there was a long war, and it lasts until this day, because of this other fall [i.e. in addition to Adam and Eve's sin].[47]

Guillaume Audebert, in turn, appears to have claimed to have learned such heresies from Guillaume Faure de Pechermer, and here is further evidence of a conspiracy against him. According to Guillaume Féraut, the latter told Guillaume Audebert and himself what apparently happened next in the narrative above, when Lucibel fell. This was that when God observed his kingdom depleted (*pauperatum*) on account of the fall, he asked of those around him 'Does anyone want to be my son, and for me to be his father?' When no one answered, Christ, who was God's steward, replied 'I want to be your son, and I will go wherever you send me.' And then God sent Christ as his son to Earth to preach in the name of God, and there Christ went.[48] Guillaume Faure, again, was at the heart of what was 'heretical' at Castelsarrasin.

But other people, too, supposedly made statements relating to the corruption of the material world and its implications for the believer. Guillaume de Frussenet had apparently once said that it was not God who made man, bread, wine or grain, but the prostitution (*putaria*) of the earth did this.[49] We saw that Pierre de Penne apparently declared to Pierre Seilan that God neither

---

[46] D22, fol. 32r; Duvernoy, *Le catharisme I*, pp. 63–4.

[47] D22, fol. 12r–v. This is reminiscent of various Cathar stories about the Fall noted in Duvernoy, *Le Catharisme I*, pp. 57–9.

[48] D22, fol. 26r–v.

[49] D22, fol. 227v.

destroyed nor created anything material.[50] Raimond de Rodolos asserted that Aimeric de Na Regina had said that God was not born (*non venerat*) of the Blessed Virgin but *omumbraverat se*: literally, he 'shadowed' or 'disguised himself', so she did not give birth to him but only appeared to be pregnant and the child only appeared to be born, a concept that would be encountered by the inquisitor Jacques Fournier at Montaillou early in the fourteenth century.[51] In addition, he said that God was not present at the mass – just the greedy prelates.[52] Bernard Bort de Cambise, tried at Montauban, mocked the idea that blessed bread was the body of Christ.[53] If consecrated bread was the body of Christ, he said, he would have a full stomach for the whole year.[54] Pierre de Noye went further, making that joke about the size of Christ's body.

Incoherence: mere background noise?

We need to be clear that not all 'unorthodox' beliefs were necessarily dualist or Waldensian and some do not seem to have made sense within any known cosmological system. For example, what can we make of Guillaume Féraut's evidence that Guillaume Audebert had told him that the *perfecti* preached that cattle and horses laboured in Heaven, dragging manure and working in the sky as they did on earth?[55] There are other elements of heretical belief and practice that are difficult to relate to our concept of dualist or other heretical beliefs. Jean Duvernoy has written most about what we could call 'core' beliefs, based on his great knowledge of Cathar texts and Languedoc depositions. As a result, he doubts the validity of the claim by Gausbert Sicard de Courande that a house for *perfectae* was consecrated on his lands.[56] No such ceremony is attested elsewhere and would in any case be meaningless within dualist cosmology, with its abhorrence of matter and denial that ritual or faith or grace could change the fecund status of earth and make it become 'special'.

But other evidence from Quercy points to Gausbert not being unique in wanting 'special places'. It concerns the ritual site at Corbarieu, near Montauban, to which, as we have heard, sick and dying people are recorded as travelling in order to receive the *consolamentum*. It was there that Bernarde Targuier had heard it preached that God was not made visible, that the host was not the body of Christ, that one could not be saved by baptism and marriage; and she had believed it.[57] Hugues du Port of Montauban had a house there, perhaps a hostel like the one he ran at Montauban. There he

---

[50] D21, fol. 217r–v.
[51] D22, fol. 31v. For discussion of this explanation of the Virgin birth see Duvernoy, *Le catharisme I*, 84.
[52] D22, fol. 31v.
[53] D21, fols. 255v–6r.
[54] D21, fol. 254r–v; DPC, pp. 168–9.
[55] D22, fol. 26v; Duvernoy, *Le catharisme I*, pp. 77–8.
[56] D21, fol. 231r; DPC, pp. 126–7.
[57] D22, fol. 3r.

admitted having received *perfecti*, and there several *consolamenta* took place.[58] Perhaps the link between ritual and appropriate places for ritual was so ingrained in orthodox Christian belief that *credentes* found it difficult to disassociate themselves from it. Perhaps *consolamenta* seemed 'better' if they were done at Corbarieu, and perhaps Gausbert Sicard wanted this blessing done irrespective of Cathar beliefs about physical matter.

Similarly paradoxical, as throughout Languedoc, we have a good many references to Cathars blessing bread. Guillaume Pellegri of Gourdon, for one, ate bread blessed by them,[59] as did Rixende de Luzech.[60] Pierre de Noye of Castelsarrasin ate bread blessed by several groups of *perfecti*.[61] The practice is difficult to interpret if Cathars considered all created matter tainted, even food; blessing it did not change this. But was it always the *perfecti* who set the 'belief' agenda? The blessing may have been understood as cleansing, and a replacement for Holy Communion. It was certainly important to many believers. Perhaps, like the attachment to ritual sites and 'special' places, this was a compromise ritual; meaningless to the heretics, it neither helped nor harmed. Its value was that it engaged believers in communities of solidarity.

Another unusual account of heretical practice is that of Bernard Estève of Montauban, who tells us that he prayed with *perfecti*, performing genuflections with them, and also beating his chest.[62] Duvernoy notes that this is the only mention in any inquisitorial document of such a ritual and posits that it might have been a novitiate practice.[63] If it was, we have no other record of it among Cathars. It does sound rather like a strange ritual observed of heretics in Périgord in *c*.1000, whose belief and practice I consider to have been Bogomil-derived.[64] It seems highly unlikely that such a practice had survived and been adopted by thirteenth-century Cathars. However, the Périgord document was recirculated in the 1160s, quite possibly in response to the Cathar threat. It is possible that either Bernard Estève or Pierre Seilan had encountered reports of such a practice.

Weighing it all up
While we have examples of apparently incoherent and incompatible beliefs existing alongside Catholicism, Catharism and Waldensianism, undermining

---

58 D21, fol. 265r–v; DPC, pp. 186–7.
59 D21, fols. 186v–7r.
60 D21, fol. 227r.
61 D22, fol. 28r.
62 D21, fol. 290r.
63 DPC, p. 229 note 327.
64 C. Taylor, 'The letter of Héribert of Périgord as a source for dualist heresy in the society of early eleventh-century Aquitaine', *Journal of Medieval History* 26 (2000), pp. 313–49. See also M. Frassetto, 'The sermons of Adémar of Chabannes and the letter of Héribert. New sources concerning the origins of medieval heresy', *Revue Bénédictine* 109 (1999), pp. 324–40, *cf.* Lobrichon, 'The chiaroscuro of heresy'.

my suggestion that there were clear and distinct confessional choices to be made in Quercy, we should also remember that many deponents recalled being in a transitional stage between beliefs; they responded to what they encountered, evaluated it and attempted to make choices based on it. For example, Guillaume de Broile had assisted in discussion, probably of the New Testament, 'in the presence' of Waldensians, and had discussed the nature of creation with Cathars.[65] Pierre Raimond Roque had listened to Waldensian sermons and believed them to be good people. He listened to Cathar sermons and preaching three, no, four times, he said. He believed the Waldensians to be good men. Then he said he believed the same of the Cathars.[66] The debate had not settled his mind and he remained a rare thing in Quercy, someone who did not know what he thought.

In contrast, Bernard Raimond of Montauban, also tried at Moissac, sought out both sects to find out more about them, desiring to make an informed choice. He found the Waldensians to be good men, but he found the *perfecti* to be better, having discussed the matter with someone else as well, and became attached to them thereafter, accompanying his Cathar sister from Toulouse to Montauban and being involved in the 1223 Cathar council at Pujols in the Agenais, to which he led a *perfectus* and where he saw other heretics and listened as they preached.[67] In other words, having made a conscious decision as to which belief system he was the most convinced by – Catholicism, Waldensianism or Catharism – he became one of the most important *credentes* in Quercy.

The Quercy documentation also gives us insight into a very exciting process taking place in the early decades of the thirteenth century: public debates between the heretical sects. Such disputations seem to have usually taken place at Montauban, perhaps because there were most Waldensians there. Pierre Bacou of Montauban assisted Waldensians in the dispute with Cathars noted above. The brothers Raimond and Jacques Carbonnel of Montauban, Waldensian adherents, helped arrange a disputation with Cathars.[68] Guillaume Carbonnel also assisted in a dispute, perhaps the same one, and favoured Waldensians.[69] Guillaume Laurent assisted in a dispute, but does not appear to have been an adherent of either party very actively.[70] François, the clerk at Montcuq, also admitted having assisted in such a debate.[71] At Gourdon, Pana, the Waldensian adherent who 'loved Pierre de

---

[65] D21, fols. 263r–v.

[66] D21, fols. 231v–2r.

[67] D21, fols. 242r–3r, 286r. The council was attested by the papal Conrad von Urach in 1223: Mansi, *Concilia*, XXII, 1204–6. On the literature and its significance, see Taylor, *Heresy*, pp. 226–8.

[68] D21, fol. 234r–v.

[69] D21, fol. 254r.

[70] D21, fol. 250v.

[71] D21, fols. 219v–220r.

Vals like an angel from God', had allowed *perfecti* and Waldensians to dispute in her house.[72] Galtier d'Arcambal only encountered Waldensians because they were disputing in his house.[73] En Gorse of Montpezat received heretics in his house and also heard a debate between *perfecti* and Waldensians.[74] It was in part through witnessing such a debate that Guillaume de Broile had encountered both sets of belief.[75]

We must surely consider that similarly 'informed' thinking took place in relation to the teaching of the Catholic clergy. Indeed, our impression of an indolent Catholic clergy in Languedoc, not interested in their flock, breaks down again in the context of Quercy, where some priests fought hard for the souls in their care. We have numerous accounts of Cathars and clergy debating their beliefs. In *c.*1220, for example, Guillaume Faure de Pechhermer had seen the *perfecti* Guillaume de Cavelsaut, Raimond Grimoard and Bernard de la Mothe in the home of Arnaud Pagan, where they were debating with two priests of the town, in which debate he, Arnaud and Arnaud's wife Pétronille had assisted.[76] The Durand brothers Bernard and Gausbert had *perfecti* in their house for three days and there they debated with a priest.[77] Guillaume Barrère, noted above for his extensive involvement with the *perfecti*, not least the Montolieu network with Barthélémy de Carcassonne at its heart, had sometimes doubted which was the best faith, the Roman or that of the heretics. In spite all of this, he said, he had never stopped believing in the Catholic faith.[78]

As such, I cannot escape the conclusion that the people in audiences such as these – and there were many of them – were aware of which sets of beliefs the clergy held and which sets they labelled as 'heretical'. Through debates the laity came to a decent understanding of what was 'wrong' about the two dissident sets of belief in relation to what the priests taught and what the 'heretics' also taught about themselves and each other.

We turn now to evidence of organisational structures in the heretical sphere, to explore if and how heretics in Quercy operated and the impact this had. We cannot resolve the question of whether there was a Cathar 'church' on the basis of the Quercy evidence. Only occasionally do deponents give evidence concerning formal structures among the sectarians. Ideas and beliefs seem to have mattered more; at least, the inquisitors do not seem to have devoted a great deal of time to extracting the sort of information through which histo-

---

72 D21, fols. 194v, 203v.
73 D21, fols. 195v, 196v–7r.
74 D21, fol. 308v.
75 D21, fol. 263r–v.
76 D22, fol. 4r–v.
77 D21, fol. 286v; DPC, pp. 222–3.
78 D21, fol. 221r–v.

rians and medieval commentators came to the conclusion that there was a Cathar 'church'. But there is some evidence of this sort nonetheless.

Quercy and a Cathar 'Church'

Hierarchy

Pierre de Penne's sentence, awarded by Pierre Seilan, includes the following: 'Item, he did not believe in any of the sacraments of the Church and believed that the only church was the *heretical* church, and that no one was saved through the Roman Church, but that everyone was saved in the heretical church.'[79] This fits the inquisitorial discourse too neatly. The account has been 'interpreted' by the court, just as the other depositions of *credentes* supposedly calling Cathars 'heretics' must have been. If we are certain that Pierre de Penne did not consider Cathars to be 'heretics', which he certainly did not, we cannot be sure that he made an equally neat assertion about a Cathar 'church'. Unlike the more ambiguous and nuanced assertions made by deponents above, this casts doubt on there being something that Cathars in Quercy called a 'church', and we should also keep in mind that *ecclesia* in the depositions could perhaps merely refer to the concept of a devotional community that had been expressed in the vernacular.

Furthermore, people referred to as Cathar bishops and deacons by historians – men such as Vigouroux de la Bacone, Bernard de la Mothe and Guillaume de Caussade – are not necessarily or consistently given these titles by deponents in Quercy. In Doat 21 we have few references to heretical titles at all. Typical of references to Vigouroux is the record that Géraude de Lacoste of Montcuq received 'Vigouroux and his *socius*' in her home and heard him preach.[80]

However, we have other evidence concerning Cathar organisational structures that seems indeed to have been offered by deponents. The evidence indicates that whether heretical titles were apparently attributed to heretics by deponents very much depended on the inquisitors' preference. Brother Ferrer's court and that of Bernard de Caux in particular recorded such details. We have mention of several Cathar 'deacons'. Raimond Aimeric is attributed the title *diachonus* by Arnaude de la Mothe,[81] and Guilabert de Castres is *episcopus*.[82] Her uncle Bernard de la Mothe is *haereticus* sometimes,[83] but other times *diachonus* of Lanta.[84] Significant *credentes* interviewed by Bernard de

---

[79] D21, fol. 217r–v.
[80] D21, fol. 222r; DPC, pp. 106–7.
[81] D23, fols. 3r, 5v.
[82] D23, fol. 17v.
[83] In Doats 21–3 generally.
[84] D23, fols. 7r, 15v.

Caux were aware of organisational structures as well. Raimond Jean d'Abia is recorded as referring to Bernard de la Mothe as both *haereticus*[85] and *diachonus haereticorum*.[86] He refers to the heretic Raimond-Bernard in the same way,[87] and to Guiraud de Gourdon of Caraman also as a heretical deacon.[88] De Caux has Guillaume Faure de Pechermer referring to Guilhabert de Castres, the single most significant *perfectus* in Languedoc in the 1220s, as *episcopus haereticorum* when he met him at Toulouse.[89] In contrast, Guillemette de Sapiac is recorded as telling Pierre Seilan that she saw Guiraud Abit and his *socius*.[90] Abit is known to historians as the Cathar bishop of the Carcassès from *c.*1227 to 1228.[91] That he is not named as such by Guillemette could reflect Pierre Seilan's wider preferences concerning what was recorded and what was not.

On the question of Cathar 'dioceses', I have argued elsewhere that the heresiarch Vigouroux de la Bacone, to whom we have many references in Quercy, was Cathar bishop not only of the Agenais, with which he is usually associated in the sources, but also bishop of the heretics in Quercy from *c.*1220;[92] and furthermore that in 1223 he and the heretic Barthélemy de Carcassonne caused a schism between the 'mitigated' and 'absolute' forms of dualism, that he was reconsoled at Pujols in the Agenais by Barthélemy into the moderate order, and that Barthélemy replaced him as bishop of the Agenais. I still support Bernard Hamilton's conclusions on what was occurring within the Cathar hierarchy of the Agenais.[93]

I would also maintain that Vigouroux was one of the most important heresiarchs to operate in Quercy, but am now less sure that he was recognised as 'bishop' of Quercy's heretics. The question of his jurisdiction is not answered by the wealth of references to him and may not have been significant to

---

[85] D23, fols. 262r, 633.

[86] D23, fol. 273v.

[87] D23, fol. 267v.

[88] D23, fol. 267r. He is not connected to the lords of Gourdon in Quercy.

[89] D22, fol. 6r.

[90] D21, fols. 240v–1r; DPC, pp. 144–5 note 248.

[91] For example in Roquebert, *L'epopee*, I, p. 100.

[92] See Taylor, *Heresy*, pp. 177–9 and 'Authority and the Cathar heresy', pp. 172, 173–4. *Cf.* Duvernoy, *Le catharisme II*, p. 231.

[93] The papal legate Conrad von Urach, an ally of the crusade in Languedoc since 1217, stated in 1223 that a certain Barthélemy of Carcassonne had been sent into the Agenais by a new 'pope' of the Cathars, a heresiarch in Bosnia, in order to achieve the resignation of the Cathar bishop *Vigorosus de Bathona* and that after he had convinced Vigouroux to resign, at a Cathar council at Pujols, just south of Villeneuve-sur-Lot, the latter retired to the Toulousain and Barthélémy took over the running of his church: Hamilton, 'The Cathar council of Saint Félix', pp. 23–53. His case relates to the authenticity of the evidence for the Cathar council at Saint-Félix de Caraman in the 1170s. On the career of Vigouroux de la Bacone, see also Taylor, *Heresy*, pp. 225–31 (pp. 226–7); Y. Dossat, 'Un évêque Cathare originaire de l'Agenais', pp. 623–39; Duvernoy, *La catharisme II*, pp. 70–1, 263.

ordinary believers or those tolerant of heretics, however neatly a detailed reading of the sources can be made to fit this version of events.[94] Furthermore, Georges Passerat places the community of Beaucaire, where Guillaume de Caussade was the dominant heresiarch, under the jurisdiction of the Cathar bishop of Albi.[95] However, both Pons Grimoard, as *seneschal*, and the inquisitors related to Guillaume de Caussade's Beaucaire in a quercinois context. As such, there was either a dispute between the Cathar dioceses of Agen and Albi concerning lower Quercy, or there was an overlap of influence there, or the matter was not significant enough to contemporaries to be referred to in depositions. The first two possibilities could be read into the accounts of men such as Rainier Sacconi and into the sources for the schism of 1223, but is all but absent in the depositions, even those recognising that Vigouroux was *a* bishop (i.e. bishop, but perhaps of somewhere else, such as Agen). However, while I would accept the existence of Cathar dioceses on an institutional level for the *perfecti* at least, I do not think it is possible, or especially useful, to see the heretics of Quercy under the rigid jurisdiction of any one Cathar bishop.

One of the most important *credentes* at Montcuq was one of its lords, Bertrand de la Roque-de Montcuq. His sentence is evidence of the close linkage between Montcuq and the Agenais heretics, including their bishop. Among other things, Bertrand admitted directing *perfecti* 'in the house of Vigouroux' (*in domo Vigoros*), probably referring to Castelmoron-sur-Lot in the Agenais, where the heresiarch is known to have had property.[96] He said that he saw Vigouroux and his *socius* at Moissac, and was asked by Vigouroux to act as an escort for him.[97] Bertrand's account has the concept of Cathar hierarchy as the peg on which everything else hangs. In fact, the first item in it is an admission of having received Guillaume de Caussade and his brother Guiraud, both *perfecti*, in what sounds like a meeting between them and another, unnamed, *perfectus*.[98]

I have to confess also to having previously underestimated the significance of Guillaume de Caussade in Quercy,[99] not appreciating the extent of his activity other than at Caussade itself.[100] Duvernoy makes the case for his

---

94   Taylor, *Heresy*, p. 228.
95   'Cathares en Bas-Quercy', esp. pp. 149–50.
96   Taylor, *Heresy*, pp. 228–9.
97   D21, fol. 219r–v. Duvernoy suggests that this Vigouroux is not necessarily Vigouroux de la Bacone (DPC, note 186). The account makes perfect sense, however, if we consider Montcuq's geographical position in relation to the Agenais and Castelmoron, where Yves Dossat has established Vigouroux had a house: above, Chapter 5, p. 158.
98   D21, fol. 219v.
99   Taylor, 'Authority and the Cathar heresy', p. 173, *cf.* Passerat, 'Cathares en Bas-Quercy', pp. 149–65.
100   See above, Chapter 4, pp. 137, 140, 147.

being a deacon,[101] and we have observed that his family were very influential at Beaucaire, where Guillaume the miller pointed out to credulous women-folk that it was 'Holy Guillaume', not St Martin, who had had a mill built for them. The *credens* Eustache received a greeting there from the heretic via François the clerk,[102] and Pierre Vidien de Valtauren was sent by Jauffré de Caussade to fetch Guillaume, although the latter would not come.[103] This heresiarch was influential at Montcuq, as we shall see, some distance indeed from Caussade and Beaucaire, further strengthening the impression that Montcuq was highly significant to Cather networks and that it was Mont-cuq's connections with Gourdon, the Agenais and Bas-Quercy that facilitated the conversion of the Vaux and Bouriane.

We have other references to networks of heretical organisation beyond Quercy and even beyond Languedoc involving not merely transporting or concealing heretics. Their numerousness indicates that from the 1220s Quercy was far from peripheral in terms of southern French and even international heretical structures. The *credentes* of Montcuq were very involved again. Guillaume Varrera was involved in the Aude network with Barthélemy de Carcassonne at its heart. On someone's orders (we do not discover whose) he had led heretics from Montolieu to Toulouse.[104] Durand Vairet, also of Montcuq, was with heretics at Martel and beyond Quercy at Laure. He was even involved in seeking advice concerning getting a heretic set free.[105] In other examples, Guillaume Faure de Pechermer gives us accounts of people from Castelsarrasin with leading *perfecti* at Toulouse and notes connections between Montauban heretics and those of Lantarès, Caraman and Agen.[106] Finally, we should note that heretics and believers in Quercy were locked into heretical networks extending into Italy. Bernard Estève of Moissac had gone to Italy and seen Cathars in three places in Cremona.[107] Guillaume de Caus-sade was able to commission Arnaud de Peyre of Montcuq to accompany the heretic's sister and niece to Cremona, where the latter believed they were to become *perfectae*.[108] Arnaud Rufet of Montauban saw *perfecti* at Milan.[109] We can see, therefore, that Quercy was far from peripheral to heretical networks in western Europe.

---

101 *Le catharisme II*, pp. 230–4 esp. note 86, 257–66, esp. 284. See also Albe, *L'hérésie … en Quercy*, pp. 15–16.
102 D21, fol. 228r.
103 D21, fols. 228v–9r, and see DPC, p. 123.
104 D21, fol. 221r–v.
105 D21, fols. 220r–21r.
106 D22, fols. 8v–9r.
107 D21, f. 290r. Although he may have been something of a fantasist, being the same *credens* who told Pierre Seilan that heretics had taught him to beat his chest when he prayed (see above, p. 196).
108 D21, fol. 226r–v.
109 D21, fol. 263r.

Heresy in disguise

One of the most intriguing aspects of the Quercy evidence is the revelation that Catharism infiltrated monastic institutions. This is wonderful material to work on because one reason, according to the established models, why the heresy was taken up by the lesser nobles to the extent that it was was that monastic institutions were few and far between, with provision for women being lacking in particular. We have noted that in the twelfth century there was no lack of houses to patronise and aspire to enter, Cistercian Obazine being the best example. In *c*.1170, from the evidence in Chapter 2, no fewer than three noble women of Quercy looked to end their days at Coyroux, and their men-folk likewise looked to Obazine, as in the case of Arnaud de la Roque-de Linars.

But all was not as it seemed. From several deponents we hear that Linars, a house for women protected by the de la Roque-de Linars and the de Goulême, only masqueraded as a Catholic abbey. It was actually a house of *perfectae*, including during the crusade, when its occupants disguised themselves in the habits of nuns.[110] Arnaude de la Mothe spent a short time there and revealed that at that time its six women were *perfectae* 'in nuns' habits'. Also, at Augustinian Lativia (modern Lécune), Prioress Raimonde de Mazerac was a *perfecta* for four or five years, and her house concealed several others like her. Her family, the lords of Saint-Jean-de-Mazerac, were connected to the de Caussade, as we know from the testimony of Guillaume Donadieu de Mazerac. She asked Pierre Seilan whether the Blessed Virgin had suffered giving birth like other women, and whether she had suckled Jesus bodily. She was to be expelled from her abbey and placed in a stricter monastery.[111]

Perfectae, as we have noted, were far less mobile than their male counterparts, and so when they did confine themselves it was in different circumstances. These houses were probably little different in practice from houses run by women such as Jeanne d'Avignon in towns, being the way in which women chose to practise their faith, except that we hear that at times of danger their own robes had to be exchanged for those of nuns. In contrast, male heretics entered supposedly orthodox abbeys more immediately to conceal themselves. Our best example is that of Cistercian Belleperche, close to Castelsarrasin, whose order first ruled against its monks sheltering heretics in 1218. Nonetheless, they were sometimes welcomed, or at least tolerated, at Belleperche before the inquisition.[112] This was perhaps due to the social status of those heretics entering the abbey. One of them was none other than Falquet de Saint-Paul, a lord of Moissac, who sheltered there along with Bernard

---

110 D23, fols. 7v–8r.

111 D21, fol. 307r; DPC, pp. 13, 236–7; Albe, *L'hérésie … en Quercy*, p. 16.

112 On Belleperche see Kienzle, *Cistercians, Heresy and Crusade*, pp. 171, 215, although I cannot extrapolate from this sort of evidence, as she does, that some Cistercians sympathised with Cathars.

d'Alegre-de Borrel until the Dominicans themselves arrived in the region and Falquet fled for Italy.[113] Bernard d'Alegre-de Borrel himself continued to live at the abbey, according to Bernarde Targuier.[114] But when, in the early 1240s, Rostanh de Bressols led Raimond Estève, a condemned heretic, to the abbey apparently expecting to find him asylum, the monks were too afraid to take him in, as Brother Otto recounted to Jean Vital, Pierre Galaup and Bernard de Crousilles.[115] Otto and his brothers were not alone in fearing to shelter *perfecti* in the inquisitorial period. By the 1240s the heretics were living hand to mouth and continually having to move on for fear of staying in one place too long. They lived stressfully and clandestinely for years, destitute if support networks such as those we have noted as giving them food, shelter and holding money for them broke down, and ever fearful of betrayal, which could come from one's nearest and dearest, as we have seen.

But we should consider as well the safety of their supporters. *Credentes* were tied through formal and informal bonds of obligation to heretics. Depending on their own social status and contractual obligations, many of their helpers must have been unwilling. Even if one merely sheltered a heretic and no case could be made against you regarding worse crimes, personal freedom could be snatched away, as could the house in which the heretic had been received. In fact, Cathars became a liability from 1229. Surely only the most devoted of their followers can have genuinely welcomed the dissidents as they sought safe places to stay.

Unwelcome guests and ritual impositions

In 1274 a nurse of the hospital at Saint-Antonin-Noble-Val told the inquisition that Guillemette Badoel had told her, a long time ago, that once at Castelnau-Montratier she saw three women she believed were *perfectae* leaving a house near the castle, but that when they saw her they went back inside and stayed there.[116] Here we gain a glimpse of what it must have been like to live the hunted, persecuted life of a heretic, in this case Cathars. But we should also fear for the owner of the house in question. From such accounts we gain the impression that life was extremely stressful for the *perfecti*, but should note also that it must have been likewise for those protecting them.

Many records give us further insight. Guillaume Roudat of Montcuq had concealed and kept safe some *perfecti* and those helping them, enabling them to make their escape when someone came searching for them.[117] We heard from Pons Grimoard (see Chapter 4) that heretics already hiding in a house

---

[113] D22, fol. 3r; Guillaume Pelhisson, *Chronique*, pp. 56–9; Douais, *Documents*, p. 95; DPC, p. 231 note 331.

[114] D22, fol. 3r.

[115] D22, fol. 12r.

[116] D25, fols. 58v–59r; DPC, p. 16.

[117] D21, fol. 215v.

at Lauzerte took refuge in the tower when he arrived, only revealing themselves later. We have a similar reference at Moissac. On one occasion when *perfectae* had been arrested there Raimond de Bénac was told by some fearful person, who he did not identify, to hurry to the heretics hiding in the latter's house and get them also to climb up into the tower, which he did.[118] Arnaud de Sapiac junior was entrusted with taking heretics to a certain house, but no one there wanted to receive them and so he led them away again. He let them hide on the porch of his own house so that they would not be seen by men they were hiding from, but they asked him if they could stay in the house itself. He refused, but instead led them to another man they knew, who did shelter them.[119] Hugues Jauffré was paid seventy *solidi* as what appears to have been danger money for sheltering them.[120]

Such evidence demonstrates that people were afraid to accommodate heretics in general but also that they might take pains to keep heretics out of their houses more specifically for fear of being dispossessed by the bishop or inquisitor. Pierre-Raimond Boca, tried at Montauban, who admitted many crimes of the regular sort, would also admit only to having received a *perfectus* on his porch (*in portico sua*). Duvernoy suggests that this strategy, like Arnaud de Sapiac's, was intended to save his house from destruction, because he had not let them inside.[121] Rather like vampires, then, it could be unwise to invite them across the threshold. A visit by *perfecti* – being able to host and feed them and take part in ritual life with them – was an honour and a blessing, but also a burden on many levels.

With intra-sectarian activity, nothing was straightforward. Take gift-giving *by* Cathars. This was not an act of pure generosity anymore than was the famous Occitan noble largesse. For Cathars, gifts seem to have been a way of creating and also dominating bonds of reciprocity in which they were not only supported economically but in which they merely deigned to reciprocate. Gift-giving demonstrated that they were well-connected and not entirely dependent on the recipient *credens* anyway – having, by implication, goods and money in surplus. This is not unlike the relationship between Catholic clergy and laity. They required and expected gifts from supporters, but had so many of these that they too could demonstrate generosity, downgrading the status of the gift-giver thereby. The surplus came, by implication, from more elite donors. Was it good to get a gift from a Cathar, in fact? Did it do more than demonstrate the superior standing of the elect? We should note here quite a stark contrast with Waldensians, who do not appear to have given gifts, only to have received goods, and practical ones at that.

---

118 D21, fol. 304r.
119 D21, fols. 267v–8r.
120 D21, fol. 297v.
121 D21, fol. 232r; DPC, pp. 128–9 note 234.

Furthermore, because of the dualists' dietary regime, the believer must have been pleased when their turn at accommodating the *perfecti* coincided with one of their frequent periods of fasting. Of the two sects, the *perfecti* were the most demanding to support in terms of their dietary requirements. Their dietary regime dominated a host's household to the extent that new pots had to be bought and kept for the use of the *perfecti* in case the believer accidentally contaminated their food by placing it in a vessel that had at another time contained meat.

Cathar aloofness concerning the material world did not prevent them from indulging in highly structured ritual performances, demanding adoring, genuflection, requests for blessings and prayers to God, and participation in rituals such as the *appareillamentum* and *melioramentum* as well as the *consolamentum*.[122] Guillaume Faure de Pechhermer, among others, recalled such rituals. Gausbert de Clusel said that 'when he came upon them he always inclined his head and said 'Bless us' (*Benedicite*).[123] This drew attention to their superior status, in recognition of their purity and the fact that they, out of everyone, knew that they would be 'saved'.

The *credens* could be saved as well, of course, but only if they were to 'die in the hands' of the pure. This involved the most significant ritual of all, the transforming of the believer into a *perfectus* or *perfectae* themselves, the *consolamentum* administered at the point of death: this was what was meant by dying 'in their hands'. We have observed that *perfecti* were paid both in kind and in money for performing the ceremony, and also that believers sometimes travelled to other places – we hear specifically of Corbarieu and Villemur – to receive this sacrament, even if they were very ill. Otherwise they arranged for heretics to come to their house to perform it.

But the role in this ceremony of the ordinary believer, as opposed to be person about to be 'consoled', is ambiguous. Many examples have been noted of people both being present at *consolamenta* and also assisting at them. We have observed that Huguette of Gourdon had assisted at her husband's, for instance. Bernard de Latour, in another example, had conveyed sick people to the heretics and helped during the ceremony at En Roques's home.[124] Guillaume d'Eysses, tried at Gourdon, who had accompanied them on their flight at Easter in 1229, had received them in his house and allowed them to perform there the *consolamentum* of Jeanne de Castelnau, which he witnessed.[125]

However, sometimes *credentes* were explicitly excluded from the ceremony. In *c.*1223, Guillaume Faure de Pechermer had attended the *consolamentum* of

---

[122] Jean Duvernoy has written most on the subject of Cathar rituals. See, in particular, *Le catharisme II*, pp. 203–16.
[123] D21, fols. 293r–4r; DPC, pp. 233–4 and note 336.
[124] D21, fol. 186v; DPC, pp. 34–5 and n. 78; Combarieu, *Dictionnaire*, p. 134.
[125] D21, fol. 201v.

Etienne Sanche at the latter's house, but the heretics had shooed him from the room when the ceremony actually started, he said, and had done the same even to Etienne's wife, Raimonde.[126] Neither was it something that the most ardent and tested adherent would do routinely as part of their supportive role in the heresy. For all his extensive involvement in the heresy, Pierre de Noye said he had never seen a *consolamentum* take place.[127] Unfortunately we lack even one account of what took place at *consolamenta* in Quercy, and no great insight can be given into the ritual itself from this evidence base alone.

In contrast, Waldensians were so much simpler in their demands on the believer. Their distinctive ritual was the collective re-enactment of the Last Supper on Maundy Thursday, which they commemorated as Christ had commanded. Of the approximately 165 people who admitted contact with Waldensians at Montauban, 30 had either helped at the Waldensian celebration of the Last Supper (*interfuit cene Valdensium*) or had eaten at it. Pons de la Jonquière of Montauban, for example, had assisted at the ritual and, during it, had eaten and drunk bread and wine blessed by the Waldensians.[128] Pierre de la Barrière had assisted on two occasions and eaten fish and bread and wine similarly blessed.[129] Raimond Hugues assisted also.[130]

But they ate the same food as the people supporting them, and prayed the same prayers. The Waldensians also taught prayers, to Na Sauris of Montcuq, for example,[131] and Pérégrine Gasc said the same of the Waldensians at Moissac in 1244. They held Easter Sunday as special; Arnaud Capre shared meat with them then.[132] Otherwise, the major differences between Catholics and Waldensians were that Waldensians were not licensed to preach, let alone perform or undermine sacraments, which in Quercy we hear that they did. From Na Coutes we learn that they preached on Easter day, and she also tells us about their hearing confessions and administering penances.[133]

Just as the inquisitor distinguished between the two sects using evidence for ritual participation such as this, so can the historian. Furthermore, it is evident that people in Quercy made a distinction also. In accordance with my suggestion that few individuals engaged at any deep level with both heresies, Raimond Gastaud of Montauban is untypical in Quercy in having engaged in specific ritual practice with both sects: he celebrated the commemoration of the Last Supper with Waldensians, but greeted and adored *perfecti* and asked

---

[126]   D22, fol. 7v.
[127]   D22, fols. 28v–29r.
[128]   D21, fol. 249r–v.
[129]   D21, fol. 231v.
[130]   D21, fol. 255r.
[131]   D21, fol. 222v.
[132]   D21, fol. 257v.
[133]   D21, fols. 241v–2r.

of them *Benedicte*.[134] Hedging one's bets in this way was unwise in the event, and Raimond was sent to Constantinople for two years by Pierre Seilan.

The sort of material above gives the impression of heresy in Quercy from an anthropological, synchronic perspective; a 'snapshot' of heretical life, if you like. But heresy was a diachronic process rather than a characteristic of Quercy. The contexts in which it grew and changed will be discussed further in Chapter 7.

---

[134] D21, fols. 261v–2r.

7

The Reshaping of Quercy

Between c.1200 and c.1250, because of what happened to it in military and political terms, Quercy ceased to be a borderland between Aquitaine and Languedoc, politically influenced by both Toulouse and the Poitevin-ruled Limousin. Instead, even its northern lords reorientated themselves towards Languedoc. They did so in confessional terms also. The latter in particular is almost incredible when we consider the devotional life of Quercy south of the Dordogne, focused on the Cistercians of the Limousin and influenced politically by its viscounts, whom the lords of Gourdon joined in the defence of orthodoxy in 1209. I have highlighted the fact that the lords of Gourdon cannot be demonstrated to have encountered heretics at close quarters until the 1214 siege of Casseneuil in the Agenais, during which Ratier de Castelnau-Montratier, along with numerous *perfecti*, was protected by its lord Hugues de Rovignan. But, by the end of the wars, Quercy had been corrupted and its leading castellans induced to likewise protect, if not actually 'believe in', the quarry the crusaders sought. We shall now address the reasons for this *volte face*.

The Social Impact of the Invasion

As observed in Chapter 3, in August 1212 Montcuq was abandoned by its *bailli* Guiraud de Montfabès and the *castrum* was given to Baudouin of Toulouse. The lords of Lolmie, a castle pertaining to Montcuq, became Baudouin's vassals. The lords of Mondenard were already his allies, Armand de Mondenard having supported his operation in lower Quercy in 1211. But, along with Ratier de Castelnau-Montratier, who was the most important member of the family of Gourdon in the Vaux, the lords of Lolmie and Mondenard conspired to have their new master murdered in 1214 and saw the plan through.

We also know that the pope had envisaged that 'heretical' or otherwise uncooperative lords of Languedoc would be replaced by others loyal to Rome: loyal politically as well as in terms of personal belief. This was his major strategy for opposing the *perfecti*. So, in 1212 the lords of Gourdon, established patrons of Obazine, allies of the viscounts of Turenne, rivals of Raimond VI for authority within the Vaux in any case and with rights at Montcuq themselves, could not have been better placed to take control of the Vaux decisively.[1] The installation of Baudouin of Toulouse at Montcuq was surely the point at which the lords of Gourdon and their allies in the Vaux began reconsidering their position with regard to the crusade: hence the rebellion in 1214.

There is no evidence of the political disaffection of Bertrand de Gourdon himself manifesting itself until 1217–18, and the path he chose was more complex than that of Ratier de Castelnau-Montratier. He had performed homage to Simon de Montfort in 1211 and, despite presumably being perturbed by events in 1212–14, did so again in 1217.[2] However, he took up arms in support of Toulouse in its great siege of 1217–18, and in January of the latter year was reprimanded for this by the pope.[3] Yet on 25 May 1218 de Montfort gave 'to our dear and faithful' (dilecto et fideli nostro) Bertrand de Gourdon 100 *livres* of Cahors as rent for *Caselliges* (probably Lamothe-Cassel) in exchange for a third declaration of fealty.[4] Shortly after the attempted relief of Toulouse, therefore, Bertrand de Gourdon was in favour again with the crusader's leader. He performed homage three times to the French king also, in 1211, 1226 and 1227.[5] He had then secured clerical allies in 1233, joining the Confederation of Rocamadour, and he probably also gave the castle of Moulin, at nearby Nôtre-Dame-des-Neiges, to the deacons of le Vigan, saving his reduced right to demand hospitality there, now for merely five of his knights.[6]

It would be easy to see the lords of Gourdon and others of the Vaux as fickle and cynical in their alliances, not least when we consider their initial, probably genuine, enthusiasm for crusading, their willingness to submit both to the abbot of Cîteaux as the crusade's leader in 1209 and ultimately to a new French overlord, Simon de Montfort, a man in no sense their social superior but with whom it was wise to be friends. However, we should not simply understand the situation in Quercy as being one in which lords such as these were forced simply to acknowledge a new count of Toulouse, or lord of Montcuq, for that matter.

The new lords demanded the types of social relationships with vassals that were the basis of militarised society in northern and eastern France, whence

---

[1] Taylor, *Heresy*, p. 239, and below, and see chapters 2 and 4 for Guiraud de Gourdon-de Montcuq, Bertrand de Gourdon-de Montcuq and Bernard de Gourdon, all at Montcuq.

[2] Taylor, *Heresy*, pp. 195, 221, 239.

[3] See above, p. 101.

[4] *HGL*, VI, 514–15. *Cf.* Bulit, who does not use the crusade sources and places the first homage of Bertrand de Gourdon to de Montfort in 1218 and in the context of the confirmation of the latter in 1215 of his legal status as count of Toulouse: *Gourdon*, p. 64 and see p. 78.

[5] AD Lot F. 98; *HGL*, VIII, 1119.

[6] The contents of this charter were communicated in person to Roger Bulit by Edmund Albe, Quercy's best known archivist, but subsequently lost: Bulit, *Gourdon*, p. 65.

the crusaders hailed. Fiefs were no longer essentially about the distribution of rights to revenues, the social glue discussed in Chapter 2 that acknowledged status through wealth but preserved horizontal relationships established between free social equals. Fief holding now also meant that vassals were obliged to provide men-at-arms for the crusaders' campaigns, and that castles would be seized from uncooperative vassals. In 1212, therefore, the lords of Lolmie became vassals not only of a new master, but vassals of a far more dependent type than previously known, meaning a significant shift in what constituted their obligations.

Likewise, when Bertrand de Gourdon became the vassal of Simon de Montfort for *castra* pertaining to his family in the Bouriane and Vaux – some of which were originally allods associated with the family as bishops and protectors of the see of Cahors, others of which were perhaps held by the second or third generation of families such as the d'Arcambal originating within the garrison of Gourdon – the crusader considered them his to grant or withhold. Furthermore, he considered the ties between himself and his new vassal as superseding other obligations and relationships that the lord of Gourdon had or might enter into. Bertrand's previous lord, Raimond VI, had not thought in this way. It was not only political masters that were changing, therefore, but cultures also. Resistance to this, as much as anything, may have lain behind alliances made and broken after 1209.

This understanding also helps us to explain the dense networks of increasingly dissident political and familial association that culminated ultimately in three nodes of rebel authority in the western half of Quercy: the castellans of Gourdon, the elite of Castelsarrasin and the lords of Caussade. The lesser nobles within these spheres of authority drifted into their chosen confessional circle too, in the case of Caussade and Castelsarrasin. I would further suggest that in spite of the fact that Bertrand de Gourdon, the chief lord of Gourdon in his lifetime, merely tolerated heretics and did little to encourage them, and at least once sent them away, the next generation, Fortanier's, turned its back on family tradition and was more welcoming when Cathars and Waldensians first attempted to infiltrate Gourdon. I would suggest that this was in part an empathy with the 'good Christians' as they arrived *en masse* in the early days of the inquisition: they were refugees from Roman authority, which was no longer acknowledged by powerful nobles in central and northern Quercy, whether or not they had adopted any 'counter-church'.

Just to remind ourselves that heresy was not ubiquitous, that such concentrations really did exist and as such need explaining, we should note that the east of Quercy, dominated by the Benedictines and the lords of Cardaillac (who also performed homage to the crown in 1243),[7] was all but immune to heresy. Not only were its authorities spotless in terms that the inquisitors

---

[7] *HGL*, VIII, 1119.

were interested in, but they had crusaded and, unlike the de Gourdon, had never been attacked by the crusade. Taken together, the names and places represented in the Rocamadour charter of 1233, for example, fall into three spheres: Cahors, Figeac and Gourdon. The names of lords and towns of the Gourdon area signing in 1233 overlap very extensively with those in which heresy was identified (they are listed below). Those from the area around Figeac and Cahors, to a town or lord, did not.[8] Thus the confessional preference of the power at the centre of such secular networks could affect the complexion of the wider group. This is not entirely surprising and has been suggested of other regions, but can be evidenced as well as asserted of Quercy.

Client Lords: Protectors of Heretics

Indeed, R. I. Moore notes more generally of Languedoc that it was the more minor nobility that acted as the most significant protectors of Catharism.[9] M. Lambert observes that '(o)nce sympathy for Catharism was established in a *lignage* it could travel both horizontally through family connections and downwards through lines of dependency'.[10] While I would stress the 'could' in Lambert's statement in terms of families, and be wary of asserting that it necessarily *did*, this and his observation on lines of dependency holds for Quercy also. Indeed, Quercy is an example of Moore's and Lambert's assertions. James Given further observes of these heretical networks that they came into their own as part of strategies for surviving inquisition. By drawing neighbours whose orthodox sympathies were compromised into client relationships with them, nobles helped to secure themselves solidarity from those dependent on them for protection.[11] Something similar is demonstrable in the Agenais.[12] Client relationships between the greater and lesser lords reflect relative economic power, military association, shared patronage of particular abbeys and relative abilities to forge independent political relationships. These relationships, between disaffected leading nobles and the networks of influence extending from their *castra* – between themselves and the more minor castellanies in lower Quercy, the Vaux and Bouriane – were decisive in structuring resistance to the crusade in Quercy and resistance to the evils wrought by men who also called themselves Christians, but who

---

8   Those of Figeac were Galhard and Raimond d'Assier and their men; Déodat and
     Guillaume de Bouyssou; the unnamed knights and men of Thémines, Camboulit,
     Lentilhac, Sénaillac; and the lords and towns of Faycelles, Felzins, Bio, Issepts, Fons.
     Those of the Cahorsain were Corn, Anglars and Livernon.
9   Moore, *Origins*, p. 237.
10   Lambert, *The Cathars*, p. 68.
11   Given, *Inquisition, passim*.
12   Taylor, *Heresy*, p. 166.

attacked other Christians, stealing their livelihood and the status that went with holding Occitan fiefs.

The lords of Gourdon and their circle

The lords of Gourdon are the most obvious nucleus of social and political influence to have been promoting heretical adherence throughout the network they dominated. The solidarities appear to have held. We have no evidence that anyone informed on Bertrand or Fortanier or their kin in other towns, even though records as brief as Pierre Seilan's sentences often do make reference to other named individuals where relevant. The loyalty of client lords appears to be been assured, and Bertrand himself does not appear to have given evidence against his knights or other people in the *castrum*. The case is all the more compelling because Given's schema does not necessarily assume heretical *belief* on the part of the leading lords themselves, and we have noted in the case of Bertrand de Gourdon that he was ambivalent on the matter. Indeed, he was giving out very mixed messages to lesser lords wondering which way to jump.

So, what did the sphere of authority and loyalty of the lords of Gourdon consist of?[13] In addition to Gourdon itself, the most significant *castra* which pertained directly to the family were Salviac[14] and Castelnau-Montratier,[15] and they also controlled the viscounty of Saint-Cirq.[16] But they had numerous other castles and *castra* within their sphere of influence. We know that in 1119 the following men were associated with the lords of Gourdon in their donation to Cluny of Mont-Saint-Jean: Ebrard 'le Cot' and his son Arnaud, Giraud d'Arcambal and his brother Séguin, Bernard-Hugues de la Roque, Guillaume de Fénelon, Guiraud de Goulême, Reynaud de Rouffilhac and Gausbert and Bertrand de Pestillac. These early twelfth century toponyms all appear in Pierre Seilan's register. In addition to these, other small castles and settlements lying very close to Gourdon in the twelfth and early thirteenth centuries were Peyrilles,[17] le Bouscot, Léobard, le Boulvé, Lavercantière, Goudou, Rampoux, Prouillac, Laborie, Milhac, Frayssinet, Concorès, Peyrignac, Cazals and le Vigan. Of these toponyms only the last five are *not* represented in Pierre Seilan's register. This evidence attests to both continuity in Gourdon's domination of the Bouriane and the thoroughness with which confessional diversity, or at least a toleration of it, had infiltrated a region once notable for its patronage of great monastic houses.

---

13 I discuss the lords of Gourdon in many places throughout the book; please consult the index for further references.

14 Held by Guillaume de Salviac-de Gourdon.

15 Held by Ratier de Castelnau-Montratier.

16 See above, p. 45.

17 Held by Aimeric II de Gourdon-de Castelnau. See above, p. 105. The lords of nearby Fages were vassals of the lords of Gourdon in the twelfth century. See above, p. 106 n. 91.

The lords of Goudou, for example, were tied into the political networks focused on Gourdon, on the one hand, and heresy, on the other. They were a client family of the de Gourdon, Fortanier I having founded their castle, which dominated what would become Labastide-Gourdon.[18] It was also the lords of Gourdon who conceded its customs, in 1238, withholding some rights for themselves. Although the de Goudou boasted an abbot of Marcilhac, Raimond de Goudou, by 1235,[19] three family members would be guilty of heretical involvement in 1241–2. Arnaud 'Rectus' de Goudou shaved a *perfectus* and was given a bonnet in return.[20] Gaillard de Goudou received *perfecti* at his house at Labastide and ate with them. He had also promised their followers that he would not betray them.[21] Pierre-Guillaume de Goudou saw Waldensians and listened to them preach for three days and believed them to be good men. He is described as *faiditus*, implying that he had perhaps fought with the lords of Gourdon but been deprived of his castle.[22]

Another castle under the influence of the lords of Gourdon was Goulême. Six members of its lords and two of the de Goulême-de Milhac were convicted by Pierre Seilan at Gourdon. But the clan, like the de Gourdon, had been donors to Obazine. Between 1165–6 and 1172–3 three brothers of the family – Guillaume, another Guillaume and Pons – had ceded to the abbey rights they had to the lands of Arnaud de la Roque-de Linars,[23] another family associated with the lords of Gourdon since 1119.[24] Arnaud himself had been interested in the monastic life to the extent that in 1170–1 he ceded to Obazine rights on his own land on the banks of the Alzou and the church at Ginouillac for 400 *solidi* and a promise of eventual admission to the abbey of himself, and also of his legitimate sons. We know that Arnaud made it: as both a layman and a *conversus* he witnessed charters, in the latter capacity in 1183–4.[25] In fact, the de la Roque were among Obazine's major benefactors between 1160 and 1174.[26]

We know of at least another eight family members acting as donors or witnesses at Obazine in the period in which the lords of Gourdon were donors. For example, in 1170–1 the brothers Guitard and Guiraud de la Roque

---

[18] See above, p. 58.

[19] The lords of Gourdon still had some rights there in 1285, which were confirmed by Fortanier II in 1266: http://www.quercy.net/qmedieval/histoire/monog_albe/labastide_murat.html#Seigneurie (last accessed 6/8/09).

[20] D21, fols. 195v, 197r; DPC, pp. 56–7 note 120 (where he identifies Arnaud 'Cedus' as Arnaud Rectus).

[21] D21, fols. 193r, 213r.

[22] D21, fols. 195v, 197v–8r.

[23] *CO*, nos. 211, 356.

[24] See above, p. 58.

[25] *CO*, nos. 313, 576, 620, 619. We also know of an Arnaud de Linars de Castello (no. 619).

[26] *CO*, nos. 148, 152, 173, 178, 192, 286, 338, 366, 348, 358, 361.

gave up lands they held in the Limousin to Obazine.[27] They were still under the influence of Gourdon by 1200. Hugues de la Roque was a signatory in 1233 to the Rocamadour document. However, the generation after that of Arnaud the *conversus* would be investigated by the inquisitors at Gourdon, and also at Montauban, Montcuq and Almont. En Roque himself was in fact one of the most significant *credentes* tried at Gourdon. We have also seen that Linars, the abbey under their protection, had become a nest of *perfectae*.

From further afield, from a family represented at Gourdon in the inquisitor's register but originally from the Dordogne, we have the *credens* Pierre de Verneuil.[28] It was his ancestors who witnessed the charter of Mont-Saint-Jean in favour of Cluny in 1119, and who ceded rights to the church at Calès to Obazine in 1168–9. Here they were, with a descendant sentenced for his engagement in religious dissent.

Turning to the Vaux, aside from Castelnau-Montratier, *castra* held or heavily influenced by the lords of Gourdon were Sauveterre,[29] Montcuq,[30] Montaigu[31] and Mondenard.[32] Men of other settlements in the Vaux noted in Chapter 3 as working in military alliances with Bertrand de Gourdon and Ratier de Castelnau-Montratier were Araimfré de Montpezat, Bertrand de Pestillac, Hugues de la Mothe and Ratier de Caussade. These were the lords significant enough for the sources to record as Quercy's opposition to the crusade. Of these families, all would be associated with heresy a generation later.

A second secular network overlapping with a 'heretical' one is entirely different, in that the lord at its heart was a leading heresiarch and neither an ambivalent warrior, like Bertrand de Gourdon, nor a latter-day convert, like Fortanier.

The de Caussade and their network of support

In Chapter 2 we saw how the viscounty of Monclar and the seigneurie of Montpezat were concentrated within one family by the countand were his vassals for it. We also observed that the influence of other viscounties of south-western Quercy, ones that had secured the boundary between the lands of Toulouse and those of Rodez and Albi, was undermined. It is possibly that this made room in south-eastern Quercy for the increasing significance of the

27   *CO*, no. 338, and see chapter 2.
28   D21, fols. 192r, 202r.
29   Held by Guiraud de Gourdon-de Sauveterre-de Mondenard. See above, p. 136.
30   Held in part by Guiraud and Bertrand de Gourdon-de Montcuq. See above, p. 147.
31   Held by Guillaume de Gourdon de Salviac and also Arnaud and Bertrand de Montaigu, both allies of Gourdon in the war. See above, pp. 96, 101. Pierre, Bernard and Raimond de Montaigu lived at Montcuq. The last of these was an especially important *credens*. See pp. 135, 180.
32   Held by Bertrand and Armand. The former was an ally of the lords of Lomie and Ratier de Castelnau-Montratier in 1214. The former was a crusader.

honour of Caussade and its heretical lords, as opposed to that of Raimond VI,[33] just as we have observed that it did for the de Gourdon in central Quercy. Caussade's heretics are more often associated with Cathars in Albi, who were more numerous than those of Quercy in *c*.1200, and we have seen that this may explain what prompted an attack on the town in that curious first wave of the crusade in 1209. It may also account for the crusade's activity in the area, discussed in Chapter 3, possibly initiated by the Cistercians established at La Garde Dieu.

The crusaders' efforts were not sufficient to snuff out heresy in the Caussade area. In the 1230s and 1240s the lords of Caussade of whom we know were Jauffré, Pierre, Ratier (the ally of Bernard de Cazenac in 1217), the *perfectus* Guiraud,[34] his sister and niece, both *perfectae*,[35] and, most significantly, his brother Guillaume de Caussade, known as the Cathar deacon of Lanta. Guillaume Donadieu de Mazerac, one of the knights of Caussade, was the most important witness against Guillaume and his family in Doat 23, as we have seen. From him we learn that the lords of Lautardia, la Garrigue and la Pradelle were client lords at manses near Caussade. The lords of Caussade are also referred to in Doat 21 and 22. We have heard of members of the de Caussade at Montauban, Bertrande and Bernard Teissier. Pons Grimoard gave evidence against the de Caussade in the 1230s and confessed to Bernard de Caux that he had encountered Guillaume de Caussade hiding at Beaucaire and done nothing about it.[36]

We have other evidence of connections between Caussade and the lords, *credentes* and heretics of Beaucaire and also Montalzat. Guillaume the miller of Beaucaire and Pierre Vidien de Valtauren worked for them, as we have seen, and Guillaume Donadieu's evidence also connected the de Caussade to lesser lords of la Garrigue-de-Caussade, la Pradelle and the de la Garde, knights of Montalzat. The latter knights, Bertrand, Bernard and Guiraud, were also vassals of the count for what they held at Montalzat 1232,[37] making them another example of a 'compromised' family seeking an alliance at the region-wide level after 1229, once it was safe to be an ally of Toulouse again.

Indeed, we could make the case that the count was almost reckless in terms of the company kept in Quercy from quite an early date, establishing there a network of actually fairly suspect officials who in turn would oversee the establishment of heresy throughout southern Quercy. These allowed Castelsarrasin to become one of the most important 'heretical' towns in Quercy.

---

[33] As noted in DPC, p. 27.

[34] According to Bertrande de la Roque de Montcuq: D21, fol. 219r.

[35] According to 'Eustache', convicted at Beaucaire: D21, fol. 228r.

[36] D22, fol. 37r.

[37] D143, fol. 98 is reproduced in AD Lot F, laisse 123. It was witnessed by Déodat Barasc, among others.

The Heretical and Secular Elite at Castelsarrasin in 1228

In addition to the extensive evidence addressed in Chapters 4–6 discussing the role of local *credentes* at Castelsarrasin in support of heresy – people such as Pons Grimoard and Guillaume Faure de Pechermer – we should note the role of Bernard de Cazenac and Vigouroux de la Bacone in the revival. It began before the Peace, in 1228, when Castelsarrasin was retaken by Bernard de Cazenac, the mercenary vilified by the crusaders but now an Occitan hero. As we have heard from several witnesses, he met with Pons Grimoard, soon to become seneschal of Quercy for the count of Toulouse, and with notables including Guillaume Faure de Pechermer, Raimond Jean d'Abia, Aimeric de Bressols, Raimond-Guillaume de Barètges and Hugues de Cavelsaut.

There is no reason to suspect Bernard de Cazenac of anything worse than the willingness to work in a town full of heretics and their supporters, of all persuasions, in a culture essentially alien to him but tolerable because of the political rewards: the chance to build a political base far from Turenne. It is ironic, therefore, that it was his activity, not that of Raimond VII, or even the Grimoards, that appears to have facilitated the resilience of the heresy in lower Quercy. It was a mantle that the other men of 1228 would take up.

Raimond VII did clearly did not appreciate the scale and nature of the heretical communities protected by his vassals and allies in Quercy. Not only did the lords in the region lose their enthusiasm for the crusade and join the south in resistance to the invasion: some also relaxed their opposition to heresy in their towns and castles, drawing existing 'heretical' retainers into relationships of mutual protection, and some even embraced heretical teachings. But, in spite of this revival, the Peace of 1229 would herald the violence of inquisition. Quercy's complex devotional tapestry would be dismantled beyond recognition within a generation.

But before this, in 1228, a renaissance in heretical authority was taking place also. Catharism survived the captivity of Castelsarrasin from 1212 to 1228 because the town had surrendered to the crusaders in the former year, and so its people were able to keep the properties, in which they hid heretics. But leading heresiarchs evidently stayed away for the most part, for their safety. Thus Bernard de la Mothe reappeared at the 1228 meeting, as we heard in Chapter 4. He was working as an agent of the Cathar 'bishop' of Toulouse, Guilhabert de Castres.[38] He preached at Castelsarrasin and was adored, although not by de Cazenac. The latter came from the world of the Dordogne and, whatever the crusaders considered he and his ally the viscount of Turenne had done wrong, there is no evidence of any heretical involvement on their part. In de Cazenac's case, however, he was prepared

---

[38] For his activity in *c.*1223–6 as Guilhabert de Castres' envoy see sources cited above and also Hamilton, 'The Cathar council of Saint Félix', pp. 49–51.

at the very least to turn a blind eye to the renewed presence of the Cathars in Castelsarrasin.

Vigouroux de la Bacone also reappeared. His career will be discussed further below, but Castelsarrasin was where he based himself in Quercy. He was three times in the town in *c.*1224[39] as well as being in evidence in 1228. Guiraud Guallard stated in 1243 that he had seen Vigouroux in *c.*1228: once at Moissac on the quayside, about to be led into a house owned there by Guillaume Faure de Pechermer of Castelsarrasin itself, and twice at the home of Arnaud de Bressols at Castelsarrasin, once with Bernard de La Mothe. On each occasion he was in the company of the most important families of heretical supporters in lower Quercy.[40] He was also encountered at the Faure household in Castelsarrasin, with de Cazenac again, at the home of Arnaud de Bressols, close to its hospital, and preaching to many of the town's leading families at a meeting also attended by Guillaume Salomon, Cathar deacon of Toulouse.[41] He was there again in *c.*1231.[42]

Now we address what the evidence suggests about what we could call the shape and progress of the Cathar presence in Quercy in the context of dominant nodes of support.

The changing geography of heresy

I have argued elsewhere[43] that the *perfecti* of Quercy were under the authority of the Cathar bishops of Agen, one of whom was Vigouroux de la Bacone, bishop by 1223. In that year he was reconsoled by the schismatic Barthélemy de Carcassonne, a 'moderate', or 'mitigated, dualist', removed as bishop and replaced briefly by Barthélemy. In 1229, from its stronghold at Montségur in the Pyrenees, the leaders of the 'absolute dualist' community to which Vigouroux had previously belonged re-established a bishop for the Agenais, one 'Tento'. Vigouroux was reconsoled, this time back into the absolutist *ordo*, and became Tento's 'elder son' (*filius maior*), or apprentice, intended

---

[39] D22, fols. 44v–5v; Taylor, *Heresy*, p. 229.

[40] D22, fols. 13v–14r, 14r–v, 16r–v, 20v and 21v. The inquisitors apparently found this witness's evidence problematic. Two of the above references are repeated accounts of the same event but with different dates ascribed. In addition, he says that Vigouroux was again at Castelsarrasin in *c.*1235 (ibid. fols. 19r–v), although it is almost certain that he was dead by then (see below).

[41] D22, fols. 4v–5r, 9v–10r, 13v–14r, 14v, 15v–16r, 19v, 20r–v, 20v–21r, 21r–v, 21v, 22r–v, 23v–24r, 35r, 36r–v and 45r–v; D23, f. 265r; Griffe, *Le Languedoc … 1209–29*, p. 177; Passerat, 'Cathares en Bas-Quercy', p. 160. See D22, fols. 15v–16r also for a meeting at Castelsarrasin with another set of important heretics not from the Bas-Quercy region. They are Sernin, Pons Dairos and Pons Guilhabert. The meeting is not dated, however, and so it is difficult to know what significance to attach to it.

[42] D21, fol. 18v.

[43] Taylor, *Heresy*, pp. 181, 183, 184, 185, 196, 225–31, 233–8.

to follow him as bishop. Vigouroux remained thus until at least 1232 and was recalled in depositions and sentences in Quercy and elsewhere. But in the following year Vigouroux and Tento returned to Montségur as refugees escaping the early inquisitions. Even so, Vigouroux was taken, and almost certainly executed at Toulouse in 1233, by which time he was a Cathar bishop again, according to Aubri de Trois-Fontaines.

I have also suggested that no Cathar heresiarch had much influence beyond lower Quercy, where Catharism was well established by 1204, until c.1220. Before that, it was limited to Montauban, Moissac and most significantly Castelsarrasin. Catharism is in evidence for the first time in the Vaux in the early 1220s, but only at Montcuq. Vigouroux was reported there as a *perfectus* three times. He is also recorded three times at Castelsarrasin in c.1224 as well as being in evidence in 1228 and in c.1231: in other words, before and after he was *filius maior* and formally attached to the Agenais. It does seem that he was devoted to the heretics and *credentes* of Quercy.

Turning to Montcuq, its walls were destroyed as part of the Peace agreement. It was the only town in Quercy above the Tarn that this applied to,[44] and so probably reflects a perception of its confessional ambivalence. In 1230 Guiraud de Gourdon-de Sauveterre performed homage for what he held there to Raimond VII.[45] But even though the count stationed a *bailli* there from 1229, heretical traffic between Quercy and the Agenais passed through it.[46] Not only did Othon de Berètges and François the clerk encourage this process, but men of Montcuq who were in the sphere of the lords of Gourdon were also implicated. They were Bernard de Gourdon, Guillaume-Bertrand de Montcuq and Bertrand de la Roque-de Montcuq, all convicted there in 1241, as we have seen.

It was in the context of the Peace of 1229 that Pons Grimoard became seneschal of Quercy, controlling Castelsarrasin as his capital and supplanting Bernard de Cazenac, who was not someone the crusaders and inquisitors would have tolerated. When Pons was appointed he was given instructions by Raimond VII to disrupt the inquisition. He was not instructed to protect heretics, but, as we have seen, he did this also. Pons was not entirely successful in either case. In 1234 210 people were burned at Moissac. It was very probably following this that heretics became more prominent in central and even northern Quercy. Like the crusade, the inquisition also created refugees, who migrated toward the Lot and beyond until established in the Bouriane.

---

[44] Ibid., p. 221.
[45] *HGL*, VIII, 1957.
[46] Taylor, *Heresy*, p. 238.

A Reassertion of Orthodoxy

We now return to the business of ten members of Quercy's elite escaping sentencing by Pierre Seilan in 1241–2. They were two members of the Pellegri family of Gourdon, four of the Foulcaut of Montauban, the lady of Saint-Paul (Moissac), François the clerk of Montcuq and two lords of Gourdon. Some mitigating circumstance or intervention meant that no sentence was recorded by their names and crimes by Pierre Seilan's clerk. In the case of the lords of Gourdon and the Saint-Paul the inquisitors were aware that they were dealing with people from important noble families, the most important in the Bouriane and lower Quercy, in fact. The Foucault, too, were socially very significant and we noted that Pierre Raimond Foucault would be among the elite of Montauban who took the oath of loyalty to the crown in 1243 after the murders at Avignonet.

But the lack of sentences cannot have been the result of status, or not of status *per se*. Other important people were *persona non grata* by 1243, when knights, lords and townspeople signalled their loyalty to the crown by signing pledges to that effect. As we have seen in Chapter 5, this latter process excluded members of families such as the Carbonnel and de la Roque who had been convicted, and other members of their families came to the fore as a result, as did other families with no stain of heresy upon them at all. Yet the high status of the ten cannot have been a negligible coincidence either. If status itself did not save them, in one case at least we can see what probably did. This is because we know that on 7 March 1242 Guillaume de Gourdon-de Salviac gave up rights and lands near Léobard and Salviac to the abbey of Obazine to establish and support a daughter house. He gave them in perpetuity and the grant was of all rights of lordship. Nôtre-Dame-de-Gourdon, more commonly known as L'Abbaye Nouvelle, was the first Cistercian abbey in Quercy north of the Aveyron. The site chosen for the building of the house itself – begun in 1260 and completed in *c.*1280 – was le Pech Gisbert, on the Céou.[47]

We could say that Guillaume saved his line from disgrace.[48] In December 1241 heresy had been discovered at Gourdon and its immediate lords were undone. By 24 March 1242 the family's guilt in tolerating heresy at Sauveterre, Montcuq and Castelnau-Montratier would be discovered. But Guillaume himself, and Salviac also, would emerge free from the taint of heresy by the time that Pierre Seilan was finished. We have no evidence that heresy was ever tolerated on his property. In this context, knowing that his family's

---

[47] *GC*, I, pp. 187–8 is summarised in *CO*, spplt. 1304, and see pp. 13–14 and note 1. See also Leblanc, 'L'Abbaye nouvelle près de Gourdon', pp. 49–75 (pp. 50–1); Lacoste, *Quercy*, II, p. 253; E. Albe, 'L'abbaye nouvelle', in *Dictionnaire du département du Lot* (Paris, 1911), I, col. 33; Bulit, *Gourdon*, p. 71; Lartiguaut, *Histoire de Quercy*, p. 121.

[48] Leblanc agrees: 'L'Abbaye nouvelle près de Gourdon', p. 51.

guilt and his innocence was a realistic outcome of the crusade, he seems to have intervened on behalf of his misguided kin. Leblanc even suggests that it was the inquisitors rather than the Cistercians who selected the exact spot where the house would be situated.[49]

The inquisitor arrived in the Vaux, probably at Montcuq, on 10 February 1242. Two days later Guillaume was at Castelsarrasin, where he met Raimond VII and made a complete submission, performing homage for all of his lands in Quercy.[50] He received them back 'because of services he had performed for the count', although his new lord distinguished the lands from their surplus produce, reserving the right to usufruct for himself.[51] Guillaume then travelled to Obazine, where he made the donation, for which he was the vassal of Raimond VII; this certainly happened with the count's prior knowledge and approval of the strategy.

The chief lords of Gourdon therefore appear to have escaped sentencing through the drastic action taken by Guillaume de Gourdon-de Salviac. We also know that this intervention took place after their trial but before the book of sentences was actually drawn up: that is, at the stage where sentences were being allocated. It seems quite plausible that the other eight who escaped sentencing at this stage had also made significant agreements with inquisitors.

L'Abbaye Nouvelle was not only a generous gift, and one which perhaps mitigated against the crimes of the de Gourdon, but was almost certainly perceived as a guarantee of orthodoxy in northern Quercy; one that would succeed where distant Beaulieu, Figeac and Rocamadour had failed, and where Lativia and Linars had actually succumbed to heresy. Therefore, it is not necessary to suggest that the criminals or their defenders escaped justice through bribery, even if the rest could have afforded donations as grand as that of Guilluame de Gourdon-de Salviac, which seems unlikely. Instead, I am suggesting that sentences were commuted in return for a policed reconciliation with orthodox practice. L'Abbaye Nouvelle was not envisaged simply as a prize for the Cistercians but was part of the process whereby the presence of monks could secure the orthodoxy of a region.

Others escaping punishment may likewise have been able to make promises to actively contribute to the reform of what was, by now, endemic disregard for orthodox authority. Feuchter prefers this effective 'negotiation' with

---

[49] Ibid.

[50] *HGL*, VI, 735–6, citing *Catalogue des Manuscrits … de Colbert* (Paris, 1908), no. 1067. *HGL* says Colbert but *cf.* Teulet, *Layettes*, II, 463b–4a, no. 2953, which says that he did homage to Raimond VII for his part of the castles of Gourdon and Salviac. He also did homage for lands in Périgord, according to the *HGL* narrative, adding weight to the case that he had married Hélis de Montfort.

[51] The charter tells us that this accord was in part because the two men were apparently related: *HGL*, VI, 736. The editors are not able to shed light on this relationship, and neither can I.

the inquisitors in the case of notables convicted at Montauban, positing a mass commutation of sentences to do good works.[52] These people had influenced their political clients and social milieu in matters of doctrine and the recognition of devotional legitimacy once before, in the twelfth century, had done so 'incorrectly' in the 1220s, and should do so once again under the watchful gaze of new Cistercian neighbours. It may be that they, too, had someone like Guillaume de Gourdon to act as guarantor of their conduct and activity. Certainly the authorities needed such people in place at Gourdon, Moissac, Montauban and Montcuq, from what we know of their heretical pasts.

We might ask whether such donations were worth the cost. More was surrendered by the de Gourdon than was equivalent to the cost of a handful of penitential pilgrimages, and this may be true in some way for the others. But their crimes were of such magnitude that the punishment would surely have involved a long, as well as an expensive, exile. Furthermore, those with recorded sentences remained *personae non gratae* politically. If I am correct, then their donations were *instead* of sentencing, not as alternative penances, as in the case Feuchter makes for Montauban.

My argument has been that inquisitors were interested in uncovering and punishing heresy, not merely constructing it, even though some of this indeed took place. It would be illogical to consider that they were turning a blind eye to the activity of leading *credentes* in the region, and there is no precedent for lax or corrupt practice on the part of these inquisitors. Rather, they were hated for their thoroughness. How may we account, therefore, for what, in spite of the case I have just made, perhaps still has the ring of a corruption of inquisitorial values?

In fact, if the donation saved the castellans of Gourdon from sentencing, it did not entirely rehabilitate either them or their town. It is notable by its absence in the oaths taken in 1243 to reaffirm the loyalty of the region after Avignonet. It cannot be a coincidence that, of the lords of Gourdon, only Guillaume de Gourdon-de Salviac signed such an oath.[53] Bertrand and Fortanier de Gourdon, Guiraude de Gourdon-de Sauveterre and Bernard de Gourdon-de Montcuq did not. They were not fit for such an alliance, although they surely sought it. The contrast with their earlier position as major donors to Obazine and fervent crusaders is marked.

Gourdon itself was as yet incapable of carving out an 'orthodox' identity for itself, whether or not a town can be considered 'heretical' as an entity or not. The compromised position of Pierre and Galtier Pellegri could not have helped matters either, and we should note once more the unusual sentence of Guillaume Pellegri: the requirement to support a priest, perhaps reflecting

---

[52] Feuchter, 'Le pouvoir de l'inquisition', *passim* and see above, pp. 000 and 000.

[53] *HGL*, VIII, 1980.

something of the spirit of the burden and privilege undertaken by the lords of Gourdon themselves in founding an abbey.

We should consider things from a slightly different perspective also, that of Guillaume de Gourdon-de Salviac himself. While those deponents sentenced in 1241–2 were carrying out their penances and his kinsmen at Gourdon, Montcuq and Castelnau-Montratier were politically marginalised, there was an important realignment taking place of the most aggressively anti-Cathar forces with influence in Quercy aside from the inquisitors: the Limousin Cistercians and the count of Toulouse. In 1242, as well as escaping the attention of the inquisitors, perhaps justly, he had tied himself tightly into an alliance involving both of them.

By February 1244, however, Fortanier himself would be permitted to do homage to the count for *everything* that he held and which pertained to him in Quercy, including Saint-Cirq, and even beyond it:[54] a total submission to authority that was both Occitan and orthodox. It was wiser than Bertrand's course of action – performing homage to the crusaders several times by 1226, performing it likewise to the crown in that year, but at the same time working secretly with Bernard de Cazenac and others. He had made himself a target for the inquisitors by the 1240s in spite of probably having no time himself personally for the teaching of the heresiarchs he encountered. With Guillaume de Gourdon-de Salviac's help the family was rehabilitated to the extent that in 1246 Bernard de Caux and Jean-de-Saint-Pierre would be aided in an inquest by another Guiraud de Gourdon, evidently a prior of the cathedral clergy at Cahors.[55]

There are two further observations to make about the properties donated to Obazine in 1242 by Guillaume de Gourdon-de Salviac for the establishment of L'Abbaye-Nouvelle, which were Albe-Cassange, Prevairies, *Gros-Cayrou*, *Maires*, *Males-Mouliers* and the manses and other property held by him at Aurimont, Pradel, *Ginèbre* and Pech-Foulque, with all their 'men, fiefs, rights and lands'. The rights donated were to a spring at *Maireguet* and over the men and lands of Blanzaguet. He also exempted the monks from *péage*, and from customs and exactions on all his other estates, 'for themselves, their goods and their men'.[56] The first point concerns the locations themselves.[57]

---

[54] AD Lot F. 123 summarises and partly transcribes 'Cartulaire de Raimond VII' (from D143, fol. 82r; Teulet, *Layettes*, II, 549a–b, no. 3226). The prestigious witness list includes the bishop of Albi, the count of Comminges and the viscount of Narbonne, as well as two lords of Quercy: Bertrand de Cardaillac and Déodat Barasc. See also Combarieu, *Dictionnaire*, p. 209; Bulit, *Gourdon*, p. 69.

[55] See Albe, *L'hérésie … en Quercy*, p. 19.

[56] The modern French place-names are given by Barrière in *CO*, spplt. 1304.

[57] The modern editor of Obazine's cartulary, Bernadette Barrière, gives the likely modern French versions of the medieval place-names. I cannot locate *Gros-Cayrou*, *Maires*, *Males-Mouliers* and *Ginèbre*. *Mairaguet* is perhaps just north of the Dordogne at Pinsac.

There is a Pradel near Gourdon itself and another in the north near Creysse.[58] Pech-*Fourque*,[59] Prevaires,[60] Aurimont[61] and Albe-Cassange[62] are hamlets in the modern commune of Salviac. Pech-Fourque lies south-west of the abbey, between it and Salviac; Aurimont is just to the west of the abbey; Prevaires just to its north; and Albe-Cassange is just to its south-east. None of these place-names are represented in Pierre Seilan's register. Indeed, there are *no* toponyms in the register that can be associated with Salviac. This is rare for the trial at Gourdon, which is otherwise surrounded by place-names so represented. My first point, therefore, is that the Salviac region reflects the confessional preference of its most immediately dominant lord, again supporting my observations about lords and their influence over the people of settlements associated with them.

My second point concerns the nature of what was donated, in that it supports my case that Occitan fiefs were not 'lands'. They were only one form of alienated property among the set of 'men, fiefs, rights and lands' in the charter. But neither were they the same thing as 'rights', in that, like 'lands', 'rights' are not synonymous with 'fiefs' in 'men, fiefs, rights and lands'. 'Fiefs' are not even as closely associated in the list with 'lands' as 'rights' themselves are. Furthermore, rights could also be something 'owned', like Guillaume's right to the spring at Maireguet, like his ancestors' rights to woods at Mont-Saint-Jean. Rights could also be to subordinate men, retainers, as well as to lands, as at Blanzaguet. In fact, fiefs were just one way of redistributing revenues, and feature only marginally in what was donated, along with 'men, lands, rights, customs, péage, and exactions'. Guillaume's fiefs, therefore, were simply one way in which he supported himself, collecting on someone or something or some activity actually 'owned' by another. And we know who this other party was because, as of a few days earlier, Guillaume held everything he had in Quercy of Raimond VII. Indeed, it seems likely that what he held of the count in early 1242 he held from him already, because he performed homage to him in 1241, and the lords of Gourdon do not seem to have had other lords except for the crusaders and Capetians.

The donation of lands surrounding the Céou valley in 1242 carried with it all claims that could be made on it in any way by Guillaume or anyone else in his family. It was confirmed as such on 10 March 1244.[63] This was the kind of donation that Obazine, like Cîteaux and like all abbeys by the thirteenth century, wanted. The only things he could not give were the things that he

---

58 There is also one at Cours. My thanks to Peter Biller for identifying these possible locations.

59 Again identified by Peter Biller.

60 Combarieu, *Dictionnaire*, p. 192.

61 Ibid., p. 7.

62 Visible on local maps.

63 *CO*, spplt. 1313 summarises *GC*, I, 188.

held as fief of the count of Toulouse, because they were not his. But Obazine could now collect on these even if it not own them.

Heresy after Bernard de Caux

Although the Cathars in Quercy survived the crusade and even increased in number in its aftermath, we hear of few further incidents after the mid-1240s. The heresy did continue at Montauban into the 1250s to an extent, but Guillaume de Pelhisson describes the heightened level of fear in the region. Catharism in lower Quercy was all but crushed by the scale of punitive activity in that decade and, crucially, the officials of Raymond VII lost the freedom to operate outside of his agenda. Even the devotional complexion of lower Quercy changed. The Dominicans founded a convent at Montauban in 1251–2.[64] At Castelsarrasin leading families in the 1260s were making concessions to Grandselve.[65] In central Quercy, where it had arrived more recently, Catharism was apparently eliminated most easily, in spite of a handful of convictions in the 1270s.[66] Cathars were apparently still in evidence in the valley of the Vers, however, which joins the Lot from its right bank, and on the plateau at Cours. They supposedly had a little library in caves.[67]

To the east, the de Cardaillac remained important and won the abbacy of Obazine for Guiraud III de Cardaillac (1254–67).[68] The post-inquisitorial period saw a flurry of foundations in addition to l'Abbaye Nouvelle. The Cistercian monastery of Espagnac established a convent for Augustinian canonesses at Saint-Eulalie.[69] The military orders were established in Le-Grand-Prieuré-des-Dames in 1259.[70] The Knights Hospitaler founded commanderies in Quercy at La Tronquière (1250), Espédaillac (1257) and Assier (1280).[71]

But the fact remains that by the end of the crusade the northern Languedoc was typified by not only political rebellion against the papally sponsored invasion, becoming more and more closely identified with the French state as that strategy was, but ideological rebellion also in the form of tolerance of heresy. In this the lords of upper Quercy in particular flew in the face of their traditional lords, the house of Saint-Gilles, as well as of the French and the clergy. Heresy was no more 'natural' to them than was its persecution but, ironically given dualist indifference to political struggle, Catharism became allied with the defence of southern French autonomy. As Moore has noted in

---

64 E. Magnou-Nortier, 'Dans la tourmente (xiie–xive siècles)', in *Le diocèse de Toulouse*, ed. P. Wolff, Histoire des diocèses de France, n.s. 15 (Paris, 1983), pp. 76–7.

65 AD Haute-Garonne ms. Lat. 202, 106 (edited in Blaquière and Dossat, 'Les cathares au jour le jour', pp. 264–6); Guillaume Pelhisson, *Chronique*, pp. 58–9; HGL, VIII, 1869.

66 See Albe, *L'hérésie en Quercy*, p. 23.

67 Lartigaut, *Histoire de Quercy*, p. 109.

68 CO, 13.

69 Combarieu, *Dictionnaire*, pp. 229–30.

70 Juillet, *Templiers et Hospitaliers*, pp. 173–315.

71 Ibid., p. 79.

general terms of the response to Occitan Catharism, its repression was much greater than the threat it posed actually warranted.[72] Indeed, it was a hammer to crack a nut and the region's lords responded as destructively. In the over-reaction to heresy which justified the violence against Quercy the crusade had made havens for Catharism and Waldensianism in some of the most Catholic castles and towns of Languedoc.

---

[72] *Persecuting Society*, p. 151.

Conclusion

After Raimond VII died in 1249 Quercy went to the crown as had been agreed in 1229. Royal commissioners obtained new oaths from the consuls of Castelsarrassin, Montauban and Moissac, and from lords such as Dorde Barasc, Fortanier de Gourdon and Bertrand de Cardaillac.[1] Alphonse divided the administration of Languedoc into four regions, Quercy and the Agenais comprising one, with four new seneschals.[2] In 1251 Alphonse of Poitiers, the king's brother, and Jeanne de Toulouse, the dead count's daughter, toured Quercy, visiting Lauzerte and Montauban in particular.[3] This is tantalizing, as Catharism survived at Montauban and Caussade in a small way into the 1250s.[4] The royal couple may indeed have 'seen' a heretic, 'but without knowing them to be such'.

In accounting for the rise and fall of heresy in Quercy, I have argued the following.

On the nature of heresy in Quercy

Heresy was partially constructed and understood through the categories of belief and activity imposed on it by inquisitorial records, influenced in their turn by polemical treatises and early manuals for inquisitors. But it was nonetheless a reality external to the texts. I have tried to demonstrate that the focus of the inquisitor on investigation before punishment undermines the notion that his methodology essentially entailed him using such received knowledge of Catharism and Waldensianism to reproduce and confirm that same knowledge through his practice in the courtroom. The concern of the inquisitor was, in the first instance, to identify heresy and understand its nature. To achieve this he needed a methodology that met this aim, as well as being stress-inducing for the communities and individuals in the midst of which he implanted himself. Its results are reflected in the records the inquisitors left. If we are careful about how we use these – understanding the function of both the formulaic and idiosyncratic content to the inquisitor – we

---

[1] HGL, VI, 810–11, 812.

[2] HGL, VI, 823 and VIII, col. 1284.

[3] HGL, VI, 822.

[4] AD Haute-Garonne ms. Lat. 202, 106, in Blaquière and Dossat, 'Les cathares au jour le jour', pp. 264–6; Albe, L'hérésie ... en Quercy, pièces justificatives i. 40.

can extract at least some of that external reality of heresy from them, and a good deal besides about heresy and the societies and individuals it touched in its various forms.

One thing we learn is that people distinguished between differing beliefs and weighed them up against each other rationally, on the basis of what their exponents taught and what they themselves observed about the world. Another is that they knew that such ideas were contested and could be dangerous. Even if they were merely encountered rather than actively sought out – and even if they were not fully understood, let alone adhered to – some ideas crossed a line that had been drawn in the sand by people who knew about such things. We can therefore say that 'heresy' was a concept that medieval people understood. Deponents knew what it was, as opposed to what it was not, by 1240, even if the distinction had been passed down to them by those same people drawing the line. Thus they concocted various strategies to negotiate a way around the situation in the courtroom: having been a child at the time of encountering it, other people being more guilty of it, not having taken part in rituals when others had, not knowing heretics to be such, being threatened by other people into silence, and so on. None of these made a person innocent, and they were to no avail. Indeed, once condemned, these adherents were 'heretics' too.

To the historian, on the other hand, 'heretic' as a *concept* means someone knowingly at odds with the teachings of the Roman faith, and choosing this path. Many people in Quercy clearly did this. However, 'heresy' is not useful to historians as a descriptive category if we try to juxtapose it with 'orthodoxy'. We would be assuming a polarity and antithesis between them that may not have existed in the minds of most people in Quercy before the inquisition. What we have in Doat 21–23 are traces of at least three competing belief systems – the Roman faith, Waldensian and dualism – that overlap and do not emerge as entirely coherent and distinctive in any given incidence in the inquisitors' records. We can use this generalisation for Quercy to prove something helpful in talking about 'heresy' in the high medieval Languedoc more widely, and even beyond it. This is that we should indeed use the term 'Cathar' to describe what the inquisitors translated from the vernacular as *hereticus*. Or, if we do not, we have to find another name to distinguish clearly between those people about whom inquisitors asked 'Did they teach that God did not make what was visible?' and Waldensians, who taught exactly what the inquisitor himself believed about creation. Certainly, terms such as 'dissident' or 'good people' will not do where we have more than one dissident sect in which individuals were considered to be good people. Many deponents 'considered to be good people' both 'heretics' and Waldensians, but otherwise distinguished between them. Inquisitors considered them both to be 'heretics', but found a way to distinguish between them also. Thus *heretici* in the sources should be understood as people who did not believe that God created the world: dualists, or rather, because there were many kinds of dualists in other countries, 'Cathars', and also someone condemned for involvement with them.

But the depositions do not reveal only 'dualists' and Waldensians. Some of the 'surplus' slipping through the net constructed to catch heresy and considered worth recording by the inquisitor is apparently eccentric, and also eclectic in not always conforming to identifiable belief systems. Sometimes it owes more to a parallel and equally pervasive current, anti-clericalism. Other notions, we might posit, drew on folkloric and oral tradition, although we can rarely prove this. But sometimes it transcends strikingly the commonplaces of dualism found in the sentences and depositions and echoes Cathar tracts ordinarily encountered in highly literate circles: those of the *perfecti* themselves or those of Cathar-turned-inquisitors. Even more astonishing is where it resembles stories told by dualists of the Balkans and Asia. I have noted several of these, which occur within a small subset of all the depositions that must have been made and recorded in inquisitorial manuscripts sadly lost long ago. That such traces of humble lives are lost forever is the more tragic, but we cannot help but wonder whether they took echoes of dualist creation stories with them.

Finally, just as we could try to approach inquisitors and their records less passionately, so we should the heretics. Their status as victims should not in itself elicit our sympathy. There are several facets of their belief and lifestyle that undermine the empathetic picture painted of them by Reformation and Occitan-centred historiography, and in some popular Anglophone literature also.

For one, dualism absolves the believer of responsibility for what takes place on earth. Only the proscription of harming living things and producing more of them, introduced into medieval dualism by the Bogomils, divides Catharism from the nihilism of the Paulicians, from whom the Bogomils acquired their dualist cosmology.[5] Salvation was determined by the believer's ritual state at the point of death rather than by a lifetime of correct belief and practice. For other Christians, the devotional life included remorse for past sins; for Cathars, evading past sins was all that mattered. I may be being harsh. The *perfecti* themselves practised rigid abstinence to the extent of suffering when, strictly speaking, this was not necessary for salvation if the *consolamentum* was performed at the point of death. Doing far more than this bare minimum, they preached, comforted and, above all, as we know from many depositions, they 'saved'. Nonetheless, they broadcast their abstinence, shunning impure hospitality, and this afforded them veneration in their lifetime, great status and the social power that went with being the focus of networks of solidarity and collective identity. Frugal though they were,

---

[5] J. Hamilton and B. Hamilton (eds. and trans.), *Christian Dualist Heresies in the Byzantine World, c. 650–c. 1405* (Manchester, 1998), p. 44.

their chosen path meant that other people had to support them economically; the Quercy evidence points to this at least. Waldensian brothers and sisters evidently had status too, but they demanded less and gave more for this, in economic terms.

On Why and How Heresy Prospered in Quercy

Even if it is true of Languedoc and its relationship to twelfth-century dualism in the 1160s and 1170s, when Papa Nicetas arguably preached a new doctrine, and in the 1170s and early 1180s, when violence was first threatened against Cathars, that many people did not really distinguish clearly between or identify entirely with any of the Roman church, 'Waldensianism' or 'Catharism', it is inconceivable that after 1184 secular leaders at least were not aware of what was acceptable belief and practice and what was not. In lower Quercy secular lords and comital officials by and large did not have to respond to heresy on a significant scale until the early 1200s. In fact, we can possibly narrow this down as far as saying that in 1204 they were made welcome almost officially, because a meeting took place at Castelsarrasin between *perfecti* and powerful men that certainly had political as well as devotional content.

However, twelfth-century Quercy, in particular north of the Tarn-Aveyron-Garonne, was not a society in which we might predict that heresy would gain purchase. Even below this river network Quercy undermines several features of our more generalised understanding of Languedoc in the twelfth and early thirteenth century. Firstly, there was no devotional malaise or vacuum for heresy to fill. Instead, there was a strong relationship between the laity and abbeys within and beyond Quercy. In lower Quercy there were no fewer than nine Cistercian houses. The bishop dominated the Cahorsain. The Benedictine abbeys shaped the east and the Gourdon–Turenne alliance with Obazine in the Limousin did likewise in the north. There were even abbeys for women in Quercy – Lativia, Linars and les Oleiras – and we have five noted examples of women of knightly and noble families who aspired to enter Obazine-Coyreux. If anything, it was perhaps the case that in some instances clerical influence and authority was *too* strong. For example, as we have seen, the revenues of Linars and of churches at Gourdon pertained to le Vigan from 1143, not to the lords of Gourdon. This was an arrangement guaranteed by the bishop.

So, perhaps, a second possibility, and as Andrew Roach suggests, is that heresy was an economic choice. Towns in lower Quercy vied with St Théodard, Moissac and Belleperche for economic rights. This could have been a contributing factor in the creation of conditions in which lords became predisposed to tolerating heresy. The lords of la Roque, for example, gave so much to Obazine in the 1100s that they in any case had to slow down, but nonetheless looked to engage with some form of Christianity nonetheless. The same could be said of the knights of Arques and Saint-Michel-des-Bannières, among others.

However, there is a paradox inherent in the ways that the clergy of Languedoc are viewed by historians. The Occitan clergy was supposedly ineffectual, a laughing stock, but at the same resented by those from whom it aggressively demanded tithes. It was both weak and strong, in other words. But there is no such paradox in most of Quercy, where the church was powerful and at the centre of cultural and devotional life. It would be undermined in favour of dissident religious beliefs for social and political rather than economic reasons. Where clashes between the laity and clergy did concern economic matters they related to urban liberties and there is no indication beyond the bishops' polemic that 'heresy' was involved. Nonetheless, economic motives of a sort did lie behind some of the political choices made by people in Quercy who also tolerated heretics, as we shall see.

Thirdly, heresy did not run in families. Although there are many 'heretical' families, in that they might contain individuals found guilty of associating with heretics to some greater or lesser degree, the family as a whole was only very rarely allied to one particular sect, the Pellegri being the most significant exception. Individuals appear to have been far more sectarian, as we have seen. The Foulcaut of Montauban were very rare in having several members who associated with both sects. Furthermore, because we have such a great deal of evidence that families embraced both heretical sects – Cathars and Waldensians – we can also infer what we might have learned from 'negative depositions', had they survived: that families straddled the 'heretical' and 'orthodox' worlds. This is supported by the non-depositional evidence for orthodox activity, namely charters of foundation and patronage of churches and abbeys. We know of a *perfectus* called Bernard Carbonnel at Montauban, and Pierre Carbonnel was involved with both sects, but the family also patronised the Franciscans of the town. The de la Roque rose from being clients of the lords of Gourdon to being great patrons of Obazine, and signalled their submission to the crown in 1243, but they were likewise implicated heavily at Gourdon, Montauban, Linars and Caussade. The d'Arcambal founded Belleperche and signed for Cahors in 1233 while also being rivals in a purely secular sense of the bishop, but they had extensive heretical involvement elsewhere. Even as Bishop Pons of Saint-Martin d'Antéjac served Quercy, and as his family provided consuls at Cahors, four of them were sentenced for heresy at Almont. The de Jean and d'Arcambal at Cahors were only orthodox where they patronised the friars, but they and the Carbonnel and de la Roque were involved with the sects elsewhere. The de la Mothe provided a prior at Saint-Pierre-des-Cuisines but numbered at least four *perfecti*. If anything, urban identities and cultural dynamics shaped devotional activity.

But this does not supply us with the whole answer. Behind the situation whereby individuals took to associating with devotional outlaws to the extent that some of the leading lay supporters had notorious *perfecti* and *credentes* in their families there was an imposed cultural shift that turned Quercy against the crusade and against its one-time allies in the Roman church. Thus, by the time the inquisitors began operations in Quercy, secular leaders were turning a blind eye to the clergy's enemies. This situation arose because of changes wrought by the invasion. In accounting for the success of heresy in Quercy, therefore, we should look not only for the characteristics Quercy shared with the rest of Languedoc but also to factors unique to the county.

The former kinds of characteristics include the nature of the twelfth-century Occitan fief.[6] It was the right to direct or indirect income from estates and offices, held alongside property owned outright, which conferred and expressed legal freedom and implied social equality with other propertied people, including those lords from whom fiefs were held. Pierre Bonnassie makes this easiest to understand by suggesting that we should see the fief as a gift, the giving of which entailed both patronage and reciprocation, with counter gifts being made at the same time. For example, in 1240 Vital de Montcuq and Fons de Mondenard jointly rendered the castle of Mondenard to the count in their own name and those of its other lords.[7] There followed a charter of customs and *utages* (sic) conceded by the count 'to the knights and inhabitants of the castle of Mondenard'.[8] The fief was transferred via horizontal ties, rather than down through a chain of command, even though this also existed.

Another shared Occitan characteristic is that towards the end of the century the *castrum* replaced the manse as the significant unit of political and economic activity (within such manses we perhaps find the 'lost peasants' of Quercy, now exploiting the rural sphere as townspeople, with a foot in both worlds). Increasingly, fiefs entailed rights to these urban revenues held by vassals of *castra* overlords. But during the crusade the lords controlling both *castra* and traditional castles, even those loyal to the crusade, were suddenly expected to do homage for them, and to hold them as vassals of new northern lords, as though by right of conquest. If a man such as Ratier de Castelnau-Montratier wanted people to hold fiefs 'of' him – the rights to parts of what he owned or was owed, in his *castrum* or elsewhere, thus working to cement social bonds and tie clients to him politically – he was supposed to suffer at the same time the indignity that he himself held his town only at the will and whim of a northern lord such as Baudouin of Toulouse or Simon de Montfort. Accordingly, Ratier de Castelnau-Montratier – and, along with him, the lords of Lolmie, Gourdon, Barasc, Mondenard, Montaigu, Montpezat, Pestillac, la Mothe and Caussade – defected in the period 1214–18. They began to throw off their northern masters and reorientate themselves along regionalist rather than confessional lines such as they had drawn in 1209. Being allies of Rome

---

6   See above, Chapter 2, pp. 62–5, 69–70.
7   Transcribed from the cartulary of Raimond VII fol. 35 into AD Lot F, laisse 125.
8   Noted in AD Lot F, laisse 125, in Occitan, and confirmed at Sauveterre.

had not benefited them and had even diminished them, rendering them either displaced or dependent. Even so, this was not an easy choice to make, and the most important lay lord in Quercy, Bertrand de Gourdon, did not throw off his confessional allegiance until 1218.

We should not look upon Quercy as stuck in the past in terms of its rejection of 'French' models of social organisation. Its rebels were not reactionaries. Indeed, they were just beginning to prosper in new ways economically as nucleated settlements replaced the manse. Their economic dynamism was giving them access to new revenues from *castra*, such as taxes on profit, or from property sales and rents. In this sense, economics do indeed help to account for why Roman-imposed masters were opposed.

But the indignity of losing one's legal parity with other lords was more significant. As such, by the time that Quercy was uniting itself through the rhetoric of the Peace of 1229, some of the lords involved and others besides were allowing heresy to expand its influence at Moissac (through the actions and inaction of the lords of Saint-Paul and Othon de Berètges), Montauban (the de la Mothe), Castelsarrasin (Pons Grimoard and Guillaume Faure) and Montcuq (Othon again). Just as Bob Moore and James Given have stressed, their choices impacted in turn on lesser and client families, who were themselves encouraged into cultural identification with the enemies of the crusade.

The sphere of the lords of Caussade is a good example. The struggle against heresy at Caussade may have begun as early as 1209, but Catharism was deeply entrenched there, was vibrant in the 1230s and the reach of its heretical lords was long. Associated with them were knights such as the lords of Valtauren, the de la Garrigue and de la Pradelle, all convicted. At Montcuq François the priest connected the heretics of that town and Caussade. Othon de Berètges's own deputy, Bernard de Saint-Geniès, also refrained from arresting heretics. It was discovered that Pierre de Bruelh of Montpezat, probably another comital servant, failed to arrest Raimonde de Mazerac. Her kinsman Guillaume Donadieu was another of the Caussade clients. The lords of Montaigu sanctioned heretical activity, again with connections with Caussade. The lords of Caussade also dominated Beaucaire, and their *credentes* dependents there thought highly of them.

The domination of the Bouriane by the lords of Gourdon gives us more examples of client families tolerating heretics. We have seen that the circle of families allied to Gourdon in 1119 resembles closely the list of families still associated with it in the early thirteenth century, which in turn are represented in the 1241 sentences. The de Fages-de Peyrilles, de Goulême-de Milhac, de Lascroa, d'Arcambal and others in the sphere of the lords of Gourdon all had members found guilty of support for heretics in 1241. A priest at Almont also refused to arrest heretics. He was Arnaud de la Roque, his family being clients of the lords of Gourdon. Likewise, at Moissac the servants of the Saint-Paul family had been involved in heresy, the knight Raimond Jean d'Abia not least among those they influenced.

Being visible and well-known to higher authorities themselves, these rulers ran high risks in accommodating heretics. We have seen that in 1223 Cathars were turned away at Gourdon in spite of the political disillusionment of its chief lord, so dissatisfaction did not lead naturally to religious dissidence. It required changes and dissatisfaction at a deeper, social level to change the psyche of a community, heretics who could offer new and more convincing answers to fundamental questions and the spiritual presence of belief systems that were not that of the Roman-backed invaders, whatever the extent to which the core principles of Waldensianism and Catharism were actually taken to heart.

However, we should not see toleration of heresy as an inevitable outcome of the wars and political transformation. Not all lords who were clients of the de Gourdon were implicated in heresy. In 1223 Bertrand de Gourdon gave Montbrun, a *castrum* close to Béduer, to Dorde Barasc to hold.[9] Perhaps this was by way of compensation and reward for his losses and loyalty in the crusading era, in which he and Araimfré and Guillaume Barasc had ultimately sided with the lords of western Quercy. But this family were from the east of Quercy, close to Figeac, and never tainted by heresy in spite of their southern partisanship. Instead, they were more immediately influenced by Quercy's bishop, their kinsman Guiraud Barasc-Béduer (1237–50). Again, a lord's preference was influenced by a powerful presence in his personal network.

The Aftermath of Inquisition

The inquisition almost certainly saw the end of any Waldensian presence in Quercy. As suggested, it was not *quite* the end of Catharism in Quercy, but it is nonetheless impossible not to view the inquisition as successful in its aim to eradicate the expression of dissident doctrines. Leading lords and officials were sentenced, careers of urban notables were destroyed and relationships within families and communities could never be the same. Whole communities were affected by what happened to people within them.

We have also seen that status and wealth made alternative – far more dignified and certainly prestigious – penances possible, and as part of which the names of the criminals were kept out of the papers, so to speak. As such, the de Gourdon were able to return to their former glory as patrons of Obazine. This was instead of sentencing, not an alternative penance, thus removing the stigma of heresy from the family – so successfully, in fact, that in 1246 Bernard de Caux and Jean-de-Saint-Pierre would be aided in an inquest by a Guiraud

---

[9] Bulit, *Gourdon*, p. 65; Lacoste, *Quercy*, II, 216.

de Gourdon, prior of the cathedral clergy at Cahors,[10] and by 1249 a Guillaume de Gourdon, the archpriest at Montpezat, was involved in resolving the affair between the bishops and the consuls at Cahors.[11]

But there is a good deal we do not know about the immediate aftermath. Because the towns of the 1243–4 record are not those investigated in 1241–2, we cannot get data for the most interesting questions, such as what happened to the towns of 1241–2 after Pierre Seilan left. Did those sentenced to depart on pilgrimages do so? Did they return, and what then? What happened to those individuals we have encountered for whom we have no evidence post-dating their trial? In the case of the relapsed – not least Arnaude de la Mothe and Pons Grimoard – we must assume that they were burned. Guillaume Faure we know was to be either sentenced to perpetual incarceration or exiled. We know that several other people tried by Bernard de Caux were still awaiting sentencing when the record that appears in Doat 22 was concluded in late January 1244, and we do not know the outcomes for others tried by Brother Ferrer. Such silences are frustrating not least because we want to know the fate of deponents to whom we have extended historical empathy.

A final observation takes us back to Quercy in its context as ally of Raimond VII. Even before 1229 he was no friend of the heretics, and after this date he was compelled and policed in this matter anyway. But in Quercy we can see that he was not as vigilant as he is assumed to have been in terms of the servants he appointed. Pons Grimoard may have appealed to him because he shared an antipathy towards the Dominicans. His family contained several *perfecti* and adherents of both sects, his friends and neighbours were likewise involved, and we know that he had sought to undermine the inquisitors on the count's orders, if we interpret them from Pons's perspective. Notorious as the Grimoards must have been in terms of their confessional complexion, the count could scarcely have chosen a less appropriate servant. It is unlikely that he knew of Pons's darker activities in office, such as failing to arrest the *perfectus* Guillaume de Caussade at Beaucaire. Likewise, it is quite probable that he did not know that his *bailli* for Moissac and Montcuq, Othon de Berètges, had let Vigouroux de la Bacone escape from his custody in the 1220s until it, too, came to the attention of the inquisition.[12]

But this is really as generous as we can be to the count, who seems to have allowed his officials a free hand. When we consider the scale of the convictions in 1241–2, a lack of knowledge on his part of what was happening in Quercy from the late 1220s onwards, under his nose, seems astounding. If he had selective blindness about the moral quality of his allies and servants he was no less guilty than his father had been of tolerating error. The very least

---

[10] See Albe, *L'hérésie ... en Quercy*, p. 19.
[11] D118, f. 70; AD Lot, F. liaise 176; *IRC*, no. 41.
[12] Given, *Inquisition*, esp. pp. 39, 169.

we can say is that a commitment to erasing heresy from his lands cannot have been foremost in his mind when his servants in Quercy were appointed.

However, if it seems possible that Raimond VII did not appreciate the scale and nature of the heretical communities protected by his vassals in Quercy, the same did not apply to the relationship between these leaders and the knightly families they had surrounded themselves with. The lords in the region not only lost their enthusiasm for the crusade and joined the south in resistance to the invasion, but also, in some cases, relaxed their opposition to heresy in their towns, drawing existing retainers into relationships of mutual protection. And some even embraced its teachings.

Bibliography

Unpublished primary sources

Cahors, Archives départementales du Lot
Archives départementales du Lot, laisse E. ter 21; laisse F. 98, 123, 125, 176, 177, 365; laisse J. 634
Archives municipales de Cahors, charters 1, 9, 26, 30, 52, AA1, AA58, BB1, CC50, DD1, DD2, DD8, FF2, HH1 and *'Le Livre noir'*
Archives municipales de Gourdon, charter AA2

Montauban, Archives départementales de Tarn-et-Garonne (Montauban)
Archives départementales de Tarn-et-Garonne, charter AA1 and laisse G. 541, 662, 692
Archives municipales de Montauban: *'Te igitur'*

Paris, Bibliothèque nationale de France
Ms. Lat. 5219
Mss. Fonds Doat, 21, 22, 23, 117, 118, 119, 122, 143, 153

Published primary sources

The Accounts of Alphonse of Poitiers, 1243–1248, ed. F. X. Hartigan (Lanham and London, 1984).

Albanès, J. H. (ed.), *Gallia Christiana novissima. Histoire des archévêchés, évéchês et abbeyes de France*, 7 vols. (Montebéliard and Valence, 1895–1920).

Annales ecclésiastiques et politiques de la ville de Figeac en Quercy, diocèse de Cahors, ed. J. F. Debons (Toulouse, 1829).

Archives historiques de La Marche et du Limousin, ed. M. Léroux et al., 4 vols. (Limoges, 1887–92).

Bernard Gui, *Manuel de l'inquisiteur*, ed. and trans. G. Mollat, 2 vols. (Paris, 1926–7).

Bernard of Fontcaude, *Adversus Waldensium sectam*, PL 204, 793–840.

Bruel, A. (ed.), *Recueil des chartes de l'abbaye de Cluny*, 6 vols. (Paris, 1876–1903).

Bull, M. (ed. and trans.), *The Miracles of Our Lady of Rocamadour* (Woodbridge, 1999).

Cartulaire de l'abbaye cistercienne d'Obazine (xiie–xiiie siècles), ed. B. Barrière (Clermont-Ferrand, 1989).

Cartulaire de l'abbaye de Beaulieu (en Limousin), ed. M. Deloche (Paris, 1859).

Cartulaire de l'abbaye de Berdoues, ed. J.-J. Cazauran (The Hague, 1905).

Cartulaire de l'abbaye de Cadouin, ed. J.-M. Maubourgnet (Cahors, 1926).

Cartulaire de l'abbaye de Conques en Rouergue, ed. G. Desjardins (Paris 1879).

Cartulaire de l'abbaye d' Uzerche (de xe au xive siècles), ed. J.-B. Champéval (Tulle, 1901).

Cartulaire de l'abbaye de Vigeois en Limousin (954–1167), ed. M. de Montégut (Limoges, 1907).

Cartulaire de la Selve: la terre, les hommes et le pouvoir en Rouergue au xiie siècle, ed. P. Ourliac and A.-M. Magnou (Paris, 1985).

Cartulaire de Tulle, ed. E. Albe, *Bulletin de la société archéologique de Borda* (1923).

Cartulaires des abbayes de Tulle et de Roc-Amadour, ed. J.-B. Champéval (Brive, 1903).

Catalogue des actes de Simon et d'Amaury de Montfort, ed. A. Molinier (Paris, 1874).

Catalogue des actes des comtes de Toulouse III: Raimond V (1149–1194), ed. E.-G. Léonard (Nîmes and Paris, 1932).

Charte des coutumes de Cajarc, ed. L. Combarieu and F. Cangardel (Cahors, 1879).

Chartes, chroniques et mémoriaux pour servir à l'histoire de la Marche et du Limousin, eds. A. Leroux and A. Bosvieux (Tulle, 1886).

Chartes du Limousin antérieures au xiiie siècle, ed. A. Leroux (Tulle, 1900).

Chartier du monastère de Sarlat, ixe–xiie, ed. G. Marmier, *Bulletin de la société historique et archéologique du Périgord* 11 (1884), pp. 450–82.

Chronica magistri Rogeri de Houedene, ed. W. Stubbs, 2 vols. (London, 1868–71).

The Chronicle of William of Puylaurens: The Albigensian Crusade and its Aftermath, trans. W. A. and M. D. Sibly (Woodbridge, 2003).

Combarieu, L. and P. Lacombe (eds.), *Te Igitur* (Cahors, 1888).

Congar, Y., 'Arriana haeresis comme désignation du néo-manichéisme au xiie siècle', *Revue des sciences philosophiques et théologiques* 43 (1959), pp. 449–61.

Corpus Juris Canonici, ed. A. L. Richter and E. A. Friedberg, 2 vols. (Lepizig, 1879; rprt. Graz, 1955).

d'Achery, L. (ed.), *Spicilegium*, 2 vols. (Paris, 1723).

de Vic, C. and J. Vaissète (ed.), *Histoire générale de Languedoc*, revised by A. Molinier, 16 vols. (Toulouse, 1872–1904).

Delisle, L. and E. Berger (eds.), *Recueil des actes d'Henri II, roi d'Angleterre, concernant les provinces françaises et les affaires de France*, 3 vols. in 2 (Paris, 1916–27).

'Deposition de Guillaume Donnadieu d'Elves', ed. Y. Dossat, *CF* 3 (Toulouse, 1968), pp. 290–8.

Douais, C. (ed.), *Documents pour servir à l'histoire de l'inquisition dans le Languedoc* (Paris, 1900; rprt. 1977).

Dufour, E. (ed.), *Documents inédits pour servir à l'histoire de l'ancienne province de Quercy* (Cahors, 1868).

Durand de Huesca, *Liber antiheresis*, ed. J. Duvernoy, *Archivum Fratrum Praedicatorum* 16 (1946).

Duthu-Latour, H. et al., *Les villes du Quercy au moyen âge: consulats-économie-société, 1250–1350* (Cahors, 2003).

Duvernoy, J. (ed. and trans.), *Chronique de Guillaume Pelhisson* (Paris, 1994).

Duvernoy, J. (ed. and trans.), *L'inquisition en Quercy: le registre des pénitences de Pierre Cellan, 1241–1242* (Castelnaud la Chapelle, 2001).

Fénié, B. and J.-J. Fénié, *Toponymie occitane* (Bordeaux, 1997).

Fournier, P. F. and P. Guébin (eds.), *Enquêtes administratives d'Alphonse de Poitiers, arrêts de son parlement tenu à Toulouse et textes annexes, 1249–71* (Paris, 1959).

François, M. (ed.), *Le livre des miracles de Notre-Dame de Rocamadour* (Rocamadour, 1973).

Gams, P. B. (ed.), *Series episcoporum ecclesiae catholicae*, 3rd edn (Leipzig, 1931).

Gervase of Canterbury, *Opera historica*, ed. W. Stubbs (London 1879)

Guillaume de Puylaurens, *Chronique*, ed. J. Duvernoy (Paris, 1976; rprt. Toulouse, 1996).

Guillaume de Tudela et al., *La Chanson de la Croisade Albigeoise*, ed. and trans. E. Martin-Chabot, 3 vols. (Paris, 1960–72).

Guillaume Pelhisson, *Chronique* suivie du récit des troubles d'Albi (1234), ed. and trans. J. Duvernoy (Paris, 1994)

Hamilton, J. and B. Hamilton (eds. and trans.), *Christian Dualist Heresies in the Byzantine World, c. 650–c. 1405* (Manchester, 1998).

Histoire de la guerre des albigeois, Anon., in *RHF*, XIX, pp. 114–92 and *HGL*, VIII, pp. v–vi, 5–205.

Les miracles de Nôtre-Dame de Roc-Amadour au xiiie siècle, ed. and trans. E. Albe, 2nd edn (Toulouse, 1996).

Maisonneuve, H. (ed.), *Études sur les origines de l'inquisition*, 2nd edn (Paris, 1960).

Mansi, J. D. (ed.), *Concilia*, introduction and 53 vols. (originally *Sacrorum conciliorum nova et amplissima collectio*, 53 vols. (Florence, 1759–1927)) (rprt. Graz, 1960–61).

Migne, J. P. et al. (eds.), *Patrologiae cursus completus, series Latina*, 217 vols. (Paris, 1852–1904, with 4 vols. index and 5 vols. supplementum 1958 74).

Molinier, A. (ed.), *Correspondance administrative d'Alphonse de Poitiers*, 2 vols. (Paris, 1894–1900).

Pataki, T., 'Hommages rendus aux vicomtes de Turenne (1163–1304)', *BSEL* 109 (1988), pp. 111–12.

Percin, J. J. (ed.), *Monumenta conventus Tolosani ordinis fratrum praedicatorum* (Toulouse, 1693).

Pierre des Vaux-de-Cernay, *Histoire Albigeoise*, ed. and trans. P. Guébin and H. Maisonneuve (Paris, 1951).

Pierre des Vaux-de-Cernay, *Hystoria Albigensis*, ed. P. Guébin and E. Lyon, 3 vols. (Paris, 1926–30).

Pierre des Vaux-de-Cernay, *The History of the Albigensian Crusade*, ed. and trans. W. A. and M. D. Sibly (Oxford, 1998).

Rainerius Sacconi, *Summa de Catharis et Pauperibus de Lugduno*, in *Un Traité néo-manichéen du xiiie siècle: Le Liber du duobus principiis, suivi d'un fragment de rituel cathare*, ed. A. Dondaine (Rome, 1939), pp. 64–78.

Sancti Stephani Lemovicensis cartularium, ed. J. de Font-Réaulx, *Bulletin de la société archéologique et historique du Limousin* 69 (1922).

Teulet, A. et al. (eds.), *Layettes du trésor des chartes*, 5 vols. (Paris, 1863–1909).

The Song of the Cathar Wars, trans. J. Shirley (Aldershot, 1996).

Thonnat, G. (ed.), *Documents généologiques, historiques sur les familles nobles et notables du Haut-Quercy* (Cahors, 1977).

Vaissière, A. (ed.), 'Documents relatifs à l'histoire de la maison de Turenne', *Bulletin de la société scientifique, historique et archéologique de la Corrèze* 7 (1885), pp. 310–402.

Wakefield, W. L. and A. P. Evans (ed. and trans.), *Heresies of the High Middle Ages* (New York, 1969; rprt. 1991).

Wolff, P. (ed.), *Documents de l'histore du Languedoc* (Toulouse, 1969).

Works of reference

Albe, E. (ed.), *Inventaire des archives municipales de Cahors, i:i: xiiie siècle* (Cahors, 1915).

Albe, E. (ed.), *Inventaire raisonné et analytique des archives municipales de Cahors*, 3 parts: 1 (Cahors, 1915); 2. *BSEL* 41 (1920), pp. 1–48 and *BSEL* 43 (1922), pp. 1–28; 3. *BSEL* 47 (1926), pp. 1–150.

Balteau, J. et al. (eds.), *Dictionnaire de biographie française*, vol. 1– (Paris, 1932–).

Bequart, N. (ed.), *Guide des archives de la Dordogne* (Périgueux, 1970).

Combarieu, L., *Dictionnaire des communes du Lot* (Cahors, 1881; rprt. Nîmes, 2000).

Combarieu, L. (ed.), 'Inventaire mss. des archives communales de Cahors' (Cahors, 1864) (unpublished guide, AD Lot).

Combarieu, L. (ed.), 'Inventaire mss. des archives communales de Figeac' (Cahors, 1885) (unpublished guide, AD Lot).

Combarieu, L. (ed.), 'Inventaire mss. des archives communales de Gourdon' (Cahors, 1869 and 1877 supplt.) (unpublished guide, AD Lot).

Combarieu, L. (ed.), 'Inventaire mss. des archives hospitalières de Figeac' (Cahors, 1888) (unpublished guide, AD Lot).

Combarieu, L. (ed.), *Inventaire sommaire des archives départementales antérieures á 1790: Lot*, 3 vols. (Cahors, 1883–1900).

Couderc, C. (ed.), *Manuscrits de la bibliothèque de Cahors* (Cahors, 1888).

d'Alauzier, M. (ed.), 'Inventaire ms. des archives communales de Cajarc' (Cahors, 1960) (unpublished guide, AD Lot).

d'Alauzier, M. (ed.), 'Inventaire ms. des archives communales de Capdenac' (Cahors, 1944) (unpublished guide, AD Lot).

de la Chenaye-Desbois, F. A. A. et al., *Dictionnaire de la noblesse*, 3rd edn., 19 vols (Paris, 1969; rprt. of Paris, 1863–77)

de la Torre, M., *Lot: le guide complet de ses 340 communes* (Paris, 1990).

Duboys, A. et al., *Biographie des hommes illustres de l'ancienne province du Limousin* (Limoges, 1854).

Lacombe, O. (ed.), *Inventaire sommaire des archives departementales (de la Corrèze) antérieures de 1790*, 4 vols. (Paris, 1869–1911).

Latouche, R., *Archives de Tarn-et-Garonne* (Montauban, 1920).

Maisonobe, M. et al. (eds.), *Inventaire sommaire des archives départementales antérieures á 1790: Tarn-et-Garonne* (Montauban, 1894).

Mathieu, G. et al., *Archives départementales de la Corrèze. Répertoire numérique des séries antérieures à la Révolution et de leurs suppléments* (Tulle, 1912).

Méras, M., *Guide des archives de Tarn-et-Garonne* (Montauban, 1972).

Prat, R., *Guide des archives du Lot* (Cahors, 1971).

Souchal, G., *Archives départementales antérieures á 1790. Corrèze* (Tulle, 1955).

Bibliography

Secondary sources

Albe, E., 'L'abbaye nouvelle', in *Dictionnaire du département du Lot* (Paris, 1911).

Albe, E., *L'hérésie albigeoise et l'inquisition en Quercy* (Paris, 1910).

Albe, E., *Les institutions religieuses de Gourdon* (Gourdon, 1926).

Albe, E., *Les marchands de Cahors à Londres au xiiie siècle* (Cahors, 1908).

Albe, E., 'Les religieuses hospitalières de l'Ordre de Saint-Jean de Jerusalem au diocèse de Cahors', *Revue de l'histoire de l'église de France* 27 (1941), pp. 180–220.

Albe, E., 'Titres et documents concernant le Limousin et le Quercy: les possessions d'Obazine dans la diocese de Cahors et les familles du Quercy', *Bulletin de la société historique et archéologique de la Corrèze* 32:1 (1910), pp. 417–60, 511–609.

Albe, E. and A. Viré, *Le prieuré-doyenné de Carennac, archéologie et histoire* (Brive, 1914).

Amalric, J.-P., *Histoire de Quercy* (Toulouse, 1993).

Ames, C. C., *Righteous Persecution: Inquisition, Dominicans, and Christianity in the Middle Ages* (Philadelphia, 2009).

Arnold, J. H., *Belief and Unbelief in Medieval Europe* (London, 2005).

Arnold, J. H., *Inquisition and Power: Catharism and the Confessing Subject in the Medieval Languedoc* (Philadelphia, 2001).

Arnold, J. H., 'Inquisition, text and discourse', in *Texts and the Repression of Heresy*, eds. C. Bruschi and P. Biller (York, 2003), pp. 63–80.

Arnold, J. H., 'The historian as inquisitor: the ethics of interrogating subaltern voices', *Rethinking History* 2 (1998), pp. 379–86.

Asad, T., 'Medieval heresy: an anthropological view', *Social History* 11 (1986), pp. 345–62.

Aubrun, M., *Moines, paroisses et paysans* (Clermont-Ferrand, 2000).

Audisio, G., *'Les Vaudois'. Naissance, vie et mort d'une dissidence (xiie–xvi siècles)* (Turin, 1989), translated by Claire Davidson as *The Waldensian Dissent: Persecution and Survival c.1170–c.1570* (Cambridge, 1999).

Aurell, M. (ed.), *Les cathares devant l'histoire. Mélanges offerts à Jean Duvernoy* (Cahors, 2005).

Aurell, M., 'Les sources de la Croisade albigeoise: bilan et problématique', in *La croisade albigeoise*, ed. M. Roquebert (Carcassonne, 2004), pp. 21–38.

Aussel, M., 'Noël 1241: Gourdon au temps de l'inquisition', *BSEL* 117 (1996), pp. 91–117.

Ayma, L., *Histoire des évêques de Cahors* (translation of G. Lacroix, *Series et acta episcoporum Cadurcensium*), 2 vols. in 4 (Cahors, 1621; rprt. Cahors, 1878/9).

Barber, M., *The Cathars: Dualist Heretics in the Languedoc in the High Middle Ages* (Harlow, 2000).

Barrière, B., 'Les abbayes issues de l'érémitisme', *CF* 21 (Toulouse, 1986), pp. 71–105.

Barthelémy, D., 'Castles, barons, and vavassors in the Vendôme and neighbouring regions in the eleventh and twelfth centuries', in *Cultures of Power: Lordship, Status and Process in Twelfth-Century Europe*, ed. T. N. Bisson (Philadelphia, 1995), pp. 56–68.

Barthélemy, D., *La mutation de l'an mille, a-t-elle eu lieu? Servage et chevalerie dans la France des xe et xie siècles* (Paris, 1997).

Barthélemy, D., *The Serf, the Knight and the Historian* (Ithaca and London, 2009).

Baudel, E., *Une évolution de ville: Cahors-en-Quercy* (Cahors, 1928).

Bazalgues, G., *À la découverte des noms de lieux du Quercy et des communes du Lot* (Gourdon, 2002).

Beauvillain, J., *Le couvent des Dominicains de Cahors* (Toulouse, 1976).

Bec, P., *Nouvelle anthologie de la lyrique occitane du moyen age*, 2nd edn (Poitiers, 1970).

Belperron, P., *La croisade contre les Albigeois et l'union du Languedoc à la France (1209–1249)*, 2nd edn (Paris, 1967).

Benjamin, R., 'A Forty Years War: Toulouse and the Plantagenets, 1156–96', *Historical Research* 61 (1988), pp. 270–85.

Berlioz, J. (ed.), *Les pays cathare* (Paris, 2000).

Berman, C., *Medieval Agriculture, the Southern French Countryside and the Early Cistercians: A Study of Forty-Three Monasteries* (Philadelphia, 1986).

Berman, C., *The Cistercian Evolution: The Invention of a Religious Order in Twelfth-Century Fance* (Philadelphia, 2000).

Bertry, L., *Histoire de la ville de Tulle* (Tulle, 1900).

Biget, J.-L., 'À la source, un anticléricalisme et un évangélisme', in his *Hérésie et inquisition dans le midi de la France* (Paris, 2007), pp. 38–62.

Biget, J.-L., *Hérésie et inquisition dans le midi de la France* (Paris, 2007).

Biget, J.-L., 'Introduction: Le "catharisme", une histoire en devenir', in his *Hérésie et inquisition dans le midi de la France* (Paris, 2007), pp. 7–35.

Biget, J.-L., 'La dépossession des seigneurs méridionaux. Modalités, limites, portée', in *La croisade albigeoise*, ed. M. Roquebert (Carcassonne, 2004), pp. 261–300.

Biget, J.-L., 'L'art cistercien dans le Midi toulousain', *CF* 21 (Toulouse, 1986), pp. 313–70.

Biget, J.-L., 'L'anticléricalisme des hérètiques d'après les sources polémiques', *CF* 38 (Toulouse, 2003), pp. 405–45.

Biget, J.-L., 'Le Poids du contexte', in his *Hérésie et inquisition dans le midi de la France* (Paris, 2007), pp. 106–41.

Biget, J.-L., 'Les "Albigoise". Entrée dans l'histoire', in his *Hérésie et inquisition dans le midi de la France* (Paris, 2007), pp. 142–69.

Biget, J.-L., '"Les Albigeois": remarques sur une dénomination', in *Inventer l'hérésie? discours polémique et pouvoirs avant l'Inquisition*, ed. M. Zerner et al. (Nice, 1998), pp. 219–56.

Biget, J.-L., 'Les bons hommes sont-ils les fils de Bogomils? Examen critique d'une idée reçue', *Slavica occitania* 16 (2003), pp. 133–88, revised as 'Un phénomène occidental' in his *Hérésie et inquisition dans le midi de la France* (Paris, 2007), pp. 63–105.

Biget, J.-L., 'Notes sur le système féodale en Languedoc et son ouverture á l'hérésie', *Heresis* 11 (1989), pp. 7–17.

Biget, J.-L., 'Un phénomène occidental', in his *Hérésie et inquisition dans le midi de la France* (Paris, 2007), pp. 63–105.

Biller, P., '*Curate infirmos*: the medieval Waldensian practice of medicine', in his *The Waldenses, 1170–1530: Between a Religious Order and a Church* (Aldershot, 2001), pp. 49–67.

Biller, P., 'Goodbye to Waldensianism?', *Past and Present* 192 (2006), pp. 3–33.

Biller, P., 'Medieval Waldensian abhorrence of killing pre-c.1400', in his *The Waldenses, 1170–1530: Between a Religious Order and a Church* (Aldershot, 2001), pp. 81–93.

Biller, P., 'The Cathars of the Languedoc and written materials', in *Heresy and Literacy, 1000–1530*, ed. P. Biller and A. Hudson (Cambridge, 1994), pp. 61–82.

Biller, P., 'The Preaching of the Waldensian sisters', in his *The Waldenses, 1170–1530: Between a Religious Order and a Church* (Aldershot, 2001), pp. 125–58.

Biller, P., '*Thesaurus Absconditus*: the hidden treasure of the Waldensians', in his *The Waldenses, 1170–1530: Between a Religious Order and a Church* (Aldershot, 2001), pp. 97–110.

Biller, P., 'Through a glass darkly: Seeing medieval heresy', in *The Medieval World*, ed. P. Linehan and J. L. Nelson (London/New York, 2001), pp. 308–26.

Biller, P., *The Waldenses, 1170–1530: Between a Religious Order and a Church* (Aldershot, 2001).

Biller, P., '*Topos* and reality of the heretic as *illiteratus*' in his *Medieval Waldensians* (Woodbridge, 2001), pp. 169–90.

Biller, P. and A. Hudson (eds.), *Heresy and Literacy, 1000–1530* (Cambridge, 1994).

Bisson, T. N., *Assemblies and Representation in Languedoc in the Thirteenth Century* (Princeton, 1964).

Bisson, T., 'The "Feudal Revolution"', *Past and Present* 142 (1994), pp. 6–42.

Blaquière, H. and Y. Dossat, 'Les cathares au jour le jour. Confessions inédites de cathares quercynois', *CF* 3 (Toulouse, 1989), pp. 259–98.

Bondéelle-Souchier, A., *Bibliothèques cisterciennes dans la France médiéval* (Paris, 1991).

Bonnassie, P. (ed.), *Fiefs et féodalité dans l'Europe méridionale (Italie, France du Midi, Péninsule Ibérique) du xe au xiiie siècle* (Toulouse, 2002).

Bourin, M., 'France du Midi et France du Nord: deux systèmes anthroponymiques?,' in *L'anthroponymie. Document de l'histoire sociale des mondes méditerranéens médiévaux*, ed. M. Bourin et al. (Rome, 1996).

Bourin, M., 'How changes in naming reflect the evolution of familial structures in southern Europe, 950–1215', in *Personal Names Studies of Medieval Europe: Social Identity and Familial Structures*, ed. G. T. Beech et al. (Kalamazoo, 2002), pp. 3–13.

Bourin, M., *Villages médiévaux en bas Languedoc: genèse d'une sociabilité: xe–xive siècles* (Paris, 1987).

Bousquet, J., *Le Rouergue au premier Moyen Age (vers 800–vers 1250)*, 2 vols. (Rodez, 1992).

Boyle, L., 'Montaillou revisited: *Mentalité* and methodologie', in *Pathways to Medieval Peasants*, ed. A. J. Raftis (Toronto, 1981), pp. 119–40.

Brenon, A., 'Catharism in the family in Languedoc in the thirteenth and fourteenth centuries: an investigation based on inquisition sources, in *Urban and Rural Communities in Medieval France*, ed. K. Reyerson and J. Drendel (Leiden, 1998), pp. 291–304.

Brenon, A., 'Le catharisme méridional: questions et problèmes', in *Les Pays cathare*, ed. J. Berlioz (Paris, 2000), pp. 81–100.

Brenon, A., 'Le faux problème du dualisme absolu', *Heresis* 21 (1993), 61–74.

Brenon, A., *Le vrai visage du Catharisme* (Portet-sur-Garonne, 1988).

Brenon, A., *Les archipels cathares: dissidence chrétienne dans l'Europe médiévale* (Cahors, 2000).

Brenon, A., *Les femmes cathare* (Paris, 1992).

Brenon, A., 'Les heresies de l'an mil: Nouvelles perspectives sur les origines du Catharisme', *Heresis* 24 (1995), pp. 21–36.

Brenon, A., '"Vaudoisie" en Languedoc, xie–xive siècle', in *Les Pays cathare*, ed. J. Berlioz (Paris, 2000), pp. 125–46.

Brown, E. A. R., 'The tyranny of a construct: feudalism and historians of medieval Europe', *American Historical Review* 79 (1974), pp. 1063–88, reprinted in *Debating the Middle Ages: Issues and Readings*, ed. L. K. Little and B. H. Rosenwein (Oxford, 1998), pp. 148–69.

Brunn, U., *Des contestaires au 'Cathares': Discours de réforme et propaganda antihérétique dans le pays du Rhin et de la Meuse avant l'inquisition* (Paris, 2006).

Bruschi, C., '"Magna diligentia est habenda per inquisitorem": precautions before reading Doat 21–26', in *Texts and the Repression of Medieval Heresy*, ed. C. Bruschi and P. Biller (York, 2003), pp. 81–111.

Bruschi, C. and P. Biller (eds.), *Texts and the Repression of Medieval Heresy* (York, 2003).

Bruschi, C., *The Wandering Heretics of Languedoc* (Cambridge, 2009).

Bulit, R., *En pays de Bouriane: Gourdon en Quercy, des origines au xixe siècle* (Gourdon, 1923; rprt. 1997).

Burnham, L. A., *So Great a Light, So Great a Smoke: the Beguin Heretics of Languedoc* (Ithaca and London, 2008).

Cameron, E., *Waldenses: Rejections of Holy Church in Medieval Europe* (Oxford, 2001).

Castaing-Sicard, M., *Monnaies féodale et circulation monétaire en Languedoc (xe–xiiie siècles)* (Toulouse, 1961).

Cazanave, A., 'Hérésie et société', *Heresis* 13/14 (1990), pp. 7–61.

Cazes, J.-P. et al., 'Les conséquences de la croisade sur les forteresses seigneuriales, l'apport de l'archéologie: Termes, Fenouillet, Montaillou', in *La croisade albigeoise*, ed. M. Roquebert (Carcassonne, 2004), pp. 369–84.

Champeval, J.-B., *Figeac et ses institutions religieuses* (Cahors, 1898).

Cheyette, F. L., 'George Duby's *Mâconnais* after fifty years: reading it then and reading it now', *Journal of Medieval History* 28 (2002), pp. 291–317.

Clarke, J. J., *Oriental Enlightenment: The Encounter between Asian and Western Thought* (London and New York, 1997).

Clavaud, F., *Cajarc, consulat de Haut-Quercy aux xiiie et xiv siècles. Etude démographique* (Paris, 1989).

Clozier, R., *Le Quercy* (Paris and Grenoble, 1953).

Combarieu, L. and F. Cangardel, 'Gourdon et ses seigneurs du xe au xive siècle', *BSEL* 6 (1880).

Constable, G., 'Renewal and reform and in religious life: concepts and realities', in *Renaissance and Renewal in the Twelfth Century*, ed. R. L. Benson and G. Constable (Oxford, 1982), pp. 37–67.

Coulon, J., *Catus-en-Quercy, des origines au xie siècle* (Gourdon, 2003).

Cruceus, G., *Histoire des évêques de Cahors* (Cahors, 1878).

Cursente, B., 'Le castrum dans le pays d'Oc aux xie et xiie siècles', *Heresis* 11 (1989), pp. 19–25.

Cursente, B., 'The French Midi reflected in personal names', in *Personal Names*

Studies of Medieval Europe: Social Identity and Familial Structures, ed. G .T. Beech et al. (Kalamazoo, 2002).

Daymard, J., *Le vieux Cahors* (Paris, 1908; rprt. Roanne, 1978).

de Cathala-Coture, A. et al., *Histoire politique, ecclésiastique et littéraire du Quercy*, 3 vols. (Montauban, 1785).

de Gournay, F., 'Le fief en Rouergue (xe–xiie siècle)', in *Fiefs et féodalité dans l'Europe méridionale*, ed. P. Bonnassie (Toulouse, 2002), pp. 203–20.

de Vic, C. and J. Vaissète, *Histoire générale de Languedoc*, revised by A. Molinier, 16 vols. (Toulouse, 1872–1904).

Débax, H., *La féodalité languedocienne* (Toulouse, 2003).

Débax, H., 'Fief et castrum: le fief dans les serments de fidélité languedociens du xie siècle', in *Fiefs et féodalité dans l'Europe méridionale (Italie, France du Midi, Péninsule Ibérique) du xe au xiiie siècle*, ed. P. Bonnassie (Toulouse, 2002), pp. 137–43.

Débax, H. (ed.), *Les sociétés méridionales à l'âge féodale: Espagne, Italie et sud de la France, xe–xiiie s. Hommage à Pierre Bonnassie* (Toulouse, 1999).

Dedieu, H., 'Quelques traces de religion populaire autour des frères mineurs de la province d'Aquitaine', *CF* 11 (Toulouse, 1976), pp. 229–49.

Delagrange, R., *Cadouin. Histoire d'une relique et d'un monastère* (Bergerac, 1912).

Delluc, G. and J. Secret, *Cadouin: une aventure cistercienne en Périgord* (Périgueux, 1965).

Dobelmann, S., *La langue de Cahors, des origines à la fin du xvie siècle* (Toulouse, 1944).

Dondaine, A., 'Aux origines de valdéisme. Une profession de foi de Valdès', *Archivum Fratrum Praedicatorum* 16 (1946), pp. 191–253.

Dondaine, A., 'Durand of Huesca et la polémique anti-cathare', *Archivum Fratrum Praedicatorum* 29 (1959), pp. 268–71.

Dondaine, A., 'Le manuel de l'inquisiteur (1230–1330)', *Archivum Fratrum Praedicatorum* 17 (1947), pp. 85–194.

Dondaine, A., 'L'origine de l'hérésie médiévale: à propos d'un livre récent', *Rivista di storia della chiesa in Italia* 6 (1952), pp. 47–78.

Dossat, Y., 'A propos du chroniqueur Guillaume de Puylaurens', in his *Église et hérésie en France au xiii siècle* (London, 1982), pp. 47–52.

Dossat, Y., 'De Vaudès à Saint-François à Montauban', *CF* 8 (Toulouse, 1973), pp. 403–13.

Dossat, Y., *Église et hérésie en France au xiiie siècle* (London, 1982).

Dossat, Y., 'La repression de l'hérésie par les évêques', *CF* 6 (Toulouse, 1971), pp. 217–51.

Dossat, Y., 'Le chroniqueur Guillaume de Puylaurens était-il chapelain de Raymond VII ou notaire de l'inquisition toulousaine?', in his *Église et hérésie en France au xiii siècle* (London, 1982), pp. 343–53.

Dossat, Y., 'Le massacre d'Avignonet', *CF* 6 (Toulouse, 1971), pp. 343–58.

Dossat, Y., 'L'inquisiteur Bernard de Caux et l'Agenais', in his *Église et hérésie en France au xiii siècle* (London, 1982), pp. 75–9.

Dossat, Y., 'Les cathares dans le documents de l'inquisition', *CF* 3 (Toulouse, 1968), pp. 71–106.

Dossat, Y., *Les crises de l'inquisition toulousaine au xiiie siècle (1233–1273)* (Bordeaux, 1959).

Dossat, Y., 'Les Vaudois méridionaux d'après les documents de l'inquisition', *CF* 2 (Toulouse, 1967), pp. 207–42.

Dossat, Y., 'Opposition des anciens ordres à l'installation des mendients', *CF* 8 (Toulouse, 1973), pp. 263–306.

Dossat, Y., 'Un évêque Cathare originaire de l'Agenais: Vigouroux de la Bacone', in his *Église et hérésie en France au xiiie siècle* (London, 1982), pp. 623–39.

Dossat, Y., 'Une figure d'inquisiteur: Bernard de Caux', *CF* 6 (Toulouse, 1971), pp. 253–72, and in his *Église et hérésie en France au xiii siècle* (London, 1982), pp. 47–52.

Douais, C., *Essai sur l'organisation des études dans l'ordre des frères prêcheurs au XIIIe et au XIVe siècle (1216–1342)* (Paris, 1884).

Douais, C. (ed.), 'Saint Raymond de Peñafort et les hérétiques: Directoire à l'usage des inquisiteurs aragonais, 1242', *Le moyen âge* 12 (1899), pp. 305–25.

Dufour, E., *La commune de Cahors au moyen âge* (Cahors, 1846; rprt. Marseille, 1976).

Dufour, J., *Les évêques d'Albi, de Cahors et de Rodez des origines à la fin du xiie siècle* (Paris, 1989).

Duhamel-Amado, C., *Genèse des lignages méridionaux: l'aristocratie languedocienne du xe au xiie siècle* (Toulouse, 2001).

Durand, A., *Les paysages médiévaux du Languedoc (xe–xiie siècles)* (Toulouse, 2003).

Durieux, F.-R., 'Approches de l'histoire franciscaine du Languedoc au xiiie siècle', *CF* 8 (Toulouse, 1973), pp. 79–100.

Duroy, G., *Histoire de Turenne* (Paris, 1880).

Duvernoy, J., '"À l'époque, l'église ne poursuivait pas les Vaudois": éssai de chronologie du valdéisme languedocien', in his *Cathares, Vaudois et Béguins: dissidents du Pays d'Oc* (Toulouse, 1994), pp. 153–61.

Duvernoy, J., 'Albigeois et Vaudois en Quercy d'après le registre des pénitences de Pierre Seilan', in his *Cathares, Vaudois et Béguins: dissidents du Pays d'Oc* (Toulouse, 1994), pp. 85–97.

Duvernoy, J., 'Albigeois et Vaudois en Rouergue', in his *Cathares, Vaudois et Béguins: dissidents du Pays d'Oc* (Toulouse, 1994), pp. 99–110.

Duvernoy, J., 'Aux origines du valdéisme: une profession de foi de Valdèisme', *Archivum Fratrum Praedicatorum* 16 (1946), pp. 232–5.

Duvernoy, J., 'Droit coutumier d'origine romaine et féodalité occitane', *Heresis* 11 (1989), pp. 29–40.

Duvernoy, J., 'Hérésie et tolerance dans le Midi au xiiie siècle, in his *Cathares, Vaudois et Béguins: dissidents du Pays d'Oc* (Toulouse, 1994), pp. 63–8.

Duvernoy, J., 'La noblesse cathare en Languedoc', in his *Cathares, Vaudois et Béguins: dissidents du Pays d'Oc* (Toulouse, 1994), pp. 69–84.

Duvernoy, J., *Le Catharisme I: La religion des Cathares* (Toulouse, 1976).

Duvernoy, J., *Le Catharisme II: L'histoire des Cathares* (Toulouse, 1979).

Duvernoy, J., 'Le problème des origines du catharisme', in his *Cathares, Vaudois et Béguins: dissidents du Pays d'Oc* (Toulouse, 1994), pp. 39–52.

Duvernoy, J., 'Les albigeois dans la vie sociale et économique de leur temps', *Annales de l'institut d'études occitanes 1962–3* (1966), pp. 64–72, and in his *Dissidents du pays d'Oc: Cathares, Vaudois et Béguins* (Toulouse, 1994), pp. 205–14.

Duvernoy, J., 'Les origines du movement vaudois', *Heresis* 13/14 (1990), pp. 173–98.

Edwards, A. D., 'La fondation de l'université de Cahors', *CF* 5 (Toulouse, 1970), pp. 266–73.

Enjalbert, H. (ed.), *Histoire de Rouergue* (Toulouse, 1987).

Erikson, K. T., *Wayward Puritans: A Study in the Sociology of Deviance* (New York, 1966).

Escande, J. J., *Histoire de Périgord*, 2nd edn (Sarlat, 1955).

Fage, R., *Les états de la vicomté de Turenne*, 2 vols. (Paris, 1894).

Faucher, J., 'Contribution à l'histoire de la vicomté de Turenne', *Bulletin de la société historique et archéologique de la Corrèze* 60 (1938), pp. 61–94.

Feuchter, J., 'Pierre Sellan. Le pouvoir de l'inquisition à travers ses peines. Le cas de Montauban (1241)', in *Inquisition et pouvoir*, ed. G. Audisio (Aix-en-Provence, 2003), pp. 235–55.

Feuchter, J., 'Pierre Sellan, un viellard expérimenté', in *Les inquisiteurs. Portraits de défenseurs de la foi en Languedoc (xiiie–xive siècles)*, ed. L. Albaret (Toulouse, 2001), pp. 41–55.

Flamari, E., *Esquisse d'histoire. Vicomté de Turenne* (Limoges, 1940).

Frassetto, M., 'The sermons of Adémar of Chabannes and the letter of Héribert. New sources concerning the origins of medieval heresy', *Revue bénédictine* 109 (1999), pp. 324–40.

Friedlander, A., 'Heresy, inquisition and the crusader nobility of Languedoc', *Medieval Prosopography* 4 (1983), pp. 45–67.

Galabert, F., *Montpezat de Quercy* (Marseille, 1976).

Gardel, M.-E., 'Conséquences de la croisade sur le milieu castral: l'exemple de Cabaret', in *La croisade albigeoise*, ed. M. Roquebert (Carcassonne, 2004), pp. 349–68.

Gardel, M.-E., *Vie et mort d'un castrum: Cabaret, archéologie d'un village médiéval en Languedoc (xie–xiiie siècles)* (Cahors, 2004).

Gaussin, P.-R., 'Les communités féminines dans l'espace Languedocien de la fin du xie à la fin du xiv siècle', *CF* 23 (Toulouse, 1988), pp. 299–332.

Ginzburg, C., 'The inquisitor as anthropologist', in his *Clues, Myths and the Historical Method* (London, 1990), pp. 154–64.

Given, J. B., *Inquisition and Medieval Society: Power, Discipline and Resistance in Languedoc* (Ithaca and London, 1997).

Given, J. B., 'Les inquisiteurs du Languedoc medieval: les elements sociétaux favorables et contraignants, in *Inquisition et Pouvoir*, ed. G. Audisio (Aix-en-Provence, 2003), pp. 57–71.

Graham-Leigh, E., *The Southern French Nobility and the Albigensian Crusade* (Woodbridge, 2005).

Griffe, E., *Le Languedoc cathare (1190 à 1210)* (Paris, 1971).

Griffe, E., *Le Languedoc cathare au temps de la croisade (1209–29)* (Paris, 1973).

Griffe, E., *Le Languedoc cathare et l'inquisition (1229–1329)* (Paris, 1989).

Griffe, E., *Les débuts de l'aventure cathare en Languedoc (1140–1190)* (Paris, 1969).

Grimal, P., *Le Quercy*, 2nd edn (Paris, 1998).

Guiraud, J., *Histoire de l'inquisition au moyen âge*, 2 vols. (Paris, 1935–8).

Hamilton, B., 'The Albigensian Crusade', in his *Monastic Reform, Catharism and the Crusades (900–1300)* (London, 1979), pp. 1–40.

Hamilton, B., 'The Cathar council of Saint Félix reconsidered', in his *Monastic Reform, Catharism and the Crusades (900–1300)* (London, 1979), pp. 23–53.

Hamilton, B., *Monastic Reform, Catharism and the Crusades (900–1300)* (London, 1979).

Hamilton, B., *The Medieval Inquisition* (London, 1981).

Hamilton, B., 'Wisdom from the East: the reception by the Cathars of Eastern dualist texts', in *Heresy and Literacy, 1000–1530*, ed. P. Biller and A. Hudson (Cambridge, 1994), pp. 38–60.

Hautefeuille, F., 'La seigneurie de Castelnau-Montratier au xie et xiie siècle', *BSEL* 113 (1992), pp. 255–71.

Havet, J., 'L'hérésie et le bras séculier au moyen âge jusqu'au XIIIe siècle', *Bibliothèque de l'École des Chartes* 41 (1880), pp. 498–507.

Higounet, C., *Le conté de Comminges de ses origines à son anexion à la Couronne*, 2 vols (Toulouse/Paris, 1949).

Higounet, C., *Mouvements de populations dans le Midi de France du XIe–XVe siècle* (Paris, 1953).

Higounet, C., *Paysages et villages neufs de moyen âge: receuil d'articles de Ch. Higounet* (Bordeaux, 1975).

Higounet, C., 'Structures sociales, "castra", et castelnaux dans le sud-ouest Aquitaine (xe–xiie siècles)', in *Structures féodales et féodalisme dans l'occident méditerranéen (xe–xiiie siècles)*, eds. P. Toubert et al. (Rome, 1980), pp. 109–16.

Higounet-Nadal, A., *Histoire de Montauban* (Toulouse, 1984).

Higounet-Nadal, A., *Histoire de Quercy* (Toulouse, 1993).

Higounet-Nadal, A., *Histoire de Rouergue* (Toulouse, 1993).

Imbart de la Tour, P., *Les paroisses rurales du ive au xie siècles*, 2nd edn (Paris, 1979).

Juillet, J., *Les monastères des femmes en Quercy au xiie siècle* (Marseilles, 1982).

Juillet, J., *Templiers et hospitaliers en Quercy: les commanderies et prieurés sur le chemin de Notre-Dame de Rocamadour* (Grenoble, 1999).

Kaelber, L., 'Weavers into heretics? The social organisation of early thirteenth-century Catharism in comparative perspective', *Social Science History* 21 (1997), pp. 111–37.

Keck, C., 'L'entourage de Simon de Montfort pendant la Croisade albigeoise et l'établissement territorial des *crucesignati*', in *La croisade albigeoise*, ed. M. Roquebert (Carcassonne, 2004), pp. 235–44.

Kienzle, B. M., *Cistercians, Heresy and Crusade in Occitania, 1145–1229* (York, 2001).

Kienzle, B. M., 'Hélinand de Froidmont et la prédication cistercienne dans le Midi (1145–1229)', *CF* 31 (Toulouse, 1997), pp. 37–67.

Lacabane, J.-L., *Observations sur la géographie et l'histoire du Quercy et du Limousin (à propos d'une brochure sur les divisions territoriales du Quercy)* (Paris, 1862).

Lacarrière, C., *Histoire des évêques de Quercy, des saints, des monastères, des principaux événements du Quercy* (Martel, 1876; rprt. Nîmes, 2004).

Lacoste, G., *Histoire générale de la province de Quercy*, 4 vols. (Cahors, 1883; rprt. 2004).

Lafforgue, A., 'Naissance d'une ville (12e et 13e siècle)', in *Histoire de Montauban*, ed. D. Ligou, 2nd edn (Toulouse, 1992), pp. 25–50.

Lambert, M. D., *The Cathars* (Oxford and Malden, 1998).

Lambert, M. D, *Medieval Heresy: Popular Movements from the Gregorian Reform to the Reformation*, 3rd edn (Oxford, 2002).

Lappara, E., *Cardaillac en Quercy et son histoire* (Cardaillac, 1982).

Lartigaut, J., *Histoire de Quercy* (Toulouse, 1993).

Lartigaut, J., 'Le testament d'une grande bourgeoise de Cahors, Sébélie de Jean, veuve d'Arnaud Béral (1286)', *BSEL* 113 (1992), pp. 103–24.

Lartigaut, J., *Les campagnes de Quercy* (Toulouse, 1976).

Lartigaut, J., *Puy-l'Évêque au moyen âge. Le castrum et la châtellenie (xiiie–xve)* (Bayac, 1991).

Le Bret, H., *Histoire de Montauban*, 2 vols., 2nd edn (Montauban, 1941).

Le Roy Ladurie, E., *Montaillou, village Occitan de 1294 à 1324* (Paris, 1975).

Lea, H. C., *The Inquisition of the Middle Ages: Its Organization and Operation*, intr. W. Ullmann (rprt. of H. C. Lea, *The History of the Inquisition of the Middle Ages*, 3 vols. (New York, 1887), vol. 1, chapters 7–14, London, 1963).

Leblanc, G., 'L'abbaye nouvelle près de Gourdon', *Mémoires de la société archéologique du Midi de la France* 27 (1961), pp. 49–75.

Lefavrais-Raymond, A., and D. Laporte, *Histoire de Béduer en Quercy* (Béduer-en-Quercy, 1996).

Léglu, C., 'Vernacular poems and inquisitors in Languedoc and Champagne, c.1242–1249', *Viator* 33 (2002), pp. 117–32.

Léon, M., *Histoires de Quercy autour de Crayssac* (Bayac, 1989).

Lerner, R. E., *The Heresy of the Free Spirit in the Later Middle Ages* (Los Angeles and London, 1972).

Ligou, D. (ed.), *Histoire de Montauban*, 2nd edn (Toulouse, 1992).

Limayrac, L., *Étude sur le moyen âge. Histoire d'un commune et d'une baronnie du Quercy (Castelnau-Montratier)* (Cahors, 1885).

Lobrichon, G., 'The chiaroscuro of heresy: early eleventh-century Aquitaine as seen from Auxerre', trans. P. Buc, in *The Peace of God: Social Violence and Religious Response in France around the Year 1000*, ed. T. Head and R. Landes (Ithaca and London, 1992), pp. 80–103.

Macé, L., *Catalogues raimondins. Actes des comtes de Toulouse, ducs de Narbonne et marquis de Provence (1112–1229)* (Toulouse, 2008).

Macé, L., *Les comtes de Toulouse et leur entourage: xiie–xiii siècles: rivalités, alliances et jeux de pouvoir* (Toulouse, 2000).

Magnou-Nortier, E., 'Dans la tourmente hérétique (xiie–xive siècles)', in *Le diocèse de Toulouse*, ed. P. Wolff, Histoire des diocèses de France, n.s. 15 (Paris, 1983), pp. 47–83.

Magnou-Nortier, E., 'Fidélité et féodalité méridionales d'apres les serments de fidélité (xe–début xiie siècle)', *Annales du Midi* 80 (1968), pp. 457–84.

Magnou-Nortier, E., *Foi et fidélité* (Toulouse, 1976).

Magnou-Nortier, E., 'Formes féminines de vie consacrée dans les pays du Midi jusqu'au début du xiie siècle', *CF* 23 (Toulouse, 1988), pp. 193–216.

Magnou-Nortier, E., 'La noblesse Toulousain: essai sur son histoire médiévale', in *La noblesse au moyen âge, 11e–15e siècles*, ed. P. Contamine (Paris, 1976), pp. 154–74.

Magnou-Nortier, E., *La société laïque et l'église dans la province écclesiastique de Narbonne (zone cispyrénéenne) de la fin du viiie à la fin du xie siècle* (Toulouse, 1971).

Magnou-Nortier, E., 'La terre, la rente et la pouvoir dans le pays de Languedoc pendant le haut moyen âge, ii: La question du manse et de la fiscalité foncière en Languedoc pendant le haut moyen âge', *Francia* 10 (1982), pp. 21–65.

Magnou-Nortier, E., 'La terre, la rente et la pouvoir dans le pays de Languedoc pendant le haut moyen âge, iii: Le pouvoir et les pouvoirs dans la société aristocratique languedocienne pendant le haut moyen âge', *Francia* 12 (1984), pp. 58–118.

Magnou-Nortier, E., *Les structures sociales de l'Aquitaine, du Languedoc et de l'Espagne au premier âge féodale* (Paris, 1969).

Magnou-Nortier, E., 'La "féodalité" méridionale, a-t-elle existé? Réflexions sur quelques sources des xe, xie et xiie siècles', in *Fiefs et féodalité dans l'Europe méridionale*, ed. P. Bonnassie (Toulouse, 2002), pp. 167–201.

Magnou-Nortier, E., 'Note sur le sens du mot *fevum* en Septamanie et dans la marche d'Espagne, à la fin du xe et au début du xie siècle', *Annales du Midi* 76 (1962), pp. 141–52.

Manteuffel, T., *Naissance d'une hérésie: Les adeptes de la pauvreté volontaire au moyen âge*, trans. A. Posner (The Hague, 1970).

Marsac, M., 'La châtellenie et les seigneurs de Moncuq', *Bulletin de la société historique et archéologique du Périgord* 98 (1971), pp. 89–98.

Martin, J., *Venice's Hidden Enemies: Italian Heretics in a Renaissance City* (Berkeley, 1993).

Massabie, L., *Question de prééminence entre les abbayes de Conques et Figeac* (Figeac, 1879).

Molinier, C. M., *L'inquisition dans le midi de France* (Paris, 1880).

Moore, R. I., 'Nicétas, Emissaire de Dragovitch, a-t-il traversé les Alpes?', *Annales du Midi* 85 (1973), pp. 85–90.

Moore, R. I., 'Postface', in *Inventer l'hérésie? discours polémique et pouvoirs avant l'Inquisition*, ed. M. Zerner et al. (Nice, 1998), pp. 263–9.

Moore, R. I., *The Birth of Popular Heresy* (London, 1969).

Moore, R. I., *The First European Revolution, c.970–1215* (Oxford, 2000).

Moore, R. I., *The Formation of a Persecuting Society: Power and Deviance in Western Europe, 950–1250*, 2nd edn (Oxford, 2008).

Moore, R. I., *The Origins of European Dissent* (London, 1977).

Morghen, R., *Medioevo cristiano* (Bari, 1951).

Mousnier, M., 'Implantations monastiques et encadrement des populations en Gascogne Toulousaine dans la première moitié du xii siècle', in *Crises et réformes dans l'Église, de la réforme grégorienne à la préréforme: Actes du 115e Congrès national des sociétés savantes, Section d'histoire médiévale et de philologie, Avignon, 1990* (Paris, 1991), unpaginated.

Mousnier, M., 'Les conséquences de la croisade dans l'économie des abbayes cisterciennes', in *La croisade albigeoise*, ed. M. Roquebert (Carcassonne, 2004), pp. 301–22.

Mousnier, M., *La Gascogne toulousaine au xie–xiie siècles* (Toulouse, 1997).

Mousnier, M., 'Grandselve et la société de son temps', *CF* 21 (Toulouse, 1986), pp. 107–26.

Muessig, C., 'Les sermons de Jacques de Vitry sur les cathares', *CF* 31 (Toulouse, 1997), pp. 70–83.

Mundy, J. H., *Liberty and Political Power in Toulouse 1050–1250* (New York, 1954).

Mundy, J. H., 'Urban society and culture. Toulouse and its region', in *Renaissance and Renewal*, ed. R. L. Benson and G. Constable (Oxford, 1982), pp. 229–47.

Napoléone, A.-L., 'Urbanisme et habitat à Figeac aux xiie, xiiie et xive siècles', *Mémoires de la société archéologique du Midi de la France* 58 (1998), pp. 67–92.

Ourliac, P., 'Réalité ou imaginaire, la féodalité toulousain', in his *Les pays de la Garonne autour de l'an mil* (Toulouse, 1993), pp. 89–102.

Ouliac, P., 'Le servage à Toulouse aux xiie et xiiie siècles', in his *Études d'Histoire du droit médiévale* (Paris, 1979), pp. 133–47.

Passerat, G., 'Cathares en Bas-Quercy: entre l'église de l'Agenais et celle de l'Albigeois', in *Europe et Occitanie: les Pays Cathares* (Carcassonne, 1995), pp. 149–65.

Pataki, T., *Cressensac, essai historique d'une commune dans la vicomté de Turenne* (Cressensac, 1984).

Pataki, T., 'Hommages rendus aux vicomtes de Turenne (1163–1304)', *BSEL* 109 (1988), pp. 111–12.

Pataki, T., *Les institutions seigneuriales de la vicomté de Turenne jusqu'en 1350* (Cahors, 1988).

Paterson, L., *The World of the Troubadours* (Cambridge, 1993).

Pegg, M. G., 'Historiographical essay: On Cathars, Albigenses, and good men of Languedoc', *Journal of Medieval History* 27 (2001), pp. 181–95.

Pegg, M. G., *The Corruption of Angels: The Great Inquisition of 1245–1246* (Princeton and Oxford, 2001).

Perié, J.-F., *Cahors: le cathédrale* (Toulouse, 1991).

Périé, R., *Histoire politique, religieuse et littéraire du Quercy, à partir des temps celtiques jusqu'en 89*, 2 vols. (Paris, 1861–5; rprt. Nîmes, 2002).

Peters, E., *Heresy and Authority in Medieval Europe* (Philadelphia, 1980).

Petit-Dutaillis, C., *The French Communes in the Middle Ages*, trans. J. Vickers (Amsterdam and Oxford, 1978).

Plantadis, J., *Histoire de Tulle des origines à nos jours* (Tulle, 1913; rprt. Marseille, 1977).

Poly, J.-P., 'Régime domanial et rapports de production "féodaliste" dans le Midi de la France (viiie–xe siècles)', in *Structures féodales et féodalisme dans l'occident méditerranéan (xe–xiiie siècles)* (Rome, 1980), pp. 57–82.

Pradalie, G., 'Les sauvetés castrales', in *Genèse médiévale de l'anthroponymie moderne*, ed. M. Bourin-Derruau (Tours, 1989), pp. 29–35.

Rey, R., *La cathédrale de Cahors et les origines de l'architecture à coupoles d'Aquitaine* (Cahors and Paris, 1925).

Reyerson, K. L., *Society, Law, and Trade in Medieval Montpellier* (Aldershot, 1995).

Reyerson, K. L. and J. Drendel (eds.), *Urban and Rural Communities in Medieval France: Provence and Languedoc, 1000–1500* (Leiden, 1998).

Reynolds, S., *Fiefs and Vassals: The Medieval Evidence Reinterpreted* (New York, 1994).

Ribaucourt, C., 'Les mendiants du Midi d'après la cartographie de l'"enquête"', *CF* 8 (Toulouse, 1973), pp. 25–33.

Richard, J., 'Châteaux, châtelains et vassaux en Bourgogne au xie et xiie siècles', *Cahiers de civilisation médiéval* 3 (1960), pp. 433–47.

Roach, A., 'The Cathar economy', *Reading Medieval Studies* 12 (1986), pp. 51–71.

Roach, A., *The Devil's World. Heresy and Society, 1100–1300* (Harlow, 2005).

Roche, J., *Une église cathare. L'évêché du Carcassès: Carcassonne, Béziers, Narbonne, 1167–début du XIVe siècle* (Cahors, 2005).

Roquebert, M., 'Le "déconstructionisme" et les études cathares', in *Les cathares devant l'histoire*, ed. M. Aurell (Cahors, 2005), pp. 105–33.

Roquebert, M., *L'épopée Cathare*, 4 vols. (Toulouse, 1970–89).

Roquebert, M., *Les Cathares de la chute de Montségur aux derniers bûchers, 1244–1329* (Paris, 1998).

Roquebert, M. (ed.), *La croisade albigeoise* (Carcassonne, 2004).

Rosenwein, B., *To Be a Neighbour of Saint Peter: the Social Meaning of Cluny's Property, 909–1049* (Ithaca, 1989).

Runciman, S., *The Medieval Manichee* (Cambridge, 1947).

Scellès, M., *Cahors: ville et architecture civile au moyen âge (xiie–xive siècles)* (Paris, 1999).

Šemkov, G., 'Le contexte socio-économique du catharisme au Mas-Saintes-Puelles dans la première moitié du 13e siècle', *Heresis* 2 (1984), pp. 35–53.

Shaw, I. P., 'The ecclesiastical policy of Henry II on the Continent', *Church Quarterly Review* 151 (1951), pp. 137–55.

Sol, E., *L'église de Cahors sous les Carolingiens et Capétiens* (Paris, 1938).

Stock, B., *The Implications of Literacy: Written Language and Models of Interpretation in the Eleventh and Twelfth Centuries* (Princeton, 1983).

Sumption, J., *The Albigensian Crusade* (London, 1975).

Tardif, A., 'Documents pour l'histoire du *processus per inquisitionem* et de l'*inquisitio heretice pravitatis*', *Nouvelle revue historique de droit français et étranger* 7 (1883), pp. 669–78.

Taylor, C., 'Authority and the Cathar heresy in the northern Languedoc', in *The Origins of Heresy and Persecution in the Middle Ages: Essays on the Work of R. I. Moore*, ed. M. Frassetto (Leiden, 2005), pp. 139–54.

Taylor, C., *Heresy in Medieval France: Dualism in Aquitaine and the Agenais, c.1000–c.1250* (Woodbridge, 2005).

Taylor, C., 'Innocent III, King John and the Albigensian Crusade (1209–1216)', in *Pope Innocent III and his World*, ed. J. C. Moore (London, 1999), pp. 205–27.

Taylor, C., 'The letter of Héribert of Périgord as a source for dualist heresy in the society of early eleventh-century Aquitaine', *Journal of Medieval History* 26 (2000), pp. 313–49.

Thouzellier, C., *Catharisme et Valdéisme en Languedoc à la fin du xiie et au début de xiiie siècle*, 2nd edn (Paris, 1966).

Thouzellier, C., *Un traité cathare inédit du début du xiiie siècle* (Louvain, 1961).

Toubert, P. et al., *Structures féodales et féodalisme dans l'Occident méditerranéen (xe–xiiie siècles)* (Rome, 1980).

Tulard, J. et al., *Brigands en Rouergue, xie–xixe siècle* (Rodez, 1993).

Vauchez, A., 'Les origines de l'hérésie cathare en Languedoc, d'après un sermon de l'archevêque de Pise Federico Visconti (1277)', *Società, istituzioni, spiritualità: studi in onore di Cinzio Violante*, 3 vols. (Spoleto, 1994), II, pp. 1023–36.

Vauchez, A., 'Lay people's sanctity in western europe: evolution of a pattern (twelfth and thirteenth centuries)', in *Images of Sainthood in Medieval Europe*, ed. R. Blumenfeld-Kosinski and T. Szell (Ithaca, 1991), pp. 21–32.

Verdon, L., *La terre et les hommes en Roussillon aux xiie et xiiie siècles* (Paris, 2001).

Vicaire, M.-H., 'La province dominicaine de Provence, 1215–1295', *CF* 8 (Toulouse, 1973), pp. 36–77.

Wakefield, W. L., 'Friar Ferrier, inquisitor', *Heresis* 7 (1986), pp. 33–41.

Wakefield, W. L., *Heresy, Crusade and Inquisition in Southern France, 1100–1250* (London, 1974).

Wakefield, W. L., 'Heretics and inquisitors: the case of Le Mas-Saintes-Puelles', *Catholic Historical Review* 69:2 (1983), pp. 209–26.

Wakefield, W. L., 'Heretics as physicians in the thirteenth century', *Speculum* 57 (1982), pp. 328–31.

Wakefield, W. L., 'Les assistants des inquisiteurs temoins des confessions dans le manuscrit 609', *Heresis* 20 (1993), pp. 57–65.

Wakefield, W. L., 'Pseudonyms and nicknames: inquisitorial documents of the Middle Ages', *Heresis* 15 (1990), pp. 9–22.

White, S., 'Debate: The "Feudal Revolution", Comment 2', *Past and Present* 152 (1996), pp. 205–23.

Wickham, C., 'Debate: The "Feudal Revolution", Comment 4', *Past and Present* 155 (1997), pp. 196–208.

Wildhaber, B., 'Catalogue des établissements cisterciens de Languedoc aux xiiie et xive siècles', *CF* 21 (Toulouse, 1986), pp. 21–44.

Wolff, P., *Commerce et merchands de Toulouse, vers 850–vers 1450* (Paris, 1954).

Wolff, P., 'Le problème des Cahorsins', *Annales du Midi* 62 (1950), pp. 229–38.

Wolff, P., *Histoire de Toulouse* (Toulouse, 1958).

Wolff, P., *Histoire du Languedoc*, 2nd edn (Toulouse, 2000).

Wolff, P., 'Inventaires villageois du Toulousain', *Bulletin philologique et historique jusqu'à 1610 (1965)* (Paris, 1968), pp. 481–544.

Wolff, P., 'La noblesse Toulousain: essai sur son histoire médiévale', in *La Noblesse au Moyen Age, 11e–15e siècles*, ed. P. Contamine (Paris, 1976), pp. 154–74.

Wolff, P., *Regards sur le Midi médiéval* (Toulouse, 1978).

Woods, S., *The Proprietary Church in the Medieval West* (Oxford, 2006).

Wyffles, C., 'Les Cahorsins en Flandre au xiie siècle', *Annales du Midi* 103 (1991), pp. 307–21.

Zammit, J., 'Approche anthropologique des populations médiévales du Languedoc au début de xiiie siècle', *Heresis* 2 (1984), pp. 55–61.

Zerner, M., 'Le déclenchement de la croisade albigeoise: retour sur l'affaire de paix et de foi', in *La croisade albigeoise*, ed. M. Roquebert (Carcassonne, 2004), pp. 127–42.

Zerner, M. et al. (eds.), *Inventer l'hérésie? discours polémique et pouvoirs avant l'Inquisition* (Nice, 1998).

Zerner, M. et al., *L'histoire du Catharisme en discussion: Le 'concile' de Saint-Félix (1167)* (Nice, 2001).

Zerner, M. and H. Piéchon-Palloc, 'La croisade albigeoise, une revanche', *Review historique* 267 (1982), pp. 3–18.

Websites and electronic sources

Albe, E., *Labastide-Murat*: http://www.quercy.net/qmedieval/histoire/monog_albe/labastide_murat.html#Seigneurie

Duvernoy, J. (ed.), *Cahiers de Bernard de Caux, 1243–1247*: http://jean.duvernoy.free.fr/text/pdf/bdecaux.pdf

Unpublished sources

Chiu, H. 'The Intellectual Origins of Medieval Dualism' (unpublished M.Phil dissertation, University of Sydney, 2009).

Index

Page numbers in *italics* refer to figures.

YORK MEDIEVAL PRESS: PUBLICATIONS

God's Words, Women's Voices: The Discernment of Spirits in the Writing of Late-Medieval Women Visionaries, Rosalyn Voaden (1999)

Pilgrimage Explored, ed. J. Stopford (1999)

Piety, Fraternity and Power: Religious Gilds in Late Medieval Yorkshire 1389–1547, David J. F. Crouch (2000)

Courts and Regions in Medieval Europe, ed. Sarah Rees Jones, Richard Marks and A. J. Minnis (2000)

Treasure in the Medieval West, ed. Elizabeth M. Tyler (2000)

Nunneries, Learning and Spirituality in Late Medieval English Society: The Dominican Priory of Dartford, Paul Lee (2000)

Prophecy and Public Affairs in Later Medieval England, Lesley A. Coote (2000)

The Problem of Labour in Fourteenth-Century England, ed. James Bothwell, P. J. P. Goldberg and W. M. Ormrod (2000)

New Directions in later Medieval Manuscript Studies: Essays from the 1998 Harvard Conference, ed. Derek Pearsall (2000)

Cistercians, Heresy and Crusadse in Occitania, 1145–1229: Preaching in the Lord's Vineyard, Beverly Mayne Kienzle (2001)

Guilds and the Parish Community in Late Medieval East Anglia, c. 1470–1550, Ken Farnhill (2001)

The Age of Edward III, ed. J. S. Bothwell (2001)

Time in the Medieval World, ed. Chris Humphrey and W. M. Ormrod (2001)

The Cross Goes North: Processes of Conversion in Northern Europe, AD 300–1300, ed. Martin Carver (2002)

Henry IV: The Establishment of the Regime, 1399–1406, ed. Gwilym Dodd and Douglas Biggs (2003)

Youth in the Middle Ages, ed. P. J. P. Goldberg and Felicity Riddy (2004)

The Idea of the Castle in Medieval England, Abigail Wheatley (2004)

Rites of Passage: Cultures of Transition in the Fourteenth Century, ed. Nicola F. McDonald and W. M. Ormrod (2004)

Creating the Monastic Past in Medieval Flanders, Karine Ugé (2005)

St William of York, Christopher Norton (2006)

Medieval Obscenities, ed. Nicola F. McDonald (2006)

The Reign of Edward II: New Perspectives, ed. Gwilym Dodd and Anthony Musson (2006)

Old English Poetics: The Aesthetics of the Familiar in Anglo-Saxon England, Elizabeth M. Tyler (2006)

The Late Medieval Interlude: The Drama of Youth and Aristocratic Masculinity, Fiona S. Dunlop (2007)

The Late Medieval English College and its Context, ed. Clive Burgess and Martin Heale (2008)

The Reign of Henry IV: Rebellion and Survival, 1403–1413, ed. Gwilym Dodd and Douglas Biggs (2008)

Medieval Petitions: Grace and Grievance, ed. W. Mark Ormrod, Gwilym Dodd and Anthony Musson (2009)

St Edmund, King and Martyr: Changing Images of a Medieval Saint, ed. Anthony Bale (2009)

Language and Culture in Medieval Britain: The French of England c.1100–c.1500, ed. Jocelyn Wogan-Browne et al. (2009)

The Royal Pardon: Access to Mercy in Fourteenth-Century England, Helen Lacey (2009)

Texts and Traditions of Medieval Pastoral Care: Essays in Honour of Bella Millett, ed. Cate Gunn and Catherine Innes-Parker (2009)

The Anglo-Norman Language and its Contexts, ed. Richard Ingham (2010)

Parliament and Political Pamphleteering in Fourteenth-Century England, Clementine Oliver (2010)

The Saints' Lives of Jocelin of Furness: Hagiography, Patronage and Ecclesiastical Politics, Helen Birkett (2010)

The York Mystery Plays: Performance in the City, ed. Margaret Rogerson (2011)

Wills and Will-making in Anglo-Saxon England, Linda Tollerton (2011)

York Studies in Medieval Theology

I   *Medieval Theology and the Natural Body*, ed. Peter Biller and A. J. Minnis (1997)

II *Handling Sin: Confession in the Middle Ages*, ed. Peter Biller and A. J. Minnis (1998)

III *Religion and Medicine in the Middle Ages*, ed. Peter Biller and Joseph Ziegler (2001)

IV *Texts and the Repression of Medieval Heresy*, ed. Caterina Bruschi and Peter Biller (2002)

York Manuscripts Conference

Manuscripts and Readers in Fifteenth-Century England: The Literary Implications of Manuscript Study, ed. Derek Pearsall (1983) [Proceedings of the 1981 York Manuscripts Conference]

Manuscripts and Texts: Editorial Problems in Later Middle English Literature, ed. Derek Pearsall (1987) [Proceedings of the 1985 York Manuscripts Conference]

Latin and Vernacular: Studies in Late-Medieval Texts and Manuscripts, ed. A. J. Minnis (1989) [Proceedings of the 1987 York Manuscripts Conference]

Regionalism in Late-Medieval Manuscripts and Texts: Essays celebrating the publication of 'A Linguistic Atlas of Late Mediaeval English', ed. Felicity Riddy (1991) [Proceedings of the 1989 York Manuscripts Conference]

Late-Medieval Religious Texts and their Transmission: Essays in Honour of A. I. Doyle, ed. A. J. Minnis (1994) [Proceedings of the 1991 York Manuscripts Conference]

Prestige, Authority and Power in Late Medieval Manuscripts and Texts, ed. Felicity Riddy (2000) [Proceedings of the 1994 York Manuscripts Conference]

Middle English Poetry: Texts and Traditions. Essays in Honour of Derek Pearsall, ed. A. J. Minnis (2001) [Proceedings of the 1996 York Manuscripts Conference]

Manuscript Culture in the British Isles

I   *Design and Distribution of Late Medieval Manuscripts in England*, ed. Margaret Connolly and Linne R. Mooney (2008)

II   *Women and Writing, c.1340–c.1650: The Domestication of Print Culture*, ed. Anne Lawrence-Mathers and Phillipa Hardman (2010)

III   *The Wollaton Medieval Manuscripts: Texts, Owners and Readers*, ed. Ralph Hanna and Thorlac Turville-Petre (2010)

Heresy and Inquisition in the Middle Ages

Heresy and Heretics in the Thirteenth Century: The Textual Representations, L. J. Sackville (2011)